50 BATTLES THAT CHANGED THE WORLD

THE CONFLICTS THAT MOST INFLUENCED THE COURSE OF HISTORY

William Weir

BARNES & NOBLE

NEW YORK

2005 Barnes & Noble Books

ISBN 0-7607-6609-6

Printed and bound in the United States of America

06 07 08 09 10 M 9 8 7 6 5 4 3 2

Dedication

For my favorite warrior, Major Alison M. Weir, USAF

Contents

Introduction

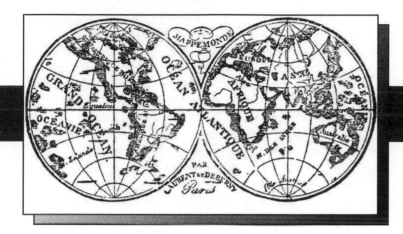

Any attempt to list the 50 most important battles in all history is necessarily subjective. To list them in order of importance is an even greater exercise of chutzpah. Nevertheless, people have been listing decisive battles since Sir Edward Creasy, a lawyer who taught history, a century-and-a-half ago.

Other compilers include General J.F.C. Fuller, a professional soldier; Captain B.H. Liddell Hart, who was gassed and injured early in his career and had to leave the army—he then became a journalist, and Fletcher Pratt, who was a writer by trade. Each brings a distinctive flavor to the enterprise. Fuller is very strong on battles that were fought on land. He's less interested in sea power and far less interested in air power. Liddell Hart emphasizes his strategic theory—the superiority of the indirect approach. He, and to some extent Fuller, preaches the gospel of small, highly trained armies rather than the mass armies we've had in every major war since those of the French Revolution. Pratt's *The Battles that Changed History* has the distinct tang of salty air, although most of the early battles it covers were fought on land. Pratt also has the most openly Occidental orientation.

"[O]ne of the most striking features of Western European culture," he writes, "has been its ability to achieve decisive results by military means. It may even be the critical factor, the reason why that culture has encircled the world. Not that the Far East and Africa have been lacking in great battles or great victories, but their results have had less permanent effect on the stream of world history."

It might be hard to convince a Russian that the victories of Genghis Khan and the consequent subjugation and isolation of his country for three centuries didn't have much effect on the stream of history. Considering that the Mongol conquests brought such Chinese innovations as cheap paper, movable type, the astrolabe, and gunpowder to Europe, it might be difficult to convince anyone else, either.

In this book, I've attempted to avoid this kind of bias. But it's necessary to consider who we are and where we are. What's important to this author—an American living at the juncture of the 20th and 21st centuries—and to his audience would probably not be important to a Chinese person in the 13th century.

It's been fairly easy to avoid a bias in favor of any particular military approach. I'm the son of a career U.S. Navy officer and the father of a career U.S. Air Force officer, but I'm a dedicated civilian. Service as an army combat correspondent and regimental public information NCO in the Korean War gave me a slightly broader picture than most GIs get, but the main thing I learned was when to keep my head down. Some of the military in my upbringing may have rubbed off, though. Large proportions of the articles I've written have concerned military history and weapons. Of my four previous books, one, *Fatal Victories*, was entirely military history. Another, *Written With Lead*, was about legendary American gunfights, including such military events as the Battle of Saratoga and Custer's last stand. Still another, *A Well Regulated Militia*, detailed the history of the American militia.

- Every battle has some effect on history. How do you decide which had the most?
- The basic criteria for picking the importance of the battles that changed the world are:
- How big a change did the battle make, and how much does that change affect us?

One way is to decide what's really important to us and how did we get to enjoy it. Most people would put freedom and democracy high on any list of desirable things. Consequently, Marathon, which preserved the world's first democracy, holds the number-one spot. Order, not anarchy, is also highly desirable. Justinian, Narses and Belisarius, by crushing the Nika revolt, made the world's most widely used code of law possible. Bunker Hill, and to a slightly less extent, Saratoga, ensured the independence of the United States. So, in a much less direct way, did Jackson's victory at New Orleans. The Allied victories in World War II, particularly the Battle of Britain, were the latest battles to guarantee democracy.

Another approach is to look at the currents of history. The ancient Greeks saw history, to a large extent, as a record of the conflict between East and West. That is certainly a viable idea. There are, in a very general sense, two cultures in the world—Western and Eastern. The former would include ev erything from the Orthodox-influenced culture of Russia to the secular culture of the United States. The latter would include the Far Eastern culture of China and Japan, both deeply non-Western in spite of a Western veneer, and a wide variety of other cultures, many of them Islamic. Neither the East nor the West has managed to absorb the other, but it wasn't for want of trying. This struggle, too, goes back to Marathon. It continues through Alexander, Crassus and the seemingly interminable conflicts between Christianity and Islam.

The West has been unable to absorb the East, but it certainly was able to dominate it. There are a string of decisive battles that helped bring that about. At Diu on the Indian Ocean, Portuguese sailors destroyed a Muslim fleet in 1509. That crippled the thriving Arab trade with India and China. Dar es Islam began to shrink economically. Ten years later, Hernan Cortes landed in Mexico. Two years after that, he had conquered—for the first time since Alexander—a non-European empire, which opened a trade route to the Far East across the Pacific. Russia's conquest of Kazan in 1552 initiated European expansion overland to the Far East. A generation later, the defeat of the Spanish Armada energized the English to push west across the Atlantic and conquer North America.

The latest trend in world history seems to be that the Western political domination of the world is ending. In 1940, there was only one independent country in Africa. Europeans owned the rest of the continent. Today there are no colonies in Africa. Most of Asia and the Far Eastern islands, except, China, Japan, and Japan's colony, Korea, were also owned by Westerners. Today none of it is. In a way, the battles of the American Revolution started the trend. The United States became the first independent country in the New World. The rest of the Americas followed. In 1905, Togo's Japanese showed that non-Caucasians equipped with modern technology could beat Caucasians equipped with comparable technology. In 1914, von Lettow Vorbeck's black African soldiers proved that, man for man, they were the equal of Caucasians. But none of the colonial countries could field the military equipment the Japanese could. It took a European country, Ireland, to demonstrate how a weak nation could win its independence from a strong one.

History is full of odd twists like that.

Battle 1

Marathon, 490 BC
A View from the Mountains

Who fought: Greeks (Mitiades) vs. Persians (Datis).

What was at stake: The survival of democracy.

Callimachus studied his Persian opponents from the heights above the plain of Marathon. As expected, there was a lot of cavalry—mostly horse archers. There were also foot archers and infantry spearmen. It was hard to estimate their number, spread out as they were. There had to be at least as many as the 10,000 Athenians and 1,000 Plateans he commanded. There were probably many more. The Great King had unlimited resources. The Persian infantry were not as well armored as the Greeks, and their spears were shorter. But the Persian strength was always their cavalry, both lancers and horse archers. Plains like Marathon made it possible to use cavalry effectively, but plains were scarce in Greece. That was most likely why the Persians chose to land here, a two-days-march away from Athens. If only the Spartans would arrive soon. With Spartan reinforcements, the Greeks, although all infantry, might be able to drive the Barbarians into the sea. (To the Greeks, all foreigners were "barbarians," who made sounds like "bahbahbah" instead of speaking Greek.)

Greeks charge Persians at Marathon.

The Greeks had sent Pheidippides, a professional runner, to ask for Spartan assistance. The Spartans were willing, but they said that because of a local religious festival they'd have to delay their departure. Meanwhile, the Athenians and their Platean allies had been holding the mountain passes. The 10 generals, each commanding an Athenian regiment, could not agree whether they should continue holding their ground or whether they should attack the Persians. Although Callimachus was polemarch, or titular commander, he had only one vote in the counsel of war. Field command, when it came to fighting, rotated among the generals, each one having a day to command the entire army. Miltiades, one of the generals, was rabidly anti-Persian. He had been badgering Callimachus to vote in favor of attacking. So far the polemarch had not made up his mind.

Callimachus could think of no Athenian general who ever had to make such a momentous decision. It might determine the fate of an idea that was radically new in the civilized world—rule by the people, democracy. For as long as anyone could remember, kings, who claimed some sort of connection with the gods, ruled Greece. Then most cities overthrew their kings and accepted rulers (strongmen called tyrants) who claimed no divine connection. Now Athens had deposed its last tyrant, Hippias, and passed laws against tyrants.

The whole situation was very strange. The Great King, Darius, had ordered his son-in-law, Mardonius, to depose tyrants among the King's Ionian Greek subjects. The tyrants had led the subject Greeks in an unsuccessful revolt. Darius replaced the tyrants with pseudo democracies. The Ionian citizens could make their own laws, but all would have to be approved by the Great King. One of the tyrants deposed was Miltiades, the general who so ardently wanted to attack the Persians. Miltiades had a personal grudge. Born in Athens, he was an Athenian citizen. But he had become tyrant of the Cheronese (modern Gallipoli). When he fled back to Athens, he was tried under the anti-tyrant law. But while tyrant, Miltiades had conquered the island of Lemnos and given it to his home city. This earned Miltiades enough favor in Athens to win him not only acquittal, but election as one of the generals. There was still, however, a faction in Athens that despised the former tyrant.

Athens and Eretria had helped the Ionian rebels, which, the Persians said, was why they were there. They were going to punish Athens and Eretria for their meddling. But Callimachus knew that Darius wanted all of Greece, and many Greek cities had already submitted to him. The biggest holdouts were Athens and Sparta.

Suddenly Callimachus saw movement in the Persian army. The Barbarians had begun moving their horses toward the shore where their 600 ships were beached. Callimachus made up his mind. It was time to attack now, Spartans or no Spartans.

The Great King

The Greeks called Darius, the Emperor of Persia, the "Great King." In Susa, his capital, he waited for word from the Aegean. The Greeks were a headache. As long as some were outside the empire, they would incite those who were inside, to rebel. But conquest of Greece would not be easy. Mardonius had learned that. After putting down the Ionian revolt, he continued into mainland Greece. Thessaly had submitted, but the semi-nomadic Thracians had put up a stiff fight before they accepted Persian rule. Then the sea intervened. A tremendous storm wrecked the Persian fleet that had been supplying the Persian army. Mardonius had to withdraw.

Greece was mostly barren and mountainous. The Greek cities depended on commerce for food. No large army could live off the land in Greece. Such an army would have to be supplied by sea. But the sea was treacherous. And the Greeks were worse. Just 45 years earlier, the warships of one small Greek city, Phocaea, had destroyed a Carthaginian fleet twice its size. The Carthaginians were colonists of the Phoenicians, who supplied Persian naval power. Greek sailors had colonized not only the Ionian coast of Asia Minor, but the Dardanelles, the Crimea, Cyrene in Africa, Massillia (modern Marseille), and both the Mediterranean and Atlantic coasts of Spain. If the Greek cities united, they could wipe out any fleet Darius could muster.

Fighting Greeks on land was not much easier. The Greeks had devised a military system that was ideal for their narrow mountain valleys. It was all infantry, based on heavy infantry protected from head to foot by heavy armor. The Greek *hoplite* wore a bronze helmet that covered everything but his eyes and mouth, an armor corselet, and greaves to protect the part of his legs visible from behind a huge bronze-faced shield. Arrows would not penetrate his armor except at close range. He carried a long spear, with a short sword as a secondary weapon. The Greek heavy infantry attacked in long, straight lines many ranks deep, called a phalanx. They marched in step, keeping time with the music of flutes. Greek mercenary hoplites were in demand all over the civilized world. Man for man, they were the best infantry in the world.

Greece, then, could only be conquered with overwhelming numbers, which would have to be supplied by sea. But depending on ships, in the face of Greek naval power and the stormy Aegean, was risky in the extreme. The conquest of Greece would require subtlety.

But Darius had not gotten to where he was by being stupid. He had usurped the throne of Persia, restored Cyrus the Great's crumbling empire, and extended its borders into India, across the Hellespont into Europe, up into the barren steppes of Turkestan and down the Nile into the deserts of Sudan. Darius would not try to overwhelm the Greeks. He would wage war on their minds.

By posing as a patron of democracy, Darius had convinced many Greeks that Persian overlordship was no bad thing. They had given his envoys earth and water as tokens of submission. But the Spartans had thrown his envoy into a well to get water, and the Athenians dropped Darius's representative into a pit to gather earth.

Psychological warfare against Sparta was almost impossible. The city-state was run like an army; dissent was also impossible. But Athens had opposing factions. Darius sent agents to the Athenians who hated Miltiades. They pointed to flourishing democracies in Ionia and promised that if the Athenian out-party opened the city gates to Persian troops, they would be the in-party. The Athenian dissenters pointed out that there was no way they could do that while the in-party controlled the army. The Persian agents promised to lure the army out of the city. The Athenian traitors agreed to help.

Darius's plan called for a swift strike directly across the Aegean. The expeditionary force would be comparatively small—only what could be transported on 600 ships. It would quickly take tiny Eretria, then lure the Athenian army away from the city. With their troops away, the Athenian traitors would let the Persians in, and Athens would be conquered before help arrived from Sparta or anywhere else.

Mardonius had been wounded on his expedition to Greece, and he hadn't been notably successful. Darius gave the command to his nephew, Artaphernes, and a Median general named Datis. Datis, a brave and experienced soldier, would actually command.

The military mind

Datis was a good commander. He had to be to have achieved his rank without being an ethnic Persian. But he wasn't subtle. When he attacked Eretria, on the island of Euboea, the Eretrians resisted for six days. Then traitors opened the city gates to the Persians. It is not known whether or not Persian agents had approached them before the attack, but it seems likely. What is known is that Datis, once inside, followed standard operating procedure. He sacked the city, burned the temples, and carried the inhabitants off into slavery. Then Datis embarked for the trip to Marathon.

He waited for the Athenian army to appear, as expected. Then he waited for the signal telling him the gates of Athens would be open. He waited and waited. He knew that if he didn't get the signal soon the Spartans would arrive and there would be hell to pay.

If he had a bit more imagination, Datis would have known that sacking Eretria after traitors had opened the gates was not a good way to encourage the Athenian fifth column.

Finally, Persians and Greeks both saw someone signaling the Persian army by flashing sunlight from a polished bronze shield. Datis ordered his army to embark.

Dunkirk for Datis

The cavalry, Persia's greatest strength, went first. Meanwhile Callimachus had voted in favor of attack. As luck would have it, today was Miltiades' day to command. Miltiades lined up his troops with the center only four ranks deep in order to make his line as long as the Persian line. He kept the wings eight ranks deep in order to

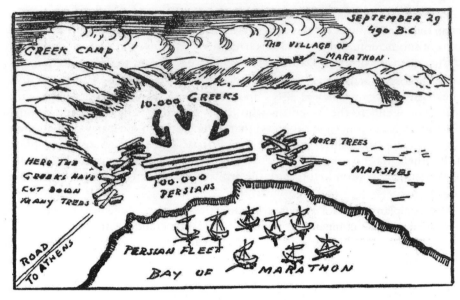

SEPTEMBER 29
490 B.C

GREEK CAMP

THE VILLAGE OF
MARATHON

10.000 GREEKS

MORE TREES

HERE THE
GREEKS HAVE
KUT DOWN
MANY TREES

100.000
PERSIANS

MARSHES

ROAD
TO ATHENS

PERSIAN FLEET

BAY OF MARATHON

Opposing forces at Marathon.

repel flank attacks by any cavalry that hadn't embarked. The flutes tootled, and the hoplites set out with their traditional slow march, keeping all ranks dressed, each man crowding behind the shield of the man on his right.

When the Greeks were about 200 yards away, the Persian archers began shooting at the bronze glacier approaching them. Their arrows bounced off the Greeks' armor. And the glacier turned into an avalanche. The Greek array switched to double-time and swept down on the Persians.

Ethnic Persians and Sakas (Iranian nomads related to the Scythians) held the center of the Persian line. They fought desperately against the weakened Greek center, suffering appalling losses. The Greek spears were longer and their armor was heavier. The Persians actually climbed over the Greek shields to hack at the shield-bearers with axes and daggers. The Greek center bent back.

Meanwhile, the Greek wings, eight ranks deep instead of four, continued to advance. As the Greek line bowed in the center, the wings turned inward. The Persians were caught in a double envelopment, crowded into a dense mass where their bows were useless.

The Persians turned and fled back to their ships. The Greeks pursued. They only captured seven of the ships, which shows that a great mass of the Persian army got away. It was now headed for Athens, and sea travel was faster than marching over the mountains.

The great race

Miltiades, Callimachus, and the rest of the Greeks knew about the signal. It seemed that in spite of the fate of Eretria, traitors were ready to surrender Athens to the Persians. They called on Pheidippides, who had run to Sparta to ask for help, to inform Athens of the victory. Speed was absolutely essential, the generals emphasized. The professional runner had never run so fast. He staggered into Athens crying,

"Nike, Nike!" and dropped dead. The traitors knew now that the Athenian army had beaten the Persians and was on the way home. Any notion of welcoming Darius's troops was forgotten.

The Athenian army made a forced march over the mountains in one day. The Persians found the city closed and their enemies ready for another fight. They went home.

Darius's son, Xerxes, decided to have another go at the Greeks. This time, he sent an enormous army into Greece. The Persians swarmed down the peninsula, overwhelming opposition and burning Athens. Then the disaster Darius had foreseen occurred. A Greek fleet, following the directions of Themistocles of Athens, lured the Persian navy into constricted waters near the island of Salamis and wiped it out. Xerxes had to withdraw the bulk of his army. He left Mardonius with a small force he believed could subsist on the countryside. The next year the combined phalanxes of many Greek cities annihilated the Persian army. Democracy did not die.

1

Marathon, 490 BC

Battle 2

Emperor Justinian.

The Nika Rebellion, 532 AD
Civilization on the Edge

Who fought: Imperial forces (Justinian) vs. Constantinople mob (Green and Blue leaders).

What was at stake: The rule of law.

The hangman was probably new. He certainly didn't know his craft. And his ignorance almost killed Western civilization.

It wouldn't have taken much to kill Western civilization in the year 532. In distant Britain, which had not seen a Roman soldier in more than a century, the Saxons had recovered from the defeat the man known as "Arthur the Soldier" had inflicted on them at Mt. Badon, 16 years earlier. Their chiefs, Cynric and Ceawlin, were preparing new invasions. But Arthur had another project on his mind—he was preparing to battle his own son, Medraut (or Modred). The savage Franks owned Gaul and western Germany. The Visigoths, defeated by the Franks, ruled Spain. Across the Straits of Gibraltar, the Vandals controlled the province of Africa, the breadbasket of the Empire, and all of the Mediterranean. Italy, including Rome itself, was under the sway of the Ostrogoths.

The once-mighty Roman Empire consisted only of the Balkan Peninsula, Asia Minor, Syria, and Egypt. It was menaced not only by the barbarians in the west, but

16

by the civilized and powerful kingdom of Persia in the East. To the north, the Huns, despite the destruction of Attila's empire, were still the best cavalry in Europe. They and their allies, the Heruls, a Hunnicized German nation, remained a threat, and a new threat was joining them. The Slavs, a people savage enough to make the Huns look like exemplars of civilization, were massing on the Balkan boundaries.

But to the people of Constantinople, capital of the Empire, these external threats were not as serious as the internal troubles. The emperor, Justinian, had coped well with the external problems during the five years he wore the purple. Surprisingly well. When the Persians attacked, Justinian had put a young, unknown officer named Belisarius in charge of the Imperial forces. At Daras, Belisarius lured the Persians into a trap and scattered their army.

But another of the emperor's appointments, John of Cappadocia, was bringing disaster at home. As praetorian prefect, or chief financial officer, John was balancing the budget by levying crushing taxes and curtailing essential services. John's measures were driving small farmers out of business. They began swarming into Constantinople, where they strained the city's relief facilities and increased its crime rate.

Even more serious was religious dissension. Paganism among the Romans was defunct. The two principal Christian sects in Constantinople, however, showed no Christian charity toward each other. Quarreling between the Catholics and the Monophysites was continuous and often violent. Three men to be hanged had committed their murders in one of those quarrels.

The factions

The men belonged to street gangs sponsored by two factions known as the Blues and the Greens. They took their names from the colors of the chariots they entered in the Hippodrome races. The government recognized the factions and established them as civilian militia divisions charged with defending the walls of the city. With official recognition came political affiliation, and, after Christianity became the religion of the Empire, affiliation with either the Catholics or the Monophysites. The Blues were Catholic and supported Catholic emperors; the Greens were Monophysite and supported Monophysite emperors. The factions sponsored street gangs, called partisans. The partisans dressed like Huns. They shaved the front of their scalps and let their hair grow long in the back. They wore Hunnish trousers and boots and shirts with baggy sleeves. Inside the sleeves, they carried daggers.

A large crowd had assembled to watch the execution on January 10, 532. The three men were marched to the scaffold and nooses placed around their necks. When the floor gave way beneath them, the three bodies dropped.

But two of the bodies dropped all the way to the ground. The ropes had broken. After a moment of embarrassment, the hangman and his assistants hustled the two convicts—one a Green, the other a Blue—back up on the scaffold and tried to hang them again. The ropes broke again.

The executioners were stunned. The crowd murmured. Was God sending them a sign? A crowd of monks from a nearby monastery rushed up to the prisoners and carried them to a boat, rowed them across the Golden Horn and gave them sanctuary in a church. The city prefect, who had condemned the men to death, sent guards to the church to seize the men as soon as they stepped out.

18 Nika!

That pleased neither the Blues nor the Greens. Three days later was the Ides of January, a traditional occasion for chariot races. As tradition demanded, the emperor appeared at the Hippodrome. Both the Blues and the Greens implored him to pardon the fugitives. He gave them no answer. As the 22nd race began, a cry went up from all parts of the Hippodrome, "Long live the humane Greens and Blues." It must have shocked any neutral observers (if there were any). The Greens and Blues had never agreed on anything before.

That night, a mob of Blues and Greens demanded that the prefect remove his guards. He refused. The mob burst into his headquarters, killed several officials, opened the jail, and released all the prisoners. Then the rioters set fire to a number of buildings. The fire spread, and many more buildings burned, including the huge church of Hagia Sophia.

Justinian holding court.

Rioting went on and on. The mob was organized. Officers of the Green and Blue factions—high-ranking Romans—provided the leadership. The partisans, the dispossessed farmers, and the armed retainers of the great magnates supplied muscle. To identify themselves, the rioters shouted the traditional cheer of a winning faction at a chariot race—"Nika!" (Victory!). Historians later named this movement the Nika Rebellion.

The two regiments stationed in the city refused to move. Belisarius, who had returned triumphant from the Persian War, led his private army of retainers against the rioters, as did another general, Mundus, who had arrived leading a group of Herul auxiliaries. The mob, however, swarmed around the soldiers in the labyrinthine streets of the city and attacked them from all sides. The troops could accomplish nothing.

On January 18, a week after the failed hangings, Justinian, his empress Theodora, Belisarius, Mundus, their troops, and a few picked officials were huddled in the palace while the Blues and Greens assembled in the Hippodrome crowning a new emperor. John of Cappadocia urged the emperor to flee.

Although probably none of the participants realized it, the moment was a turning point in history. If Justinian had fled, his dreamed-of project, the codification of Roman law, would probably never have happened. The civil and criminal law of most of Europe, Africa, and the Americas is based on Justinian's code. The law in the United Kingdom, most of the United States, and the rest of the world, although not based directly on the Roman code, is strongly influenced by it.

The shape of civilization for the next two millennia depended on the actions of as unlikely a cast of characters as fate had ever brought together.

First, there was the emperor, Justinian, who had been born Peter Sabbatius on a small farm in Illyria, north of Greece. His uncle, Justin, years before had joined the army. Justin could barely read and write, but he learned enough about military tactics to become count of the Excubitors, commander of one of the elite units of the army.

Stationed in the capital, Justin sent for his nephew and arranged for his education. Peter became Justin's secretary. To Justin, that meant confidential agent.

Succession to the throne in the Roman Empire did not depend on heredity. Theoretically, the senate, the army, and the populace proclaimed the emperor. Actually, the army did most of the choosing, with the factions playing an important part in the process. When the old emperor died, Peter's intrigues with military and religious officials resulted in Justin becoming emperor. Justin gave Peter the rank of patrician and promoted him to Master of Soldiers, or commander-in-chief of the armed forces. When Justin became ill, he made his nephew co-emperor. Peter Sabbatius changed his name to Justinian. When Justin died, Justinian became sole emperor. A tall, cadaverous, and humorless man, he shared the throne with his wife, Theodora, who had an even stranger background.

The empress, a pretty dark-haired woman, was much younger than Justinian, who was now about 50. She had once been an actress, which in those days was practically synonymous with prostitute. Also, she was a Monophysite, and Justinian was a Catholic. But when Justinian met her, long before he became emperor, he fell madly in love. He wanted to marry Theodora, but the empress Euphemia—herself a former slave—forbade a wedding. The patrician and the former prostitute married after Euphemia died.

In spite of their differences, and in spite of her background, Theodora remained passionately loyal to Justinian all her life, and he to her. At this moment, her voice resolved a crisis.

"If you wish, O Emperor, to save yourself, there is no difficulty," she said. "We have ample funds. Yonder is the sea, and there are the ships. Yet reflect whether, when you have once escaped to a place of security, you will not prefer death to safety. I agree with an old saying 'Purple makes a fair winding sheet.'"

Justinian agreed, too. He wasn't ready to die, though. He had a plan. But the plan depended on two other unlikely people: Belisarius and the emperor's private secretary, Narses.

Belisarius, not yet 30, had also married an actress, a friend of Theodora. The wedding, in fact, had taken place shortly before the riot. Antonina's affair with Belisarius may have had something to do with the young soldier's rise in the world. In the war against Persia, he had fully justified the emperor's faith in him. In Constantinople, though, his best efforts had been futile. His success in carrying out Justinian's plan would depend on the performance of the man who had to play the hardest role: Narses. And Narses was the most unlikely of this entire unlikely group.

Justinian planned to make him grand chamberlain, the second most powerful civilian in the Empire. But Narses had once been a slave. He was also a eunuch, castrated as a boy in his native Persarmenia (the portion of Armenia occupied by Persia), so he could be a servant in Persian harems. Somehow, he ended up in the slave market of Constantinople, and somehow, he attracted the attention of Justinian.

Justinian was impressed with the slave's intelligence, loyalty, and capacity for hard work. The emperor had no need for a harem guard, but he could always find a use for brains. Narses, about four years older than Justinian, became a free man and rose rapidly in the imperial service. He was not only smart, but also generous and gregarious. These characteristics made him one of the most popular of court officials. And he was also, as he was to prove at this time, utterly fearless.

Justinian told Belisarius and Mundus to take their troops to the two entrances of the Hippodrome. Once again they would meet the rioters. But this time, Narses would prepare the way for them.

To Narses, he gave a bag of gold. The skinny little eunuch entered the Hippodrome alone and unarmed, walking through the howling mob that had already killed several hundred people. He circulated through the Blue section, waving to acquaintances and approaching important Blues. He reminded them that Justinian was a Catholic and had favored the Blues during Justin's reign. He pointed out that Hypatius, the man they were now proclaiming emperor, was a Green. He asked how they could support a Green. And he passed out the gold. The Blue leaders conferred quietly with each other. Then they unobtrusively spoke to their followers. Suddenly, in the middle of the coronation, all of the Blues turned and streamed out of the Hippodrome. The Greens were stunned. Before they could recover from their surprise, the soldiers of Belisarius and Mundus attacked. The Greens had no chance to organize. The soldiers killed 30,000, and Justinian had no more trouble with the factions.

The emperor was now free to rebuild the fire-ravaged city and build a new Hagia Sophia, a church still considered one of the marvels of the world. He could now start the reconquest of Africa and Italy—a Herculean task actually performed by Belisarius and the incredible Narses. Finally, Justinian could commence his greatest accomplishment: the codification of the law. Thanks to that, the rule of law, not the changing whims of a succession of tyrants, became established in Western civilization.

Battle 3

Digging in on Breed's Hill.

Bunker Hill, 1775 AD
A Fort on the Hill

Who fought: Americans (William Prescott) vs. British (William Howe).

What was at stake: American independence.

As the sun rose over Boston Harbor, an officer on the *HMS Lively* noticed something strange on the hill behind Charlestown. He trained his telescope on the hill. The damned rebels were building a fort. In fact, it was almost completed. The officer immediately informed his captain, who opened fire on the rebel position. But a few minutes later, *Lively* received an order from Adm. Samuel Graves to cease fire.

In his headquarters in Boston, Lt. Gen. Thomas Gage, too, was aware of the fort. This was absolutely intolerable. Gage had spent most of his life in North America, fighting for the king. He had married a New Jersey woman and planned to retire to a country house he had purchased in New York. This ragtag band of peasants, led by the most improper young radicals, was trying to plunge his country into anarchy. Gage had already requested reinforcements to help him deal with the situation. He got 3,000 additional soldiers, bringing the British forces in Boston to 5,000. London felt that this number would be adequate to handle dissidents in a town of 20,000. Gage did not. He also got less welcome reinforcements—three new major generals,

Henry Clinton, John "Gentleman Johnny" Burgoyne, and William Howe, three of the most ambitious officers in the service. Each of them, Gage knew, coveted his command.

Through his efficient intelligence organization, which included spies in the highest rebel councils, Gage knew that the dissidents had been hoarding ammunition and weapons, even cannons. He had sent a force composed of the flank companies—the grenadiers and the light infantry, the army's elite—to confiscate those stores at Concord. But the rebels had spies, too. The stores were gone. What the troops found at Concord was a horde of armed farmers who drove them all the way back to Charlestown. The rebels fired at the troops from houses and from behind stone walls. There seemed to be thousands of them. The fight must have convinced them that they were the equals of British regulars. After the fight, they besieged Boston. Now they were building a fort on Breed's Hill, as if they were real soldiers. But they'd run like rabbits when they had to face *attacking* regulars, Gage thought.

Meanwhile, he wanted to give the rebels an immediate reaction to the fort they had built overnight. He called his new staff generals together. Burgoyne was a writer, a playwright. He told Gentleman Johnny to draft a message to Graves, asking the admiral to resume the cannonade of the rebel fort. It had to be persuasive. Graves, a senior member of Britain's "senior service," would never take orders from an army man, even though the task of obliterating the fort would be the army's. Besides, Graves still bore a grudge against Gage because of a dispute he had had with the general's father years before. After the note to Graves had been sent, Gage wanted to hear how his generals thought they should handle the fort.

Rabble in arms

If Gage could have visited the rebel encampments, the numbers he saw would have troubled him. Militias from all over New England were there, as well as troops from the Middle Colonies and even from the South. But he would have been heartened by the confusion. Artemas Ward, commander of the Massachusetts militia, was nominally in command under the Massachusetts Committee of Safety. But militia officers were all throwing their weight around. Gen. Israel Putnam of Connecticut, who had commanded troops in the French and Indian War, was particularly pushy.

The Americans had fortified positions at the entrances to Boston and Charlestown. Those two towns occupied a pair of twin peninsulas, almost islands, projecting like huge pollywogs into the harbor. (In those days, the Back Bay section of Boston really was a bay.) Each peninsula was linked to the mainland by a narrow, flat neck. There were no troops permanently in Charlestown. Putnam proposed fortifying Bunker Hill, the highest point on the Charlestown peninsula. This would prevent the British troops from using Charlestown as a staging area, as they had before the raid on Concord. It could also close most of Boston Harbor.

Other militia generals protested that the hill would be too easy to isolate, given the Royal Navy's absolute control of the harbor. But nobody could stop Putnam from leading troops into the peninsula under cover of night. On the other hand, nobody made any arrangements for relief of the troops who would do the digging or even for supplying them with water, food, and ammunition. With Putnam went Col. William Prescott of Massachusetts, Col. Richard Gridley, a trained military engineer, and 1,200 armed farmers, who would do the digging.

When they got to the top of Bunker Hill, they decided it would be better to fortify Breed's Hill—lower, but steeper, and closer to the British. Gridley traced the

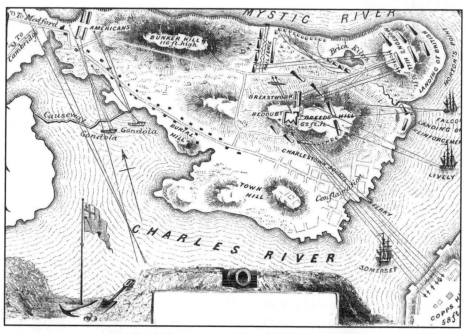

Map showing location of British and American forces.

outlines of a fort, and Putnam ordered his men to dig. The fort was to be an earth-work 130 feet square with 12-foot walls rising from a dry moat.

Prescott, who would have the field command on Breed's Hill, had his men start fortifying the flanks of the fort. They threw up breastworks down the Mystic River side of the hill and into woods bordered by a swamp. On the other side of the peninsula, the waters of Boston Harbor were too far away to permit building fortifications down to the beach. Prescott sent a detachment into the village of Charlestown. By sniping from the houses they might delay a British sweep. There was still a gap beyond the woods on the left. Prescott sent Capt. Thomas Knowlton with some Connecticut militia to plug it. They dug in behind a rail fence with a stone foundation. Below the bluffs above the Mystic shore, Col. John Stark and two regiments of New Hampshire militia took over the end of the fence and built a stone wall that ran across the beach into the river.

Work on the fortifications was briefly interrupted when *Lively* began shooting, but it continued after the cease-fire. Then the whole fleet opened fire, as well as army cannons across the bay. The naval guns were not designed to fire on hilltop forts at close range. Most of their shots were too low. The digging continued. A soldier named Asa Pollard went down the hill to get water. As he was returning, his head suddenly disappeared, and a geyser of blood erupted from his neck. A cannon ball had decapitated him. The Americans took cover. But Prescott got up on a parapet and walked up and down as he ordered the troops to continue digging.

Prescott noticed a nattily dressed young man coming up for the rear. As he came closer, the colonel recognized Dr. Joseph Warren, chairman of the Committee of Safety and president of the Provincial Congress. Warren had just been named a major general. Prescott offered him the command.

"I shall take no command here," Warren said. "I came as a volunteer with my musket to serve under you."

At British headquarters, Henry Clinton had a suggestion. Clinton, born in New-foundland, raised in New York, and blooded on Europe's battlefields, proposed landing on Charlestown Neck. It was a strip only 35 yards wide, and doing so would cut the rebels off.

Gage snorted that there was no need for subtlety. The rebels would run when face-to-face with real troops on the offensive. That would be a greater blow to their morale.

William Howe opposed both plans. Howe was the brother of Lord Augustus Howe, the inventor and master of light infantry tactics. James Wolfe, the conqueror of Quebec, considered William Howe the most daring and brilliant young officer in the army. Howe had led Wolfe's assault on the Plains of Abraham.

Howe pointed out that troops landing on the swampy neck, where there was no cover, would be caught between rebels to the north and rebels to the south, both on high ground. The tides permitted landing and evacuation at limited times of the day, and then only at a spot a half-mile from the neck. Howe proposed landing at Moulton's point, east of Charlestown, in front of Breed's Hill. It would not be a simple frontal assault, however. One detachment, under Brig. Gen. Robert Pigot, would enter Charlestown Village and march on the fort. Pigot would not attack. He would just hold the rebels in place while the rest of the army delivered the knockout punch. Howe, leading the grenadiers—18th-century shock troops—and battalion companies, would attack the hastily dug fortifications on the Mystic River side of the fort. But the light infantry, Howe's favorite arm, would deliver the keystroke. The light infantry, wiry men picked for their agility and trained to think for themselves, would jog up the Mystic River beach, hidden by the bluffs, and turn the rebels' flank. They would then attack the rebels behind the breastworks just as the grenadiers and battalion companies were about to charge.

After landing, Pigot's detachment came under sniper fire. Pigot asked for artillery support. The British ships responded by firing hot shots (cannon balls heated red hot), and carcasses (hollow shot filled with a flaming mixture of tow and tar), into the town. The village was soon a roaring furnace. Pigot led his troops around the town and up toward the fort. On the British right, Howe mustered his troops in three waves.

"I shall not desire any one of you to go a step farther than where I go myself at your head," he told them. He meant it.

Behind the breastworks, the slowness of the British advance and the silence of the British field pieces puzzled the Americans. The advance was slow because the Redcoats were plowing through deep grass that hid stone walls and ditches. The field pieces were silent because they were six-pounders and they had been supplied with 12-pound shot.

Hidden from both the Americans behind the breastworks and the British main body were the light infantrymen. There was nothing slow about their advance. They were double-timing up the beach four abreast toward what looked like a deserted stone wall. The light company of the Royal Welch Fusiliers led the column.

When the Welshmen were 100 feet from the wall, there was a deafening blast and a cloud of smoke. The light company of the Royal Welch Fusiliers ceased to exist. The King's Own light infantry, behind the Royal Welch, slowed for fraction of a second, then leveled their bayonets and charged before the rebels could reload. They leaped over the bodies of their comrades and were yelling in fury as a second volley blasted them. No soldiers could reload that fast. The light company of the 10th Infantry paused. There was a third volley. The whole light infantry column stampeded to the rear.

Behind the wall, John Stark cast a baleful eye over his three lines of prone militia-men, dampening any desire to pursue the enemy or even cheer.

"Reload and wait," he said.

If the fourth company had continued to charge, the battle would have been over.

All of this was hidden from the men following Howe. The grenadiers, the first wave, fired a volley at the silent breastworks when they were 80 yards away and charged at double-time. They had covered about 30 yards when rebel heads and musket muzzles appeared above the earth wall. There was an ear-splitting crash and a cloud of white smoke. Howe looked around. Instead of a line behind him, there were clumps of men and individuals standing alone. The survivors fired back but hit nothing but dirt. The rebels fired again. The grenadiers headed down the hill. The battalion companies in the second wave marched through them and fired. They hit nothing. The rebels began firing as fast as they could.

"An incessant stream of fire poured from the rebel lines," a British officer wrote later. "It seemed a continuous sheet of fire for near 30 minutes."

Howe screamed at his troops and waved his sword, but the British troops ran to the rear.

Pigot's troops, as they neared the fort, had the same experience.

"General Burgoyne and I saw appearances on the left of the army which made us shudder," Clinton wrote after watching the action from Copp's Hill in Boston. "In short, it gave way." Clinton rounded up reserves and took them across the bay. Once there, he formed up the walking wounded into another unit.

Howe was not about to let Clinton steal a victory from him. He and Pigot reorganized their troops, light infantry, grenadiers, and battalion companies together, and took them up the hill 15 minutes after the repulse. There was no subtlety this time. It was a simple frontal assault against an entrenched enemy. It was a simple bloodbath. The Redcoats were again repulsed.

On the hill, most of the rebels had been without sleep or food since the previous night. Now they were running out of ammunition.

For his third assault, Howe organized the troops into deep columns so that a whole line would not be exposed to fire at the same time. As soon as the British were in range, the Americans opened fire. The rebels fired until their ammunition gave out. Some fired pebbles and nails in place of bullets. The British swept over the fort, but the rabble militia did not stampede.

The rebel retreat, wrote Gentleman Johnny Burgoyne, was "no flight: it was even covered with bravery and military skill."

Out of the 1,800 Americans who saw action, 449 were killed or wounded. One was Dr. Joseph Warren, slain in the last few minutes of the fight. The British losses were 1,060 killed or wounded out of 2,600.

"A dear bought victory," Henry Clinton commented. "Another such would have ruined us."

Another such was not needed. The British had gained an unimportant hill. The Americans had gained confidence. At Concord, they had intimidated the British by their numbers, but their shooting was remarkably poor. They were nervous because they were committing treason and were firing on what was probably the best army in the world. At Bunker Hill, they stood up to a superior British force and beat them back until they ran out of ammunition.

If the Americans decided to resist, the British faced a hopeless situation. The colonies were a land mass 1,000 miles wide and 1,000 miles deep. The population was a quarter of that of Britain and Ireland combined, and it was largely self-sufficient. There was no vital center, although Philadelphia was the second-largest English-speaking city in the world. It was across 3,000 miles of ocean. In short, it was too big to be conquered by any forces available in the 18th century

Battle 4

Alexander the Great.

Arbela, 331 BC
A Field Prepared for War

Who fought: Greeks (Alexander the Great) vs. Persians (Darius).

What was at stake: Western civilization.

Every Greek knew the Persian Empire was huge, but never before had it been so obvious. The army Darius III had assembled was not a million strong as some ancient writers assert. That figure is absurd. It was, however, many times larger than the 40,000 foot and 7,000 horse in Alexander's army. The Greeks saw that the Persian line was so long that it could easily envelop both of their flanks. Both Persian wings were held by cavalry. Some of them were heavy cavalry with both riders and horses wearing armor. The rest of the horsemen were light cavalry, the dreaded horse archers of the steppes. Between the cavalry wings were two lines of infantry. In the center of the first line stood mercenary Greek hoplites, flanking the Persian "Immortal" infantry, Darius's *corps d'elite*. And in the center of the Immortals was the Great King himself.

Front and center of the whole Persian army were 15 elephants, beasts the Macedonians had never seen before. On either side of the elephants were 100 chariots with scythe blades on their wheels. Darius apparently was banking heavily on the chariots. He had leveled the field in front of his army so the chariots could operate efficiently.

That was typical of Darius—strategically stupid. That levelled field kept his army tied in place more rigidly than if he had shut it up in a fortress. The army not only couldn't move; it couldn't even change front if Darius were to use his chariots. Darius did not see the problem, but his opponent did.

Alexander

The young king of Macedon had many faults: He was ruthless, was capable of breathtaking cruelty, and possessed of a superhuman ego. But he was not stupid—especially strategically. He scouted the Persians' position, captured orders detailing the arrangements of their army units, and let them wait. For days Darius waited behind his leveled field until Alexander decided to come and get him.

Alexander had beaten the Persians twice before. The first time, he led his heavy cavalry across the Granicus River and drove off the 20,000 Persian light cavalry opposing him. Then the rest of his army crossed and defeated 20,000 mercenary Greek infantry under Memnon of Rhodes. Alexander let the Persian prisoners go home and massacred the Greeks, calling them traitors.

The notion that all Greeks should unite in a crusade against the Persian Empire was a legacy Alexander had inherited from his father, Philip II of Macedon. Philip fully accepted the traditional belief that there were two classes of humans: Greeks and "barbarians." And he had a practical reason for promoting the belief: Greeks would only unite when faced with a common enemy, and Philip wanted the Greeks united under him.

The idea of the ancient and cultured Greek city-states being led by a Macedonian king repelled many Greeks. Macedonians were Greek hillbillies who were so behind the times they still had kings. Philip achieved his aim by developing an army that utterly outclassed any forces in the Greek city-states. After defeating them, he formed a league that included all mainland Greek city-states but Sparta, a city for which he had only contempt. Then he invaded Persia.

The Macedonian king didn't get far. But that was only because he was assassinated. Revolt broke out in Greece, but Alexander quickly put it down. He proved that he could operate the machine his father had invented.

The base of the Macedonian military machine was a new kind of phalanx. The Macedonian phalangites had metal helmets and greaves, but no bronze corselets. They had 18-foot long spears called sarissas, instead of the 8-foot Greek spears. They had smaller shields than the huge, bronze-faced hoplite shield and longer swords. They could move faster than the Greek phalangites, and they could maneuver in small battalions as well as long lines.

Philip used the phalanx to hold the enemy in place, but he used the heavy cavalry to knock it out. The elite heavy cavalry ("the King's Companions") were armed with helmet, corselet, shield, sword, and spear. Macedonians, unlike most Greeks, were horsemen. At this time, no cavalry in the world had stirrups. Only a rider trained from childhood could keep his seat on a horse while thrusting with a spear. For scouting and harassing the enemy, Philip had light cavalry armed with bows or javelins and swords. Alexander later added a corps of super heavy cavalry, the *Sarissophoroi*, which used the long infantry spear.

Philip invented a new kind of soldier to provide a link between the heavy cavalry and the phalanx. These "hypaspists" wore helmets and carried shields heavier than the Macedonian phalangites' but lighter than those of the hoplites. Their spears were

Alexander the Great's empire.

similar to the old hoplite weapon. They were more mobile than the phalangites and could fight either as a phalanx or in extended order.

Philip's most mobile infantry were his archers, slingers, and javelin throwers, who wore little armor. For really long-range fighting and siege work, he had artillery—ballistas and catapults. These had been used by the Greek states in Sicily and Italy, but seldom in the Greek peninsula. Philip's engineers invented a new and much more powerful kind of artillery that used twisted sinew cords instead of a bow to throw projectiles.

The Macedonian army was a far more complex affair than the old Greek phalanx. It was also better trained. Philip had the world's first standing army, raised by the world's first universal military service.

After putting down the cities that rebelled following his father's death, in the course of which he leveled the city of Thebes and massacred 6,000 Thebans, Alexander recruited troops from other Greek states for the Persian expedition. The Granicus battle wasn't much of a test for his army. He outnumbered the Great King's forces, and Memnon of Rhodes had foolishly tried to hold the riverbank with cavalry instead of his heavy infantry. Alexander secured a hold in Asia Minor, then marched down the Mediterranean coast to take the Persian naval bases. He wanted to secure his rear before pursuing the Persian army.

This time, Darius himself appeared at Issus with a large army in Alexander's rear. Alexander maneuvered the Persians into a cramped space where their numbers didn't count for much and led his Companions in charge after charge, aiming at the Persian king. Darius fled, leaving his weapons and family behind.

Instead of following the defeated Persians, Alexander completed his conquest of the coastal cities and proceeded into Egypt, where he was hailed as a god. This was no big deal to the Egyptians—all their pharaohs had been gods. But it seemed to be a revelation to Alexander. He decided that he had been chosen by heaven to rule the world. His tutor, Aristotle, had taught him that there were two classes of humans: Greeks and barbarians. Alexander could not understand why, if he ruled both Greeks and barbarians, one group was better than the other. He decided that all men were brothers and the gods had chosen him to reconcile their differences. He took his troops to the East to complete his assignment.

Meanwhile, Darius raised another army and hoped to intercept Alexander by the Tigris River, north of the city of Arbela. On a plain called Gau Gamela, or camel pasture, Darius drew up his army and leveled the field.

Quality vs. quantity

Alexander eventually moved his troops up to face the Persians. He built a fortified camp and waited some more. Parmenio, his second-in-command, suggested a night attack on the massive Persian army. "I will not steal a victory," said Alexander. He was not just being chivalrous. Alexander always depended on exact timing and precise movements. That might not be possible at night. So the Macedonians slept soundly in their camp while the Persians, expecting a night attack, stayed up all night wearing their armor and holding their weapons.

At sunrise, Alexander led his troops up to the leveled field. Then he did something the Persians had never seen before: He moved his army obliquely to the right. It was a kind of giant-scale version of the "right oblique, march" familiar to any veterans of the U.S. Army's "dismounted drill." The right wing of Alexander's army would be the first to contact the Persians. The Macedonian king was there, leading his Companions and Sarissophoroi in person. A screen of light infantry covered the advance. To foil any flanking attacks by the enormous Persian army, Alexander had several infantry and cavalry divisions behind his own flanks. They could face right, left, or to the rear as needed.

Darius noticed that the Greeks, while moving forward, were also moving away from his prepared field. To stop that movement, which would frustrate his chariots, he sent his heavy cavalry to charge the Greek right. Alexander met the charge with Greek mercenary cavalry. The Greeks were driven back, but Alexander charged the enemy horsemen with his own heavy cavalry. Meanwhile, Darius unleashed his chariots.

The chariot had been the ultimate weapon a thousand years before this. It was a mobile missile platform, with a driver and one or two archers. All other soldiers could move only as fast as their feet could carry them, so it was easy for charioteers to concentrate overwhelming firepower wherever needed. Then soldiers learned to ride, and cavalry replaced chariots as the mobile arm. Cavalry could occasionally be used as a shock weapon, but only the most expert riders on the best trained horses could get their mounts to crash into a steady line of spear points. A charioteer, standing *behind* a pair of horses, never could. Darius's scythe chariots could only be successful if the Greeks panicked. They didn't. The archers and javelin men shot down both charioteers and their horses. The panicked horses that escaped ran around the battalions of phalangites and were captured by the grooms in the Macedonian camp. All the Persian charioteers had accomplished was to demonstrate why chariots had been obsolete for centuries.

What the elephants did was unknown. Whatever it was, it had no effect on Alexander's army. It seems most likely that they suffered the same fate as the chariots.

While battling the Persian horsemen, Alexander sent one of his cavalry divisions to flank the would-be flankers. The Persians, menaced from the rear, stampeded off the battlefield. The Persian cavalry attack had opened a gap in the Persian front. Alexander noticed the gap. He detached his Companions , some hypaspists, and four battalions of phalangites and led them in a charge straight at Darius. The Persian emperor dropped everything and galloped away, running for his life. Most of the Persian army followed him. The Persian right wing, however, had ridden around the Greek left wing and attacked the camp. They were trying to rescue the family Darius had left behind after Issus. Alexander turned and charged to the rear. The Persians were finally routed. The Macedonians pursued the remnants of the Persian army for 35 miles, slaughtering thousands.

The fruits of victory

Alexander rode into Babylon and proclaimed himself the new Great King of Persia. In Babylon he learned that the Spartans had attacked the troops he left in Greece and that Sparta was now part of his empire. Then he went on campaigning, conquering tribes and cities through Iran and Turkestan and into what is now Afghanistan, Pakistan, and India. But he did not forget his notion of the brotherhood of man, which he demonstrated in Babylon by holding a mass marriage of 7,000 of his troops to Persian women according to the Persian rites. He adopted Persian administrative methods and employed Persian officials.

Before Alexander, Persia had seemed to be on the verge of accomplishing with diplomacy and money what it had failed to do with military power. The Great King was taking sides in Greece's incessant civil wars. After the Peloponnesian War, Sparta had become the chief power in Greece. Spartan hegemony in the Aegean Islands was destroyed in the Battle of Cnidus. The victorious fleet was Greek, but the Great King had paid for it. Later, in 384 BC, the Great King arranged a peace among the warring Greek states. In this "King's Peace," Persia again got undisputed sovereignty over the Ionian Greeks in Asia Minor. Athens, Sparta, Thebes, and Corinth all took turns lording it over other Greeks, and all took Persian money for enterprises, which in the long run benefited only Persia. The Persian Empire was like a great black hole, sucking the small Greek states into it by economic gravity.

Alexander changed that. He obviously did not preserve democracy from extinction at the hands of Persia. He almost made it extinct in Greece. But the idea had already crossed the Adriatic to Italy, where the Roman Republic was growing stronger annually. Slowly the idea of people ruling themselves would spread over the world. It would die in some places but spring to life in others. What Alexander did was shift economic, as well as military, power from Asia to Europe. The idea of the rights and duties of citizenship did not die, even under Alexander and his successors. Because of his conquests, Europeans would never become the slaves of a divine king, as in Persia or Egypt.

Alexander added an idea of his own to both Europe and Asia. The brotherhood of man has had even rougher sledding than democracy, but we've come a long way from the Great King, and even from Aristotle.

Battle 5

Crusaders take Jerusalem.

Hattin, 1187 AD
The Franks

Who fought: Crusaders (Guy de Lusignan) vs. Muslims (Saladin).

What was at stake: The fate of Christianity or Islam.

"So formidable is the charge of the Frankish chivalry with their broadsword, lance and shield, that it is best to decline a pitched battle with them until you have put all the chances on your own side."

So advised the Byzantine emperor, Leo the Wise. Leo was thinking of the knights of the Carolingian Empire, but the techniques of Charlemagne's knights had been adopted all over Europe when the crusades began. Still, perhaps because the first Crusaders were overwhelmingly French or Norman, to Byzantines and Muslims alike, all Westerners were "Franks." And Leo's advice was still sound.

War in Europe—a moist mass of peninsulas and islands, covered with forests and broken up by rivers and mountains—meant fighting at close quarters. Knights were encased in heavy mail, and foot soldiers wore as much armor as they could afford. Often the knight's huge charger, or *destrier*, was also armored. The destrier's saddle let the knight put all his weight and his horse's weight, too, behind a lance thrust. The lance and the sword were the Western knight's only weapons, and the charge was his only tactic. Horsemen of the steppes, unhampered by woods or many rivers, covered wide areas in their skirmishing. They depended mostly on the bow and usually charged only after their foes had been thoroughly softened up by archery. Asian tactics left little room for infantry, except in sieges.

The Frankish footmen, who had beaten the Romans, Goths, Vandals, Huns, and Arabs for centuries, had not forgotten how to fight. They were armed with spears and shields, and also with a new weapon: the recently reinvented crossbow. Anna Comnena, a Byzantine princess, described the device she saw in the hands of the first Crusaders:

**Richard the Lionhearted feared
he would not reconquer Jerusalem.**

> "It is a weapon unknown to Greeks and to the Barbarians. This terrible weapon is not worked by drawing its cord with the right hand, and holding it with the left hand. The user rests both his feet against the bow, whilst he strains at the bow with the full force of his arms...When the cord is released, the arrow leaves the groove with a force against which nothing is proof. It not only penetrates a buckler, but also pierces the man and his armour through and through."

The Crusaders' military system was based on the close coordination of crossbowmen, infantry spearmen, and heavily armored knights. The disciplined spearmen kept the Turkish horse archers away from the knights, who led their destriers until they were ready to fight. Between every two spearmen was a crossbowman who shot down Saracens before they could get close enough to hit anything with their bows. If the frustrated Muslims tried to break through the Christian lines with a mass attack, the infantry opened its ranks and the mounted knights charged. As at Marathon, the Westerners had heavier armor and carried longer spears. Unless there was an enormous imbalance of numbers the Muslims always lost.

The Turks

When Mohammed's followers rode out of Arabia and into the Roman lands of North Africa, Syria, and Mesopotamia, they discovered they had allies. The conflict between the Catholics and the Monophysites (see The Nika Rebellion, pg. 16) was still going on. The Catholics were in control in Constantinople, so the Monophysites in the Near East welcomed the Muslims as liberators. Their Prophet had taught the Arabs that Christians and Jews were "people of the book" and must be tolerated, so the conquest went smoothly.

After they were established, Muslim rulers bought pagan Turks as slaves, converted them, and made them soldiers, called mamluks. In time, the mamluks overthrew their masters and became rulers.

Compared with the Arabs and Persians, the Turks were barbarians. They did not understand all the subtleties of Islam, such as why they must make special allowances for

Christians and Jews. This was one reason why the Crusaders were in the Holy Land. The other was the desire of the pope to channel the energies of the nobles and knights away from fighting each other and slaughtering Christian peasants.

The Turks, like the Christian knights, loved fighting, even fighting each other. The so-called Seljuk Empire broke up into a welter of rival sultanates, sheikh-doms, and emirates. At the height of this confusion, the Franks appeared and carved out the Crusader principalities.

Then a new leader, a Kurdish sultan who called himself El Malik en Nasir Salehed-Din, appeared. Saladin, as the Franks called him, conquered the petty Muslim states one after another. Then he turned his attention to the Christians.

Saladin.

For eight years, King Baldwin IV of Jerusalem, a leper who assumed royal powers at 16, outmaneuvered and frustrated the great Saladin. Then, Baldwin the Leper, one of history's most underrated generals, died. When he knew death was near, King Baldwin appointed his brother-in-law, Guy de Lusignan, regent, but Guy proved so inept the King dismissed him and appointed Count Raymond of Tripoli instead. But when Baldwin died, his sister, Sybilla, organized a coup d'etat that made her husband king.

More than Byzantine politics

King Guy quickly proved that he couldn't control his own barons, let alone Saladin. Count Raymond, who thought he should be king, and Reynald de Chatillon, were the two most uncontrollable barons. Reynald, who spent years in a Muslim prison, was a fanatic who said he was not bound by any oath sworn to an infidel. He was also a bandit and a pirate who had robbed and killed Christians as well as Muslims. When Reynald broke the truce with Saladin by attacking a Muslim caravan, the Sultan besieged his castle, but was driven away by King Baldwin and forced to sign another truce. But before that happened, Raymond had protected his own interests by signing a separate truce with Saladin.

When Guy became king, the Master of the Temple, Gerard of Ridfort, urged him to move against Raymond. Saladin, however, sent word that he would support the Count of Tripoli with his army. Then Saladin asked Raymond for permission to cross his territory to raid Acre. Raymond agreed, provided the raid lasted no more than 24 hours and no Christians were harmed.

Saladin's 7,000 cavalry were returning from their visit to Acre when they encountered a band of 130 knights under the Master of the Temple at Sephoria. The knights were an embassy from Guy to Raymond. Gerard didn't hesitate; he ordered an attack. Fortune favors the brave, but not the absurd. Almost all the Christians were killed. Gerard got away. Now that war had begun with the Muslims, Raymond made his peace with Guy and joined the army the King was raising. By stripping castles of most of their garrisons and emptying the treasury to get cash, Guy had assembled 1,200 knights, 2,000 Turcopole light cavalry, and 10,000 infantry. Saladin, though, raised a much bigger army. He besieged Tiberias, where Raymond's castle was located.

Surprisingly, Raymond, renowned for devotion to his own interests, advised against attempting to relieve Tiberias. The fortress was strong, he said, and his wife, Princess Eschiva, could hold out for a long time. It was midsummer. Saladin would find little fodder for his huge cavalry force. He'd have to give up the siege soon. And if Tiberias should fall, the loss of Princess Eschiva was not as great as the loss of the country.

Raymond's counsel was good, but nobody trusted him. Both Reynald and Gerard of Ridfort opposed him. Reynald lived to fight Muslims, and Gerard wanted to live down the shame of running from the fight at Sephoria. As a compromise, Guy brought the army up to Sephoria. The town was near Tiberias, and it had plenty of water and fodder. If Saladin attacked them there, he was bound to lose. But that night, Gerard sneaked into Guy's tent and shamed the King into trying to relieve Tiberias.

The dry well of Hattin

The plan was to drive directly at Saladin's water supply, the Sea of Galilee. Without water, the Muslims would have to withdraw. The tactics would be the time-tested Christian pile driver. Cavalry and infantry were heavily armored. The poorest foot soldiers wore quilted or felt jackets that were amazingly arrow-resistant.

"I have seen soldiers with up to 21 arrows stuck in their bodies marching no less easily for that," wrote Beha ed-Din Ibn Shedad, a Muslim official and friend of Saladin.

He did not, however, see them marching easily in July. The heat was scorching. Metal armor became searing hot where it was exposed to the sun. Many men had emptied their canteens before noon. The Turkish and Arab horsemen seemed to be everywhere. They swarmed around the Christians, shooting arrows and dashing back into clouds of dust. The crossbowmen tried to reply, but they couldn't cock their crossbows while walking. The men had to stop, hold their bows with their feet, and draw their bowstrings with both hands. Every time the crossbowmen stopped, the whole army had to stop. Coordination between crossbowmen, infantry spearmen, and cavalry was the essence of Crusader tactics.

The Turcopole cavalry fought in the Turkish manner, but they were overwhelmed by the masses of Muslim light cavalry. The Christian knights charged again and again, but the more agile Muslim horses scampered away from each charge. To the heavily armored knights, the weather was a more dangerous foe than the Muslims. Some knights actually suffocated to death in their closed helmets. Then the Templars (the rear guard) sent word that their horses could go no farther. Guy saw the village of Hattin, and where there were houses, there must be water. He ordered a halt at the village. When they arrived, though, the Crusaders found that the well was dry and the village abandoned. But the men were too exhausted to move on.

Saladin surrounded the village and distributed more arrows to his troops. He brought up 70 camels loaded down with more arrows. He set up his tent on a hill where he had a good view of the battlefield. Unlike the Crusader leaders, Saladin was a strategist, not a fighter. He hated war, was inept with weapons, and was never in the forefront of his troops.

On the second day of the battle the Muslims set fire to the scrub, and the Christians, already suffering horribly from thirst, fought right through the blaze. When Guy attempted to rally the soldiers, they lost cohesion, and the Muslim attacks became more effective. They were dying of thirst, and the Sea of Galilee was only three miles away, all downhill after crossing a ridge.

"Let's save ourselves!" a foot soldier shouted. A disorganized mass of infantry stampeded for the ridgeline. But the spearmen and crossbowmen were unable to coordinate their efforts. And they were too tired to fight anymore. Some could no longer even stand. They surrendered. Beha ed-Din saw one Muslim soldier tie up and lead away 30 Christian infantrymen.

Raymond of Tripoli gathered his knights, charged the ring of horse archers and broke through. Guy and his remaining men tried to make a stand on a hill, but the Muslims swept over them.

The battle was over. Almost all the Christian fighting men in Palestine had been killed or captured. Saladin sent most of the surviving Crusader infantry to the slave markets, but he beheaded all of the Templars and Hospitalers. He kept the other nobles for ransom. He didn't get much ransom. Prisoners he liked, such as King Guy, he released without ransom. And if ransom as late in coming for the other knights, he had them butchered for the entertainment of his dinner guests.

Immediately after the battle, Saladin had the Crusader leaders sent to his tent. He gave Guy a goblet of chilled rose water. Guy drank a portion and passed the cup to Reynald de Chatillon. Saladin became angry because he had vowed to personally behead Reynald.

"Remind the King," Saladin said to his interpreter, "that it is he, not I who gives drink to this man."

A little later, the Sultan asked Reynald to renounce Christianity. As he expected, the Crusader contemptuously refused. Saladin swung his sword, but, inept as always, he cut off Reynald's arm instead of his head. The Sultan's embarrassed attendants immediately beheaded the baron.

The beginning of the end

Saladin released Guy on the condition that he leave the Holy Land. Guy immediately broke his promise. He went to Tyre, hoping to renew the fight, but the garrison there refused to admit him. In Europe, however, the Holy Roman Emperor and the kings of England and France started a new crusade. The Emperor died en route, but the French and English arrived. Richard the Lionhearted almost got to Jerusalem, but he realized that a garrison there could easily be cut off by the Turkish and Arab horse archers. Only a full field army could resupply Crusaders in Jerusalem. Richard signed a truce with Saladin. The Crusaders were able to hang on to a greatly reduced portion of the Holy Land for another century, but the crusading cause was defunct.

Given the demographics, that result was inevitable. What gives Hattin its greatest importance is its effect on the Muslims, not the Christians. It convinced them that the ancient tactics of the horse archer, demonstrated centuries before by the Scythians and the Parthians, could not be beaten. The Arabs knew about saltpeter, which they called "the snow from China," and its use in gunpowder long before the Europeans, but they neglected to develop guns. Cannons and the clumsy muskets the Europeans made could not be used by horse archers and would be useless against them.

So the lords of Dar es Islam sat back, confident of their invincibility, and grew fat siphoning riches from the trade between Europe and the Far East. And three centuries later, as we'll see in the next battle, the roof fell in.

Battle 6

The OTTOMAN EMPIRE before 1453.

Diu, 1509 AD
Franks on the Water

Who fought: Portuguese (Francico de Almeida) vs. Turks and Egyptians (Husain Kurdi).

What was at stake: Trade with the Far East and India, and the rise or fall of Christendom or Dar es Islam.

"Kansuh al-Ghawri came to power [as Sultan of Egypt]," wrote the Arab chronicler Ba Fakhi al-Shihri. "He dispatched a mighty fleet to fight the Frank, its commander being Husain Kurdi. Entering India he stopped at Diu.

"The expedition fell in the year 13 (1507-8 AD). It had an engagement with the Frank, but was defeated and returned to the Arabian coast.

"This was the first appearance of the Franks, may God curse them, in the (Indian) Ocean seizing (Muslim shipping)."

Thus al-Shihri passed over what turned out to be not only the worst defeat yet suffered by the forces of Islam, but a turning point in the centuries-long conflict between the Cross and the Crescent. Shanbal, another contemporary Arab chronicler, gives only a bit more detail:

36

"In this year [1508-9 AD] the Frank took Dabul, looting and burning it. In this year also, the Frank made an expedition against Gujerat and attacked Diu. The Emir Husain, who was at that time in Diu fighting the Holy War, went forth to meet him, and they fought an engagement at sea beyond the port. Many on the Frankish side were slain, but eventually the Franks prevailed over the Muslims, and there befell a great slaughter among the Emir Husain's soldiers, about 600 men, while the survivors fled to Diu. Nor did he [the Frank] depart until they had paid him much money."

The "Franks" were really Portuguese. In the battle at Diu where "many on the Frankish side were slain," Portuguese casualties came to 32 dead and 300 wounded. The Muslim death toll rose to at least 1,500. But the loss to Islam was too great to be measured in mere casualties. To understand what happened, we have to go back several centuries.

The world of Islam

A millennium and a half after the birth of Christ, Christianity was almost totally confined to Europe. But in half that time, Islam had spread from Arabia over the whole eastern shore of the Mediterranean, then east through Mesopotamia, Persia, Afghanistan, northern India and into Indonesia and the Philippines. It had traveled west to Egypt and across North Africa and into Spain. Muslims crossed the Sahara and converted the Negro empires of West Africa. The religion of the Prophet had spread south along the east coast of Africa, where Arabs had established colonies long before Mohammed. Muslim muezzins called the faithful to prayer in Central Asia where Turkish and Mongol tribes had once practiced shamanism.

The Crusades, troublesome as they were at the time, had ultimately benefited Dar es Islam. The Christians had acquired a taste for the goods of the East. They craved the silk of China and the pearls of Persia, the spices of Indonesia and the gold of India. And all of the trade routes were in Muslim hands. Occasionally Europeans like the Poles might travel overland to China, but such ventures were rare. The caravans that trudged along the old Silk Road were all Turkish Muslims.

The sea routes from the east, which handled much more trade, were also a Muslim monopoly. Arab dhows from Arabia and Africa crossed the Indian ocean. The round trip was slow, because the dhows depended on seasonal winds, but the volume of trade was immense—and immensely valuable. Goods from China, India, and Persia ended up in Egypt, where they were shipped to Europe in Venetian bottoms. The Indian Ocean route was safe from the Europeans. To reach that ocean, the Christians would have to cross Muslim lands. The only other way would be to go around the whole continent of Africa—an unthinkable trip.

Muslim rulers grew rich from the trade—especially the mamluk rulers of Egypt. Egyptian wealth aroused the envy of the Ottomans, a more recent influx of Turkish nomads who had founded an empire based on Anatolia.

The Ottoman Empire was expanding in all directions. In the east, it fought the Persians, and in the west, it sacked that bastion of Christianity, Constantinople, and flowed into the Balkans. In the north, it drove through the Caucuses and into Russia. In the south, it claimed Syria and Mesopotamia. The Ottomans seemed to be invincible. The heart of the empire's army was its light cavalry bowmen, the service that had proven so effective in the Crusades. As in all Middle Eastern and Central Asian lands, the light cavalry were the nobility. Infantry were serfs or slaves. The Ottoman sultans, though, had developed a new kind of slave infantry. Their Janissaries had been taken from Christian parents in infancy, raised as Muslims and trained in the military arts until they were old enough to be soldiers. Most of them were archers, but a few had been given guns. Unlike most Muslims, the Ottomans saw a use for gunpowder. The Janissaries' muzzle-loading matchlocks had neither the range nor the accuracy of the Turkish bow, but the Turks found that in some cases, firing from ships or fortresses, they were handier. The Turks had big guns, too, huge cannons that could shatter most stone walls with one shot. The Turks saw that cannons had value in naval warfare as well as sieges. They mounted cannons in the bows of their galleys to supplement the galleys' rams. And as the 16th century dawned, they got a chance to learn the value of ship-borne guns.

The land of war

The Ottomans referred to Europe as "the land of war"—the place where they would go only to fight. The name was appropriate in more ways than one. For five centuries before the First Crusade, invaders had overrun Europe. Goths, Huns, Avars, Bulgars, Magyars, Vikings, and Moors had attacked the Christian kingdoms from all sides. Under these barbarian attacks, the civilization of Rome had disappeared. Urban life was almost extinguished and Europe had become semi-barbaric. The First Crusade was launched in 1096. Just 82 years before that, Brian Boru smashed the last great Viking expedition outside Dublin, and the Byzantine emperor Basil the Bulgarcide wiped out the last attack on civilization by Central Asian nomads. Muslims still held most of Spain and Portugal.

About the only arts that developed in Europe during this period were the military arts. The Europeans were busily practicing them on each other when Pope Urban II incited them against the Muslims. The techniques developed for war in Europe, however, did not work in the deserts of the Near East.

In spite of their failure, the Crusades were not a total disaster for Europe. They brought the semi-barbaric Westerners in contact with the Eastern Roman Empire as well as with the civilization of the Islamic lands. Learning got a jump-start. Universities were founded and grew. Ancient philosophers, who were almost forgotten, were studied again. So were ancient mathematicians and engineers. The mechanical ingenuity that had produced the crossbow (which so amazed Anna Comnena) was turned to peaceful arts. Millers began grinding grain with water or windmills. Miners dug deep for coal, iron, copper, and precious metals. Masons built towering Gothic cathedrals. Metal founders learned how to cast enormous bronze bells for those cathedrals.

Society began to change, too. The armored knight was no longer supreme. Scottish pikemen had defeated English knights, Flemish infantry, French knights; and Swiss halbardiers, Burgundian knights. At Crecy, Poitiers, and Agincourt English archers had mowed down French chivalry by the thousands. As the power of the nobility declined, the power of the merchants and artisans grew.

Commerce increased by land and sea. Food production increased. Farmers adopted better plows, and fishermen went even farther abroad. Sailors from the Mediterranean met sailors from the Atlantic, and each group learned from the other. The design of ships and maritime rigging advanced farther in the 14th and 15th centuries than it had in the previous two millennia.

The two biggest Atlantic powers, England and France, became enmeshed in the Hundred Years War. France won the war, but it was ravaged and took a long time to recover. The war had hardly ended when England plunged into the Wars of the Roses. So the smaller Atlantic powers took the lead in exploring the ocean. Spaniards and Portuguese discovered the Azores and the Canary Islands.

These voyages of discovery were not made in the pursuit of knowledge for its own sake. The Ottoman Turks were still advancing in Europe. There was a legend that off in Central Asia or Africa was Prester John, a Christian priest-king, who might be induced to attack the Muslims from the rear. Prester John was not pure myth. Coptic Christian monks from Abyssinia (modern Ethiopia) had visited Portugal. And the Pope had sent envoys to see the Great Khan, some of whose subjects were Christian. Perhaps ships could find a sea route to the land of Prester John. To Iberian Christians, skirmishing with Iberian Muslims, the Crusades were not some long-ago wars. "Here we are always on crusade," a Spanish knight told an English visitor.

The Venetians, the Genoese, and the Turks controlled the Mediterranean, but they could never go far into the Atlantic. The principal Mediterranean warship was the galley. Galleys had sails, but in combat they used only oars for propulsion. Galleys were long, narrow, low, fast, and maneuverable in calm water but unmanageable and dangerous in rough seas. Because rowers propelled them, galleys had enormous crews. No galley could carry enough food for a long trip. Thousands of years before this, Phoenician mariners in the pay of Egypt had sailed around Africa. But it took them three years to do it. They had to land every autumn to plant wheat. They stayed until the grain was ready to harvest, then pushed on.

The sailors of Europe's Atlantic seaboard developed ships that could make long trips on the high seas. They were much wider and higher than galleys, and only sails propelled them. They could sail against the wind. Their crews were small. One of them would stand no chance against a galley that boarded it.

For protection, they relied on guns. Not three or four forward-facing guns like those of a galley, but rows of guns along the side. They had two, sometimes three, gun decks, with cannons poking through gun ports that could be closed in high seas.

The Ottoman Turks had guns, but their artillery technology was far behind that of the Europeans. Centuries of casting bronze church bells had made Europeans the world's best makers of large castings. Then the bronze casters found it was not too hard to adapt their skills to making cast iron guns. European shock warfare, between masses of heavily armored men, also promoted the development of hand-held guns that could penetrate heavy armor.

Passage to India

To the Portuguese, the trip around Africa was another part of their endless crusade. In 1415, they captured the Moorish port of Ceuta. Ceuta was a terminus of the trans-Sahara caravans that brought gold and ivory up from Central Africa. The Portuguese learned that there were riches to be had all the way to India. Their exploration was methodical. They explored 100 leagues a year, establishing trading posts and making treaties with native rulers as they moved south. The farther south they got, the farther they got from civilization, culminating in the Bushmen at the southern tip of Africa.

"The inhabitants of this country are brown," wrote a sailor known as Old Alvaro, who accompanied Bartomeu Dias on the first Portuguese expedition to round the Cape and continue on to India. "All they eat is the flesh of seals, whales and gazelles and the roots of herbs. They are dressed in skins and wear sheaths over their private parts."

But the eastern coast of Africa proved to be completely different from the western coast. Here the Portuguese saw no impoverished tribesmen living in grass huts. They found port cities, with stone piers and many-storied buildings. In the cities were people of many races: blacks, Indians, Persians, and Arabs. Most of the inhabitants of the ports were of mixed race. Almost all were Muslims except for a few Hindus. They had never seen Christians. They at first took the white Portuguese for Turks or Arabs.

Dias had skirmishes with the emirs of Mozambique and Mombassa, but he made an ally of the emir of Malindi. Then he crossed the Indian Ocean and landed at Calicut. Muslim merchants in Calicut induced its Hindu ruler to turn against the Portuguese, and Dias was lucky to escape and sail back to Portugal.

Pedro Alvares Cabral led a second Portuguese expedition to Calicut. On the way to India, Cabral accidentally discovered Brazil. In Calicut, the Portuguese had more trouble with its ruler, and after helping the Rajah of Cochin, who was at war with Calicut, they returned to Portugal. King Manoel then sent Vasco da Gama, who had first reached the Cape of Good Hope, against Calicut. The troops of Calicut were besieging Cochin when da Gama arrived. The firepower of the Portuguese fleet routed the besiegers. The Portuguese followed up this success by seizing key points on the Indian Ocean shores and destroying all Muslim shipping they could find.

Conquest of the sea

In 1505, the king and council of Portugal decided to consolidate all their enterprises in "the Indies." Manoel appointed Francisco de Almeida viceroy and gave him command of the greatest fleet ever sent out from Portugal.

Meanwhile, Muslim rulers in East Africa, South Arabia, and India had been complaining to the Sultan of Egypt about the attacks of "the Frank." The Venetians, too, urged their Egyptian ally to do something. The Sultan needed no persuasion: Egypt was already feeling the pinch. The Egyptian sultan sent a message to his rival, the Ottoman sultan, and the two Muslim powers agreed to cooperate. They concentrated an enormous fleet at Jeddah on the west coast of Arabia and sailed down the Red Sea. The Muslim admiral, Husain Kurdi, headed for Diu, a Muslim port.

Almeida's fleet had arrived at Cochin. Hearing that there was a concentration of Muslim ships at Diu, he sent his son, Lorenco, with a few light ships to scout the area. The Turco-Egyptian fleet trapped Lorenco, and he was killed. The Turks skinned his body, stuffed it with straw, and sent it to the Sultan in Constantinople. Before Almeida could concentrate his forces, the Muslims had sailed back to Arabia.

Two years later, Husain returned with even more ships. The great majority were galleys, mounting three cannons in the bow over the big bronze beak used for ramming. There were 200 ships, thousands of rowers, and 1,500 soldiers for boarding enemy craft. Besides swords and spears, the soldiers carried bows or matchlocks. They had grappling irons for seizing ships and fire pots for dropping on their decks. Husain was going to settle the "Franks" once and for all.

When the Muslims returned, Almeida was ready. Burning with a desire for revenge, he led his ships up to Diu. He had 17 ships, but all were larger and far better armed than Husain's galleys. As soon as the Muslim scout ships reported seeing Portuguese sails, the Muslims left the port and rowed toward them. The ocean was rougher than the Red Sea or the Mediterranean. The galleys couldn't make as much speed as they expected, and it was harder to keep in line.

Instead of charging straight ahead, as usual in combat between galleys, the Portuguese turned broadside. Then they opened fire. They fired thundering salvos, drowning out the sound of the comparatively few Muslim guns. Few Muslim ships got close enough to ram or board. Portuguese fire shattered the galleys. Cannon balls plowed through the banks of oarsmen, leaving masses of gore and mangled bodies. As an Indian writer put it, "Courage availed nothing against artillery, and their fragile craft were sunk in batches." By nightfall, the Muslim flagship had been sunk, along with most of the other galleys. The surviving Egyptians and Turks ran their ships aground and fled into the city.

The Egyptian mamluks, weakened by the loss of the Oriental trade, were the first to suffer. The Ottomans conquered them eight years after Diu. In the following century, the Turks made three more attempts to dispute mastery of the Indian Ocean with the Portuguese. All ended the same way. The Portuguese eventually lost control of the ocean, but they lost it to the Dutch, who were followed by the English and French. The Indies trade, that great source of wealth, was lost to Islam forever.

A Genoese sailor, Christoforo Columbo, inspired by da Gama's feat in reaching the Cape, began trying to sell his plan of sailing west to reach the East. The Portuguese said his plan was based on faulty mathematics. (It was.) But the Spanish bought the idea. Columbo sailed in 1492, right after the Spanish drove the last Muslims out of Spain.

When the 15th century began, Islam seemed about ready to dominate the world. That prospect sank in the Indian Ocean off Diu.

Battle 7

Hurricanes on the ground.

The Battle of Britain, 1940 AD
Hitler's Delusion

Who fought: British (Winston Churchill) vs. Germans (Adolf Hitler).

What was at stake: The survival of democracy.

The mighty French army, touted as the best in the world, had collapsed like a punctured balloon. The British expeditionary force had dashed back to Britain, leaving almost all of its equipment and not a few of its men. France was finished; Britain was on the ropes. Adolf Hitler was so confident the British would make peace that he had no plans for continuing the war against them.

"The British have lost the war, but they don't know it," Hitler told General Alfred Jodl. "One must give them time, and they will come around."

Hitler thought the British Empire was a stabilizing force in the world. As historian A.J.P. Taylor points out, Hitler believed that if Britain were conquered, the Americans and the Japanese—the other two of the world's three great naval powers—would divide its empire. Britain's huge navy would certainly go to the United States. Hitler wanted Britain to be a junior partner in his crusade against Bolshevism. He didn't want it to be a former power, like France.

The British hesitated. Prime Minister Neville Chamberlain and his foreign minister, Lord Halifax, said on May 27, 1940, that they might discuss terms if "matters vital to the independence of this country were unaffected." Even Winston Churchill said he might be willing to make peace if Hitler wanted only the overlordship of Central Europe and the return of former German colonies. But the next day, he rejected the notion.

In July, Hitler decided that the British had had enough time. He ordered preparations of "Operation Sea Lion," the invasion of Britain. To most of the world, Britain looked like another pushover. Germany's enormous army and air force had conquered Poland, Denmark, Norway, Belgium, the Netherlands, Luxembourg, and France.

Spitfires attack.

Hitler and his generals knew better. The English Channel might look like a wide river on a map, but it was 20 miles wide at its narrowest—plenty of room for the Royal Navy to operate. The *Luftwaffe* would have to prepare the way. Although the Luftwaffe was easily the world's most powerful air force, it, unlike the air forces of most other major powers, had not been designed for strategic bombing. Italy's Giulio Douhet and America's Billy Mitchell had preached that in the next war, air power was the only force that would count. Air forces would destroy the enemy's surface forces, his means of production, and even his cities before he could mobilize. Britain's Royal Air Force had been established to fight just such a war. The Luftwaffe, on the other hand, had been created to provide close support for the army. Hitler's friend, Hermann Goring, the Luftwaffe chief, had been an ace fighter pilot in "von Richtofen's Circus," with 22 confirmed kills over the World War I Western Front. Goring scorned the heavy bomber pilots as "truck drivers" and considered fighter pilots modern knights.

On July 16, Hitler issued Fuhrer Directive No. 16, "Preparations for a landing operation against England." The Luftwaffe was to destroy naval vessels and coastal defenses, prevent air attacks, and "break the initial resistance of enemy land forces and annihilate reserves behind the front." Goring viewed this rather large order with a cocky fighter pilot's optimism.

"The Fuhrer has ordered me to crush Britain with my Luftwaffe," he told his generals on August 1. "By means of hard blows, I plan to have this enemy, who has already suffered a crushing moral defeat, down on his knees in the nearest future, so that an occupation of the island by our troops can proceed without any risk." With German planes hitting Britain from Norway, Denmark, the Low Countries, and France, Goring believed, four days would be all he'd need.

The tight little island

As a fighting force, the British Army was almost defunct. Britain's navy might be strong, but its air force looked almost as hopeless as its army. Goring could concentrate 800 Bf 109 fighters, 300 Bf 110 long-range fighters, 400 Ju 87 dive-bombers (the dreaded Stukas), and 1,500 Dornier, Junkers, and Heinkel bombers. In 1938, at the time of the Munich crisis, only six of 30 RAF fighter squadrons had modern Hurricane or Spitfire fighters. And between May 10 and June 4, the RAF had lost 430 front line fighters over France.

One of the things Goring did not know, though, was that the British had greatly increased their fighter production. In 1940, Messerschmidt was producing only 140 Bf 109s and 90 Bf 110s a month. Vickers and Hawker were producing 500 Spitfires and Hurricanes a month. The Bf 109 was a superb fighter, but no better than the Spitfire, and it had a range of only 125 miles. The German bases closest to England were more than 20 miles away; most were more than 50 miles away. The bases in Scandinavia were much farther. Operating from the closest bases, the 109s could spend no more than 25 minutes over England.

British pilots shot down would land in England; if they were extremely unlucky, they'd land in the Channel, which was controlled by British ships. Lucky German pilots would also land in England, and unlucky ones would land in the Channel. In either case, they'd be out of the war. Fighting on home ground also made maintenance of British planes easier. The RAF was able to keep more than 600 Spitfires and Hurricanes operational at all times. The Germans never had more than 800 Bf 109s ready for combat.

Even more important, a British team under Robert Watson-Watt had invented radar, and British radar stations covered all of the island's eastern and southern coasts. The Germans had a primitive form of radar, but they had no idea that their enemies had a far more sophisticated system. Their radar systems let the British pinpoint German attackers and concentrate fighters to meet them.

Air war

In spite of Goring's bombast, the initial Luftwaffe attack didn't look like much. It started July 10 with raids on England's south coast and ships in the channel. The Germans sent 20 or 30 aircraft on each raid. They sank a number of merchant ships but didn't touch the Royal Navy. By July 31, the Germans had lost 180 planes; the British, 70.

The operation established two facts:

1. The Bf 110, later to become a great night fighter, was totally outclassed by both the Spitfires and the Hurricanes.
2. The Stuka was a flying coffin in aerial combat.

On August 1, Hitler officially issued Fuhrer Directive No. 17, ordering the Luftwaffe to "overpower the English air force with all the forces at its command in the shortest possible time." That prompted Goring's "hard blows" announcement, but "Operation Eagle" didn't get under way for a week, and even then it was so disorganized that Goring didn't proclaim "Eagle Day" until August 13.

The "Eagle" raiders attacked British air bases, but only once the radar stations. A raid on the Spitfire factory on August 13 cost the Germans 45 planes to the British

13. On August 15, the Luftwaffe lost 75 planes to the RAF's 35. That day Goring withdrew all the Stukas from the battle and reorganized the Luftwaffe command. From now on, Goring ordered his generals, concentrate on RAF fighter bases. The new strategy began to pay off. On August 24, the Luftwaffe flew 1,000 sorties and destroyed 22 RAF fighters. It lost 38 of its own planes, but not all were fighters. Between August 24 and September 10, the RAF lost 290 fighters. The Luftwaffe lost 380 planes, but only half were fighters. The German raiders were coming in waves. After the British intercepters had dealt with one wave, they landed to refuel. Then a second Luftwaffe wave bombed them on the ground.

It looked as if the Germans were going to win the Battle of Britain. But time was running out. The autumn gales would rule out any chance for a seaborne invasion. Hitler had set the date for a channel crossing at September 15.

The birth of "the Blitz"...

The night of August 24–25, 10 German bombers, sent to bomb a fuel storage area, panicked and dropped their bombs on the heart of London. The British retaliated with a raid on Berlin. It was totally ineffective—not the city-crushing stroke envisioned by Douhet—but it made Hitler furious. He would punish the evil English by bombing London. Goring had told him the Luftwaffe had wiped out most of the RAF. Now, Hitler thought, he could break the spirit of his enemies and make invasion easy. On September 7, the Luftwaffe concentrated all its forces on London. And the British began to rebuild their air bases and increase their production of fighter planes.

What followed was a British epic. The Luftwaffe sent hundreds of planes against a city defended by masses of barrage balloons, 2,000 anti-aircraft guns, and 750 fighter planes. The German planes did a considerable amount of damage to London, but they never broke the spirit of British civilians. And the British armed forces got stronger.

...And the death of "Sea Lion"

The bombing of London, what the British called "the Blitz," continued through most of the war. But the Germans lost the Battle of Britain. If they had begun the battle with massive raids on British air bases and airplane factories, it may have been different. But they did not. Just when Germany seemed to be making progress, they switched to bombing cities. The storms began at the end of the summer, and, by that time, Britain was far stronger than it was in June. Hitler postponed Sea Lion, then cancelled it on September 17. It would never be resumed.

The Battle of Britain did not guarantee that Hitler would lose the war, but it was a long step, perhaps the longest step, toward that end. From now on, he would conduct his operations in the East with an increasingly powerful enemy at his back. That unconquered enemy was as close to the lands he occupied as Santa Catalina Island is to Los Angeles or Long Island is to New Haven, Connecticut. It not only had one of the world's largest navies, but it was developing an air force that would surpass the Luftwaffe in every way. And it provided a base for millions of new enemy troops from across the seas.

Battle 8

Constantinople, Part I, 1203 AD
An Inconvenient Contract

Who fought: Crusaders and Venetians (Enrico Dandolo) vs. East Romans (Alexius III and Alexius IV).

What was at stake: Constantinople's role as a bulwark against the Turks.

On the face of it, the contract looked like a windfall. A group of French knights wanted transportation to Egypt to begin a new crusade. The five-year truce Richard the Lionhearted and Saladin signed had ended, and both Saladin and Richard were dead. The leader of the knights, Boniface of Montferrat, was willing to pay the Venetians well for carrying his army across the Mediterranean. Egypt, Boniface told the Doge of Venice, was the most vulnerable part of Islam, and the key to the Holy Land.

But to the Doge, Enrico Dandolo, Egypt was something else: It was Venice's leading trading partner.

A lesser man would have resigned himself to losing either the ferry contract or the lucrative trade with Egypt. Dandolo did neither. He sent a message to Saphadin, Saladin's brother, who was now Sultan of Egypt, telling him not to worry. Then he spoke with his council.

Dandolo cared nothing for crusades. His only concern was Venice. Now 80, he had fought the Pisans, the Genoese, and the Byzantines for control of the eastern

46

Mediterranean. His city was now the greatest power on the inland sea. In one of his battles with the Byzantine Greeks, he had suffered a blow on the head that killed his eyesight. Though his eyes were useless, there was nothing wrong with Dandolo's hindsight or foresight. He could look back at the years of strife between Venice and Constantinople, including a massacre of all Italian merchants in the Byzantine capital. He remembered, too, that when Saladin had captured Jerusalem, Isaac Angelus, the Greek emperor, had sent his congratulations. He could also look forward to a Venetian thalassocracy based on Crete, Rhodes, Cyprus, and the Greek islands. The Great Council, the ruling body of the Venetian Republic, endorsed the Doge's plan.

An army held hostage

Dandolo agreed with the Crusaders to transport 4,500 knights, 4,500 horses, 9,000 squires, and 20,000 heavily armed soldiers called sergeants to Egypt. He would also supply 50 warships and their crews and furnish the army with nine months' rations. In return, the Crusaders would pay Venice 85,000 silver marks—four marks for each horse and two for each man—and give the Venetians half of the booty they captured. The contract would last for one year from the day the fleet sailed. The Crusaders borrowed 5,000 marks from Venetian bankers as a down payment. Dandolo put them up on the island of Lido, several miles from Venice, and began building a fleet. When the fleet was ready, Dandolo asked for his money but the Crusaders didn't have it.

"You shall not depart from the island until we are paid," he said. Then he made them a proposal. The King of Hungary had stolen the city of Zara from Venice, Dandolo said. (Actually, Venice never held Zara, but the North European rustics didn't know that.) If the Crusaders would take back the city, Dandolo would forgive their debt.

The Crusaders besieged Zara. Some of them deserted and went to the Holy Land alone, but most remained. They took Zara and asked for their passage to Egypt.

Dandolo's crusade

It was too late, the Doge told them. The winter storms would make passage to Egypt impossible—they'd have to wait until spring. It was, after all, their fault, because they were so late in paying their debt. Meanwhile, Pope Innocent III had excommunicated all the Crusaders who attacked Zara for having shed Christian blood after taking the cross. A little later, realizing that his wily Italian compatriots had taken in this crowd of northern bumpkins, he revoked the excommunication but warned them not to do it again.

Then a young man named Alexius Angelus appeared at the Crusader camp. Alexius was the son of the Greek emperor, recently deposed by a usurper who was also named Alexius. The crusaders didn't know it, but Prince Alexius was part of a scheme hatched by the blind Doge. If Dandolo could use the Crusaders to restore him to power, Prince Alexius would become a Venetian puppet.

Putting young Alexius on the throne would not be an easy task. Constantinople was the strongest city in the world. For centuries, it had defeated Goths, Huns, Avars, Slavs, Magyars, Russians, and Arabs trying to take it. On the other hand, Dandolo controlled the world's most powerful navy, and now he had the world's most powerful army under his thumb.

Prince Alexius was persuasive. Geoffroi de Villehardoin, one of the crusader leaders, recalled that Alexius offered:

Firstly, if God permits you to restore his inheritance to him, he will place his whole empire under the authority of Rome, from which he has long been estranged. Secondly, since he is well aware that you have spent all your money and now have nothing, he will give you 200,000 silver marks and provisions for every man in your army, officers and men alike. Moreover, he himself will go in your company to Egypt with 10,000 men, or, if you prefer it, send the same number of men with you; and furthermore, so long as he lives, he will maintain, at his expense, 5,000 knights to keep guard in the land overseas.

The Crusaders sailed to Constantinople.

Assault

The Crusaders sent an envoy to the usurper, Alexius III, to tell him they had come to restore Prince Alexius to his throne. If the current emperor would step down, he could live as a wealthy man. If not, he would not live at all. Alexius III did not abdicate. Then the invaders took Prince Alexius up to the city walls in a small boat.

"Here is your natural lord," they told the crowds on the walls. "Rally to his side and no harm will come to you." The crowds gave no sign that they recognized young Alexius.

The next day, Dandolo's host launched the assault. The Byzantine army lined up on shore to meet them. The Crusaders hesitated, but the Doge said his ships would clear the way. Catapults and ballistas on the fore and stern castles of the warships hurled boulders and spears at the Greek soldiers. Crossbowmen in the fighting tops and decks shot clouds of bolts. The Greeks fell back. The Crusader assault boats scraped ashore and dropped their drawbridges. Armored knights rode ashore with lowered lances. The Greeks turned and ran back into the city, breaking down the bridge that led to the entrance. The Greeks still held the harbor, a narrow arm of the sea called the Golden Horn. They had stretched a chain across it from the city to the fort of Galata on the other side. The Crusaders besieged the fort. The Greeks sallied out but were beaten back. The Crusaders followed so closely the Greeks couldn't close the gate of the fort. While the French were taking the fort, the Venetians attacked the chain. They sent galley after galley crashing into the chain. The chain snapped.

Dandolo wanted to attack the city's sea wall. It was only one wall, whereas the land side had a double wall, with the space between the two ramparts so constricted that getting over the second wall would be most difficult. The French, however, protested that they were landsmen. They needed terra firma beneath them when they fought. The crusaders lined up their siege engines and crossbows, opened fire, and attacked a gate tower with scaling ladders. The Varangian Guard, English and Scandinavian mercenaries who had been in imperial service since Viking times, held the tower. The Varangians used the big Danish battleaxe, which chopped through the Crusaders' armor with frightening facility. The French failed.

Dandolo, meanwhile, launched his own forces against the sea wall. He had built scaling towers, equipped with drawbridges, on the decks of his ships. Again, the Venetian catapults banged and crossbows snapped. The warships closed in. This time, the Greeks shot back with their own engines and archers. The Venetian crews moved back.

The old Doge told a sailor to bring him the banner of St. Mark, the flag of his city-state. Holding it before him, Dandolo screamed at the sailors he could not see, "Put me ashore, you craven dogs!"

Constantinople waterfront.

The ship pulled up to the bottom of the wall. A dozen men leaped out to shield their Doge, who jumped off the ship. Up on the ship's tower, the drawbridge thumped down, and Venetian soldiers charged over it to the wall. The other warships now joined them, and Venetians and Greeks were soon battling all along the sea wall. Dandolo's men captured 25 towers on the wall and moved into the city. The Emperor called his men, who were fighting the French, to stop the Venetians. The Italians retreated before the assault, but they set fire to the houses between them and the Greeks. The wind from the sea blew the fire back toward the imperial troops, and the Venetians fortified their captured towers. The emperor then led his army out of the city to attack the French.

"We had no more than six divisions while the Greeks had close on 60, and not one of them but was larger than ours," Villehardoin recalled. "However our troops were drawn up in such a way that they could not be attacked except from the front."

The Crusaders "took all the horse-boys and cooks who could bear arms and had them fitted out with quilts and saddle cloths [for armor] and copper pots [for helmets]," wrote Robert de Clari, one of the Crusaders. The Crusaders could not advance, for fear of being outflanked, and the Greeks had no desire to fight on a narrow front where their numbers would mean little. The Emperor slowly withdrew into the city.

That night, Alexius III and his household sneaked out of Constantinople. The people of the city let old Isaac out of his dungeon and opened the city gates. Invincible Constantinople had fallen.

The second siege

Isaac was broken in spirit and blind, so Prince Alexius joined him as co-emperor. The real power in Constantinople, however, belonged to Enrico Dandolo, a man just as blind as Isaac and far older.

The Crusaders asked Prince Alexius, now Alexius IV, for the money and men that he had promised. Alexius and Dandolo pointed out that the usurper still held most of the empire. When that was recovered, Alexius could pay his debt. But both Alexius and Dandolo knew that there were not 200,000 silver marks in the treasury. Nor was there money in the treasury to pay the 10,000 mercenaries Alexius had promised.

Some of the Crusaders asked Dandolo to take them to Egypt without the money or mercenaries. Dandolo said he could, but there were only two months left on the contract. He would not be able to supply them after those two months. He pointed out that Alexius had already given them 100,000 marks (half of which, under the agreement, went to Venice). If the new Emperor could settle his empire, he'd surely pay the rest. The Crusaders might want to help him do that. If they did, he'd make his fleet available for another year free of charge. The Crusaders agreed to help.

Meanwhile, the Pope heard about the attack on Constantinople. He was furious, but he learned that his own papal legate had blessed the enterprise, so he couldn't excommunicate the Crusaders. He decided to make the best of it and take advantage of Alexius's offer to bring the Orthodox Church back to Rome.

In Constantinople, there was rioting between the French and the Greeks. Finally, the Crusaders got tired of the Emperor's stalling. They said they'd take their payment by force. The Emperor called up his troops and drove them out of the city. Then the son-in-law of the usurping Alexius III, Alexius Ducas, nicknamed Murzuphlus, led a coup and deposed both Isaac and Alexius IV. The first died of natural causes and the second was strangled.

The Venetians and Crusaders again attacked the sea wall, but they were beaten back with heavy losses. The Greeks had always been able to outnumber the soldiers crossing the drawbridges from the towers. Dandolo had the ships tied together so he could land twice as many men at each point. Still the Westerners could make no headway until a gust of wind drove two ships against the wall, and soldiers from them immediately got on the wall. The Greeks had not seen that attack coming, so the Crusaders and Venetians were able to establish a foothold. As the Greeks moved against them, other Venetian ships hit undefended battlements. By the day's end, the Westerners held three towers. They opened some city gates, and armored knights charged the Greek troops on the streets. When night fell, Murzuphlus and his army fled.

The bitter fruits of victory

The French and Venetians split the spoils, and French knights established fiefs in Greece and forgot about crusading. Venice took over the Aegean Islands, achieving Dandolo's dream. Relations between the Greeks and the Latins, as the French and Venetians were called, had never been good. Now they were as bad as they could be. The Pope never realized his dream of Christian unity.

Constantinople had been the bulwark of Christendom against the forces of Islam for centuries. Dandolo's crusade had wrecked the Empire's infrastructure and set it up for conquest by the Ottoman Turks a couple of centuries later (see Constantinople, Part II, pg. 145). Even worse, it set a deadly precedent. The Pope had not approved the conquest of Constantinople, but he had recognized the new Latin Empire. The precedent of crusading against Christians was set. Later in Innocent's reign, he authorized a crusade against the Albigensian heretics in France. Instead of relying on moral suasion, the church had turned to naked force. Soon all Christian groups, both supporters and enemies of the papacy, adopted the idea. That culminated in the terrible religious wars of the 16th and 17th centuries—collectively, the most disastrous event in the history of Western civilization.

Battle 9

Tsushima, 1905 AD
"Russian prestige will do the rest"

Who fought: Russians (Zinovi P. Rozhestvensky) vs. Japanese (Togo Heihachiro).

What was at stake: Narrowly, control of Manchuria; broadly, unquestioned Western domination of the Far East.

Russia, in the time-honored fashion of European colonial powers, was taking over the Chinese territory of Manchuria. First, it got a concession to run the Trans Siberian Railway through a strip of Chinese territory. Then she got a long-term lease on the Liao Tung Peninsula, where it planned to build a naval base, and then permission to build and operate a branch railroad from the Trans Siberian to the peninsula. Russia was establishing what was then called a "sphere of influence" in Manchuria.

That concerned Japan, which was trying to establish its own sphere of influence in Korea. Russia and Japan entered negotiations, but Russia was always finding reasons why no conclusion could be reached. While the diplomats talked, Russia secured China's permission to send troops to the Yalu River, the border between Manchuria and Korea. Japan broke off diplomatic relations with Russia.

Then, on February 8, 1904, the Japanese Navy, under Admiral Togo Heihachiro, attacked the Russian ships at Port Arthur. Two days later, Japan declared war on

Russia. In his sneak attack, Togo hit three Russian ships. The next day he had a brief fight with Russian ships off Chemulpo (modern Inch'on) in Korea, sinking a cruiser and a gunboat. Neither action had much effect on either navy. On paper, Russia was a major naval power. It had more battleships than any country except for Britain or France. In the Far East alone, Russia had seven first-class battleships to Japan's six, nine first-class cruisers to Japan's eight, and 25 destroyers to Japan's 19. And the Far East fleet was by no means the bulk of Russia's navy. It had equally powerful fleets in the Black Sea and the Baltic Sea.

On land, the apparent discrepancy was even greater. Russia had some 4,500,000 trained soldiers; Japan had 283,000. The catch was that the Russian troops in the Far East had to be supplied by the Trans Siberian Railway. The railroad, for most of its length, was a single track. It was laid across tundra that turned into shifting morass every spring. And at Lake Baikal, in central Siberia, there was a gap in the line. In winter, goods could be hauled 30 miles across the frozen lake, but in warm weather shipments had to move over 100 miles of miserable roads. It took a full month to move a battalion to the Far East. In the whole area between Lake Baikal and the Pacific, there were only 138,000 Russian troops.

That might have aroused the traditional fear of "Asiatic hordes" (although Russia had three times the population of Japan), but Russian authorities weren't worried. Asked if his procrastination during negotiations might not provoke a war, the Russian foreign minister said there would be no war. All Russia needed in Manchuria was "one flag and one sentry. Russian prestige will do the rest." And if it really did come to a crunch, Russian naval power would be decisive. Japan, after all, was a group of islands. And while numbers might be decisive in land fighting, it was different at sea. Navies depended on science and mechanics. The "little yellow monkeys" just couldn't match Europeans there.

"Our plan of operations should be based on the assumption that it is impossible for our fleet to be beaten," the Russian Naval Staff reported.

The Russian naval commanders in Manchuria weren't so sure. Although they had more heavy warships than Togo, they let the Japanese land at Chemulpo on February 17 and move through Manchuria toward their base, Port Arthur. On August 10, to escape the Japanese troops ringing Port Arthur, the Russian fleet put to sea. It was trounced by a smaller Japanese fleet and driven back to the harbor. So far, all that the Russian Navy had demonstrated was its incompetence. Worse was to come.

The voyage of the damned

The Russian Black Sea fleet was bound by treaty not to pass through the Dardanelles, but there was no such restriction on the Baltic Sea fleet. That fleet, under Admiral Zinovi Petrovitch Rozhestvensky, had seven battleships and a number of cruisers and destroyers. On October 15, it was dubbed the Second Pacific Squadron and ordered to relieve Port Arthur. It almost never got there.

Togo's sneak attack had unnerved the Russian high command. Russian intelligence agents in Denmark reported Japanese torpedo boats in the North Sea. In the North Sea mist, Rozhestvensky's men thought they saw those torpedo boats and opened fire. They hit some other Russian warships and sank one British trawler. The "torpedo boats" had been English fishing boats. The British Royal Navy prepared to intercept Rozhestvensky. The Russian government hastily apologized.

After firing (without effect) on some Swedish, French, and German ships they mistook for Japanese, the Russians reached Tangier. Pulling out of that harbor on their way to round the Cape of Good Hope, they snagged the underwater telegraph cable, cutting off communications with Europe for four days. At Dakar, they met the first of 60 German colliers the Russian government had contracted to refuel the fleet. The Russian Navy, unlike the navies of Britain, France, Germany, and the United States, had no overseas coaling stations.

At Dakar and at Cape Town, the Russian sailors, to break the monotony, had adopted exotic pets, including monkeys, apes, and crocodiles, and brought them aboard. One pet, a poisonous snake, nearly killed a crewmember. By the time they reached Madagascar, the tropical heat and humidity had felled many Russians, including Rozhestvensky. They stayed two weeks at Madagascar, waiting for a supply ship that was to replenish the shells they had fired at inoffensive neutrals. When the supply ship arrived, the Russian sailors discovered that instead of shells, it contained 12,000 pairs of fur-lined boots and 12,000 winter coats. At French Indochina, Rozhestvensky's fleet met reinforcements. The new fleet included some coastal monitors and some decrepit warships the Russian sailors themselves called "self-sinkers."

Long before the Russian fleet got that far, Port Arthur, which it was to relieve, had surrendered on January 2. The fleet was still at Madagascar when, on March 10, Japanese troops decisively defeated the Russians at Mukden. For all intents and purposes, the war was over. But Rozhetvensky received no orders to change course. He pushed on.

Crossing the T

Togo was waiting. The Japanese ships, most of them built in Britain, were newer and faster. Their guns fired heavier shells. The Russian ships, however, carried better armor-piercing shells and the Russian armor was of better steel. The Russians entered the Straits of Tsushima, between Japan and Korea. Rozhestvensky knew the enemy was near. He ordered his heavy ships to form a line abreast instead of a column. That way, if they encountered a column of Japanese ships, they could all turn and fire broadsides at the enemy.

The maneuver was a classic naval tactic called "crossing the T." The approaching enemy fleet, one ship behind another, could fire only the guns facing forward on the first ship. The ships behind the first could not fire at all. Meanwhile the fleet that had crossed the T could fire most of the guns on each ship.

The Russian navigators, however, were not able to form a line abreast. The best they could do was two parallel columns. The Japanese approached them from the side, instead of from directly ahead. At 1:40 p.m. on May 27, the main battle fleets made contact and opened fire. The Japanese had four battleships and eight armored cruisers to the Russians' seven battleships and nine armored cruisers. It was misty, and the Russian ships, painted black with yellow funnels, were easier to see. The Japanese, ahead of most of the world in this respect, had painted their ships slate gray.

Togo took advantage of his superior speed and crossed the Russian T. Ten Japanese ships concentrated their fire on the two lead Russian battleships. One was knocked out almost immediately, the second was crippled 20 minutes later. Fire broke out on a third Russian battleship. *Mikasa*, Togo's flagship, was hit several times, and one of his cruisers was forced to drop out of the battle. The Russians tried to turn away from the T-crossing Japanese, but Togo's fleet turned with them. A half-circle of Japanese ships laid down a devastating crossfire on the Russians. Rozhestvensky was seriously wounded and transferred, unconscious, to a destroyer.

When he regained consciousness, he was in a Japanese hospital. Five of the seven Russian battleships, including his flagship, *Suvarov*, had been sunk. Three cruisers escaped to the Philippines, where their crews were interned. A cruiser and two destroyers reached Vladivostok. All together, the Russians had lost 34 of their 37 warships. Killed were 4,830 Russian crewmen, while 5,917 were captured and 1,862 were interned. The number of Japanese killed totaled 110, with three cruisers damaged and three torpedo boats sunk.

Tsushima was, except for the two battles in 1898 in which the Americans destroyed virtually the whole Spanish navy with the loss of only one seaman, the most lopsided naval battle of modern times. The Tsar had to sue for peace. Theodore Roosevelt mediated the peace. The terms, of course, were favorable to Japan. Roosevelt would have preferred that the Japanese victory had not been quite so crushing. He'd hoped the Russian and Japanese navies would balance each other. The Spanish American War, which had boosted Roosevelt to power, had made the United States a Far Eastern power. From 1905 on, Japanese and American naval men eyed each other warily. Whatever happened in the rest of the world, each knew that the other was the ultimate enemy.

Even more important, Togo and his men had shattered the notion of Caucasian superiority. That, like the long-simmering American-Japanese naval rivalry, would not come to a head for another generation or two. But it takes only a glance at a globe to see how it has changed the world.

Battle 10

Arnold takes the redoubt.

Saratoga, 1777 AD
Gentleman Johnny's Plan

Who fought: Americans (Horatio Gates and Benedict Arnold) vs. British (John Burgoyne).

What was at stake: The survival of the United States.

The King's army was marching down from Canada to end the rebellion, General Burgoyne proclaimed, and it was the duty of all loyal colonists to help it. Those who refused and sided with the rebels would suffer "devastation, famine, and every concomitant horror that a reluctant but indispensable prosecution of military duty must entail." More specifically, he said, "I have but to give stretch to the Indians under my direction (and they amount to thousands) to overtake the hardened enemies of Great Britain and America."

To be fair, Lt. Gen. John Burgoyne was bluffing. "Gentleman Johnny" had earned his nickname not by his flamboyant lifestyle but by his humanity. He had abolished flogging in his command, although it was practiced in every army, including the Continental. Burgoyne had forbidden his Indian scouts to kill civilians. He told them he'd pay only for live captives. He wasn't being totally altruistic, of course: Only live captives could provide information.

Burgoyne had witnessed the bloodbath on Breed's Hill two years before. He knew that the war could not be won without the cooperation of at least some of the colonists. As far as he could see, the center of the rebellion was New England, where the radicals had gained control of the militia and what remained of the colonial assemblies. New England was also the portion of the colonies closest to Canada. If New England could be isolated and subdued, the other colonies might abandon their ridiculous Declaration of Independence.

Gentleman Johnny had a plan, and, as a member of Parliament, he had the political connections to get it approved. He was going to move, by land and water, down Lake Champlain and the Hudson River, to cut off New England. Howe would move up the river from New York City and take the rebels in the rear. The British armies would meet at Albany. Barry St. Leger, leading an army of American Tories and Indians, would march down the Mohawk to Albany. And Tories from all over backwoods New York and New England would reinforce the King's forces. Col. Philip Skene, one of Burgoyne's Tory officers, had convinced him that the backwoods were full of Tories.

Actually, there were many loyalists in the backwoods. Sir William Johnson, who founded a fur-trading empire in western New York and Pennsylvania, had imported hundreds of them from Ireland and Scotland. Johnson, born William McShane in Ireland, was also the Mohawk chief Warraghiyagey. He had secured the loyalty of the Iroquois tribes. Johnson was dead, but his son, Sir John Johnson, and his second-in-command, John Butler, had formed Tory regiments. St. Leger was to lead them and 1,000 Mohawks under William Johnson's brother-in-law, Joseph Brant. Brant was an Indian chief educated in Connecticut and welcomed in London society.

Fair proportions of Burgoyne's army were American loyalists. One was a lieutenant named David Jones, serving in the corps led by Acting Brig. Gen. Simon Fraser. Jones had an extra incentive. His sweetheart, Jane McCrae, was waiting for him in Albany. Pretty "Jenny" McCrae, in fact, couldn't stand the waiting. She moved in with a Mrs. McNeill, a relative who had a cabin in the woods north of Albany, to be closer to her David. Mrs. McNeill, of course, was also a Tory. One of her cousins was Simon Fraser, the daring Scot who led Burgoyne's vanguard.

Jenny McCrae

The fortress of Ticonderoga, overlooking the narrow waters of Lake Champlain, was considered the Gibraltar of America. Burgoyne had Fraser circle the fort and scout out the territory. The Scot reported that a mountain overlooking Ticonderoga was not occupied. Burgoyne had cannons hauled up the mountain. When the Americans saw the guns, they abandoned Ticonderoga and fled into the woods. Burgoyne decided to pursue them instead of sailing to the end of the lake and following the road that led from there to the Hudson River.

That was his first mistake.

The English general had 7,500 men, 42 cannons, and a supply train consisting of hundreds of carts. The Americans felled huge trees across every possible trail and skirmished with his vanguard. They slowed Burgoyne's progress to about a mile a day. The British were inching through a jungle-like forest, advancing on an unseen enemy. Burgoyne had to know what was ahead of him. He sent out his Indian scouts.

One of the first things the Indians saw was the cabin of Mrs. McNeill. Two of them burst into the cabin, grabbed Mrs. McNeill and Jenny McCrae, stripped them and started back to the British camp. On the way back, they quarreled over which would receive the reward for Jenny McCrae; apparently believing the British would pay more for a beautiful young woman than for an aged widow. The Indian who lost the argument shot Jenny McCrae and scalped her.

When she got to the British camp, Mrs. McNeill told her cousin the general what happened. Fraser, beside himself with fury, went to Burgoyne. Burgoyne, too, was outraged. He ordered that the Indians be hanged. But St. Luc de la Corne, leader of Burgoyne's Indians, said that if anything happened to the murderers, he'd take all his men and go home. Burgoyne pardoned the Indians.

That was his second—and biggest—mistake.

Word of what happened spread all through New England and New York. Burgoyne had unleashed his Indians, and they were killing everyone, whether Patriot or Tory. Men picked up their muskets and rifles and set out for the American camp. The American army, which was only about half the size of Burgoyne's at the start of the campaign, grew rapidly.

Burgoyne's army, on the other hand, was shrinking. The British suffered shortages of everything, especially food. Philip Schuyler, the American commander, had ordered all the farmers in the area to destroy their crops and drive off their livestock to prevent the British from living off the land. Characteristically, Schuyler, a Hudson Valley patroon despised by the democratic New Englanders, left his own vast estate intact.

Disasters on all sides

To gather food and recruit Tories, Burgoyne sent Lt. Col. Friedrich Baum and 700 soldiers toward Lake Champlain. Baum's force consisted of British, American Tories, German mercenaries, and Indians. The Germans included 170 dismounted dragoons, encumbered by huge broadswords and bayonet-proof jackboots, which covered the knees. Baum spoke no English, but he had Philip Skene as an interpreter. Slogging through the woods, Baum heard that Patriot militia were planning to attack. He asked for reinforcements. Burgoyne sent 700 more Germans under Lt. Col. Heinrich Breymann after Baum.

Both the colony of New York and the colony of New Hampshire claimed the territory they approached. But its inhabitants called it the independent Republic of Vermont.

In New Hampshire, John Stark, who had foiled Howe's flanking movement at Bunker Hill, took 1,500 militiamen and headed west. Five hundred more militia from Massachusetts soon joined him. The Jenny McCrae story was having an effect.

Baum at first thought these armed backwoodsmen were coming to join him. They practically surrounded his force without opposition, then hit both flanks. Baum's Indians fled at the first shot. The whites were driven together in the center, and Stark launched his main attack. An American shot blew up one of Baum's ammunition carts. Baum ordered his dragoons to cut their way out with swords, but seconds later, an American bullet killed him. Baum's force disintegrated.

Just then, Breymann and his 700 Germans appeared. They were just in time to meet the Green Mountain Boys, Vermont's own army, which had arrived to help the Massachusetts and New Hampshire militia. The Germans tried to form a line and fire volleys, while the New England rustics fired from behind trees. Breymann was losing men fast; his troops were shaken. He told a drummer to beat a slow roll, the international request for a truce. To the Americans, a slow roll was just so much noise. They continued firing. The Germans stampeded from the field. By day's end, Burgoyne had lost 207 killed and 700 captured, along with four cannons. The Americans had 30 killed and 40 wounded.

While this was happening in the East, another disaster was taking place in the West. St. Leger's Tories were unpopular enough in the Mohawk Valley, but his Mohawks were hated and feared. Patriot militia reactivated old Fort Stanwix to block St. Leger. St. Leger besieged the fort. A Patriot militia force tried to break the siege, but was led into an ambush by Joseph Brant. The result was bloody and indecisive. The British abandoned the field, but the Americans were too cut up to go on.

At this juncture, Benedict Arnold, recently reassigned to the north by George Washington, appeared. He found a mentally disabled man named Hon Yost Schuyler and convinced him to tell the Indians that Arnold, who had proved his brilliance as a general in this area the year before, was coming with a huge army. The Indians believed that the mentally deficient were incapable of lying. They quickly decamped. When the Tories saw that the Mohawks were gone, they followed.

But for Burgoyne the worst news of all was that Howe was not coming. Howe had his own plan for ending the war: Capture Philadelphia, the rebel capital. Aided by the inefficiency of the British cabinet, Howe got his plan approved while Burgoyne was on the high seas. He left Henry Clinton with 4,000 men in New York City. Clinton was not about to try driving through to Albany. If he moved many men out of the city, Washington would snap it up.

While all this was going on, it occurred to Washington that something important might be happening in the north. So, along with Arnold, he sent Daniel Morgan and 1,000 riflemen. Horatio Gates, a genial Englishman who was anything but a fiery leader, had replaced the unpopular Schuyler.

Johnny rolls the dice

The American army was growing daily as armed citizens, individuals as well as militia units, arrived at Gates's camp. Gates said he was afraid to expose these raw recruits to Burgoyne's Indians, although by this time, the Indians had deserted the British. Gates put his new men to work digging earthworks a little south of Saratoga. At this point, the numerical odds had been reversed. Gates had two men for every man of Burgoyne's. Gentleman Johnny, though, never shrank from risking everything on the draw of a card. He attacked.

Simon Fraser led 2,000 men around the American left, seeking to seize a hill over-looking the rebel trenches. At Gates's headquarters, Arnold begged the commanding general to hit the British while they were in the open. Gates preferred to wait for them in his trenches. Finally, he let Arnold, commanding the left wing, send Morgan to counterattack. Morgan's riflemen drove back Fraser's scouts. Then the British light infantry appeared and pushed Morgan's men back with a bayonet charge. Arnold sent in two Continental regiments in order to stop the British. But after a hard fight, those troops, too, were driven back. Burgoyne ordered a general advance all along the line.

Arnold noticed that a gap had opened between the Fraser's corps and the main British body, led by Burgoyne. He led more troops into the gap. The British closed up, and Arnold's entire corps was engaged. Arnold rode back to ask for reinforcements, but Gates, with a horde of reserves, refused to send any. And he confined Arnold to headquarters. Meanwhile, Maj. Gen. Adolph von Riedesel, who commanded the British left, took his German mercenaries toward the sound of the guns. He hit the Americans in the flank and drove them back before darkness ended the fighting. Burgoyne had won a Pyrrhic victory. He had 600 killed, wounded, or captured. The Americans suffered 65 killed and 218 wounded. Of the troops engaged, 33 percent of the British and 10 percent of the Americans were casualties. Gates should have counterattacked, but he stayed in his trenches.

Burgoyne now heard that the rebels had cut his communications and captured most of his supply ships. And Clinton wrote that he had been reinforced and was going to move north. Gentleman Johnny had no choice but to attack.

Once again, Simon Fraser led the attack. Once again, Gates moved most reluctantly. He had already deprived Arnold of his command for being too aggressive. He allowed Morgan to take his brigade and Enoch Poor's to meet Fraser.

Morgan's riflemen performed their customary long-range carnage, and Poor's brigade, its numbers swollen to 800 by recent additions, pushed the British back with a bayonet charge. Gates allowed one more brigade to engage Riedesel's Germans, who were again moving up to support Fraser. Then Arnold, unable to contain himself, mounted his horse and led the charge against Riedesel's corps. The Germans fell back to their own trenches.

Fraser, on his big gray horse, dashed frantically up and down the line, rallying his men. The British stopped retreating and began to advance. Morgan called a rifleman named Tim Murphy, one of the best shots in the army, and told him to kill Fraser. Murphy fired twice with his double-barrel rifle, reloaded, and fired again. Fraser fell from the saddle at the third shot, and his aides carried the dying general to the rear. The British line broke. Arnold led the Americans right into the British right wing redoubt, where he was shot in the leg.

Burgoyne had to retreat, but there was nowhere to retreat to. And there was no way Clinton could reach him. He surrendered his army. Surrendered to a mob of peasants. It was unthinkable. London was shocked.

In Paris it was considered a miracle. To take advantage of the miracle, France declared war on England, and brought Spain and Holland into the fight with her. Britain, bogged down in a land war that could not be won in America, now had to face the three strongest sea powers after herself. The Revolutionary War would drag on for more than five more years, but the result was inevitable.

A new nation was created, and a rabble of peasants proved that they could successfully rule themselves without a king. A few years later, that inspired the ancient kingdom of France, and the new colonies of Latin America to do the same. The world had been changed most decisively.

Battle 11

Looting the bastille.

Valmy, 1792 AD
The Revolutionary Army

Who fought: French (Charles Dumouriez) vs. Prussians, Austrians, and Hessians (Duke of Brunswick).

What was at stake: The French Revolution and democracy in Europe.

No country was more eager for war than France, and no country was less prepared.

The Marquis de Lafayette, the Comte de Rochambeau, and others who had fought in the American Revolution helped fan the fires of revolution in France. Taxation was a problem in France, as well as in America, but in France, taxes were imposed not by a distant parliament, but by the king. The Estates General, what passed for a parliament in France, had not been summoned in almost two centuries. Finally, the agitation of the people became too much for Louis XVI. He convened the assembly.

The Third Estate, the commoners, declared themselves to be the National Assembly. They issued the Declaration of the Rights of Man and forced Louis to become a constitutional monarch with limited powers. The crowned heads of Europe began viewing France with alarm. Particularly aroused were the Holy Roman Emperor, Franz II, nephew of Queen Marie Antoinette, and the King of Prussia, Friedrich Wilhelm II. Louis knew his country was not ready for another war, so he suggested to the ministers that they declare war on Austria. The result, the king hoped, would be the defeat of the revolutionary armies and his own liberation. The revolutionaries jumped at the idea. A war, they thought, would unite their seriously divided country. War fever gripped the French population. Volunteers rushed to join the army. France sent three armies to the frontier, one of them commanded by Lafayette.

Street fighting in the French Revolution.

Lafayette was unusual. Most of the French officers had fled the country when the revolution began. That was a serious problem because most of the troops were the rawest recruits—filled with revolutionary ardor, but devoid of discipline. And in Paris, the revolutionists became ever more revolutionary. On August 10, 1792, they stripped the king of all powers. Lafayette wasn't prepared to go that far. Frustrated in his attempt to lead his troops to Paris, he fled the country.

Charles Francois Dumouriez, appointed to replace him, faced a sullen and hostile army that hated all authority figures. When he paraded his men the day after taking command, there were jeers and one soldier shouted, "*A bas le general!*" Dumouriez drew his sword and challenged the soldier to fight him. The heckler slunk back into the crowd. Dumouriez had scored a point, but he hadn't exactly transformed his troops.

Invasion

Austria had countered France's declaration of war with one of its own. Prussia joined Austria. The two countries sent armies into France. It looked as if Liberty, Equality, and Fraternity would get short shrift. Fifteen thousand Austrians entered from the Netherlands. South of them were 42,000 Prussians, 5,500 Hessians, and 4,500 French emigrés, all under the Duke of Brunswick. On Brunswick's left flank, another 15,000 Austrians crossed the Rhine. All were converging on Dumouriez. Near Lille, about 4,000 French revolutionary troops encountered a small force of Austrians. Before a shot was fired, the French dashed off the field in a screaming panic, then murdered their general.

Brunswick was esteemed the best general in Europe, a master of the maneuver-and-siege warfare that had evolved after the horrors of the Thirty Years War. That war had been fought by hordes of undisciplined mercenaries who lived off the land, slaughtered civilians, and made a desert of Germany. Eighteenth century warfare, in contrast, was fought by small, highly trained armies, which seldom touched civilians and got their supplies from well-stocked magazines in fortresses. Marshal Maurice de Saxe, one of the greatest practitioners of this type of warfare, said, "I am not in favor of giving battle, especially at the outset of a war. I am even convinced that a clever general can wage war his entire life without being compelled to do so."

It didn't look as if Brunswick would be compelled to do so. The fortress of Verdun fell after a short bombardment. Brunswick, in overall command of the allied armies, moved very slowly, but the French seemed unable to resist him. Dumouriez fell back on the Ardennes and positioned his troops to block the defiles that led through those mountains. The government ordered the southern army under Francois Christophe Kellermann to move up and help Dumouriez.

General Clerfayt, commanding the northern Austrian army, sent a detachment of light infantry and light cavalry to rush the defile at Croix aux Bois. The French defenders fled. Loss of that pass threatened to cut off the French defenders of the defile at Chesne-Populeux. They retreated to the main French body at Grandpre. The Prussians and Austrians could now flank Dumouriez.

Dumouriez retreated again. Brunswick pushed west, expecting the French to have fallen back toward Paris. But instead, Dumouriez, now united with Kellermann, had moved to the south, on the left flank of Brunswick's army. The Prussians made a wide turning motion and approached the French from the west, from the direction of Paris.

The French generals had established positions on two hills near the village of Valmy. They formed a semicircular defense line with the center facing due west. Because of sickness and the need to establish garrisons in the rear, Brunswick's forces had been reduced to 34,000 men; Dumouriez and Kellermann had 36,000 between them. But the French were the same rabble who had run away or surrendered after the first few shots.

The Duke of Brunswick.

The cannonade

Brunswick concentrated his artillery on Kellermann's army—58 guns against Kellermann's 40. Of the bombardment, the poet Goethe, who was with the Prussian army, said the cannonade, "the violence of which at the time it is impossible to describe," made the whole battlefield tremble.

The French should have fled. Brunswick looked through his telescope, but he could see nothing. Were there still any soldiers in the French trenches? He ordered the infantry to advance.

The French hadn't run. They wheeled up their artillery and opened up on the Prussian infantry. Before his men were in musket range, Brunswick halted the advance. The Duke turned to his staff and said, "*Hier schlagen wir nicht*" ("We do not fight here").

Negotiations for a truce began. Brunswick withdrew his army. King Friedrich Wilhelm finally rejected the truce and berated his general, who, if he had moved faster when the French retreated from the passes in the Ardennes, could have ended the war.

The war did not end for a long time. Not until after Waterloo. By that time, France had introduced two new ideas to military practice: mass armies and total war. More important, it became the first major European power to adopt democracy.

Battle 12

Adrianople, 378 AD
The Goths

Who fought: Romans (Valens) vs. Goths (Aletheus and Sarfac).

What was at stake: The survival of the Roman Empire (this was the beginning of the so-called Fall of Rome) and the role of cavalry (an essential component of feudalism).

Valens, the Roman Emperor of the East, beheld a most unusual sight. A huge crowd of Visigoths stood on the opposite bank of the Danube, yelling and waving their arms. They were not threatening. They were begging—begging to be admitted to the Empire.

"The multitude of Scythians [Goths]...amounted to not less than 200,000 men of fighting age," wrote the contemporary Roman historian, Eunapius. They promised "that they would faithfully adhere to the Imperial alliance if this boon were granted them."

Valens was involved in a war with Persia. He saw the Gothic warriors as a great potential reinforcement for his army. He told the generals in charge of the border guards, Lupicinus and Maximus, to allow the Goths to enter if they turned over their weapons.

He may have reflected that it's an ill wind that blows no good, or whatever the Roman equivalent of that old saw was. It had been an exceedingly ill wind for the Visigoths, and for their cousins, the Ostrogoths. The wind blew out of the East. It was called the Huns.

The Goths and Romans had been neighbors for more than a century. Their relations, with the exception of the First Gothic War (250–270) had generally been peaceful. Although moderns usually picture Goths as barbarians wearing animal skins and bent on nothing but pillage, rape, and massacre, they were Christians, had a written language, and were about as well educated as the average Roman. Many were literate in Latin and Greek as well as Gothic. One Goth, Jordanes, was an eminent historian and is one of our principal sources of information about this period. The Huns were another story.

The Huns

The Huns were true barbarians. They had no written language and no trades but herding and war. For centuries they had harried the Chinese Empire. Sometimes they dominated China. Sometimes China dominated them. During one of their struggles with the Middle Kingdom, the Huns had been fragmented. One part of the Hunnish nation fled to the west and camped on the border of Persia. They were ever afterwards known as the White Huns, after the color of the West in the symbolism of the Far East. (The North was black; the South, red; the East, blue; the West, white, and the Center, gold.) The Ottoman Turks named the Black Sea, to the north of them, and the Red Sea, to the south of them. Because of their name, some writers have said the White Huns were Caucasians (an obvious misconception). The Huns were basically Turkish, but in their periods of power, they absorbed other ethnic groups (Mongols, Manchus, and Iranians).

Power shifted rapidly on the steppes. In the fourth century, the Huns, who had been running roughshod over China, were defeated by the Avars, a Mongol people, and driven west. As they drifted along the sea of grass toward Europe, the Huns collided with the Alans. The Alans were the dominant power among the Sarmatians, an Iranian people who had replaced the Scythians as lords of central and western steppes. The Alans seem to have been great fighters, but their military ability was apparently matched by their inability to unite. Many non-Alanic tribes, like the Slavic Antes and the Sarmatian Roxalani, had Alanic leaders. And for the next few centuries, Alanic clans were to be found all over Europe, fighting in almost every battle, and fighting on both sides of each.

The Alans may have been unable to unite when they clashed with the Huns. Or perhaps the Huns just had a better military system. Like the warriors of Genghis Khan centuries later, the Huns fought in units of tens, hundreds, thousands, and, on occasion, ten thousands. They were all light cavalry, protected by leather armor, using the bow as their main weapon. According to Ammanianus Marcellinus, a contemporary Roman historian and soldier, "They fight from a distance with missiles." After the shower of arrows had demoralized a foe, "They gallop over the intervening spaces and fight hand-to-hand, reckless of their own lives; and while the enemy is guarding against wounds from saber thrusts, they throw strips of cloth plaited into nooses over their opponents and entangle them."

The Alans, like all steppe nomads, had light cavalry. But they had heavy cavalry, too. Their nobles wore iron armor and used lances as well as bows. Like the Huns, they had saddles and probably leather or wood stirrups. Saddles and stirrups made the lance a far more effective weapon than it had been for Alexander's cavalry, which had neither. But because of their decimal organization, the Huns could easily scatter before a charge of lancers and then instantly reform. The Huns replaced the Alans as the great power of the central steppes. They incorporated as many of the Alans as they could into their horde. The rest of the Alanic clans scattered. Some joined the Goths; others continued west to the borders of the steppe and the forest.

Their victory inspired the Huns to further conquests. They met another nation, similarly inspired, moving in the opposite direction. The Ostrogoths (East Goths) had learned the use of heavy cavalry from the Sarmatians. Under their king, Ermenrich, they had conquered a number of Sarmatian and Slavic tribes and were moving east. The Huns stopped that movement. Ermenrich was killed in battle and the Huns incorporated many of the Goths into their horde. The rest elected a new king, Vithimir, and retreated to the west. They found their way blocked by the western Antes.

The Ostrogoths attacked the Antes and defeated them. Vithimir then crucified the Ante king, his sons and 70 of his nobles. That, it turned out, was not a good way to escape the Huns. The Ante king and chiefs were Alans, and relatives of Alanic chiefs in the Hunnish horde. The Huns gave the Alans in their army permission to avenge their relatives. Ammanianus says, "Vithimir was made king and resisted the Halani for a time...But after many defeats which he sustained, he was overcome by force of arms and died in battle." The much-reduced Ostrogothic horde retreated farther. Acting as regents for Vithimir's young son were two chiefs, Aletheus (a Goth), and Sarfac (an Alan). The main Hunnish horde moved up, and the Ostrogoths established their camp near that of their cousins, the Visigoths. Although they spoke the same language, the two Gothic groups refused to cooperate. The Huns then made a night attack on the Visigoth camp and sent the West Goths dashing for the Roman border. The Ostrogoths followed the Visigoths but sneaked across the river instead of asking for admittance.

War

The Visigoths were supposed to turn in their weapons when they crossed the border. However, if they were willing to prostitute their wives or children, the Roman officials let them keep their arms. The Romans had also agreed to supply the Visigoths with food. They quickly forgot that promise. The Visigoths began helping themselves. So did the Ostrogoths, who had made no agreement with the Romans and were now wandering through the Empire at will.

To handle the Visigoth problem, Lupicinus and Maximus invited the Visigoth king and his nobles to a feast and then tried to assassinate them. The Visigoth leaders escaped and began making war, this time joined by the Ostrogoths. The Goths operated in widely separated bands, so it was hard for a regular army to cope with them. The Romans began using scattered bands themselves, ambushing Gothic pillagers. The Goths pulled back to their main camp, a ring of wagons near Adrianople.

Valens had left the task of running down the Gothic bands to subordinate officers. Now, though, he saw a chance to end the war with one big battle. He took command himself. Fridigern, the Visigoth King, offered to make peace if the Romans would grant him the province of Thrace. Valens rejected the offer and marched on the Gothic camp. Roman cavalry protected each flank of Valens's army, with infantry holding the center. When he saw the Roman array, Fridigern again asked for peace.

Valens sent a delegation to the Gothic wagon-camp, but before his ambassador could speak, a nervous Roman in the ambassador's bodyguard thought he saw a threatening movement behind the wagons. He shot an arrow at the Goths. The Goths shot back—all of them. The Romans fled from the rain of arrows. Their dash back to their own lines disorganized the Roman infantry. The Roman left wing cavalry charged the wagon-fort, but they couldn't break through. At that moment, Aletheus and Sarfac, leading the Ostrogothic and Alanic heavy cavalry, burst out of the woods where they had been foraging. They hit the Roman right wing cavalry and chased it off the field. Then they charged the cavalry of the Roman left wing, which was milling around the Visigothic wagons, and routed it. With the Roman horse out of the way, the Ostrogoths and Alans, now joined by the Visigoths from the fort, turned on the Roman infantry. The infantry, taken by surprise, had not formed up to meet an attack. The Goths and Alans surrounded the Roman foot soldiers and crowded them together so that they could not use their weapons. Two thirds of the Roman army—about 40,000 men—were killed. So was Valens. It was the worst Roman defeat since the Battle of Cannae, about 600 years earlier.

Aftermath

Adrianople began what military historians call the "cavalry cycle," the period when heavy cavalry, typified by the medieval knight, dominated the battlefields of Europe. It was also the beginning of the end for the Roman Empire. The Goths were now permanently established inside the Empire, an independent, wandering nation, ruled by its own kings and nobles. At times, the Goths acknowledged a shadowy allegiance to the Roman emperor, but they always acted with complete independence. Eventually, the Visigoths sacked Rome and took over Gaul and Spain. A little later, the Ostrogoths deposed the Western Emperor and seized Italy itself. The fall of the Western Roman Empire marked the birth of Western civilization as we know it.

Battle 13

U.S. Navy dive bombers.

Midway, 1942 AD
Yamamoto

Who fought: Americans (Raymond Spruance and Jack Fletcher) vs. Japanese Yamamoto Isoroku and Nagumo Chuichi).

At stake: The survival of the United States as a major power.

"If I am told to fight regardless of the consequences, I shall run wild for the first six months or a year, but I have utterly no confidence for the second or third year," Admiral Yamamoto Isoroku had told Prince Konoye Fumimaro, then premier of Japan. Yamamoto was the chief of Japan's combined fleets, operational chief of the Japanese Navy. Theoretically, he was the man responsible for carrying out the plans made by the Naval General Staff.

Actually, he also made plans. His most famous was the plan for the attack on Pearl Harbor on December 7, 1941. He pushed it through all kinds of obstacles, not the least of which was the Naval General Staff. He instituted new kinds of training for Japanese aviators, inspired the development of new types of bombs and torpedoes, and won the first naval battle in which opposing ships never came with 100 miles of each other. He won resoundingly. All the battleships in the U.S. Navy's Pacific Fleet were knocked out.

Because of Pearl Harbor, and because Admiral Ernest King, chief of naval operations, hoarded all of the newest U.S. battleships on the East Coast, what had been the world's largest navy was distinctly in second place on the world's largest ocean.

As he predicted, Yamamoto ran wild. His ships convoyed Japanese troops to the Philippines, Malaya, Burma, and the Dutch East Indies. The British sent a battleship and a battle cruiser, (*Prince of Wales* and *Repulse* respectively), to the Far East, and the Japanese sank them as soon as they arrived. Singapore, the "Gibraltar of the East" surrendered on February 13 after one week of fighting. On May 5, the Japanese took Corregidor, completing their conquest of the Philippines. They were well along in their preparations to land at Port Moresby in New Guinea, just across a narrow strait from Australia. It looked as if Yamamoto was too pessimistic when he talked to Konoye. Japan might win the war before the enormous American industrial giant could tip the scales.

But then there were a couple of bumps on the road to victory. One was tiny—an American air raid on Tokyo led by Jimmy Doolittle, a famous American air racer. It inflicted hardly any damage, but it caused consternation in Japan. The second was much bigger: Japanese and American carriers had a major set-to in the Coral Sea. The Americans lost one large carrier, the Japanese one small carrier. Japan claimed another victory. But one large Japanese carrier was so severely damaged it was out of action for months. The second lost almost all of its planes. The Port Moresby operation was postponed—indefinitely, as it turned out.

The setback in the south helped Yamamoto push through his plan for the destruction of the U.S. Navy. The Tokyo bombing helped, too. Yamamoto planned to bring the Americans to battle in the Central Pacific, near Midway Island. Midway was where some Japanese thought Doolittle's planes had been based. (They actually took off from a carrier and landed in China.)

Yamamoto's plan for Midway took advantage of the Island Empire's almost complete command of the sea. One task force was to attack the Aleutians. It would bombard the U.S. naval base at Dutch Harbor and occupy the islands of Attu, Kiska, and Adak. That attack would draw what remained of the U.S. Pacific fleet north. With the American ships away, Japanese troops, arriving in a convoy from the south, would land on Midway and establish an air base. As the American ships tried to return from the Aleutians to counter the attack on Midway, Japanese submarines, lying in wait, would ambush them. They would then be attacked by planes from Midway and from the fleet commanded by Admiral Nagumo Chuichi. Nagumo had all of the big Japanese carriers fit for service. (Missing were the two damaged in the Coral Sea). Nagumo was an old battleship admiral who commanded the fleet that bombed Pearl Harbor. Before that attack, he had been skeptical of air power. Now he was an air power enthusiast.

As the one who had developed the Pearl Harbor plan, Yamamoto was strangely less enthusiastic. He commanded the main fleet, containing almost all the rest of Japan's navy. He flew his flag on *Yamato*, an 18-inch gun bearing leviathan that, with its sister ship, *Musashi*, was the largest battleship in the world. Nagumo was to soften up the enemy and Yamamoto to finish him off.

Yamamoto fit no pigeonhole. A passionate apostle of air power, he still relied on gunnery for a final victory. He invented the carrier task force, but it was the Americans who adopted his invention. He was open to suggestions from subordinates, and he relied heavily on Commander Genda Minoru in developing the Pearl Harbor plan. But at other times he was as inflexible as a samurai sword. He had carefully plotted not only the movements of his ships, but those of the Americans. It never occurred to him that the Americans might not follow the script.

The Americans

Altogether, the Japanese had 162 ships. The Americans had 76, and a third of those were in the North Pacific Force that would never see action. The American

Japanese cruiser, Mikuma, sunk by dive bombers from the Hornet.

commander, Admiral Chester Nimitz, had, however, more ships than the Japanese expected. Yamamoto had been told that Japanese planes had sunk *Yorktown* at the Coral Sea. That big carrier, however, had been rushed back to Pearl Harbor and hastily repaired. Yard crews had done in two days a job that normally took 90. "Waltzing Matilda," as the sailors called her, was able to go to sea, but under normal circumstances, she never would have been allowed to leave the dock. The repairs were very hasty. *Yorktown* was the home of the senior of the two Hawaii-based admirals reporting to Nimitz, Frank Jack Fletcher. The other rear admiral, Raymond Spruance, had two more carriers, *Enterprise* and *Hornet*, as the heart of his Task Force 16. Cruisers and destroyers, of course, supported both carrier task forces. Up Alaska way, Rear Admiral Robert "Fuzzy" Theobold had two heavy cruisers, three light cruisers, nine destroyers, six submarines, and a bunch of Coast Guard cutters. The North Pacific Force had just been established, its ships were widely scattered, and Fuzzy Theobald had his own ideas—which did not jibe with those of Nimitz—on how to defend the Aleutians.

That's why the first Japanese blow landed without any naval opposition. No U.S. ships were in a position to oppose the Aleutian attack. The Japanese bombed Dutch Harbor and landed on Attu and Kiska. Dutch Harbor, however, was far from being knocked out, and U.S. Army Air Forces fighters from Unmak gave the Japanese pilots far more trouble than they expected. That's why Japanese troops didn't land on Adak. It was too close to Unmak.

And, of course, the Aleutians thrust didn't lure the main U.S. fleet north. That's because the Americans had an advantage neither Yamamoto nor Nagumo could guess: They had broken several Japanese naval and diplomatic codes. They knew the main attack was aimed at Midway, not the Aleutians.

They couldn't pinpoint the locations of the Japanese fleets, however. The navy had its big, slow PBY patrol planes searching the seas for a 700-mile radius around Midway, but they couldn't spot the Japanese ships because of the weather. Nagumo sent scout planes up, too, and they couldn't see the Americans. But they didn't expect to see any Americans. They believed the Americans were all up in the North Pacific.

First strikes

Nagumo's first move was to strike Midway. At 4:30 a.m. on June 4, 72 bombers and 36 fighters roared off the decks of Nagumo's four carriers.

Just 10 minutes before the Japanese pilots took off, 11 PBYs had set off on another patrol. On *Yorktown*, 10 dive-bombers began another search. Less than an hour after take-off one of the PBYs saw a Japanese carrier through the heavy cloud cover. A few minutes later, a second patrol plane reported, "Many planes headed for Midway, repeat, Midway..." Every U.S. plane on Midway took off before the Japanese planes arrived. The Marine Corps interceptors tried to stop the attackers, but the ancient Buffalo fighters weren't much opposition for the Japanese Zeros. The American anti-aircraft fire was heavy and accurate, though. A third of the attackers were shot down. In the meantime, the Midway-based bombers were attacking Nagumo's carriers.

Six navy Avenger torpedo bombers and four army B-26's armed with torpedoes attacked the Japanese. The torpedo planes couldn't break through the Japanese fighter screen and lost heavily. Not one scored a hit. Then, 16 B-17s, the army's wonder bombers, appeared. Before the war, the B-17, equipped with the Norden bombsight, was supposed to be able to demolish enemy ships long before they came close to the United States. In this case, not one of their bombs hit a Japanese ship. And in spite of Billy Mitchell, in the whole war, no B-17 ever sank an enemy warship. Hitting a stationary, sprawling factory is not the same as hitting ship that's moving between 30 and 45 miles per hour and liable to turn without notice. The U.S. submarine *Nautilus* also got into the act. It fired one torpedo that missed before it was driven away in a storm of Japanese depth charges.

Nagumo had kept a few planes in reserve armed with torpedoes and armor-piercing bombs in case any enemy ships appeared. He now ordered them below to be rearmed with incendiary and fragmentation bombs for another blow at Midway. And he had to clear the decks for the planes returning from Midway.

Aboard *Enterprise*, Captain Miles Browning, Spruance's chief of staff, had already guessed that Nagumo would order a second strike at Midway. If U.S. planes took off now, they would catch the Japanese with their planes down—refueling for the second strike. Spruance agreed. He launched all his fighters, dive-bombers, and torpedo bombers. It was risky. Fuel would be touch and go. But when they got to the target, the Japanese should be sitting ducks. Unfortunately, just at this point, Nagumo decided to change course.

Six fatal minutes

The fighters, dive bombers, and torpedo bombers flew in separate groups. Fletcher delayed launching his planes in case more Japanese ships were seen, but two hours later, he launched his planes.

Meanwhile, Nagumo had received most unwelcome news. American ships were in the vicinity, not in the Aleutians. He had the planes he prepared to bomb Midway rearmed to deal with ships.

The fighters and dive-bombers from *Hornet* missed Nagumo completely because of his change of course. *Hornet*'s torpedo squadron, Torpedo 8, spotted the enemy carriers. A torpedo bomber has to fly low and maintain a straight line. The best of torpedo planes is no fighter, and the Devastators from the American carriers were far from the best. Torpedo 8 had no fighter cover, but its commander, Lieutenant Commander John Waldron, attacked anyway. Every plane was shot down; only one aviator survived. The torpedo squadron from *Enterprise* appeared next. Ten of the 14 planes went down. Next, *Yorktown*'s torpedo planes attacked and lost the same number of planes.

The third torpedo plane attack had been wiped out at 10:24 a.m. At this point Nagumo's fleet had beaten off attacks by land-based planes, a submarine, and all of the torpedo planes of the U.S. Navy's Pacific fleet without being hit once. It looked as if he might be celebrating soon in San Francisco.

At 10:26, Lieutenant Commander Clarence McClusky, leading the *Enterprise* dive-bombers back after fruitlessly searching for the enemy carriers, noticed the carrier *Kaga*. McClusky's planes were running low on gas, but he didn't hesitate. He signaled one of his two squadrons to follow him and dived straight at *Kaga*. Lieutenant W.E. Gallaher, leading the second squadron, swooped down on *Akagi*, Nagumo's flagship. The Japanese Zeros were all at low altitude, where they had just finished shooting down the torpedo planes. One bomb penetrated to *Akagi's* hanger and detonated her torpedoes. Another exploded on the flight deck, blowing off the planes trying to refuel. Nagumo abandoned his flagship, which was later sunk by a Japanese destroyer. *Kaga* was burning from stem to stern, then an internal explosion sent her to the bottom. *Yorktown's* dive-bombers, under Lieutenant Commander Maxwell Leslie arrived just as a third Japanese carrier, *Soryu*, was preparing to launch its Zeros. Three direct hits turned *Soryu* into an inferno. Then the sub, *Nautilus*, appeared and shot three torpedoes at her. *Soryu* broke in half. The two blazing parts of the carrier went down in a hissing cloud of steam. The dive bomber attack took three minutes. It knocked out three of the Japanese Navy's four operational heavy carriers.

In five minutes, what looked like a total Japanese victory turned into the worst defeat the Empire had ever suffered. And there was more to come.

Last gasps

Nagumo did not give up. He sent the planes on the surviving carrier, *Hiryu*, to attack *Yorktown*. "Waltzing Matilda" took three bomb and two torpedo hits, which was too much for the big ship's jury-rigged repairs. Fletcher shifted his flag to a cruiser, and *Yorktown's* skipper, Capt. Elliot Buckmaster, gave the order to abandon ship. Repair crews tried desperately to save the ship, and it looked as if they succeeded. *Yorktown* was being towed back to Pearl by a minesweeper when a Japanese sub sighted it and sank both "Waltzing Matilda" and her tow ship.

Shortly before the attack on *Yorktown*, Fletcher had sent out 10 dive-bombers to search for more Japanese carriers. They found *Hiryu* just as its planes were hitting their ship. The American planes returned to *Enterprise*, refueled, and joined 14 other dive-bombers led by Gallaher to attack *Hiryu*. The U.S. flyers scored four direct hits and lost only three planes. *Hiryu* was crippled and slowly sinking. She went down with Rear Admiral Yamaguchi—a brilliant officer considered the most likely successor to Yamamoto.

Yamamoto, when he first heard of the disaster, decided to fight on with his battle-wagons. Nagumo argued against the move, and Yamamoto summarily removed him from command. But a little later, he reconsidered. The Americans had total command of the air. Reluctantly, he ordered his ships back to their bases. His six months of "running wild" were over.

There was a lot of hard fighting ahead, but Japan's advances had permanently stopped. Its industry was unable to keep up with the Americans in the production of planes and carriers, and its antiquated training methods couldn't train good pilots fast enough. And American planes and submarines were slowly choking off supplies to its far-flung troops. Before the atomic bomb exploded over Hiroshima, Japan had no oil, no merchant marine, no airframe factories, and no large cities.

Battle 14

Hastings, 1066 AD
The Bastard and the Saint

Who fought: English (Harold Godwinsson) vs. Normans (William the Bastard).

What was at stake: Whether England would be drawn out of the European mainstream and into Greater Scandinavia.

Two weeks of waiting were over. It was about 9 a.m. when William, known to friend and foe alike as "the Bastard," got his first look at the English army. Armored infantry with huge shields were drawn up on Senlac Hill, a few miles north of the town of Hastings. William had been biding his time on this narrow peninsula, foraging (the English called it ravaging) while Harold Godwinsson was busy in the north. The Bastard could have marched directly to London, but that would have meant plunging his small army into a hostile sea of semi-barbarous Northerners who could cut off his escape route. Instead, he waited for Harold to concentrate his forces here. One battle would decide the fate of a kingdom.

William was the natural son of Robert the Devil, the Duke of Normandy, and Arlette, a tanner's daughter. The bar sinister didn't bar William from inheriting his father's duchy when he was seven. The old duke had died while returning from a pilgrimage to the Holy Land.

The times were troubled, and the young duke was lucky to live to manhood. As soon as he took control, however, he quickly restored order to his duchy. With the help of Henri I of France, the 20-year-old duke wiped out the rebels' army and leveled all their castles. Then he conquered the County of Maine and added it to his domains. He could be ruthless or generous, depending on the situation. One to whom he was generous was his cousin, an impoverished English refugee named Edward. Edward was the son of a Norman mother and an English father, but his mother was also the widow of Canute the Great, the Danish king who had conquered England, Norway, and part of Sweden. He was in exile because Canute's heirs didn't want an Englishman around who might claim the throne.

A Norman knight.

Edward had no expectation of becoming a king, but after years of exile in Normandy, where he had been busy eluding Danish assassins, Canute's son, Hardicanute, brought his inoffensive half-brother back. (Edward, nicknamed the Confessor, later became St. Edward.) Then Hardicanute died. As Edward was both a half-brother of the late king and a descendant of Cerdic, founder of the ancient West Saxon dynasty, the English crowned him.

Edward's England was increasingly becoming part of Greater Scandinavia, like Iceland, Greenland, the Orkneys, and Dublin, as well as Denmark, Norway, and Sweden. English and Norse were almost dialects of the same language. There was a strong pro-Danish party in England, and most of England's greatest nobles were Danish. As in Scandinavia, the worst sentence a criminal could receive was to be declared *nithing*—his oath was worthless; he was assumed to be lying whenever he spoke; no respectable person could do business with him; and anyone could kill him without penalty. Those declared nithing often "went a-Viking": they became pirates. (In England, if not Denmark, all of those who went a-Viking for any reason were declared nithing.)

England had been Christian for centuries. But Edward, an intensely religious man, believed it was now becoming part of "the heathen North" as a result of Canute's conquest. Several of the Scandinavian kings, including Canute, had become Christian, but Edward considered their people basically pagans, if not pirates.

Edward's heritage and his long years in Normandy inclined his thoughts to favor the South. In France, Germany, and Italy, and particularly in Normandy, he saw civilization. The Normans, of course, were descendants of Scandinavians—Scandinavian Vikings, in fact—but they had absorbed the civilization of France and combined it with the vigor of the Vikings. Edward favored Normans at his court, and, childless, he hoped to have his Norman nephew succeed him on the throne. When the young man proved to be incompetent and cowardly, Edward wanted his old friend and relative, the Duke of Normandy, to get the English crown. He thought that dream had been fulfilled when his brother-in-law, Harold Godwinsson, the great earl who had been acting as Edward's assistant king, swore an oath to be Duke William's vassal.

Harold Godwinsson

Somehow, Harold had found himself in William's domain. According to William of Poitiers, Edward sent Harold to William "in order that he might confirm his promise [to make William king] by an oath." He was shipwrecked and fell into the hands of one of William's vassals, who imprisoned him. William heard about it and ordered the vassal to release Harold, who then swore to use all his wealth and influence to make William king. William of Malmesbury said Harold was on a fishing trip when he was shipwrecked. What nobody disputes, though, is that Harold swore to support William's claim to the English throne. Even Harold did not dispute it.

When Edward died, however, the English council, the Witan, named Harold king. William immediately took his case to the pope and the Holy Roman Emperor. Because of Harold's oath, both leaders supported William the Bastard. William, known as a good general and a generous leader, quickly raised an army not only of Normans, but also of Bretons, Frenchmen, and Flemings.

Harald vs. Harold

William was not the only threat to Harold. Harald Hardrada (Hard Ruler), the King of Norway, also had designs on England. Hardrada had been a Viking and a leader of the Byzantine Emperor's Varangian Guard. By devious maneuvering and hard fighting he had made himself King of Norway. He was determined to restore Canute's northern empire. He planned to grab England before William could land. He had picked up an ally from Harold's own family, his brother, Tostig. The Godwinssons were a classically dysfunctional family. His vassals, who had been incited by Harold, had ousted Tostig as Earl of Northumberland. He fled from England, became a Viking, and then joined Hardrada, the ex-Viking.

Tostig had already attacked England, but this helped Harold more than hurt him. The Viking earl raided Sandwich and kidnapped a number of men, then sailed north and landed at the mouth of the Humber with 60 ships. The northern fyrd (militia) was ready for him, though. Tostig was severely beaten and escaped with only 12 ships. His raids, however, had caused Harold to call out the militia, so he was able to respond quickly to Hardrada's invasion.

The Norwegian invasion fleet numbered 300 ships even before it picked up Tostig's Vikings. Hardrada met and defeated the militia protecting York, while Harold, his housecarls (bodyguard), and the militia—all mounted infantry—rushed north by forced marches. Hardrada was negotiating with the northern nobles over hostages and had no idea the main English army was so close. The English surprised the Norwegians and almost annihilated Hardrada's army. Both Harald Hardrada and Tostig were killed. Only 24 ships got back to Norway.

The English losses were also heavy. And the victors had no time to celebrate the victory. While he was fighting in the north, Harold learned that William had landed in the south. Harold's troops wearily climbed back on their horses and retraced their steps. Harold picked up some militia along the way. He could have had twice as many if he had waited. But he was in a great rush to stop this second invasion.

Showdown

Harold's army was about the same size as William's army—8,000 men—but it was very different. All of the English were infantry. The best armed were the royal housecarls, professional soldiers armed and equipped in the Danish fashion. They had metal helmets and long mail shirts. They wore swords and carried spears and huge

Danish axes. Some also had small throwing axes and the daggers called saxes. All carried shields, which they slung on their backs when swinging the axes with both hands. The most important nobles had housecarls of their own, equipped like the royal bodyguards. Then there was the ready militia. Every five small landholders equipped one of their number with helmet, mail shirt, and spear. Finally, there was the ordinary militia. In an emergency, every freeman had to provide military service, using whatever weapons he could find. Few of these men had armor other than shields. For weapons they had spears, woodcutting axes, clubs, and throwing clubs consisting of a stone lashed to a wooden handle. A number of militiamen had slings and a few had bows and arrows.

William's army included armored cavalry, the principal arm in continental European (excluding Scandinavia) warfare. There were 3,000 knights, 4,000 infantry spearmen, and 1,000 archers. All wore mail shirts and metal helmets. According to the chroniclers, when they heard that Harold was approaching, the Norman army spent the night in prayer. Then at dawn they began marching to meet the English.

William's army saw the English about a half-mile away. Between them and Senlac Hill was a marshy meadow broken by only a narrow strip of dry land. The marsh would make the Norman cavalry useless, so William decided to march over the dry finger of land and deploy on the other side of the marsh. It was a daring decision. The dry ground across the marsh was only 200 yards from the English line. If Harold had attacked while only a portion of the Norman army was on dry land, he would have eliminated the second threat. Why he did not is still a mystery.

The best laid plans

As soon as his army was deployed, William attacked. The plan was for the archers to soften up the English with a barrage of arrows, after which the infantry would break through the English line and the cavalry would follow up and cut down the fleeing enemy. It didn't work out that way.

The English infantry, 10 ranks deep behind the heavily armed housecarls, caught the arrows on their shields and launched their own missiles at the advancing Norman spearmen. Javelins, stones, stone-headed throwing clubs, throwing axes, and a few arrows flew out from behind the English "shield wall." When the lines of footmen closed, the housecarls' big axes easily cut through the Normans' mail. The Bretons, on the Norman left, gave way first. They fled down the hill, carrying the Breton cavalry, which had been following, with them.

The English infantry, on Harold's right, chased the Bretons right into the marsh. The Norman center, its flank exposed, fell back. It looked as if the English had won. William rounded up some cavalry and charged the English infantry. The English, disorganized and no longer a "shield wall," were routed with heavy losses. William was unhorsed in the fighting, but he got on another mount and took off his helmet to show his men he had not been killed.

His archers and infantry had failed, but William did not modify his plan. He sent his knights against the English shield wall. The fight was long and bloody, especially for the Norman knights. At length they, too, fled. Again, the English pursued them. William, though, had kept back a cavalry reserve. He led this against the flank of the English and drove them back. Norman chroniclers claimed the Norman chivalry had executed a "feigned retreat." But a deliberate retreat that looked enough like a rout to induce the English to leave the positions they had successfully defended, followed by a counterattack against a closely pursuing enemy, was impossible given the communications and command structure of an 11th century army. The Norman writers just couldn't admit that footmen had routed Norman knights—Breton infantry, yes, but not Norman knights.

After six hours of fighting, the English still held Senlac Hill. But because of the losses they had sustained, their line was shorter. William ordered a new attack, again coordinating archers, infantry, and cavalry.

Again, the archers opened the attack. This time, instead of shooting at the English directly, they aimed high so their arrows would fall on the enemy from almost directly above. As the English raised their shields to defend against the arrows, the Norman spearmen charged. One Englishman who didn't raise his shield fast enough was Harold Godwinsson. An arrow hit him in the eye. Not dead, but critically injured, Harold could do little to direct the troops. The Norman archers could not continue shooting when their own infantry closed with the English, so the English shields were in place when William's infantry arrived. The Norman foot did, however, keep the English busy. While the English and Norman infantry were slugging it out, the Norman cavalry took advantage of the shortened English line and charged its right flank. One Norman knight found Harold and cut off his leg, a wound that was quickly fatal. The English line was rolled up, and Harold's army dashed from the field.

One group of housecarls held off the Normans from behind a ravine for a while, but they were eventually destroyed. As for the rest, there was no longer a reason to fight. The king was dead. William the Bastard had become William the Conqueror.

The Norman conquest brought England into the European mainstream and out of the Scandinavian backwater. Furthermore, King William created the first centralized European state since the fall of the Roman Empire. All vassals, not just the tenants-in-chief, had to swear allegiance to him, personally. From William on, the English kings controlled their nobles more tightly than any other monarchs. Although England was not free of civil war, it was far from the chaos found in such places as France and the Holy Roman Empire. The defeat of the English was the beginning of England's rise to great power status.

Battle 15

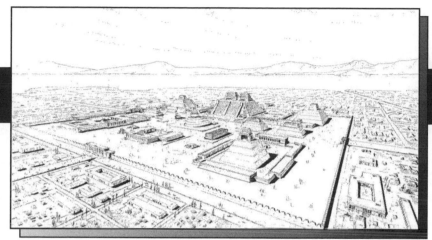

Tenochtitlan, 1520–21 AD
The Son of the Sun

Who fought: Spanish (Hernan Cortes) vs. Aztecs (Montezuma and Cuauhtemoc).

What was at stake: European domination of the New World and the opening of a Pacific trade route to the Far East.

Pedro de Alvarado was tall and handsome. To the natives, he, even more than the other fair-skinned strangers, seemed godlike. His golden hair and luxuriant blond mustache led the Aztecs, who had never seen anyone without black hair or with much facial hair, to call him *Tonatiuh*, the son of the Sun. And the laughing, high-spirited Alvarado, one of the Spanish knights who were captains of this miniscule army, had—on the surface—the sunny disposition to go with his nickname. He even fooled the Captain General, Hernan Cortes. Had he known the real Alvarado, Cortes would never have left him in charge of the tiny Spanish garrison in the Mexican capital, Tenochtitlan, because underneath the sunny exterior, Alvarado's spirit was dark, paranoid, and bloodthirsty.

This whole enterprise was mad, Alvarado knew, but that was why he'd joined it. Spain was trying to do in the New World what Portugal was doing in Africa and the Indies. People like Alvarado and Cortes were here to set up trading posts and make deals with local rulers giving Spain exclusive trading rights.

Cortes had other ideas.

His ideas didn't jibe with those of the governor of Cuba, Diego Velasquez, who had just landed a strong military force to undo Cortes's revolutionary idea, an idea only Cortes and members of his inner circle—Alvarado, Gonzalo de Cordova, Cristobal de Olid, and a handful of others—fully understood. Now Cortes was off to block the governor's attempt to block his project. He'd put too much into it to give up now.

Into the unknown

The expedition from Cuba had landed on the coast in 1519. Cortes had 11 ships with 110 sailors and 553 soldiers. The soldiers included 32 crossbowmen and 13 arquebusiers. There were also 16 horses. The natives had never seen horses, and Cortes believed that even a small number of cavalrymen would have great psychological value.

The Spanish visited several places on the mainland coast. There was one battle with the natives, and Alvarado's bold charge at a crucial moment saved the day. The Spaniards didn't conduct much trade, and they didn't make any meaningful agreements. But they acquired information and the means to acquire more information—a slave that a Mayan king had given Cortes, a Mexican girl named Malinche. She knew Nahuatl, the Aztec language, and a number of other Indian tongues. She became the Captain General's mistress and quickly learned Spanish. The Spanish soldiers called her Dona Marina.

From the coastal Totonac Indians, the Spanish learned that there was a king of kings, an emperor, far in the interior who controlled the land called Mexico, the mainland north of Yucatan and Tabasco. Cortes decided that this was the man with whom they'd have to make arrangements. From the first, the Spanish knew that the natives of the mainland were not like those of the islands. Here there were no grass huts. The mainlanders lived in stone houses and built towering stone pyramids for temples.

The emperor, they learned, lived in Tenochtitlan, a city built on an island in the middle of a large lake. The only way to enter the city was over one of three stone causeways. Each of the causeways had gaps to allow boat traffic, and drawbridges spanned the gaps. The king's name was Mocthezuma, which the Spanish pronounced Montezuma.

Montezuma

Mocthezuma II, Emperor of Mexico, had heard about the strange, bearded men even before they arrived in his territory. The man the Spanish knew as Montezuma was troubled. He was extremely religious and he knew the story of Quetzalcoatl—the fair-skinned, bearded deity, who had ruled both the Mexicans and the Mayas, then sailed off to the East. From the time Columbus landed, the people of the mainland had heard of pale-faced, bearded men who commanded thunder and lighting (with their arquebuses and cannons). Montezuma consulted the royal astrologer. The sage was not encouraging. The stars predicted, he said, that the Mexican Empire would be destroyed.

Montezuma tried to buy off the newcomers. He sent envoys to them with gifts, hoping they'd be satisfied and go away. The gifts, especially those made of gold, only made them more eager to visit him. Then Montezuma instructed his envoys to have the natives massacre the Spanish while they were admiring the gifts and enjoying the hospitality. As it turned out, that strategy didn't work either. Instead, Cortes was turning Montezuma's subjects against him.

The Aztecs were not popular in the tribes they had conquered. The conquered people, in fact, were the main source of the thousands of bleeding human hearts the Aztecs offered to their gods each year. At the opening of the temple of their principal god, Huitzilopochtli, the war god, the Aztecs offered 20,000 human hearts, freshly plucked from the bodies of victims.

At one Totonac town, Aztec tribute collectors appeared and called the Totonac chiefs to a conference. Seeing the downcast look of the chiefs after the conference, Cortes asked Malinche what had happened. She told him that the Aztecs were demanding that the Totonacs send Montezuma 20 young men and 20 young women to be sacrificed to expiate the crime of having entertained the Spaniards. Cortes demanded that the Totonacs arrest and imprison the Aztecs. The local chiefs, more terrified of Cortes than of the Aztecs, did as he ordered. That night, Cortes secretly released two of the Aztec nobles. He told them he did so out of regard for their master, Montezuma.

Montezuma.

When the Totonacs found two of their prisoners gone, they were furious. They decided to execute those remaining. Cortes talked them out of that. Instead, he said, he'd send them to his ships and hold them there. As soon as they were aboard the ships, he had the sailors take the Aztecs secretly to another part of the coast so they could make their way back to Tenochtitlan while avoiding the Totonacs.

Cortes

Although not in name, Cortes had become the emperor of the Totonacs, Montezuma's coastal subjects. To the Totonacs, Cortes was their protector against the terrible Aztecs. He did not let his own men harm them. One, who stole something from a Totonac, he ordered to be hanged. (Alvarado cut the man down, saying the troops had received the message, and the army could not afford to lose men.) Cortes settled disputes between Totonac cities that threatened civil war. He even converted the Totonacs *en massé*. He told his troops to overturn the Totonac idols, and when the gods didn't take vengeance, their worshippers adopted Christianity. Instead of making a treaty with a native ruler, Cortes was becoming a ruler himself. The next step was to make himself master of all Mexico. The Spanish authorities wanted only to establish trading posts. Conquering an empire was Cortes's own idea.

That idea terrified some of his army. They knew how few of them there were. They had horses and guns, but only 16 horses and 13 guns plus a few cannons from the ships. The Aztecs had thousands upon thousands of warriors, and they had conquered this huge empire that was bigger than all of Spain. The disaffected troops conspired to seize one of the ships and return to Cuba.

Cortes learned of the plot. He hanged two of the ringleaders and scuttled the ships. There would be no turning back.

Tlascala

Cortes and his army marched west, over mountains and up to the high plateau of central Mexico. He was accompanied by Totonac troops who were eager to smite their one-time overlords. There were two ways to approach Tenochtitlan. One was through the ancient, enormous, and opulent city of Cholula; the other, through the territory of Tlascala. The Totonacs told Cortes that the Cholulans were docile subjects of the Aztecs, not a warlike people. But, they said, don't trust the Cholulans. With the Tlascalans you always know where you stand. Cortes sent envoys to Tlascala and headed in that direction.

Cortes.

Tlascala was a federation of four mountain cantons, ancient enemies of the Aztecs. They had the same religion, language, and customs of the Aztecs. But they beat back Aztec attempts to incorporate them in the Mexican empire. In retaliation, the Aztecs cut them off from all trade with the coastal tribes. The Tlascalans detained Cortes's envoys. When the Spanish army approached, they soon learned where they stood with the Tlascalans.

The highlanders were massed in a narrow pass. Cortes estimated that there were 100,000 warriors. No Spanish estimate was less than 30,000. The Tlascalans carried shields and some of them wore quilted cotton armor and wooden helmets. For weapons they had bows and arrows, slings, javelins hurled with the *atlatl* (spear thrower), spears, and the *maquahuitl*, a flat wooden club lined with sharp obsidian blades. A shower of arrows and javelins greeted the Spanish.

Cortes shouted the ancient Spanish battle cry "San Diego y alla! (Saint James and at them!)," and led his knights in a charge, with the infantry following. The Indians did not flee. They pulled one Spanish knight from his horse and chopped both him and the animal up. The Spanish crossbows easily penetrated the Indians' shields and armor, but they were much slower to reload than the Tlascalans' bows. The arquebus blasts made the Indians hesitate, but they didn't terrify Tlascala's warriors. The Spanish advantages were their discipline—at this time the Spanish infantry was the best in Europe—their steel armor, their swords, and, above all, their artillery. The cannons blasted lanes through the mass of warriors. The Tlascalan commander eventually ordered a retreat, and the highlanders moved back like a well-disciplined army.

When the Spanish resumed their advance a couple of days later, five divisions of Tlascalans, 10,000 men each, opposed them.

"We feared death," wrote one of the soldiers, Bernal Diaz del Castillo, much later, "for we were men."

Cortes put his guns and crossbows in the first line, with the artillery on the flanks. The arquebusiers, cannoneers, and crossbowmen were to support each other, alternately loading and firing. The Totonacs, warriors who were no match for the fierce Tlascalans, he kept in the rear. The Tlascalans charged, and the Spaniards mowed them down. The cannons on the flanks kept up a crossfire of grape shot. Cavalry lancers and infantry swordsmen charged repeatedly. At the height of the battle, one of the Tlascalan division commanders, smarting from an earlier insult by his commander, withdrew his troops after persuading another division commander to join him. Then the rest of the Indian army retreated.

Xicotencatl, the Tlascalan commander, tried once more. Leading 10,000 men, he stole over the plains for a night attack on the Spanish camp. But night attacks were against Tlascalan custom, and they had no practice. There was a full moon, and a Spanish sentry saw them. Cortes's men had been sleeping fully armed, with their weapons by their side and their horses saddled. The Tlascalans suddenly heard "San Diego y alla!" and the whole Spanish army seemed to rise out of the ground and dash at them. The Indians shot a few arrows and fled.

Once again, Cortes sent an envoy to the Tlascalans. He offered them an alliance against the Aztecs. If they refused, he would raze their cities and burn their fields. The Tlascalans joined the alliance.

Cholula

While Cortes and his army were in the city of Tlascala, envoys from Cholula invited him to visit them. The Tlascalans warned against it, but Cortes knew now that Cholula would be a necessary stop. Cholula was the mecca of Mexico. It was the city of Quetzalcoatl—where the god had lived while he was instructing the inhabitants in the arts of civilization. Tlascalan scouts reported a large Aztec army camped nearby, but Cortes went ahead. He and his Spaniards entered the city, where they were warmly welcomed. The Tlascalans, hereditary enemies of the Cholulans, camped outside.

Spanish soldiers began noticing disturbing signs. Some of the city's streets were barricaded and on the flat roofs of the houses were heaps of stones that could be used as missiles. Malinche, a gregarious girl, had made friends with some women of the city. One of them asked her to stay at her house, where, she said, the Mexican girl would escape the fate of the Spaniards. Then Aztec ambassadors appeared. They gave Cortes gifts and conferred with the leading men of Cholula. Suddenly the warm relations between the Spaniards and Cholulans chilled.

Cortes befriended a couple of leading Cholulan priests and gave them many of the rich presents he had acquired from Montezuma. The priests, assured of his protection, told Cortes that he and his men were to be massacred in the city. The Aztecs had even prepared manacles for the Spaniards who were to be reserved for sacrifice. The Captain General warned the priests, unnecessarily, of the need for secrecy, then had a conference with the Cholulan chiefs. He told the chiefs that he and his army would no longer be a burden to them. They would move out the next morning. He asked only that they would meet him the next morning in the great square with porters to help his army move their baggage and artillery.

Privately, he met the Aztec ambassadors and told them he knew of the conspiracy. The Aztecs were terrified. Cortes had defeated the Tlascalans, something the Aztecs could never do, and now he knew of the conspiracy. They protested that Montezuma knew nothing of such treachery. Cortes pretended to believe them, but he made sure a strong guard watched them after that. Finally, he placed artillery at strategic spots—some guns facing into the square and others commanding the streets that led to it.

All the gateways to the square were guarded by Spanish pikemen, who remained concealed until after the Cholulan nobles appeared for the meeting in the square.

The next morning, when the square was filled with Cholulans, Cortes told them he knew of their treachery. The Cholulans said it had been ordered by Montezuma, but Cortes appeared to become even angrier because they were blaming the emperor. Then the Spanish opened fire and waded into the Indians with their swords while the pikemen blocked the exits. Cholulan warriors outside the square rushed to the rescue but were cut down by grape shot from the Spanish cannons. The Tlascalans charged into the city and attacked the Cholulans from the rear. Cortes estimated that 2,000 Cholulan men were killed; other accounts put the number at 6,000. By his orders, no women or children were harmed, but the Tlascalans took many as slaves.

The massacre is a black mark on the record of Cortes, but similar occurrences were not unusual in the early 16th century in Europe. As William H. Prescott points out in his classic *Conquest of Mexico*:

> "The atrocities at Cholula were not so bad as those inflicted on the descendants of those very Spaniards in the late war of the Peninsula [two centuries later], by the most polished of nations of our time; by the British at Badajoz, for example—at Taragona, and a hundred other places, by the French."

Cortes finally stopped the massacre, made the Tlascalans free their newly captured slaves, and appointed new leaders for the city. Then he marched on Tenochtitlan.

Tenochtitlan

The road took the Spaniards and their Indian allies over the saddle between two of the highest peaks in North America, Iztaccihuatl, and the volcano, Popocatepetl, a cone rising 17,852 feet above sea level. In the frigid air of the heights, the army could look down on the Valley of Mexico—green farmland splotched with blue lakes. On the shores of the lakes were shining cities. Some of the cities were built on piles and entirely offshore. In the center of one lake was Tenochtitlan.

On November 8, 1519, the army—400 Spaniards and some 6,000 Indians—marched along the causeway leading to the Aztec capital. The road across the salt lake was built of large stones set in cement and was wide enough for 10 horsemen to ride abreast. There were several drawbridges and in the middle of the causeway was a stone fort with towers and battlements. Montezuma welcomed Cortes in his palace, a rambling structure of marble and other stone, containing hundreds of rooms, including 100 bathrooms supplied by an aqueduct from a hilltop reservoir. He gave the Spanish general another palace, large enough to house all his Spanish and Indian troops. When the Spanish moved in, they found, in a room whose door had been bricked over, a fortune in gold and jewels.

Montezuma took Cortes on a tour of the city, showing him the public gardens, the zoo and aviary, the streets paved with cement, the canals, the palaces, and some of the dozens of temples where in each at least two or three human beings were sacrificed every day. Cortes asked Montezuma how an intelligent and noble king like himself could follow such a cruel religion and worship gods who were thought to be creatures of the devil. Montezuma's manner became frosty. These gods had led the Aztec people to prosperity and domination of this part of the world, he said. He added that he would have to offer more sacrifices to the gods for having let strangers profane their temples.

His chaplain dissuaded Cortes from trying to convert the Aztecs as he had the Totonacs, but Montezuma's people were becoming more hostile. And although the Spanish had reached Tenochtitlan, so far they had really accomplished nothing.

So Cortes asked for an audience with the Emperor. Then, accompanied by Alvarado and a few of his most trusted knights, he kidnapped Montezuma and installed him in the Spanish headquarters. Cortes and his men continued to treat Montezuma like a king, but the Aztec Emperor knew he lived in a gilded cage. He acknowledged the King of Spain, Emperor Charles V, as his feudal overlord. But the Aztec people grew more and more unhappy.

Finally, Montezuma summoned Cortes to his rooms in the Spanish palace. He said the gods of the country had told the priests that they would forsake the city unless the strangers were driven out, or better yet, sacrificed.

"I tell you this, Malintzin," Montezuma said, using the name the Mexicans had given Cortes, "because I am concerned for your safety. If you have any regard for it yourselves, you will leave the country without delay. I have only to raise my finger, and every Aztec in the land will rise in arms against you."

Cortes said he would gladly leave if he had ships. Montezuma pointed out that the Spanish general had already built several sailing ships to use on the lake. Why couldn't he do the same on the East Coast? If Cortes provided the shipwright who designed the lake ships, he (Montezuma), would provide the materials and the laborers. Cortes had to agree, but he secretly told his master shipbuilder to delay the work as much as possible. He was hoping he could find a remedy for the situation before the ships were built.

A few days later, Montezuma happily told Cortes there was no longer an obstacle to his leaving. More white men in ships had arrived on the coast. He showed the general a note in Aztec pictographs. Cortes pretended to be overjoyed. When he returned to his own quarters, he received a message from Gonzalo de Sandoval, his most efficient lieutenant, who was commanding the fort Cortes had established at Vera Cruz. Sandoval reported that Velasquez, the governor of Cuba, had sent one of his henchmen, Panfilo de Narvaez, with a strong force to arrest Cortes and take over his conquests.

The general picked 70 soldiers and left the other 140 Spaniards under the command of Alvarado. He told Alvarado to continue treating Montezuma like royalty, but not to let him leave the palace. The garrison was to stay alert, but not interfere with any of the Aztecs' normal activities. He would take his 70 men and march east, picking up reinforcements from garrisons left along the way.

"La Noche Triste"

Cortes was barely out of sight when some Tlascalans told Alvarado the Aztecs were planning to attack at the next festival. Then some Aztec nobles told Alvarado they were planning their annual festival in honor of the war god and asked if Montezuma could join them. The usual place for the celebration was in a court near the Spanish palace. The son of the Sun said he couldn't let Montezuma attend, but the Aztecs were certainly welcome to celebrate their festival near the Spanish headquarters as long as they were not armed. The Spanish soldiers, in fact, would like to be spectators.

Alvarado was thinking of duplicating Cortes's actions at Cholula. But unlike Cortes, he did nothing to verify the rumor of a rising—which he learned from the Aztecs' ancient enemies—nor did he think much about the results. As his later career in Guatemala proved, Alvarado liked to kill people, and he saw this as a golden opportunity.

At the height of the dance, the Spanish soldiers charged the 600 Aztec nobles with drawn swords and cut them all down.

The results were not what "Tonatiuh" expected. The Aztec nation rose *en masse*, and the Spanish and Tlascalans were besieged in their palace. The Aztecs burned the Spanish ships on the lake.

Cortes, meanwhile, had brilliantly surprised Narvaez in Cempoalla and captured him in his headquarters on the great pyramid. He then recruited all the interloper's troops, tripling the strength of his army. He was returning to Tenochtitlan when a messenger informed him that the Aztecs were in revolt. The streets of Tenochtitlan were still as Cortes and his men reentered the city. The Aztecs wanted all of the strangers inside where they could finish them off. In the palace, Cortes confronted Alvarado, his best friend. He was beside himself with rage.

"You have been false to your trust," he screamed. "Your conduct has been that of a madman!"

He could do nothing else. Alvarado was popular with the army, and he was both a good combat leader and a superb fighting man. And the situation was desperate.

The Aztecs attempted to storm the Spanish position, but Cortes's troops beat them back. The next day, the Spanish sallied out. Street barricades stopped the horsemen. The Spanish cannons blasted away the barricades, but there were more barricades behind them. Aztecs on the rooftops hurled stones with slings and threw spears tipped with copper, flint, and obsidian. Cortes withdrew to the palace. Later sallies were equally fruitless.

Cortes asked Montezuma to speak to his people. Standing on a rooftop, the emperor told the Aztecs the Spaniards were leaving and asked them to be patient and let the strangers leave the city. The response was a shower of missiles. One sling stone struck Montezuma on the head, inflicting a fatal wound.

Cortes soon learned that for the Aztecs, as for the Tlascalans, night fighting was not customary. He decided to sneak out at night. He had his men build a wooden bridge that could be laid down over a gap in the causeway, then lifted up and placed on the next one. He chose to take the causeway leading west. That would mean the army would have to take the most roundabout route to Tlascala, but that causeway was the shortest—only two miles long. He advised his men to travel light. His veterans took the advice, but many of the men who had arrived with Narvaez could not bear to part with all of that gold.

The night of July 1, 1520 was cool and drizzly. No Aztecs were seen on the streets as the Spanish and Tlascalans left the palace. Sandoval commanded the vanguard, containing 200 Spanish infantry. Cortes led the main body in the center, which included the artillery, most of the cavalry, and a fairly large body of infantry. Alvarado commanded the rear, with most of the Spanish infantry. The Tlascalans and other allies were evenly divided among the three divisions. The army got as far as the causeway.

Suddenly the huge drum in the temple of the war god boomed and the conch shell trumpets of the priests screeched. The Spanish rushed their portable bridge up the causeway to bridge the first gap. Cortes and his men marched across as the Aztecs, 15 or 20 men abreast, attacked the rear of the column. Aztecs in canoes appeared all along the causeway, shooting arrows and javelins at the Spanish and Tlascalans. Some even climbed the sides of the causeway. When all of the army was across the bridge, the Spanish tried to remove it and rush it up to the next gap.

They couldn't. The weight of the passing army had wedged the bridge too tightly for any humans to move.

The Aztec canoes were waiting at the next gap. Some of the knights were able to swim their horses across and many of the infantry were able to swim the gap, too. But many of Narvaez's men were dragged to the bottom by the weight of their gold. Other Spaniards were dragged into the canoes so their hearts could be laid on the altar of the war god and their bodies eaten at communal cannibal feasts. The Spanish and Tlascalans, who were able to fight their way across the second gap, had to run the gauntlet of Aztec missiles, then fight their way through the third gap. Cortes found a ford here, then he turned his horse around a led a party of troops back to help the men in the rear.

They found that the rear guard, which had borne the brunt of the heaviest Aztec attack, was practically annihilated. Pedro de Alvarado, alone and unhorsed, was holding off hordes of Indians with his lance. Then he placed the lance on the lake bottom and pole-vaulted across the gap. In his recollections, Bernal Diaz said the gap was too wide for any man to leap. But many others in the army saw the blond knight make the jump, and for centuries the place has been remembered in Mexico City as *El Salto de Alvarado*.

The whole march was remembered by the Spaniards as *La Noche Triste* (the Sad Night).

Fortunately for the Spaniards and Tlascalans, the Aztecs had stopped to strip the dead bodies, collect the rich loot—steel swords, shields, and helmets as well as gold and jewels—kill off the hopelessly wounded, and collect prisoners who would live long enough to be sacrificed. Cortes and his men reached the shore and moved rapidly through the Aztec city of Tlacopan. Once in open country, the captain general took stock. About 450 Spaniards out of 1,100 and 4,000 Indian allies out of 6,000 had been killed or captured. Forty-six cavalrymen were lost, reducing the army's horsemen to 23. All of the artillery was gone; all of the muskets had been thrown away by the fleeing troops. Only a few crossbows were left.

The road back

There was some skirmishing with small bands of Indians, but Cortes kept his army away from populated areas. They were running out of food. Then, blocking the road to Tlascala, the Spanish scouts saw an enormous army of Aztecs.

Cortes organized his troops in a long thin line so the mass of Indians could not surround it, and posted his tiny cavalry force on the flanks. He told his troopers to aim their lances at the Indians' faces and his infantry to rely on the point of the sword, rather than the edge. The Spanish fought desperately: Sandoval, Cortes, and Alvarado, particularly, performed as if battle were their natural element. But they fought with fading hope. Then Cortes noticed a gaudily costumed Indian in a litter. He took this man to be the commander. He gathered his knights and charged the Aztec general. It was almost a replay of Alexander at Arbela. But the Aztec leader, unlike Darius, did not escape. When he fell, his army fled in panic. Cortes's fortune changed almost immediately.

The next day, Cortes and his men were welcomed back to Tlascala. A few days later, delegations from the Aztecs' former vassals began arriving, pledging their support to the Spaniards. Cortes was delighted, but later found that these new allies were old enemies of the Tlascalans. The Tlascalans, it turned out, had an insane hatred for the Aztecs, and some of that spilled over on any people who had ever associated with the Aztecs. Because of that hatred the Tlascalans rejected an offer of alliance by the new Aztec emperor. The animosity, however, complicated the disposition of troops.

In Tenochtitlan, the new emperor, Cuauhtemoc, was strengthening the fortifications and enlarging the gaps in the causeways. He called on all the surrounding Indian

Aztec Drawing.

nations to help their neighbors, the Aztecs, resist the strangers. The trouble was that the surrounding nations knew their neighbors too well. Most of them wanted nothing to do with the Aztecs.

Cortes, using his Indian allies in conjunction with Spanish troops, began striking Aztec-garrisoned towns in all directions. Each success brought him more allies. Cortes had his shipwright, Martin Lopez, build 13 brigantines, which he would launch on Lake Texcoco, surrounding the Mexican capital. He armed his Spanish infantry with Indian-made copper-headed pikes to use in addition to their swords. He got unexpected Spanish reinforcements. Governor Velasquez, unaware of Narvaez's defeat, sent two shiploads of reinforcements and supplies to Mexico. The men aboard readily joined Cortes's army. Then the governor of Jamaica, seeking to establish a post on the mainland, sent three more ships. The natives drove them off, and they, too, joined Cortes. A little later, three more shiploads of soldiers, adventurers from Hispaniola, landed at Vera Cruz and asked to join Cortes.

The siege of Tenochtitlan

Once again, Cortes took his army into the Valley of Mexico. This time, he attacked the Aztec cities around Tenochtitlan one by one. He brought up the disassembled brigantines and launched them on Lake Texcoco. He sent envoys to Cuauhtemoc, offering the Emperor peace and a return to Montezuma's status as king under the protection of the King of Spain. Cuauhtemoc rejected the offer with contempt.

On May 10, 1521, Cortes launched a three-pronged attack on Tenochtitlan. Alvarado, Sandoval, and Olid commanded each column while Cortes kept a forth division and the sailing ships. First, the Spaniards destroyed the aqueduct that took water to the city from the reservoir on the hill of Chapultepec. Then they blocked the causeways and began to move up them towards the city. The Aztecs launched hundreds of canoes to attack the Spanish and their Indian allies on the causeways, but Cortes sent the brigantines against them. The crews of the sailing ships blasted the Aztec canoes with cannons and arquebuses. In a short time, there were no canoes.

Cortes's troops found themselves blocked by the enlarged breaches in the causeways. Behind the breaches, the Aztecs had built stone walls. Cortes was able to land men from the brigantines and the canoes of his Indian allies and take the Aztec defenders in the flank and rear. But there were many fortifications, and progress was slow. Cortes's men not only had to take each fort, they had to fill up the breaches behind them so the army could proceed. Finally, Cortes reached the end of the causeway. His cannons blasted down the last Aztec wall and his troops swarmed into the great plaza of Tenochtitlan. The Aztecs counterattacked and captured 62 Spaniards. They sacrificed them on the top of a pyramid as their countrymen watched. The Spanish attacked again, and again they gained footholds in Tenochtitlan. Cortes again and again made overtures to Cuauhtemoc, who again and again rejected them. The Aztecs could bring no food to their island city; they could get no water from their main reservoir.

Slowly, the Spanish and their Indian allies inched into Tenochtitlan. Cannons blasted down Aztec barricades and arquebuses, and crossbows cut down Aztec warriors before they could close with the invaders. At close quarters, Spanish steel gave the invaders the edge. Cortes had his men demolish any large buildings that the Aztecs could use as forts. By August, the Aztecs had reached the end of their rope. Cortes broke through the last fortification, and the Tlascalans and other Indians went wild. Even Cortes could not stop the massacre. His allies killed 150,000 Aztecs.

"I have never known a race to be so pitiless, nor human beings so deprived of pity," Cortes reported.

Cuauhtemoc, holding out on a small island, surrendered on August 12, 1521. Cortes congratulated him on his valor.

Birth of the New World

Cortes's conquest of Mexico was something entirely new. A European power had crossed an ocean and conquered another civilization. Before Cortes, Europeans had contented themselves with building trading posts, capturing port cities, and, at most, occupying small islands inhabited by barbarians. The Portuguese had been doing that for several generations in Africa and the Indies. The Spanish had begun to do that in the Caribbean. But after Cortes, they began to conquer and settle the mainland. Alvarado, encouraged by Cortes, cut a bloody swath through the Mayan kingdoms of Chiapas and Central America and was recognized as a *conquistador* by the Spanish crown. Francisco Pizarro led a harebrained expedition to Peru, and by several wild strokes of luck conquered an even greater empire than Mexico. The success of the Spanish led other Europeans to America—the Swedes, the Dutch, the French, and the English. The Portuguese success revolutionized trade in the Old World. The Spanish success created a New World.

It also created a new trade route: across the Pacific. Alvarado's last expedition was to cross the Pacific to the Indies. Unfortunately for him, he postponed it to rescue a Spanish officer besieged by Indians in the present Mexican state of Jalisco and was killed. But a generation later, the Spanish "Manila galleons" were shuttling across the Pacific between Mexico and the Philippines.

The New World had been integrated with both sides of the Old World.

Battle 16

Stalingrad, 1942 AD
The March to the East

Who fought: Germans (Friedrich von Paulus) vs. Russians (Georgi Zhukov).

What was at stake: The survival of the Nazi war effort and hence the survival of democracy.

Conquering the Union of Soviet Socialist Republics had always been a dream of Adolf Hitler. He was far more interested in destroying the Soviet Union than in conquering Scandinavia, the Low Countries, and France. There were several reasons. Perhaps the most important, although the hardest to understand, was ideology.

It's hardest to understand because to a reasonable person committed to neither Nazism nor Communism, the two systems were like Tweedledum and Tweedledee. Both were socialist and authoritarian. Both professed to be parties of the people (Nazi was short for National Socialist Workers' Party). However, both were controlled by all-powerful dictators: Hitler in Germany and Joseph Stalin in the Soviet Union. There were some differences: in the Soviet Union, the government owned all means of production, and in Germany, the government merely controlled them. (In both cases, the incomes of managers were vastly different from those of workers.) Soviet Communism did not include the insane hatred of Jews that was inherent in Nazism. The Communists persecuted all religions but didn't try to exterminate the followers of any.

Nevertheless, all Germans were brought up to believe that Communism was an unalloyed evil, and all Russians, Ukrainians, and other Soviet peoples were taught that Nazism was merely a disguise for untrammeled capitalism, an attempt to push the world back to the Dark Ages.

Another powerful reason for war on the Soviets was racism. German anti-Semitism was not merely hatred of a particular religion. It was based on the weird theory that Jews were a race—an inferior race that must be destroyed for the good of mankind. Racism was pervasive in Nazism. According to Nazi theorists, there were superior and inferior races. Germans, of course, were the most superior, along with their Nordic cousins, the Scandinavians, the Dutch, and the English. It went down from there. Among whites, the Slavs ranked just above the Jews. That was another reason to destroy the Soviet Union.

Then there was a practical reason. The Soviet Union was a vast country but underpopulated and underdeveloped compared with western and central Europe. Hitler wanted *Liebensraum*, living space. Germans would colonize the East and develop modern industry, and the Slavs would provide what Nature had intended them to provide: slave labor.

Today, Hitler is remembered as a power-mad warlord, who single-handedly plunged the world into World War II. Power-mad he was, and probably just plain mad as well. But unlike some other Germans—General Erich Ludendorff, for example, Hitler did not think war was the highest form of human endeavor.

"How to achieve the moral breakdown of the enemy before war has started," Hitler once said. "That is what interests me. Whoever has experienced war at the front will want to refrain from all avoidable bloodshed."

The German dictator had gone quite a distance toward the domination of Europe without war. He had bluffed the World War 1 Allies into letting him reoccupy the Rhineland, then to unite Germany and Austria, then to annex the Sudetenland from Czechoslovakia, and finally to eliminate the independence of Czechoslovakia. Germany's "March to the East" had begun.

Hitler's war of nerves failed in Poland. But before hostilities began, he guaranteed that the war in Poland would be short: he signed a pact with the Soviet Union. While German troops invaded Poland from the west, Soviet troops swept in from the east.

Up to that point, everything had gone according to Hitler's plan. The trouble was that Britain and France had treaties with Poland, and the British and French publics were sick of appeasing Hitler. Britain and France declared war and blockaded Germany. Then Winston Churchill proposed an expedition to Norway to block shipments of iron ore to Germany. But Germany moved first.

In the spring of 1940, Hitler invaded Norway, taking Denmark on the way. The move gave him more ports, making the blockade more difficult and making it easier for his submarines to put to sea. Then he invaded France, overrunning the Netherlands, Belgium, and Luxembourg in the process. The French and British armies were thoroughly defeated. That, Hitler thought, would allow him to get on with his March to the East. But Britain didn't surrender. (See The battle of Britain, pg. 42.)

Barbarossa

Hitler's ally, Benito Mussolini of Italy, caused some minor distractions by getting involved in North Africa and the Balkans. Hitler had to send troops to bail him out. But nothing interfered with the planning of Operation Barbarossa, the invasion of the Soviet Union.

At first glance, that operation might look suicidal. The Soviet Union had the largest army in the world, and it had the largest tank force in the world. Individually, its combat aircraft were no match for those of Germany or Britain, but the Soviet's air force was also the world's largest. The USSR's population was three times that of Germany, and its land area exceeded that of all non-Soviet Europe many times. Napoleon, a better general than any Hitler could call upon, had met his downfall on the snowy plains of Russia.

But Hitler had several reasons to feel confident. Soviet armor had been much less than impressive during the "dress rehearsal" for World War II (the Spanish Civil War). In the 1940–41 "Winter War" with little Finland, the Red Army had been badly mauled. And most importantly, the paranoid Stalin had almost terminally crippled the army with his purge in 1937–38. He executed most of the original military thinkers thrown up by the Russian civil war of 1918–20, beginning with Marshal Mikhail N. Tukhachevsky, the army's chief of staff. By the time the purge had ended, three of the five marshals were dead, along with 13 out of 15 army commanders, 110 of 195 division commanders, and 186 out of 406 brigadier generals. Stalin filled the vacancies mainly with old hacks who had shown their loyalty to his faction of the Communist Party.

To offset Soviet numbers, Hitler's invasion army included troops from his satellites: Italians, Romanians, Hungarians, and Slovakians. There was even a Spanish volunteer unit, although the Spanish dictator, Francisco Franco, had driven Hitler to a frenzy by refusing to join the Rome-Berlin-Tokyo Axis and allow German troops through Spain to close the Mediterranean.

Operation Barbarossa began with three main thrusts. One pushed north along the Baltic coast to take Leningrad, while a Finnish army attacked the former Russian capital from the north. A second thrust aimed directly at Moscow, the Soviet capital. The third swept down into the Ukraine, the USSR's breadbasket.

The northern thrust never took Leningrad. The Finns drove the Red Army back to the old border of Finland. Then they stopped. Hitler decided the other two thrusts were more important than the northern attack, so he did not reinforce the Leningrad thrust. Nevertheless, the Germans were able to establish a partial siege of Leningrad in which a million people starved to death.

The other two thrusts were hampered by Hitler's micromanagement. He kept shifting troops from the Moscow attack to the Ukrainian one and back again. As a result neither reached its objective before winter.

Hitler's playing generalissimo would have been even more disastrous for the Germans if Stalin were not doing the same thing.

Before Barbarossa began, Stalin was convinced that the Germans would not attack. He considered anyone who contradicted to be him a traitor. There were German overflights of USSR territory, and German patrols in Soviet uniforms crossed the border. Soviet officers, however, were afraid to pass this intelligence on to Stalin. Stalin ignored warnings he got from other governments. For instance, the United States passed on this warning: "The Government of the United States, while endeavoring to estimate the developing world situation, has come into possession of information it regards as authentic, clearly indicating that it is the intention of Germany to attack the Soviet Union."

When the Germans did attack, Stalin told his commanders not to yield an inch. The German panzer armies knifed through the Soviet lines, leaving the burned-out wrecks of thin-skinned Soviet tanks in their wake. Then they turned and surrounded the troops who, following Stalin's orders, refused to yield an inch. The German Wehrmacht captured 5,700,000 Soviet troops, most of them between June and November 1941. Of them, 3,300,000 died in captivity of starvation and maltreatment.

The war on the Eastern Front was waged with brutality unseen in any other European war of the 20th century. In a speech to his generals before the invasion, Hitler

Russian soldiers in Stalingrad.

told them that "the struggle is one of ideologies and racial differences and will have to be conducted with unprecedented, unmerciful and unrelenting harshness...German soldiers guilty of breaking international law...will be excused."

There were two results of Hitler's fanaticism; neither were favorable to Germany. First, Soviet soldiers, knowing what was in store for them, were inclined to fight to the death. In early 1942, the commander of the German 12th Infantry Division reported, "Since November last year...fierce resistance was put up and only a few prisoners taken." Second, Ukrainians, who at first welcomed the Germans as liberators from Russian oppression, joined anti-German guerrilla groups in huge numbers.

General Mud and General Winter

The German army was designed to fight in Western and Central Europe, a land with a dense network of good roads, teeming cities, and many small farms. It found itself on the Russian steppes, table-flat grasslands with few roads, almost all of them miserable, and with great distances between settlements. Now, driving deep into Russia and the Ukraine, it encountered the continental climate, something vastly different from the sea-tempered climate of the rest of Europe. To the German troops, the autumn rains were like what Noah must have witnessed from the ark. Roads became liquid. The rivers, fantastically long and wide by western European standards, flooded the surrounding land. German tanks, trucks, and even horse-drawn carts bogged down. The history of the 98th Wehrmacht division recorded, "The modern general service carts with their rubber tires and ball-bearing mounted wheels had long since broken up under the stress of the appalling tracks, and been replaced by Russian farm carts."

Worse was yet to come.

Winter descended with a ferocity that was unknown to anyone west of Russia. The German troops were completely unprepared. Supply of winter clothing had been forbidden, because that would cast doubt on the General Staff prediction that the Soviet Union would collapse before the first snow.

Hitler ordered his troops to concentrate on taking Moscow. Winter had frozen the mud, and the Germans strove mightily to take the city and get shelter from the arctic weather. But there were difficulties.

In spite of his weaknesses as a general, Stalin was a competent, ruthless civil administrator. He managed to get most of the key factories in western Russia moved behind the Urals, and now they were producing a new tank, the T 34. The T 34 was the best tank to appear in all of World War II and far better than Germany's best, the Pz KW IV. And the forces defending Moscow had a new leader, Marshal Georgi K. Zhukov, who had commanded the defenders of Leningrad. Zhukov launched a counteroffensive, using troops from the Soviet Far East and as many T 34s as he could get. The Germans were pushed back from Moscow and all along the line.

Stalin used the winter respite from German attack to court-martial defeated generals. At least one army commander and 10 major generals were executed.

Stalin's City

The German Army in the spring of 1942 was not the same organization it was the previous summer. It had 162 combat divisions facing the Red Army, but only eight were available for an all-out offensive. Three more divisions could take offensive action after a rest, 47 were able to take limited offensive action, 73 could be used for defense, and 29 for only limited defense. Two were totally useless. The Wehrmacht has 16 panzer divisions, but only 140 tanks among them—in other words, only eight or nine tanks to an armored division. On paper, it increased its strength by 23 divisions between June 1941 and July 1942. That was done, however, by reducing the battalions in each division from nine to seven and the number of men in each company from 180 to 80. Soviet tank production had exceeded Germany's even before Barbarossa. It was now churning out tanks in a growing flood behind the Urals. American trucks, planes, and other war materials were arriving by sea. The Wehrmacht was experiencing an oil shortage, and Hitler had nightmares that the allied aircraft might destroy Romania's Ploesti oil fields, his main source of the vital fluid.

Hitler knew he was at the end of the line. He could not retreat. His only chance was to capture Soviet resources to replenish his own. He would strike to the south—through the Ukrainian "breadbasket," and into the rich Caucasus oil fields. He shifted as much power as he could to the south, although he still wanted German forces in the north to take Leningrad. The oil fields of the Caucasus were the main objective, however.

"Hitler said we must capture the oilfields by autumn because Germany could not continue the war without them," Field Marshal Ewald von Kleist remembered.

There was, however, another objective to the southern drive: Stalingrad, an industrial city strung out for about 20 miles on the west bank of the Volga. In his Fuhrer Directive No. 41, Hitler said, "Every effort will be made to reach Stalingrad itself or at least to bring the city under the fire from heavy artillery so that it will no longer be of any use as an industrial or communications center." But the Caucasus were to be the main objective. Before that, however, the Wehrmacht was to execute another giant pincers movement encircling and annihilating the main Soviet forces in the Donets Corridor—the strip of land between the Donets and Don rivers. The German troops were to converge near Stalingrad.

But the Wehrmacht of 1942 was not the Wehrmacht of 1941. Because of the limited panzer power, it could attempt only small encirclements instead of the great sweeps of the previous year. And then the 4th Panzer Army ran out of fuel and had to stop. The encirclements weren't working.

Meanwhile the Soviets had been positioning their forces to meet an attack on Moscow, leaving the Germans less opposition than they could have faced in the south.

Then Stalin realized that Stalingrad—Stalin City—was endangered. He rushed troops there and again issued his "not an inch" order.

The capture of Stalingrad was assigned to Colonel General Friedrich von Paulus, one of Hitler's favorite generals, leading the Wehrmacht's 6th Army. Paulus did get into the outskirts of Stalingrad and actually reached the Volga bank, but Soviet resistance was fierce. The German infantry bogged down in room-by-room fighting in the rubble of Stalingrad's factory district. Stalingrad—Stalin's city—was now more important to Hitler than all the oil in the Caucasus. He forbade any thought of retreat.

The 4th Panzer Army had originally supported Paulus's troops in the march on Stalingrad, but then was transferred to the drive for the Caucasus oil. But Hitler took the resistance of Stalin's city to be a direct insult. He sent the 4th Panzer back to Stalingrad, fatally slowing the thrust at the oilfields. Stalin sent more troops to Stalingrad, and then appointed Zhukov supreme commander of the southern front and sent him to Stalingrad with orders to launch a massive counterattack. Zhukov considered a counterattack with his available forces to be foolish, and so it proved to be. But to refuse to obey Stalin would be even more foolish for him personally. He flew back to Moscow and convinced the Soviet dictator that a counterattack with more resources and better preparation was needed. Paulus, meanwhile was still bogged down in the rubble, and the panzer army was demonstrating that tanks are not a sure-fire solution in urban warfare. The troops of Soviet Marshal Vasili Chuikov contested every millimeter, while Zhukov allowed them only the minimum reinforcements needed to hold on.

While Chuikov held the German 6th and 4th Armies in Stalingrad, Zhukov was building up enormous forces on their flanks, held by Romanian troops. The Romanians had second-line weapons and less than top commitment to the war.

On November 19, Zhukov launched his counterattack. Five infantry and two tank armies struck the Romanians north of the city. The next day, three infantry and one tank army crossed the Volga south of the city. The 3rd and 4th Romanian armies were devastated, the German 4th Panzer Army was routed, and Paulus and his 6th Army were entombed.

Siege and surrender

Paulus radioed that he'd need 700 tons of supplies a day airlifted to hold on. The German general staff cut that to a "realistic" 300 tons and managed to supply 60 tons. Hitler ordered Field Marshal Erich von Manstein, who had masterminded the breakthrough at Sedan in the Battle of France, to break through the Soviet lines and free Paulus. Manstein was one of the best, if not the best, tank commanders in World War II. However, there is only so much a tank commander can do if he doesn't have enough tanks. Manstein failed and urged Hitler to order Paulus to break out. Hitler refused.

Winter again swept over the Russian steppes, and the Germans, still unprepared for it, fell back. Hitler promoted Paulus to field marshal on January 30. No German field marshal had ever surrendered to an enemy. The day of his promotion, Friedrich von Paulus became the first. The Soviets captured 110,000 German troops, few of whom survived captivity. Paulus survived. Hitler's favorite general became a spokesman for Soviet propaganda. After the war, he settled in East Germany.

In 1942, it was still possible for Germany to defeat the Soviet Union. But it was a long shot. If the Germans could take the oilfields in the Caucasus and hold them, they might force the Soviet military machine to grind to a halt. It's conceivable that they could then build up enough strength to swing up behind the Urals and force the Soviets to surrender. But the Germans lost any chance of taking the oilfields because of Hitler's obsession with Stalin's city.

Battle 17

Narses.

Busta Gallorum, 552 AD
The End of a Dream?

Who fought: Romans (Narses) vs. Goths (Totila and Teias).

What was at stake: Survival of western civilization in western Europe.

It looked as if Justinian's dream of regaining the Western Empire was an idle dream, after all. Belisarius, the greatest general the Empire produced in generations, had breezed through North Africa. He had wiped out the once-mighty Vandal Empire and restored control of the Mediterranean to the Romans. Then he landed in Sicily and, with the aid of the native Romans, drove the Ostrogoths back to the mainland. Conquering mainland Italy had been a tougher job, but Belisarius accomplished that, too. Or he almost did.

He had the Gothic king and his court besieged in Ravenna, their almost impregnable capital. Then the Persians attacked the eastern frontier. Justinian wanted to end the long Italian war so he could deal with the Persians. He offered to let the Goths keep Italy north of the Po. They agreed, but Belisarius refused to lift the siege. He wanted unconditional surrender. In despair, the Goths offered to recognize Belisarius as Emperor of the West if he would lift the siege. He agreed. But after he entered Ravenna, Belisarius took the Gothic king, Witigis, and his officials prisoner and sent them to Constantinople.

Justinian was outraged. First, Belisarius had disobeyed orders. Second, he had won by breaking his word. Justinian was also troubled by the thought that someday Belisarius might be tempted by an offer like the one the Goths had made. But right now, he needed him on the Persian front.

While the great general was absent, the Goths elected a new king, a vigorous young man named Totila. Totila began reconquering lost territory. When Belisarius successfully completed the latest round of fighting with Persia, Justinian sent him back to Italy. Totila, though, was a better general than Witigis, and Belisarius was unable to make headway. After much fruitless fighting, he asked to be relieved of the Italian command.

The Romans had a highly trained army, and they had a number of competent, even dashing, generals. What they didn't have was many soldiers. Conquering Italy had been many years' work for Belisarius, and everyone agreed that Belisarius was a military genius. With the resources he had available to reconquer Italy, Justinian now needed another, greater, genius—a big order. Even more important, he needed a genius he could trust—a bigger order yet. He went over the list of officers, and didn't find anyone who met either requirement. And even if he did find such a genius, he still didn't have enough soldiers. To solve that problem, Justinian turned to a highly improbable trouble-shooter, his high chamberlain, Narses. Narses was intelligent, adaptable, and utterly loyal. Further, as he was a eunuch, and well into his 70s, he could have no thoughts about starting a new dynasty. Narses did know something about what an army required. He had represented Justinian in Italy for a while, but he quarreled with Belisarius and was brought back to Constantinople. Back home, Narses had again proved his loyalty by foiling a plot by John of Cappadocia, the praetorian prefect, to assassinate Justinian.

Narses

The chamberlain was old and frail. He spent almost his whole life in offices, dictating memos and supervising archives. He was affable, generous, and highly civilized, which made him popular with lesser officials and the public. But could he recruit an army? Narses had long been a student of military theory. And, as he proved in the Nika Rebellion (see pg. 16) and in the attempted assassination, he was utterly fearless. But would the crude, barbarian Germans, Slavs, and Huns the Romans recruited for their army follow such a man? Justinian thought they would.

To find out, he sent the eunuch chamberlain north to recruit soldiers from the Heruls, a German tribe that had adopted what passed for civilization among the Huns. To the surprise of everybody but Narses, and probably Justinian, the ancient bureaucrat got on famously with the barbarians. If the Emperor is sending such an old man to form an army, the Heruls thought, he must be very wise in the ways of war.

Narses soon got a chance to prove his wisdom. A huge army of Slavs had massed on the Danube to invade the Balkans. From horseback, Narses, the one-time armchair general, directed his Heruls so adroitly the Slavs were routed with heavy losses.

While Narses was recruiting and leading barbarians, Justinian appointed his cousin, Germanus, supreme commander in Italy. Germanus took his own armed retainers and recruited an army of peasants, paying them an enlistment bonus from his own pocket. Then he died.

Once again, the emperor called on Narses. The eunuch was now to return to Italy, this time as army commander.

In addition to the Heruls, Narses recruited Huns, Slavs, and Lombards; the last were a people almost as uncivilized as the Slavs. He picked up the army Germanus had recruited, now under the command of the late general's son-in-law, Bloody John. He had Roman regular regiments, a group of Persian deserters from the eastern front and the personal bodyguards of a number of Roman magnates, including one called John the Glutton. (Every other Roman officer seems to have been named John.) It seems likely that Narses had a larger army than Belisarius had taken to Italy. It's also likely that it was not as much larger as the historian Procopius would have us believe. Procopius was the secretary of Narses' rival, Belisarius. Certainly, there is no good reason to believe that Narses' troops outnumbered those of the Goths.

A new war

In 551, at the age of 74, Narses set out for Italy. The Goths supposed that any Roman invasion would come by sea, as it always had in the past. Narses marched overland.

Totila was busy in southern Italy, but he sent one of his most able officers, Teias, to stop the Romans. Teias knew Narses had a large army, but he also knew he lacked enough ships to carry it. He would not be able to march along the coast, the Goth believed, because of all the bays, lakes, and wide rivers. (Teias had destroyed all the bridges.) So the Gothic commander concentrated at Verona, in the middle of the Po valley. According to Procopius, "He cut off all possible passage there for the enemy by making all the area everywhere around the river Po impassable and completely impenetrable by artificial means, in places making thickets and ditches and ravines, in others deep mud and standing pools." The Franks had occupied much of northern Italy, having received land from the Goths in return for their neutrality, and having seized more land while their "allies" were busy fighting the Romans. They refused the Romans peaceful passage because their army included Lombards, the blood enemies of the Franks. Narses did not want to add the formidable Franks to his enemies at this time. He decided to take the coastal route.

Narses had his troops build rafts, which the ships towed along beside the marching army. When faced with a body of water, Narses turned the rafts into floating bridges.

In the past, Belisarius and the other Roman commanders had concentrated on taking cities, turning the war into a snail-paced succession of sieges. The only result had been a long, drawn-out devastation of Italy. Narses aimed at the Gothic army. After resting in Ravenna for nine days, the Romans marched out. At Ariminum, the Gothic garrison sallied out to stop Narses' force, but their commander was killed and the Goths fled back into the city. Narses threw a bridge across the river, but he didn't stop to besiege Ariminum. Coming to another fortress, he left a few guards at the site and pushed on. Totila had stationed his forces at the main pass across the Apennines, but Narses took a little-used trail and easily crossed the range.

Totila saw that the only way Narses could be stopped would be with a pitched battle. He collected all his fighting men and advanced.

The pyres of the Gauls

Both armies camped about 14 Roman miles apart, near a place called Busta Gallorum (Funeral Pyres of the Gauls) in memory of a Roman victory over the Gauls by the consul Camillus. Totila had all the Gothic troops that weren't tied up manning garrisons, except for the men under Teias that Narses had bypassed. Narses' challenge to the Gothic power in the open field, something Belisarius had never attempted, might seem rash except for one thing: The old eunuch knew he had a superior military machine.

The Huns, the Heruls, and all the regular Roman cavalry were horse archers as well as lancers. They used the short Asian composite bow and could shoot accurately from a galloping horse. The Gothic cavalry were only lancers. Their only archers were infantry. Infantry was not highly esteemed by most military leaders at the time, whether Roman or barbarian. Ever since Adrianople (see pg. 63) infantry had been regarded as fit only for defending walls or climbing siege ladders. At least, that was the opinion of all generals except Narses. The eunuch saw that Roman infantry, trained to use both the bow and the spear with equal facility, could be invaluable in certain situations.

Narses was ready for a battle, but he gave Totila a chance to avoid one. He sent envoys to the Gothic camp advising the king that he could not forever withstand the power of the Roman Empire. Totila laughed at Narses's threat. The envoys then said, "Well, sir, fix an appointed time for an engagement." Totila said, "Let us meet in eight days."

The Roman general knew better than to trust a Goth. He prepared to fight the next day. Totila moved his whole army up the following morning. A distance of only "two spear throws" separated Roman and Goth. Narses had taken a strong position. There was only one way to get around his army, a narrow path commanded by a hill on his left. He sent 50 infantrymen up the hill in the dead of the night. When Totila saw them, he sent a force of cavalry to drive the Romans off the hill. No infantry could withstand a cavalry charge, he thought. The Roman infantry front ranks formed a wall of shields and spears; the rear ranks used their bows. The Goths were beaten back repeatedly. Totila sent another group of horsemen up the hill. The result was the same. The Gothic king resigned himself to Roman possession of the high ground. It was time for the big show.

But Teias still had not arrived. To buy time, Totila sent a Roman deserter named Coccas out to challenge any Roman to single combat. Coccas was a big man, immensely strong, who had gained a great reputation among the Goths as a fighter. One of Narses's bodyguards, an Armenian named Anzalas, rode out to meet him. Coccas charged, but at the last moment Anzalas made his horse swerve and stabbed the Gothic champion in his side. It was not an auspicious beginning for Totila. But he had another delaying tactic.

As both armies watched, the Gothic king, arrayed in gleaming purple and gold parade armor and riding a huge horse, cantered out into no man's land. His horse pranced in circles, reared, pirouetted, and ran backwards while Totila tossed his lance into the air and caught it. He was doing the mounted war dance of the Goths. Finally, he galloped back to his own lines and changed into war armor. Teias had arrived.

Narses commanded from his left flank, where he placed the best of the Romans and Huns under Bloody John. Valerian, Bloody John's uncle, and John the Glutton held the other flank with more Roman regulars. Narses placed the Lombards and some recently recruited Heruls in the center, and he made them fight on foot. These barbarians had not had the advantages of Roman discipline. Narses couldn't be sure they wouldn't flee at an inopportune time, so he took away their mobility by dismounting them. Both infantry and cavalry held the Roman flanks, and all of them had their bows strung.

When Totila saw Narses' order of battle, he decided the center was the weak point. It was held by infantry—not the disciplined Roman infantry, but the Romans' tribal allies. He ordered a cavalry charge into the Roman center.

When he saw the Gothic horsemen preparing, Narses changed his own position. He formed the infantry on his flanks into crescents, curving in towards the center. And he sent some horsemen out to the left with orders to remain concealed but to attack the Gothic cavalry from the rear when its charge failed.

Totila launched his charge—a headlong stampede aimed at the Roman center. The infantry and cavalry on the Roman flanks released clouds of arrows at the Goths. Riders fell; horses fell; horses reared and tried to turn; men and horses collided. The charge turned into pandemonium. The few Goths who reached the infantry center learned that horses can't be driven through a hedge of spears. Then the hidden Roman cavalry charged the rear of the Gothic cavalry. The Gothic horsemen were too far from their own infantry for archery support. They fled. Their infantry saw them fleeing and ran, too. The Roman cavalry rode after them, shooting all the way. Gothic bodies were spread over the fields for miles. One of them was that of King Totila.

Narses's reliance on dismounted cavalry to hold the center of his line while projecting flanks of archers shot up the enemy foreshadowed the tactics Edward III used at Crecy 794 years later. The English king's revival of the tactics of the Roman general earned him the reputation of being a military genius.

Narses sent Bloody John after the remnants of Totila's army. Then he paid off his Lombard allies and had Valerian escort them back to their own country under guard. The northern savages were far too fond of murder and rape to suit Narses.

Narses had little trouble retaking Rome. Meanwhile, the Goths crowned a new king, Teias.

Narses marched south into Campania. He was threatening the Gothic treasure stored at Cumae. As he expected, Teias rounded up all the remaining Gothic warriors and set out to save the treasure, which meant he would have to face Narses on ground of the Roman's choosing. Cut off from supplies, he tried to make a surprise attack on the Romans. The Romans weren't surprised. The Goths were outnumbered for the first time, and fought for two days. Then with Teias and most of his troops dead, they agreed to leave the Roman Empire.

Next, Narses had to deal with the Goth's allies, the Franks. The Franks were the most primitive of all the German tribes. They had no cavalry and few archers, but they were the most formidable hand-to-hand fighters in Europe. They fought in a dense mass that no cavalry could break into. First they felled approaching horsemen with their national weapon, the *francisca*, a short, heavy throwing axe that could split any shield. Those who escaped the shower of axes were skewered by the angon, a spear the Franks could either throw or thrust with, or chopped down with their long swords. Roman, Gothic, and Alanic horsemen had tangled with the Frankish footmen and come off second best.

The mistake of the Franks' previous enemies, Narses saw, was in charging those ferocious footmen. When he met them, he attacked with cavalry archers, who were able to stay out of axe-range. According to the historian Agathias, only five Franks escaped and only 80 Romans were killed.

A name to reckon with

Narses stayed in Italy for the next 13 years as Justinian's viceroy. He rebuilt roads, aqueducts, and cities, in attempt to restore a lost social order and rekindle a lost morale. He carved inscriptions on public works, like one on a bridge near Rome: "This bridge constructed by the praetorian Narses, patrician of the Empire"—the pathetic attempt of a man who could have no descendants to leave some memory of himself behind.

There was no need to embellish his reputation for contemporaries. When they looked at the withered old eunuch, they saw a master strategist. Most of his troops had gone home, but the old eunuch's reputation alone kept Italy safe. When Justinian died, his successor, Justin II, retired the ancient viceroy. (He was 87 at the time. He lived in Constantinople 10 more years.) As soon as Narses left, the Lombards poured into the Po valley.

All of Italy was not lost to the Roman Empire, however. Centuries later, when the Empire was known as the Eastern Roman, or Byzantine, Empire, Constantinople continued to control parts of Italy. There, the culture of Rome lived on in its home ground. In those areas began the movement we know as the Renaissance, or rebirth, of Western civilization. When the Eastern Roman Empire finally ended with the fall of Constantinople in 1453, the civilization that had begun in Mycenaean Greece almost three millennia before was still growing and developing.

Battle 18

Lechfeld, 955 AD
On the Road to the Abyss

Who fought: Germans (Otto the Great) vs. Magyars.

What was at stake: The end of the destructive raids of Eurasian nomads into western Europe, hence the development of Western civilization.

As the first millennium drew to a close, western and central Europe seemed to be descending into chaos. The Western Roman Empire did not fall with a crash. It dribbled away. Justinian had restored Africa and Italy, but when his viceroy, Narses (see Busta Gallorium pg. 94) left Italy, the Lombards invaded and took over much of the country. Then the Muslim Arabs invaded North Africa and went on to conquer Spain. They began raiding into Gaul, reaching what is now central France. Meanwhile, the Scandinavian Vikings were raiding everywhere. They set up bases in Brittany and Scotland, founded cities in Ireland, carved out states in England, Normandy, and Russia, and struck out in all directions.

When these onslaughts began, a conglomeration of tribal chiefs and Roman magnates who were incapable of united action led the western Europeans. A Frankish king, Charlemagne, tried to restore the Western Empire, although his domain included only parts of the old Roman Empire—Gaul, western Germany, and northern Italy. Charlemagne's empire broke up both because of rivalry among his heirs and attacks by the Arabs and Vikings. The best way to meet those raids was by heavy cavalry, highly trained and always ready to fight. And the only way the primitive economy could support those armored horsemen was by the labor of farmers in each warrior's neighborhood. Europe had been composed of landowners and peasants for centuries. It naturally followed that the landowners became the knights and the peasants the serfs. Enforcing central authority among these armed and largely self-sufficient nobles became impossible.

As the 10th century began, Viking raids had turned into full-scale invasions, with armies of pirates traveling around the countryside and wintering in armed camps. Arab corsairs were still raiding the Mediterranean coasts and an Arab fleet took the Balearic Islands from the Franks. The Slavic tribes, now organized into regular kingdoms, pressed into German lands from the east. Then a new enemy appeared.

The Magyars

The nomad nations of the Eurasian steppes were playing dominoes again. The Uighur Turks, who had driven the Arabs out of the Tarim Basin—their deepest penetration into Central Asia—were in turn defeated by the Kirghiz Turks, and the Uighurs then pushed the Pecheneg Turks west. The Pecheneg onslaught fell on the Magyars, who moved into that nomad paradise, the plains of Hungary, to join the descendants of Attila's Huns.

The Magyars, who until then seemed to have been peacefully tending their horses and cattle, reacted the way Eurasian nomads always did when they came in contact with settled peoples: They began raiding, raping, looting, killing, and burning.

The Magyars had the ancient military system of the steppes. All of the men were warriors and all of the warriors were cavalry. They were lightly armored, and their principal weapon was the composite bow—a bow composed of layers of sinew, wood, and horn, short enough to shoot from horseback, powerful enough to penetrate mail. For close fighting, they had swords and battleaxes. They could ride circles around any infantry army and shoot it to pieces without ever getting within spear range. They fought in units of tens, hundreds, and thousands and could evade a heavy cavalry charge by scattering in all directions.

The Magyars opened the new century with an attack on Bavaria in 900. Six years later, they attacked the kingdom of Moravia, pushing the Slavs out the Danube and Theiss valleys. The Magyar kings revived another steppe tradition: the protection racket, politely called tribute. If the settled people paid their annual tribute, the Magyar warriors would refrain from violent pillage. In 910, some German nobles withheld the tribute and mobilized to meet the Magyars. The nomad warriors easily evaded the knights' charges and shot down them, and even more, their horses. Then they slaughtered the dismounted knights and their infantry. After that, they went back to standard operating procedure: They killed all the men, enslaved all the women, stole all the livestock and anything of value, and burned all the villages. In 924, the Magyars launched a major offensive against the settled people, raiding all along the Danube and Rhine valleys. Striking farther and farther from their homes, they then raided northern Italy and pushed out along the Mediterranean coast into Provence. The brunt of the Magyar plague, however, fell on the eastern remnant of Charlemagne's empire, Germania.

Germania

Germania was more a theory than a state. It had a king, but the German dukes, who were not particularly respectful of his authority, elected him. The dukes themselves had trouble exercising their own authority over the horde of minor nobles who ruled the peasantry with an iron hand.

There were sporadic attempts to revive the Empire. Arnulf, the illegitimate son of Carloman, king of Germania, proclaimed himself emperor. He encouraged the Magyars to attack the Slavs, not realizing the much greater threat the nomads represented. He did, however, do something about the Vikings.

The Norse pirates had grown over-confident. At first, they had attacked settlements in small groups, killed, looted, and sailed away before any counterattacking force could organize. Now they operated in pirate armies, building fortified camps, and traveling overland on horseback. But they were neither trained to fight as cavalry nor to fight either as besiegers or besieged. In 891, Arnulf attacked a fortified Viking base at Louvain, in modern Belgium, and destroyed the pirates. That just about ended Viking raids into Germany.

It did not, however, end the threat from the Kingdom of Denmark, home of many of the Vikings. That was a bigger threat. A national army can wreak more havoc than any band of pirates.

Arnulf died after a reign of 11 years, and Germania reverted to its customary chaos. The kings of Saxony tried to keep the Danes at bay, and the kings, princes, dukes and counts of all the German states continued to pay the Magyar tribute.

In 918, Conrad of Franconia died. As king of Germania he exercised so little power as to be almost nonexistent. To replace him, the German electors were suddenly stricken with good sense. They elected Henry, King of Saxony, known for his defense against the Danes even more than for his devotion to hunting with a big bird. In 933, Henry the Fowler swooped down on the Magyar tribute collectors near Erfurt. The Magyars were not prepared to fight, not expecting an armed enemy. They fled from the charge of Henry's armored knights. That victory was enough to ensure the election of Henry's son, Otto, to succeed him.

Otto, a big, good-natured redhead, became king at the age of 28. He was an experienced soldier and, because of his quick decisions in battle and the wild charges that he led, was thought to be impetuous. But Otto was no "plain, blunt soldier." He was a man with a mission. His mission was to restore the empire of Charlemagne. It took him years. When the throne of a duchy became vacant, Otto either eliminated the dukedom by adding it to an adjoining territory or appointed one of his relatives to be duke. Naturally, that was not accomplished without fighting. There was a lot of it, but in the end, Otto was so strong he could work his will in France and Italy as well as Germany.

Rebuilding the Empire took all of Otto's time. And the Magyars took advantage of his distraction. In 937, seeking new worlds to loot, they began raiding Italy as far south as Monte Cassino, western Germany, and as far west as modern Belgium and central France. In 954, they crossed the Rhine and raided Metz, Cambrai, Rheims, and Chalons. In the spring of 955, 100,000 Magyar horsemen again invaded Germany and besieged Augsburg. But this time, Otto was ready for them.

Showdown

Otto had organized eight separate armies. All of them converged on the Magyar army on the banks of the Lech River. The mailed knights and the infantry spearmen who accompanied them hemmed the Magyars in on Lechfeld (the Lech field). The nomad horse archers didn't have room for their favorite shoot-and-run tactics. The fighting was hand-to-hand, and the mailed Germans had the advantage over the lightly armed Magyars. Even so, the fight lasted 10 hours. When it was over, the nomads had almost been wiped out. They fled back to Hungary. Fifteen years later, they all agreed to become Christians. The Magyar menace was ended forever.

In 962, the Pope crowned Otto I Emperor of the Romans. Otto, later called Otto the Great, became a successor to Charles the Great and, in theory, to all the Caesars. The empire he restored, later called by the strange name of The Holy Roman Empire of the German People, was to survive for centuries as a ghost of the empire founded by warriors from the banks of the Tiber. The ghost was not laid until Napoleon I.

More important than the re-creation of an empire is the fact that Lechfeld ended forever attacks on western Europe from the Eurasian steppes. Those attacks had started with the Cimmerians before the founding of Rome. They had come at regular intervals since Attila, consigning Europe to a dark age for half a millennium.

Battle 19

Dublin, 1916 AD
"We're going out to be slaughtered."

Who fought: Irish Republicans (Padraic Pearse) vs. British Army (W.H.M. Lowe and John Maxwell).

What was at stake: Whether small nations have a chance of winning their independence.

April 24, 1916, was Easter Monday, a holiday in the United Kingdom of Great Britain and Ireland. It had been raining for 13 of the last 14 days, so a lot of Dubliners were out on Sackville Street enjoying the fine weather. None of the strollers even paused when a marching column of green-clad men and women appeared on the street. They were the Irish Volunteers, and the Volunteers were always marching. The Volunteers were almost a joke to most Dubliners, although many recognized that they were a product of a very serious situation.

The serious situation was the Home Rule question. Britain had been on the verge of giving Ireland a parliament of its own when Sir Edward Carson, a Dublin lawyer who had moved north, organized the Ulster Volunteers and threatened civil war if the Home Rule bill became law. Carson was a Protestant, and his Protestant Volunteers feared that Home Rule would turn them into a religious minority.

"Home rule means Rome rule!" Carson shouted to his Ulster constituents. "Ulster will fight, and Ulster will be right!" Carson's ally, Randolph Churchill, proclaimed in London.

To counter Carson and his troops, the Irish nationalists in the south (mostly Catholic) organized the Irish Volunteers. A cabal of nationalists—Mary Spring Rice, Sir Roger Casement, Conor O'Brien, Alice Stopford Green, and Michael O'Rahilly—formed to buy rifles for the Volunteers. All except O'Rahilly were Protestant. To bring the weapons into Ireland, they recruited Erskine Childers, another Protestant. Both Childers and O'Brien had boats. They picked up a load of obsolete German rifles and smuggled them in. Carson didn't have to smuggle in the Ulster Volunteers' modern rifles and machine guns. Sympathetic officials and military officers simply looked the other way. Two days after the Irish Volunteers got their rifles, World War I broke out.

On Easter Monday the Irish Volunteers were carrying the old single-shot Mausers as well as a wide variety of other weapons, some military, some sporting, most of them antique. Many of the strollers were less amused when they saw who was marching with the volunteers: James Connolly and his Citizen Army. Connolly, a thickset man with a bushy mustache, was a violent Marxist labor leader. After a bitter transport workers' strike in 1913, he had organized the Citizen Army to protect future strikers from the police. Connolly, it seemed, was to be taken more seriously than the leader of the Irish Volunteers, Padraic Pearse. Pearse, a big, good-looking man with one drooping eyelid, was, after all, a poet.

The onlookers would have taken both men much more seriously if they could have heard Connolly's greeting to a friend as the march started.

"Bill, we're going out to be slaughtered," the labor leader said.

"Is there no hope at all?"

"None whatsoever." Connolly smiled and slapped his friend on the shoulder.

700 years

The English had been in Ireland a long time—700 years, Irish patriots liked to say. For much of that time, though, English suzerainty was more nominal than real. England held Dublin, originally a Norwegian city, founded by Vikings, and what was called the Dublin Pale. The real English conquest didn't get started until the Tudor dynasty. And even then, Grace O'Malley, the "pirate queen," who ruled the west coast of Ireland, was able to talk with Elizabeth as an equal.

The Tudors began the process of establishing Protestant "plantations" in Ireland after military operations characterized by frequent massacres. When a fort manned by Spanish soldiers surrendered, for instance, a young officer was detailed to lead what was frankly called a "murder band." He and his men killed all the disarmed prisoners. His name was Walter Raleigh.

Later, the bloody civil wars between Royalists and Parliamentarians that racked England, Scotland, and Ireland made things much worse. Massacre was standard operating procedure for Cromwell's forces in Ireland. Catholics were told to go "to Hell or to Connaught" (the bleak boglands of western Ireland). Penal laws forbade Catholics from practicing their religion, and until 1782, Catholic priests were forbidden to set foot in Ireland. The penalty was death. No Catholic could own property worth more than five pounds. If a Catholic owned a valuable horse, for example, a Protestant could buy it from him for only five pounds, even if the owner didn't want to sell it.

Ireland had its own parliament, but only well-to-do male Protestants could sit there. Only well-to-do male Protestants could even vote for MPs. But even well-to-do Protestants were unhappy. The Irish parliament had limited powers, and Britain treated Ireland as a colony; Irish businesses felt strangled.

The Irish rebelled in 1798. The British put the revolt down savagely. Hanging, drawing, and quartering, in which the living victim is disemboweled, was the usual method of execution, although burning alive was also used. To get information, British troops would whip every man in a village, sometimes until they died. Another method of gaining intelligence was the "tar cap." A man's head was covered with a mixture of tar and gunpowder, which was then ignited. Although the screaming victim could supply little information, his example encouraged others to talk. The main result of the 1798 uprising was that the Irish lost their parliament.

In the 19th century, the British stopped hanging priests and gave Catholics the right to maintain schools, enter professions, and vote at parliamentary elections. In the 1820s, Daniel O'Connell, a Catholic lawyer, organized tenant farmers to vote for candidates who would help them. That led to the Catholic Emancipation Act of 1829, which opened Parliament to Catholics. But the mass of the population was still miserably poor tenant farmers subject to eviction at will from landlords who let plots out to the highest bidder. There was plenty of competition for land, because the population of Ireland increased 172 percent between 1779 and 1841.

Then in the middle of the 19th century, the potato famine struck. Because of the government's gross neglect, a million and a half people starved to death while Irish estates were still shipping food to England. Another million emigrated, mostly to the United States. The Irish immigrants in America, destitute by American standards but rich by Irish standards, contributed to revolutionary movements, such as the Fenians of the late 19th century. Slowly, the British government became more liberal. Slowly, an Irish middle class began to develop. Charles Stewart Parnell, an Irish politician, became a power in Parliament. John Redmond followed him as chairman of the Irish Party. Redmond pushed the Home Rule bill through the House of Commons twice, only to have it vetoed by the House of Lords. The third time, the Lords would have no veto power. Then Carson appeared, and the war broke out. Prime Minster Herbert Asquith proposed a Home Rule law that would be suspended until the end of the war, after which Ulster would get a chance to separate from the rest of Ireland.

Labyrinthine plotting

To the British public, the prominence of Irish politicians, professionals, and writers indicated that Ireland had at last become assimilated in the United Kingdom. It was "John Bull's other island."

That was hardly the case. Those middle-class intellectuals were Ireland's leading nationalists. Some, like Arthur Griffith, leader of the Sinn Fein Party, wanted Ireland to be a constitutional monarchy, under the British Crown but separate from Britain. Others wanted a republic. Prominent among them were Pearse and his fellow poets, Joseph Plunkett and Thomas MacDonagh, all members of the Irish Republican Brotherhood, a secret society that recognized the president of the IRB as president of Ireland. The IRB had infiltrated the leadership of the Irish Volunteers. Other Republicans, like the professors Eamon de Valera and Eoin MacNeill and the labor leader, James Connolly, were not IRB members but had the same aim. Connolly, in fact, was so militantly pro-republic that the IRB leaders worried that he might wreck their plans with a premature rebellion. They kidnapped him and persuaded him to join them in the big uprising they were planning. All over the country, they told Connolly, Irish Volunteers under their IRB officers would rise up and throw out the British. Connolly agreed to join them.

The uprising was really planned by an inner circle of the IRB, in which Pearse, the IRB president, was the driving force. The planners were so afraid of informers that they didn't inform all the members of their society. They definitely didn't inform MacNeill, chairman and commander of the Irish Volunteers, or O'Rahilly, the Volunteers' treasurer. Pearse, with MacNeill's approval, had scheduled a nationwide training session for Easter Sunday. When the Volunteers turned out, the rebellion would begin.

The IRB had arranged with Roger Casement to go to Germany and secure a large quantity of captured Russian rifles and machine guns. The arms were to be landed on Good Friday by a German freighter disguised as a Norwegian ship. Unfortunately for the rebels, the British intercepted the freighter, whose captain scuttled it. Casement was landed in Ireland by a German submarine and arrested the next day.

The same night the German sub arrived, Bulmer Hobson, an IRB member who did not know of the plot, learned of the secret orders. He told MacNeill. Shortly after that, the IRB kidnapped Hobson. Then, O'Rahilly, called The O'Rahilly because he was the chief of a clan in County Kerry, learned not only about the plot, but about the kidnapping of Hobson and the failed shipment of arms from Germany. He confronted Pearse with a revolver and dared anyone to kidnap him. Then he went to MacNeill.

MacNeill told the IRB leaders he was canceling the training session. They told him it was too late, that the orders had already been given. But this was 1916, not 1798. There were telephones, automobiles, and national newspapers. O'Rahilly was one of the couriers. He drove through six counties carrying the cancellation order. MacNeill placed it as an advertisement in the newspapers. Except in Dublin, there would not be any rising worth mentioning.

The Irish Republican Army

In Dublin, James Connolly didn't care if the Irish Volunteers chickened out. He expected very little of those bourgeoisie. Connolly would lead his Citizen Army against the British alone if necessary. With him was Countess Constance Markievicz, his second-in-command of the Citizen Army. That aristocratic member of the Anglo-Irish ascendancy had stood by the socialist in the 1913 strike. She was not going to leave him in this "glorious and terrible moment."

Connolly and his troops would not have to go it alone. Volunteers like the practical mathematician, Eamon de Valera, were sure that now that the British knew a rising had been planned, they would crack down on the Irish Volunteers. There was no choice now but to fight. The poets, Pearse, Plunkett, and MacDonagh, were caught up in the idea that a "blood sacrifice" was necessary to free Ireland. They would give their lives in this fruitless rebellion, but their blood would inspire others to throw off the English yoke.

The rebels gathered in Liberty Hall, headquarters of Connolly's union, voted that an Irish republic was now in existence, that Padraic Pearse was president of Ireland, and that they were the Irish Republican Army.

As the column marched away from Liberty Hall, an automobile pulled up behind them. Looking back, they saw the grinning face of The O'Rahilly, driving a car loaded with rifles. O'Rahilly, who had worked so hard to prevent the rising, was leaving an inherited fortune, a successful business, and a devoted family to join this suicidal enterprise. He later said: "Well, I've helped to wind up the clock (he was one of the founders of the Irish Volunteers), so I might as well hear it strike."

The clock strikes

The rebels followed a plan devised by Joseph Mary Plunkett, an aristocratic poet who had never been in any army nor in any kind of a fight. The headquarters group took the General Post Office and the surrounding buildings in the heart of downtown Dublin. Edward Daly's First Battalion occupied the Four Courts of Justice, on the north bank of the Liffey, and set up barricades on Cabra and North Circular roads, several blocks north in a residential area. MacDonagh's Second Battalion took Jacobs' Biscuit Factory. De Valera's Third Battalion seized Boland's Bakery and several buildings near the Beggar's Bush army barracks in southeastern Dublin. The Citizen Army occupied St. Stephen's Green, between the Second and Third Battalions. In southwest Dublin, Eamonn Ceant's Fourth Battalion held the Dublin Union, a combination poorhouse and madhouse the size of a village.

The original plan was that the rebels would hold a "ring of steel" around central Dublin. While the British were trying to break in, the Volunteers in the west would rise with their German-supplied weapons and attack the besiegers. There were a couple of problems with the plan, aside from the fact that there would be no rising in the West.

First, there weren't enough men in Dublin to hold all the proposed strong points, and on Easter Monday, the British in and around the city outnumbered them two to one. A week later, the British numerical advantage was simply overwhelming.

Second, the plan itself was stupid. The "ring of steel" was more like a ring of Swiss cheese. The British were able to infiltrate thousands of troops between the strong points without even being seen. St. Stephen's Green, the "strong point" to be occupied by the Citizen Army, was overlooked by tall buildings. Before long, British machine gun fire from rooftops and windows drove the rebel unionists off the Green.

The fighting began like something directed by Mack Sennett. Connolly sent a party to capture the telephone exchange. As the Citizen Army troops approached the building, a woman leaned out of the building and yelled, "Go back, boys. Go back! The place is crammed with military!"

The rebels retreated. Much later, the military did occupy the building. As a result, the rebels could communicate only by runners. They did manage to cut the long distance telephone and telegraph cables. But an officer in the Castle changed into civilian clothes and bicycled to Kingstown (modern Dun Laoghaire) and alerted London.

Another IRA party was to blow up the powder magazine in Phoenix Park. But the officer in command had taken the keys to the magazine and gone to watch the horse races. The Republicans used the bomb they brought to detonate the powder to blow down the door. The door held. Instead of a tremendous blast announcing that Dublin was in revolt, there was a dull thud, inaudible a short distance away.

A party of Citizen Army men attacked the guards at Dublin Castle, the seat of British government. They threw a bomb into the guard post. The explosion stunned but did not kill the guards. The insurgents tied up the guards, then, fearing that the noise of the explosion would bring hundreds of troops flooding out of the Castle, they retreated. Actually, there were only two officers and 25 soldiers in the Castle. If the rebels had pressed on, they could have captured the entire British government.

A party of British cavalry, escorting five carts loaded with rifles and grenades, was riding along the Liffey quays. They rode right into a barricade the IRA men were erecting. The rebels opened fire. The troopers fired back and took shelter in nearby buildings. The insurgents made no attempt to follow up and capture the desperately needed weapons.

It dawned on the British that there were hostile forces in Dublin. A troop of Lancers decided that the situation called for a mounted charge on the General Post Office. A volley of rifle fire from the building killed four soldiers. The rest fled.

Then the rising changed from tragicomedy to the kind of grim drama war had become in 1916. Col. H.V. Cowan, the assistant adjutant general, called for all available troops to come to the Castle. Most of the troops made their way there without even being seen by the IRA. The route taken by the Royal Irish Regiment troops from Richmond Barracks, however, took them right by the South Dublin Union, held by Eamonn Ceant's Fourth Battalion. Instead of the bayonet charge Ceant's men were expecting, a barrage of rifle and machine gun fire hit them. The British troops (like most of those in Ireland at this time, were overwhelmingly Irish Catholics) forced the IRA men into a small corner of the sprawling Union.

The soldiers in the Castle attacked the IRA men in the neighboring Dublin City Hall. The regulars, firing machine guns and throwing hand grenades, outnumbered the insurgents seven to one. They fought from floor to floor and took the City Hall, capturing some women and wounded men. The rest of the rebels had pried up a grating and escaped into the city's sewers.

Early Tuesday, Brigadier General W.H.M. Lowe arrived at the Castle. Analyzing reports from the field, Lowe located where the rebels were holed up. He sent his troops—he had 5,000 by the end of the day—filtering through the streets to gather in attack positions. He had other troops who were skilled in metalworking armoring a pair of trucks. He called for more troops and an artillery battery. He also asked the Royal Navy for assistance. He intended to split the rebels by occupying the south bank of the Liffey, then reduce the strong points in southern Dublin, and then move in on the rebel command in the General Post Office and the Four Courts.

City under siege

Things were quiet in IRA headquarters after the cavalry attack on the GPO. Connolly was dictating orders to his devoted secretary, Winifred Carney, and passing them on to runners. Pearse was writing communiqués to be delivered to the newspapers, which had stopped publishing. Joseph Plunkett, who had left a hospital bed to join the march, was stretched out on the floor. He was dying of tuberculosis.

The O'Rahilly confronted Sean MacDiarmida, whom he believed was responsible for Hobson's kidnapping. MacDiarmida said he had ordered the kidnapping for the good of the cause, but that Hobson was well and safe.

"If he is not free tonight," O'Rahilly said, "I cannot guarantee the same for you."

MacDiarmida told an aide to release Hobson.

Out on the street, the slum-dwellers of Dublin were taking advantage of the situation and looting the stores. Frank Sheehy-Skeffington was appalled. "Skeffy" was Dublin's best-known eccentric—a nationalist, a vegetarian, an advocate of female suffrage, and a pacifist. He gathered an armload of walking sticks and went out to recruit a peace-keeping force armed with sticks to replace the police who had disappeared. A British soldier arrested him. The authorities were about to release Sheehy-Skeffington when Capt. J.C. Bowen-Colthurst, scion of the family that owned Blarney Castle, took him into custody.

Bowen-Colthurst was waging a war of his own, and he wanted Skeffy as a hostage. Accompanied by the pacifist and a party of soldiers, he encountered two boys on the way home from church. One of them tried to run, and Bowen-Colthurst ordered a soldier to shoot him. A bit later, passing a pub, he threw a hand grenade into it. He arrested the four survivors, all loyalists, and had them and Sheehy-Skeffington shot by a firing squad the next day. He killed at least two more people on Wednesday. The Castle authorities knew what Bowen-Colthurst was doing, but they made no move to stop him. He was not stopped until a Castle officer, Sir Francis Vane, went to London and persuaded Lord Kitchner, the army's commander-in-chief, to have Bowen-Colthurst confined.

On Tuesday morning, James Connolly lost a cherished illusion. He heard artillery. A dedicated Marxist, he believed that a capitalist government would never destroy private property. The guns were blasting away the barricades in northern Dublin. A little later, de Valera's position in Boland's Bakery came under artillery fire. De Valera sent a man to plant the republican flag on a unused tower 400 yards away. The British shifted their fire to the tower.

On Wednesday morning a shipload of British troops arrived from England. They were green as grass and had neither machine guns nor hand grenades. They didn't even know where they were. They hailed passing Irish girls with "Bonjour, mademoiselle." Marching to downtown Dublin, they ran into 17 IRA soldiers under Lieutenant Michael Malone. Malone, with a Mauser automatic pistol, and Section Commander James Grace, with a stolen Lee Enfield rifle, opened fire from the house at 25 Northumberland Street. Ten of the soldiers, the Sherwood Foresters, were knocked down. Their commander, Lieutenant Colonel Cecil Fane, drew his sword and shouted, "Charge!" A rifle bullet from another IRA position immediately knocked him down. Lowe, from the Castle, ordered the Sherwood Foresters by telephone to stop procrastinating and drive the rebels away. The young Sherwoods charged again and again, and the Irish marksmen cut them down in rows. Eventually, the British troops received machine guns, hand grenades, and explosives and managed to take the rebel positions. But because of the utter stupidity of the British commanders, 17 rebels had held up two regular infantry battalions for more than eight hours. Between killed or wounded, the British lost 230 men. The IRA lost eight.

The end of the rising

Defenders of the General Post Office saw a strange sight. Lumbering up Sackville Street was what looked like an iron box on wheels. Bullets bounced off it. One of the Volunteers eventually stopped it by putting a bullet through the slit where he calculated the driver sat. Both armored trucks proved their worth however, not as fighting vehicles but as a means of transporting troops under fire. The British were closing in on the GPO, but the Irish defenders seldom saw a khaki uniform. Connolly, out to inspect an outlying position, was hit in the ankle by a British bullet, which all but amputated his foot. Carried back to the post office, Connolly, whom Pearse called "the guiding brain" of the operation, continued giving orders—orders that could not be delivered.

British artillery fire got hotter. On Friday, the GPO caught fire. The blaze went out of control. The Republicans evacuated their headquarters. They released the few prisoners they had taken and moved out their wounded under a flag of truce.

The O'Rahilly led an attempt to storm a British barricade. Most of his men were cut down. He was hit and staggered into a side street. Unable to stand, he pulled out a pencil and a note from his son and scribbled a last letter to his wife on the back of the note. Then he bled to death.

Pearse and some others tried to burrow their way through the walls of adjoining buildings to get behind the British lines. On Saturday morning, as Pearse was discussing how to leave the city, he saw a family of civilians. The man, Robert Dillon, owned a bar that, with his house, had been burned down. He waved a white sheet on a pole as he and his wife and daughter approached the British barricade. The soldiers shot them all down.

"Will the retreat not involve the loss of civilian life?" Pearse asked the other officers. "Won't it be bound to lead through populous districts, whichever route we take?" The others agreed that it would.

"In that case, will you issue cease fire orders to last for the next hour," he ordered.

During the truce, Pearse tried to arrange for surrender. The British offered no terms but unconditional surrender. Pearse surrendered.

Win a battle, lose a war...

The rebels were hardly popular heroes. The Dublin population, many of whom had been burned out, all of whom had been unable to buy food or other necessities for the last week, turned out to pelt the prisoners with garbage.

The new British commander, Sir John Maxwell, instituted martial law. He had the leaders shot, two or three at a time, after secret courts martial. He rounded up scores of Irishmen, some of them loyalists, and sent them to detention in England. And he tried to cover up atrocities committed by the British forces. He had Sir Francis Vane, who had blown the whistle on Bowen-Colthurst, dismissed from the service. He denied that his troops had massacred innocent civilians in the North King Street area—even after their hastily buried bodies were found, with their hands still bound and bullet wounds in their backs.

The executions went on and on. The dying Plunkett got married right before he was shot. Connolly, dying of gangrene, had to be tied in a chair to face the firing squad. He was concerned, he told his daughter, that his fellow socialists would not understand why he took part in a nationalist uprising.

"They will all forget that I am an Irishman," he said.

...And lose a world

Connolly's countrymen remembered that they were Irish. Watching Maxwell, they decided that they would never have any real freedom under British domination. Before "the Rising," the Sinn Fein party was considered part of the lunatic fringe. But in each by-election after that, Sinn Fein scored victories. After the 1918 election, Sinn Fein controlled almost the all-Irish parliamentary seats.

The Irish MPs refused to go to London. They set up their own government in Dublin, with Eamon de Valera president of the Dail Eireann, or Irish parliament. De Valera had survived the executions because, having been born in the United States, he was an American citizen. The British tried to suppress the new government. But the Irish introduced something new in world politics. They showed how a combination of low-level warfare, directed by Michael Collins, a survivor of the Rising, and intense propaganda, directed by Erskine Childers, the man who brought the rifles from Germany, could make it possible for a small, weak country to free itself from domination by a large powerful one.

One who watched the progress of the Irish revolt intently was a photographer's assistant in Paris, a Vietnamese named Nguyen Ai Quoc. He later became famous as Ho Chi Minh.

But Ho was only one of the potential revolutionists who were inspired by the Irish example. After World War II, thousands seemed to rise out of the ground in Asia and Africa. The biggest loser, of course, was the biggest colonial power, Britain.

A failed uprising in 1916, a very small sideshow during World War I, started a chain of events that profoundly changed the world.

Battle 20

Matthias fights back.

Emmaus, 166 BC
"Everyone who has zeal for the law...follow me!"

Who fought: Jews (Judas Maccabeus) vs. Greeks (Gorgias).

What was at stake: The survival of Judaism.

The Greeks had come to the town of Modin, and Matthias knew what was in store for them all. King Antiochus wanted to destroy God's law. He had already wiped out a huge portion of the population of Jerusalem, killing all who refused to sacrifice to idols, to eat unclean meat, or to stop circumcising their male babies.

Antiochus ruled over a portion of the empire conquered by Alexander the Great, the portion Alexander had given to his general, Seleucus. Israel, which had been part of the old Persian Empire, had become part of the Kingdom of Egypt, ruled by a succession of Greek pharaohs, almost all named Ptolemy. But Antiochus, whose courtiers called him "a second Alexander," coveted Egyptian territory. When war between Egypt and the Seleucid Kingdom broke out, Ptolemy fled from his lands on the eastern shore of the Mediterranean and took refuge in Egypt proper.

During the war, Israel was divided. Some favored Ptolemy, some Antiochus. The pro-Ptolemy party dominated Jerusalem. Antiochus entered Jerusalem and slaughtered as many of the pro-Egyptian faction as he could find and sacked the great Temple. Two years later, he decided that his vast kingdom, which extended from the Mediterranean to the borders of India, had too much diversity. From now on, he commanded, all of his people would follow the same law and worship the same gods. He sent troops into Jerusalem that set up a statue of Zeus in the Temple and sacrificed swine on the Temple altars. Jews who objected, or who merely refused to worship in the Greek manner, were tortured to death.

From Jerusalem Antiochus's agents went from town to town in the ancient Kingdom of Israel, demanding that all practice the King's religion. When they got to the mountain village of Modin, the Greek officials called all the townspeople to a meeting in the marketplace. They were particularly insistent that Matthias, the priest in Modin, come. Matthias and his five sons armed themselves. According to the historian Josephus, they carried cleavers, which they were probably able to hide in their clothing.

When the crowd had assembled, the Greek official, standing in front of a newly-erected altar, addressed Matthias directly:

> "You are a ruler and an honorable and great man in this city and have many sons and relatives. Therefore, be the first to obey the King's commandment, as all nations have done, and the men of Judea and all who remain in Jerusalem; and you and your sons will be in the number of the King's friends and enriched with gold and silver and many presents."

Matthias responded in a loud voice:

> "Although all nations obey King Antiochus, so as to depart from the law of their fathers and consent to his commandments, I and my sons and my brethren will obey the law of our fathers. God be merciful to us. It is not profitable to us to forsake the law and justice of God. We will not hearken to the words of King Antiochus, neither will we sacrifice and transgress the commandments of our law to go another way."

But as soon as he finished speaking, Matthias saw another citizen of Modin approach the altar to offer a sacrifice to the idol. Beside himself with rage, Matthias drew his cleaver, dashed up to the man and chopped him down. Then he killed the Greek official. With the aid of his five sons, Matthias overturned the pagan altar. He shouted at the crowd, "Everyone who has zeal for the law and maintains the testament, let him follow me!"

Matthias and his sons then fled to the mountains, followed by many of the townsmen.

Many Jews before Matthias had fled into the wilderness. Apollonius, the Greek governor, decided not only to pursue these holdouts, but take advantage of Jewish customs while doing so. He sent troops after one group on the Sabbath. The soldiers told the Jews they could either obey the King's orders or face the consequences. The Jews refused to abandon their faith and refused to fight on the Sabbath. The Greek soldiers killed them all—men, women, and children. When Matthias and his friends heard about the slaughter they resolved that any of the strangers that offered to fight them on the Sabbath would get a fight. "And we will not all die."

Nor would they wait for the Greeks to come for them. Matthias organized an impromptu army and began guerrilla warfare. Travelling mostly at night, the Jewish army hit town after town, killing Greek troops and collaborators, throwing down pagan altars, and circumcising babies. As they expected, they received strong support from the local people.

Judas the Hammer

As the Jews also expected, The Greeks did not ignore the uprising in Israel. They began gathering troops to deal with the Jews. As the crisis was developing, Matthias died. His son, Judas, known to history as Judas Machabeus (or Maccabaeus)—Judas the Hammer—succeeded him. He earned his nickname immediately.

Apollonius concentrated a force of garrison troops in Samaria to invade Judea. Judas moved first. The Jewish army marched into Samaria before the Greeks were fully prepared and attacked. The Greeks were routed with heavy losses. And, the *Book of Maccabees* says, "Judas took the sword of Apollonius and fought with it all his life."

Seron, the commander of the Greek forces in Syria, said, "I will get me a name, and will be glorified in the kingdom, and will overthrow Judas and those that are with him, that have despised the edict of the King." He marched into Israel with most of his army, vastly outnumbering the forces of Judas. The Jews were terrified when they saw the size of his army as it approached Bethoron.

But Matthias said, "They have come against us with an insolent multitude and with pride, to destroy us, our wives and our children, and to take our spoils. But we will fight for our lives and our laws."

Then he ordered a charge while the Greeks were marching. The Jews, inspired by their leader's words, dashed at the Greeks so ferociously that the invaders, complacent about their numbers, turned tail and fled. Judas and his men pursued them down the mountain of Bethoron and into the plain. Always in classical warfare, a fleeing army was most vulnerable. The Jews slew 800 and the rest fled into the land of the Philistines.

The main thrust

In Antioch, King Antiochus decided that the Jewish rebellion was a major threat. He opened his treasury and hired an enormous army of mercenaries, bought tons of military equipment, and purchased many elephants, which were considered the ultimate weapon of Hellenistic warfare. Then the king discovered that he had spent so much on military preparations that the treasury was broke. But that was no real problem. All he needed was more tribute. So he took half the army and marched into Persia and his other eastern provinces to collect it.

He left his cousin, Lysias, in charge of the western half of the kingdom, with the other half of the army. He told Lysias to take care of Judea and Jerusalem. "[H]e should send an army against them, to destroy and root out the strength of Israel and the remnant of Jerusalem and take away the memory of them from that place."

Lysias chose three generals, Gorgias, Ptolemy (not the Egyptian king), and Nicanor, and sent them into Israel. With the army came a horde of Greek and Syrian merchants prepared to buy the Jewish slaves they were sure the army would capture. The Greeks camped on the plains, near the city of Emmaus, a short distance from Jerusalem. Jerusalem itself "was like a desert," *Maccabees* records. There was a Greek garrison in the citadel, a fortress in one corner of the city, but no civilian population. Soldiers from the citadel sneaked out and joined the Greek army to guide it through the unfamiliar country.

Meanwhile, Judas had organized his troops into a semblance of a regular army, with units of 10, 50, 100, and 1,000. Their weapons, however, were improvised and inferior to those of the Greeks, who were armed like Alexander's regulars. They set up their fortified camp on the south side of Emmaus. Judas addressed his men, urging them to fight valiantly, "for it is better for us to die in battle than to see the evils of our nation, and of the holies. Nevertheless, as it shall be the will of God in heaven, so be it done."

Judas, however, was seeking victory, not martyrdom. He and his army left the camp at night and took up a position near the Greek camp so they could attack at first light. As it turned out, Gorgias had the same idea. He took part of the army to the

Jewish camp, planning a night attack. The Greeks rushed into the Jewish camp and found it deserted.

"These men flee from us," Gorgias said. The most obvious place to flee was the nearby mountains. So he took his cavalry and infantry off to scour the hills.

While he was searching for the Jews, Judas and his men stormed the Greek camp and routed the garrison. The Jews set fire to the camp, and chased the garrison, cutting them down as they ran. They killed 3,000.

On a mountain, Gorgias and his men saw the smoke of their camp, and the dust cloud made by the retreating Greeks and the pursuing Jews. Gorgias decided it was time to return to Syria.

There was plenty of hard fighting ahead, but Israel was independent for the first time in more than 500 years—since the Babylonians captured Jerusalem and carried off part of its population. Lysias tried to restore the status quo the next year, but the Jewish army, now armed in the Greek manner, routed Lysias' men and killed 5,000. The Jewish army entered Jerusalem, cleaned out the Temple, built new altars, chose new priests, and laid siege to the citadel. Judas led his men against the neighboring nations, which had tried to take advantage of the situation, and was successful everywhere. Trouble with the Greeks of the Seleucid Kingdom continued, but the Seleucids had other troubles. They had tried to expand into Europe, but the Romans smashed their army. Then the Parthians, Iranian nomads from Central Asia, began chewing up the eastern portions of the kingdom. And the Seleucids themselves got involved in civil war and sought Jewish help. Finally, before he was killed in battle, Judas made an alliance with Rome the growing power of the West.

The legacy of Emmaus

Judas the Hammer's victory at Emmaus made possible the independence of Israel for a century. Eventually, Rome, the superpower of the Mediterranean, absorbed it. Far more important than that century of independence was the fact that it ended the persecution instituted by Antiochus. The Jewish people would undergo many more persecutions, but not until Adolf Hitler was there anything comparable to the campaign of Antiochus. Judas's victory ensured that Judaism would not die, and that Christianity, an outgrowth of Judaism, could be born.

Battle 21

Romans battling
Persians at Yarmuk.

The Yarmuk Valley, 636 AD
The Twin Beacons

Who fought: Arabs (Khalid ibn al Walid) vs. Romans (Theodorus Trithurius).

What was at stake: The expansion of Islam.

"The Roman Empire and the Persian Empire are like twin beacons that enlighten the world," the Persian ambassador once told the Roman Emperor. The two great states, the centers of Western and Middle Eastern civilizations, co-existed for generations. Their co-existence was hardly peaceful: there was almost continuous skirmishing on the border, and the Roman Christians despised the fire-worshipping Mazdians, who returned that regard. Since Crassus's ill-fated expedition against the Parthians (see Carrhae, pg. 140), however, there had been few attempts by one empire to conquer the other, and there was plenty of religious hatred *within* each empire to keep bigots busy.

That situation came to an end with the coronation of Chosroes II in Persia. Chosroes was how the Westerners pronounced his name, but it was really Kurash. He was named after a reputed ancestor, a legendary conqueror the Westerners called Cyrus the Great (who, of course, was also named Kurash). Chosroes resolved to continue the work of Cyrus—he would conquer the West.

He got off to a good start. Persian armies overran Armenia, Cilicia, and Cappadocia. Damascus, Tarsus, Antioch, and all of Syria fell to Chosroes—Kurash Parvez,

"Chosroes the Conqueror," his people now called him. He took Jerusalem and encouraged the remaining Jews to join him in killing Christians. He massacred 60,000 and enslaved 35,000 more. Then northern Egypt fell to the Persians, cutting off the Roman Empire from its main grain supplier.

The Persians were knocking on the gates of Constantinople when an African soldier, Heraclius, deposed the corrupt emperor, Phocas. The Roman Empire, really the Eastern Roman Empire, for little of it remained west of the Adriatic, was in sad shape when Heraclius arrived in Constantinople. The Persians had occupied most of the East, and the Slavs and Avars, a Central Asian nomad nation, were pressing down from the north.

Heraclius did not try to recover the lost granary, Egypt, nor the lost religious center, Jerusalem. Instead, he drove straight into Anatolia, destroyed the Persian forces there, and successively routed the armies the Shah of Shahs sent against him. The Khazar Turks of the steppes, seeing which way the wind was blowing, invaded Persia. Heraclius reached the Caspian Sea, turned south, and burned the greatest Mazdian temple in the Empire. It became apparent to his people that Chosroes the Conqueror was anything but. One of his sons murdered him and made peace with Heraclius, giving the Romans back all they had lost and then some. Meanwhile, the Avars and their Slavic vassals assaulted Constantinople. The garrison of the city beat them back with such heavy losses the Avar kingdom never recovered.

Heraclius began his campaign on April 5, 622. Five months later, deep in Arabia, an Arab who had been going around preaching morality and denouncing the worship of idols was driven out of his hometown. His name was Mohammed.

Islam

Mohammed was unpopular with the merchant princes of Mecca, but his preaching struck a chord with other Arabs. He preached the worship of one God and inveighed against drunkenness, licentiousness, and unlimited polygamy. (He set a limit of four wives to a man.) His following grew rapidly, and when he died, leadership of the movement fell to his son-in-law, Abu Bakr.

One of the tenets of Islam (Arabic for "submission") was to make war on unbelievers who refused to follow the teachings of the Prophet. The wars in Arabia quickly produced a number of talented generals to lead the forces of the faithful. The most talented was Khalid ibn al Walid.

After having united the Bedouin tribes and the kingdoms in the Arabian peninsula, Muslim armies entered Mesopotamia and Syria. They could not have picked a better time. The Roman and Persian empires had almost bled themselves white during their long war. The Persian Shah had died of the plague a year after he made peace with the Romans, leaving an infant son as heir. Heraclius, the military genius who had saved the Roman Empire, was too sick to get out of bed.

A further advantage for the Arabs was that the Roman Empire was full of religious dissension. The conflict between Catholic and Monophysite Christians (see The Nika Rebellion pg. 16) had gotten worse. The Catholics held that Jesus Christ had two natures: He was both human and divine. The Monophysite belief was that He had one nature, partly human and partly divine. Today, such an abstruse difference would be unlikely to attract much notice outside a seminary, but in the seventh century it was cause for murder and persecution.

The main strength of the Monophysites was in the southeastern portion of the Empire. The first Christians in that area were converted Jews, and Monophysite doctrine was more in accord with their former non-trinitarian belief. The people in that part of the Empire spoke Arabic or the very similar Aramaic as their first language, with Greek and Latin as second and third languages. When the Arabic-speaking Muslims swept in, the local population hailed them as liberators, not invaders. The Arabs recalled that the Prophet had declared Christians and Jews to be "people of the book," slightly misguided followers of the one true God, and should not be forced to become Muslims. In their war with the Roman armies, the native population supported the Muslims. Striking over a wide front, the Muslim Arabs surprised the Roman garrisons and took a number of cities, including Damascus.

When Heraclius heard about the Arab Blitzkrieg in Syria, he mustered a large army in Antioch and sent it to retake Damascus. Hearing that the Romans were coming, the Arabs sent word to Khalid ibn al Walid, their supreme commander, who was campaigning in Mesopotamia. Khalid ordered them to withdraw from Damascus and take up a position along the Yarmuk River, in the Golan Heights. He called for the other scattered Arab armies to meet at the Yarmuk and led his personal command of 800 men to join them.

The armies

The backbone of Khalid's armies were the Bedouin. The Bedouin were highly mobile, being mounted on horses and camels. The horsemen were cavalry, but cavalry quite unlike the Roman heavy cavalry, who wore heavy armor and used the lance as a primary weapon. The Arabs were horse archers—skirmishers who didn't close with the enemy until he was disorganized. They fought in small groups under their clan leaders and never used the mass charge that was a staple of both Roman and Persian tactics. Further, the Bedouin were as willing to fight on foot as to fight mounted. Their horsemen had none of the superiority complex that afflicted most other cavalrymen of the period.

The Roman army had changed from the days of Narses. It was no longer composed of a combination of barbarian mercenaries and the retainers of great magnates. Now it was a regular force of highly trained infantry and cavalry. The basic unit was a band of 300 or 400 commanded by a count. Anywhere from six to eight bands could be combined as a moira, commanded by a duke. The infantry were mostly light-armed archers, and at this period they were considered far less important than the cavalry. The cavalry wore metal helmets and scale armor and carried swords. They used both the bow and the lance. They were trained to maneuver in large units and could shower an enemy with a concentration of arrows or charge with massed lances depending on the circumstances.

Decision in the sand

Theoretically, Theodorus Trithurius commanded the Roman army, but it was composed of a number of largely independent units. The Muslim units had been campaigning independently, but each commander implicitly obeyed the charismatic Khalid. Arab horsemen harassed the advancing Romans until they got into the Golan, a mass of mountains and ravines unsuitable for most cavalry operations. The Arab main body deployed along the south bank of the Yarmuk. The Romans camped north of the Arab position and deployed along a wadi. The two armies remained in position for weeks during July and August, 636, while the Arabs conducted a new kind of warfare—continual skirmishing in the ferocious heat.

The Arab infantry crossed upriver and downriver of the Roman position and raided their lines. Their object was to get the Romans to pursue them. A few pursuers could be ambushed, and a major pursuit would leave an opening for a major attack. Arab forces roamed all around the Roman position looking for a chance to attack stragglers. They also became familiar with the jumbled landscape and its labyrinthine ravines.

Arab forays increased in intensity. On August 16, Khalid launched his primary attack. Arab footmen swarmed out of the hills to hit the Roman positions. For three days, the Roman lines held. On the night of April 19, a sandstorm began, driven by a scorching southern wind. The Roman horses were unable to face it and withdrew the next day. Some of the Arab auxiliaries in the Roman army followed them, then the whole Roman line collapsed. The Arabs jumped on their horses and camels and chased them, cutting down fugitives for miles. Many of the retreating Romans became lost in the ravines. The Muslims, who by this time knew the territory intimately, wiped them out.

The growth of Islam

The battle on the Yarmuk River was the first great victory of Muslim Arabs over the forces of the settled empires and kingdoms. With the Romans neutralized, the Arabs turned east and invaded Persia the next year. There, commanded by Sa'ad ibn Abu Wakkas and using Khalid's skirmishing tactics, they won another decisive victory at Kadisiyah (see pg. 245). Then another group under Amr ibn al As went west and poured into Egypt. From Egypt, newly converted Bedouin tribes rode west across North Africa, converted the native Berbers, and invaded Spain. From Persia, other Arab armies, with other new recruits, moved into Central Asia and even into China. Arab mariners from south Arabia sailed across the Indian Ocean to the East Indies and reached the Philippines.

Khalid's victory made possible the creation of *Dar es Islam*, the Land of Islam, which would be a major force in the world for at least the next thousand years.

Battle 22

U-boat torpedoes ship.

Battle of the Atlantic, 1939–45 AD
In Peril of the Sea

Who fought: Allied naval forces and shipping vs. German U-boats.

What was at stake: The survival of Britain and the Allied war effort (hence the survival of democracy).

"The only thing that really frightened me during the war was the U-boat peril," Winston Churchill recalled after World War II had ended. "It did not take the form of flaring battles and glittering achievements, it manifested itself through statistics, diagrams and curves unknown to the nation, incomprehensible to the public."

Although much of it was unknown to the public, the struggle known as the Battle of the Atlantic was no drab, colorless affair. It involved as many thrusts and counter-thrusts and as much technical ingenuity as any operation on land or in the air. No fight required more raw courage on each side and in no other battle were the stakes higher. Britain, a densely populated island, had to import half its food and all its oil. If it could be cut off from the rest of the world, its planes could not fly, its ships could not sail, and its people would starve.

Germany had a relatively small navy, and Adolf Hitler was reluctant to risk his surface ships by using them as commerce raiders. The few attempts to do so usually ended in disaster, like the sinkings of *Graf Spee* and *Bismark*. The Germans also had a number of short-range motor patrol boats ("E-boats") that did some damage to shipping, principally by mine-laying, around the British Isles. German aircraft, as we have seen, did attack shipping in British waters, but the planes, too, had short range. Almost all the German effort was by submarines.

During two world wars, Americans came to associate submarines with Germans. But at the beginning of the war, and indeed, by the end of 1941, Germany had fewer submarines than the United States. In September 1939, when the war began, Admiral Karl Donitz, chief of the German Navy's submarine division, had 57 *Unterseeboots*, and 30 of them were for use in coastal waters only. Donitz said he would need 300 ocean-going subs to blockade Britain properly, but Hitler didn't think a blockade would be necessary. Other war materials got a higher priority. Donitz didn't get his boats.

A couple of other factors kept the subs from being a serious menace until after the fall of France and the German defeat in the Battle of Britain (see pg. 42). One was that the British were able to close off the English Channel almost completely. Any submarine hoping to reach the Atlantic Ocean had to sail north around the tip of Scotland. Only eight of Donitz's U-boats had a range of 12,000 miles, making them truly oceanic. Another 18 could sail as far as Gibraltar and back. The rest couldn't leave the North Sea.

Another problem was the submarines themselves. The subs of 1941—and in fact all the submarines of World War II—were a far cry from the subs of today. Modern nuclear subs are designed to spend most of their time under water, and are most efficient when they're submerged. The submarine of World War II was a surface vessel that could dive occasionally. It used diesel engines on the surface and was faster than the average freighter, although quite slow for a naval vessel. Submerged, it used electric engines run on batteries, which had to be recharged frequently. It was painfully slow underwater—not fast enough to keep up with a fast freighter.

The fall of France solved one problem: The Germans took over the French ports on the Bay of Biscay, and the Bay of Biscay could not be choked off like the English Channel. As soon as the Germans moved in, Hitler ordered the construction of bomb-proof submarine pens on the French coast. German shipbuilders worked furiously to improve both the quality and quantity of submarines. Before the war ended, German submarines were operating in all corners of the world, and German shipyards were mass-producing boats at an astonishing rate.

On the other hand, methods of detecting submarines had, in 1941, not advanced beyond the state of the art in 1918. The most reliable method was sight. Listening devices could detect submerged subs. Sometimes the engines or propellers of the submarine itself could be heard. Sub hunters could also send out sound waves and listen for the echo if the sounds bounced off a sub, the system Americans called sonar and the British called asdic. The trouble was that a sonar man had to be an artist. Only an expert could tell the difference between an echo from a submarine and one from a whale or a coral reef. And in any case, the range of the listening devices was quite short at around 1,000 yards.

Submarine offensive

In spite of their handicaps, the German submariners opened their war with a bang. A few hours after the beginning of the war, a sub sank the passenger liner *Athena*, killing 112 people. Two weeks later, U-29 sank the aircraft carrier *H.M.S. Courageous* in what the British considered "home waters." Then a sub went right into the Royal Navy anchorage at Scapa Flow and sank the carrier *H.M.S. Royal Oak* on October 1939. Although operating only in waters close to Britain in 1939 and the first part of 1940, the submarines were sinking more ships than the British could replace. It got worse. After the fall of France, German subs intensified their attacks in the Atlantic west of Ireland and moved south to sink ships in the Bay of Biscay, off the west coast of Spain and off West Africa. Shipping to the Mediterranean and Africa suffered heavily. Particularly serious were the losses of ships carrying Nigerian oil. In April 1941, the Germans sank some 700,000 tons of merchant shipping (the average freighter displaced 5,000 tons), more than twice the British capacity to replace losses. According to A.J.P. Taylor, "This was probably the moment when Great Britain came nearest to losing the war."

Convoys

After their first heavy losses, the British rediscovered the convoy system that had been used successfully in World War I. Merchant ships sailed in groups, escorted by light naval vessels. Merchant skippers didn't like being herded like cattle, but they came to appreciate its benefits.

The ability of destroyers and corvettes to sink submarines was not what made convoys effective. In the early days, there were perhaps two or three naval vessels to escort 40 freighters, and the escorts were necessarily far apart. What convoys did was reduce the possibility of the ships being intercepted by submarines. Because they were so slow underwater, U-boats had to position themselves along sea lanes and wait for targets to appear. When ships travelling individually were strung out along the route, if a sub missed one, another would soon appear. But when they were grouped in convoys, if a U-boat skipper missed a convoy, he had a long wait before a second target appeared. He couldn't chase the convoy, because it was faster than a submerged U-boat. He couldn't surface to chase it, because the naval escort outgunned him. Two-thirds of all the ships sunk in 1941 were ships that were not travelling in convoys.

Radio intelligence played a big part in the convoy war. Convoys changed their routes frequently to leave the submarine ambushers waiting in the wrong places. German intelligence, therefore, avidly monitored British transmissions to determine convoy locations and directions. At the same time, their British counterparts were listening to German transmissions to learn where the subs were. All of this, of course, involved frantic efforts to decipher enemy signals.

Convoys did not eliminate losses. A convoy covers a wide area, and the naval escorts were seldom close enough to respond immediately to a U-boat attack. Further, World War II subs were considerably more robust than those in the last war. Depth charges had to explode very close to a submerged sub to have an effect, and surfaced subs were seldom disabled by a single shell, as they usually were in World War I. Moreover, the subs adopted a new tactic: Instead of torpedoing ships from a submerged position, they'd surface at night to attack. They were as invisible at night as if they were under water, and they were able to get away quicker. Ship borne radar could detect them, but the crude radar used early in the war was too primitive to give either early warning or accurate ranging.

Wolf packs

Submarine surface speed was the key to Donitz's strategy to counter convoys. Before the war, he had conducted experiments with surface torpedo boats that led to the "wolf pack" strategy. The wolf pack consisted of groups of subs widely scattered along the shipping routes. When a submariner saw a convoy, instead of attacking immediately, he kept his distance and radioed other members of the pack. All would then converge on the convoy. Wolf pack tactics made it harder for convoys to avoid submarines and guaranteed that when they were sighted, the attack would be massive. Wolf packs caused a big increase in sinkings during 1940 and 1941. During those years the Germans were sinking ships faster—three times faster—than the British could build them. The British, on the other hand, were not sinking German subs as fast as the German shipyards could launch new ones. During 1941, the Germans built 200 new U-boats; they had lost only 50 subs since the beginning of the war. In July 1942, Donitz finally got 300 U-boats in service.

But by that time, the Battle of the Atlantic had changed radically.

U.S. involvement

In mid-1941, the United States began to play its role. In the beginning it was in helping British intelligence gather information on submarine movements. Then President Franklin D. Roosevelt proclaimed a "defense zone" covering most of the northwestern Atlantic Ocean and ordered U.S. Navy units to patrol it. At first the American patrols merely reported sub sightings to the British. By September, they were sinking subs. In the Atlantic, the United States was waging war in fact if not in name.

Even earlier, the United States had initiated the "lend-lease" program, making war materials available to Britain without immediate payment. The most highly publicized lend-lease deal was the provision of 50 obsolete destroyers (only nine of which were fit for immediate service). Far more effective than the destroyers were the B-24 bombers and the PBY flying boats also made available. These long-range planes made possible much more extended British air patrols. At the same time, U. S. shipyards came to life after Depression-induced inactivity. Submarine sinkings dropped sharply in July 1941, while freighter launchings rose. In 1942, the Allies launched three times as many ships as they had in 1941. And most of the new ships were far faster than older freighters—almost as fast as a surfaced submarine. That would cause problems for future wolf packs.

To Hitler, the Atlantic was of secondary importance. His main concern was the conquest of the Soviet Union. That was one reason he didn't have his U-boats take more aggressive action in the western Atlantic. Another reason was that he wanted to delay the United States becoming a full belligerent. The United States was almost as populous as the USSR and even more industrialized than Germany. Hitler hoped to knock the Soviet Union out before the United States could throw its full weight into the war.

When the Japanese attacked Pearl Harbor, Hitler was bound by treaty to declare war on the United States, whether he was ready or not. The U-boats immediately carried the war to the U.S. Eastern Seaboard. The U.S. Navy was not prepared for a submarine offensive. It had no convoy system for coastal shipping, and it had too few light escort craft. In 1942, ship sinkings skyrocketed. The German submariners referred to this period as "the happy time." It wasn't happy for their victims. In some cases, the Germans gave food and water to the survivors of their attacks, telling them to "send the bill to Roosevelt." But at other times, they machine gunned the sailors in the water. Sinkings in January were triple what they had been in the previous month. In April and May, they were double what they had been in January. For the first time in almost a year, more ships were being sunk than were being replaced.

That situation did not last. The next year, freighter launchings were double what they were in 1942. American authorities managed to get seashore cities to douse their lights, in spite of protests that it would ruin the tourist season. Production of light naval ships boomed, convoys were organized, and the Americans introduced a new type of warship, the escort carrier. These pocket carriers, carrying fewer than half the number of planes aboard a regular carrier, provided continuous aerial surveillance. A submerged submarine was invisible from a ship, but unless it was well below periscope depth, an aerial observer directly above it could see its outline. And, of course, any submarine on the surface was visible for miles from a plane. The subs were forced to spend most of their time submerged, operating at snail speed. More land-based patrol planes were

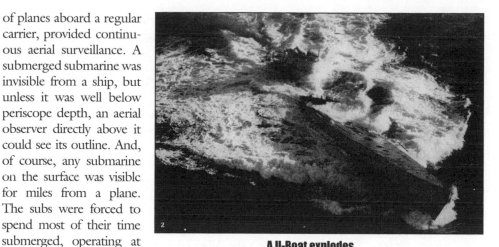

A U-Boat explodes.

put on anti-submarine duty, and they were joined by another new type of craft, the blimp. The big motorized balloons were faster than any kind of surface vessel, and they could hover motionless if need be.

Submarine sinkings increased rapidly. The Allies were now destroying U-boats as fast as the Germans could launch new ones. The average life of a U-boat grew shorter and shorter until it was only about three months. But the wolf packs weren't so easily defeated. Donitz introduced tanker submarines that could refuel his U-boats at sea. The U-boats moved away from the East Coast of the United States and began hunting off the coasts of South America and Africa. In March, 1943, ship sinkings were almost as frequent as they were in 1942. Between March 6 and 9, a convoy named SC-121 en route to Britain from Canada was attacked by wolf packs three times, and six of its 56 ships were sunk. Immediately after that, Convoy SC-122 was attacked by the same packs and lost nine ships. Between March 8 and 10, Convoy HX-229 lost 11 ships to wolf packs in a running fight across the Atlantic. At this time, there were few ships sailing individually. Most of those lost were in convoys. Sinkings remained high through May. But the U-boat war reached a turning point. Convoy ONS-5, with 42 ships, was attacked by no fewer than 51 U-boats between April 28 and May 6. Thirteen merchantmen were sunk, but the cost was five submarines—three sunk by the escort vessels and two by PBY (called Catalinas by the British) flying boats. The change became apparent in June, when sinkings dropped precipitously. The year 1943 became what a German writer later called...

"The year of the slaughter of the U-boats"

There were several reasons. Neutral Portugal saw that there was no way Hitler would win the war, so it made the Azores available as an allied air base. Naval and aerial patrols continued to intensify. Thanks to American production facilities, the Allies now had enough escort carriers, destroyers, destroyer escorts, Coast Guard cutters, and frigates to operate hunter-killer task forces independent of convoys. Old anti-submarine devices, sonar and shipboard radar, were improved. During 1942, German code-breakers had an edge on the Allies: They were able to locate convoy locations, while the Allies were in the dark about messages to submarines. Now the Allies were able decode signals to and from submarines while the Germans were ignorant of convoy movements. The Allies could route convoys around wolf packs. And the Allies introduced two new electronic weapons.

One was the high-fidelity direction finder, known as Huff-Duff to its British inventors, that could pinpoint the location of subs from their radio signals. The other was airborne radar capable of finding a sub in the blackest night and incapable of being detected by the U-boats' radar detectors. Supplemented by a new airborne searchlight, the Leigh light, airborne radar made the customary nighttime voyages from the Bay of Biscay suicidal. In May 1943, 38 U-boats were sunk in the Bay of Biscay alone, and 43 all over the world. That was more than double what all the shipyards in Germany and its occupied territory could produce. Donitz withdrew his submarines from the North Atlantic. In his memoirs, he later noted, "We had lost the Battle of the Atlantic."

But the U-boat war was not over. German subs that had been refueled by tanker U-boats, were operating as far afield as the Indian Ocean and the Pacific. Then, in 1944, the first schnorkel-equipped subs appeared. The schnorkel was a breathing device raised like a periscope. It allowed the sub to use its diesel engines submerged. The U-boat never had to surface. The wolf packs were finished, however. Huff-Duff made the necessary radio communication too hazardous. Then the Allies landed in France, and the Atlantic ports were gone.

Hand to hand

A summary of the Battle of the Atlantic sounds as if it were all technology. To the men involved, it was hardly that. To the merchant seamen and the sailors of the escort vessels, it was day after day of nerve-wracking tension, waiting for the boom of a torpedo telling you that your ship had been hit and you, if you were lucky, would soon be swimming in the freezing waters of the North Atlantic. To the submariners, it was a claustrophobic life in the most deadly of all fighting forces in World War II. The casualty rate of the German submarine force was 75 percent, 63 percent of those resulted in fatalities. Three quarters of all men who put to sea in U-boats would be killed or captured—most of them killed. No other arm of any service of any other combatant power was even close to that casualty rate.

There were times when the Battle of the Atlantic resembled the days of John Paul Jones, or perhaps Don Juan of Austria.

The destroyer *U.S.S. Borie*, an ancient four-stacker, was part of the screen for the escort carrier *U.S.S. Card*. On October 4, 1943, *Card's* group sank three of four U-boats refueling in the South Atlantic. The task force commander, Capt. Arnold J. Isbell, sent *Borie*, commanded by Lt. Charles H. Hutchins, after the fourth.

On November 1, *Borie* detected a sub and dropped depth charges. The sub surfaced. Hutchins opened fire with his four-inch gun and machine guns. The sub fired back. Hutchins tried to ram it. The old destroyer rode right over the U-boat's deck, and the American crew opened fire with small arms—rifles, submachine guns, and pistols. One sailor threw his sheath knife and hit a German trying to man the sub's deck gun.

Ramming was not a smart idea in this case. *Borie's* plates, never thick to begin with, had rusted paper-thin over the years. Seawater began pouring in its port side. After 10 minutes, the U-boat managed to get out from under the destroyer and ran away. At about 400 yards' distance, it turned and attempted to ram *Borie*. Hutchins turned his ship and fired depth charges from his stern projector into the sub's path. Three charges under the U-boat lifted it out of the water and stopped it dead only six feet from *Borie*. The U-boat backed away and attempted to flee. *Borie* pursued, firing. One four-inch shell blew the German bridge crew overboard. After a second hit, the U-boat stopped and its surviving crew surrendered.

Battle 23

Hannibal.

Cannae, 216 BC
The Impossible Dream

Who fought: Carthaginians (Hannibal) vs. Romans (Varro).

What was at stake: The survival of Rome and Western civilization.

Hannibal could see with only one eye, but he was looking into the future. He was happy with what he saw. He saw the liberation of Italy and the end of Rome's attempt to rule the world. He had already accomplished what the Romans considered impossible. He had taken an army—including war elephants—over the Alps and enlisted the ferocious Gauls. Now he knew he was about to fulfill his dream.

From his earliest childhood, Hannibal had heard about the Romans—their arrogance, their cruelty, how they bragged about warring down any nation that refused to kiss their feet. As he grew older, he learned how they had conquered the other Latin tribes, the Etruscans, the Greek cities in Italy, and the Italian Gauls. In his own lifetime, they had fought his country, Carthage. His father, Hamilcar Barca, was Carthage's most successful general in that war. He wasn't successful enough. The Romans won after a war 23 years long and forced Carthage out of Sicily. Hamilcar left, vowing revenge. The Carthaginian Senate sent Hamilcar to Spain, and he took Hannibal with him. In Spain, Hamilcar set out to conquer a new empire for Carthage. Spain had silver mines, and by controlling Spain and the adjoining coast of North

Africa, Carthage owned the Straits of Gibraltar. Beyond Gibraltar were the tin mines of Brittany and Britain and the ivory and gold of West Africa.

The heart of Hamilcar's army was his African heavy infantry, who fought in phalanx in the Macedonian manner, and his Numidian cavalry, who fought in a style all their own. These North African nomads used no bridles, guiding their racehorses with their knees so they could fight with both hands. Their main weapon was a short steel javelin, which they carried in quivers hung on their horses. Hooded, with long, flowing robes and sitting on leopard skin saddle blankets, the agile Numidians struck terror into their enemies. Hamilcar enlisted the Spaniards he met. He turned the civilized Iberians and Celtiberians into excellent heavy cavalry and infantry. The Spanish horsemen wore armor and fought with javelins, lances ,and curved short swords, sharp on the inside curve. The Greeks had adopted the weapon, and Alexander's troops had carried it to India. The modern Nepalese Gurkhas still use a version of it, called a kukri. The Spanish infantry carried a straight sword, about two feet long and double-edged. The Spanish footmen liked to fight at close quarters, using the needle-sharp points of their swords. Their blades were made of the best steel in Europe. The barbarian Celts of northern Spain also provided both cavalry

Carthaginian elephants cross the Rhone.

and infantry. They put little value on human life, their own included. They fought without body armor—even without shirts—although they wore helmets with horns to make themselves look more ferocious and carried long shields. Their weapons were long iron swords and a heavy javelin with a long iron point like the Roman *pilum*. For light infantry skirmishers, Hamilcar had the usual archers and javelin men, but also slingers from the Balearic Islands, generally considered the greatest masters of that weapon.

Hamilcar was both a general and a viceroy for the Carthaginian Senate, but his troops had become, in practice, a private army, an autonomous force. After he died, they elected Hannibal's brother-in-law, Hasdrubal, commanding general. Hasdrubal was assassinated, and the army elected Hannibal to command. He was 26.

The Carthaginians were sailors and merchants. Their military defeat and loss of Sicilian colonies did not permanently affect their business and, thanks to Hamilcar, they had more than made up their territorial losses. The Romans, who had just begun getting involved in international trade, found the Carthaginian competition irksome. They had been looking for an excuse to wipe out Carthage.

They found it when Carthage had a dispute with a Spanish city that was allied to Rome. Roman envoys came to Spain and forbade Hannibal to make war on Saguntum. He ignored them. His troops were not equipped to storm walls, but he took the city after a siege. The next year, 218 BC, the Roman envoys went to Carthage and demanded the extradition of Hannibal. The Carthaginian Senate, of course, refused. Even if they wanted to hand over Hannibal, there was no way they could. Rome declared war.

Hannibal was sure the Romans would come after him, so he sent his wife and infant son to Carthage for safety. But the Romans intended to attack Carthage as well. Hannibal's spies told him the Romans were assembling an invasion army in Sicily, under the consul Tiberius Sempronius. They planned to send another army, under the second consul, Publius Cornelius Scipio, to their ally, Massilia (modern Marseilles). Scipio was then to march overland and deal with Hannibal in Spain. Hannibal knew he'd have to protect Carthage. Instead of returning to Africa, he decided to invade Italy. That would make the Romans forget all plans to invade Africa.

He knew it was a desperate venture. If he couldn't even assault the walls of Saguntum, how could he attack Rome—one of the largest cities of the western world? The last Roman census showed 770,000 men capable of bearing arms. Carthage couldn't call up one-tenth of that. Carthage didn't even have 700,000 people—men, women, and infants—in all its African territories. Latinium had more than six million. But Hannibal remembered the aftermath of the last Roman war. The Carthaginian Senate refused to pay off the mercenary troops who had fought for it. The mercenaries revolted. In the terrible war that followed, Carthage's African dependencies revolted, too. Only Hamilcar's genius saved Carthage. Hannibal would make war on Roman territory and encourage Rome's subject peoples to revolt. That would finish the growing Roman Empire.

The impossible march

The Romans never dreamed that Hannibal would attempt to march overland from Spain to Italy. When Scipio got to Massilia, he learned that Hannibal and his army were not in Spain. They were 50 miles north of him and marching east, toward the Alps. Scipio knew he couldn't overtake an army marching as fast as Hannibal's. He sent most of his army, under his brother, Gnaeus, to wipe out Hannibal's base in Spain, while he returned to Italy to meet the invader. Attacking Hannibal's base was sound conventional strategy.

The only trouble was that Hannibal didn't need a base. He was living off the country. He was also recruiting troops as he marched. His Spanish Celts spoke almost the same language as the Gauls who inhabited what is now France, the Alps, and northern Italy. The Gauls, who had recently been beaten by the Romans, eagerly enlisted in the Carthaginian army.

Hannibal expected to get more recruits in Italy—more effective recruits. The Gauls, after all, were barbarians who didn't understand civilized warfare. In Italy, he hoped to recruit from the Greeks and Etruscans the Romans had conquered—civilized people who knew how to fight in the Hellenistic manner originated by Philip of Macedon and his son, Alexander the Great.

When the Roman heard that Hannibal was in Gaul and approaching the Alps, they dropped all plans for Africa and sent Sempronius and his army north to destroy the Carthaginian as soon as he entered Italy—assuming that there was anything left of his army after he crossed the Alps. Scipio was already on the way.

Crossing the Alps wasn't easy, but the Carthaginian army did it. Frigid weather and treacherous mountain passes killed most of Hannibal's war elephants, and mountain tribesmen killed many of his troops. Hannibal not only defeated the mountain warriors, but he recruited them into his army. Of his original army, Hannibal still had 12,000 African heavy infantry, 8,000 Spanish infantry, and 6,000 cavalry.

The gift of the war god

The Italian Gauls told Hannibal that the Roman legion was the war god's gift to the tribes of the Tiber. He soon got a chance to see it in action. Publius Cornelius

Scipio was approaching. Scipio probably didn't expect to see any Carthaginians, but he was going to block the way south just in case. Besides, the Gauls in the north had become restless, and a show of force would do them good.

On the misty bank of the Tincino River, Hannibal first saw a Roman army in battle formation. In front of them was a screen of light infantry, armed with javelins and slings. Behind them were the heavy infantry, wearing bronze helmets and iron scale armor. Each man carried two *pila*, a light one and a heavy one. The *pilum* had a wooden shaft about four feet long mounting an iron bar about three feet long and a half-inch thick. The bar was tipped with small spearhead. The legionary threw the light pilum at 20 paces and the heavy one at 10 paces. The weapon would stick in an enemy's shield, and the long iron head prevented it from being chopped off. When he got close, the legionary stepped on the haft of the pilum, pulling down the enemy's shield, and finished off his foe with a sword copied from that of the Spanish infantry. The first two lines of the Roman infantry consisted of widely separated companies, called *maniples*. The maniples of the second line covered the empty spaces between the maniples of the first line. The system made it possible for a Roman general to quickly concentrate his troops in one sector or another. It had proved its worth repeatedly, especially on broken ground while fighting enemies who used the infantry phalanx. The phalanx couldn't maintain the straight line it needed on anything but smooth terrain; the Romans in their maniples, trained to act independently, could operate on any ground. Behind the first two lines of infantry, the *hastati* and the *principes*, was a phalanx carrying the traditional long pikes. These troops were called the *triarii*. The first two lines were made up of young, active men. The triarii were veterans, not as agile as the others, but hardened by many campaigns.

Hannibal had been studying the Roman military system all his life. What interested him today was not the Roman infantry, but the cavalry. Hannibal's cavalry was a quarter of his army, all of them men who had lived their lives on horseback. The Roman cavalry wasn't one-tenth of Scipio's army, and the men were not riders but soldiers trying to sit on horses.

Hannibal unleashed his African and Spanish horsemen, along with the remaining elephants. Catching the unfamiliar scent of the elephants, the Roman horses bolted. The Carthaginian cavalry overtook the Romans and cut them down. One of those wounded was Consul Publius Cornelius Scipio. The Numidians rode around the Roman array and attacked the triarii from the rear. The Roman veterans faced about and presented a solid line of spears. Surrounding the wounded general, they moved back to the fortified city of Placentia. That night, 2,000 Gaulish auxiliaries in the Roman army came over to Hannibal. All the young Carthaginian general had to do, it seemed, was prove that the Romans were not invincible. Then the subject peoples would join their liberator.

The other consul, Sempronius, took command of Scipio's army as well as his own. The Roman Republic had two consuls as chief executive. One, in this case (Scipio) was elected from the patricians; the other, from the plebeians. It was December, and consuls would be elected in January. Sempronius was sure a victory over the invaders would ensure his reelection. He led his army—14,000 legionaries and 22,000 auxiliaries—out against the Carthaginians. After a long march in a snowstorm, which included wading neck-deep through the freezing Trebia River, the Romans suddenly stumbled on what looked like the whole Carthaginian army behind ditches and ramparts. Hannibal's fierce African and Spanish cavalry drove off the Roman horse and forced back the Roman flanks while the Roman infantry was stopped by the fortified line. At the height of the battle, another Carthaginian force that had been hidden charged the Roman rear. About 10,000 of the 36,000 made it back to the Roman camp, and Sempronius was not reelected.

Both armies went into winter quarters in January and February, Hannibal in the Po Valley, where he added thousands of Gauls to his army. Hannibal was on the move again in March of 217. He took a route to the south no Roman would expect—over the frozen Apennines and though a malarial swamp. He knew that an uninhabited natural obstacle is hardly ever the danger that a human enemy is. In the swamp, his troops marched through water for four days without finding a dry place to sleep. Hannibal caught malaria, and the fever killed the sight of one eye. But he got his army past the Roman outposts.

The great ambush

Hannibal wanted to lure the Romans into following him. He burned farms and villages, pillaged the countryside, and killed villagers. That might have brought the average Roman consul hurrying after him. But one of the new consuls was Gaius Flaminius, an experienced administrator who had held many high posts, including consul, and a talented commander who had beaten the Gauls. When Hannibal by-passed him, Flaminius asked the other consul, the patrician Servilius, to march south to cut off the Carthaginians. Then he moved out. He would catch Hannibal in a pincers.

Hannibal knew Flaminius was on his track. He led his troops to Lake Trasimeno, a lake nestled in hills with only a narrow strip of level ground along its shore. There was a fog over the lake when Flaminius's troops reached the shore. They were strung out in line beside the lake when a shower of Carthaginian javelins, arrows, and sling bullets hit them. The troops at the head of the line found their way blocked by a phalanx of African infantry, and the Spanish heavy cavalry attacked those at the back. The Romans in the middle couldn't see their enemies holding the hills above them. They couldn't concentrate or even form the kind of fighting front they had been taught. After many had been struck down, the Carthaginians charged down on them from the hills. Of the army of 40,000, Hannibal captured 15,000, including one legion of 6,000 that had surrendered as a unit—something unthinkable in the Roman tradition. The rest had been killed, including Flaminius. Hannibal re-equipped his army with the weapons and armor of the dead Romans.

More allies joined the Carthaginians, and instead of continuing south to meet Servilius, Hannibal took his army back across the Apennines and out of the swampy lowlands for rest and recuperation. The Romans elected a dictator.

The butcher's boy

Election of a dictator was an unusual, but not unprecedented, feature of Roman government. Until the next consular election, the dictator had absolute power. The Senate, the consuls, and the tribunes could not oppose him. But after his dictatorship, he had to answer for everything he had done. The dictator in this case was a patrician of patricians, Quintus Fabius, called Verrucosus, "the Warty." In a short time, he earned a new nickname, Cunctator, "the Delayer."

Fabius followed Hannibal but kept his distance. He tried to cut up Carthaginian foraging parties and shunned all Hannibal's attempts to lure him into battle. He said he was weakening Hannibal and destroying the spirit of the Carthaginian's troops. But Hannibal was pillaging central Italy, stealing everything that could be moved and destroying what couldn't. And he was receiving friendly overtures from the Greeks and the Samnites as well as aid from the Ligurians.

People began murmuring about the "Fabian strategy." One man did not murmur, but bellowed his outrage. His name was Gaius Tarentius Varro, and mention of him requires some notes on the historians of what came to be called "the Hannibalic War."

Roman writers, including historians, did not live on royalties from the sale of their books. They were either wealthy aristocrats, like Livy, or, like Polybius, dependent on Roman aristocrats—in the case of Polybius, the Scipio clan. Consequently, in this period in the Roman Republic, when there was a patrician consul teamed with a plebeian consul, the patrician is always the hero and the plebeian the goat.

Take Flaminius. Livy says he had "no experience of affairs and no military ability whatever." That is simply a lie. Flaminius was a far better general than the two blundering Scipio brothers, Gnaeus and Publius the elder, were. Of all the plebeian consuls, the historians heap the most abuse on Gaius Tarentius Varro. According to Livy, he was "reckless and passionate," "arrogant," and "superstitious," not to mention "a madman." In truth, Varro was no Flaminius. But neither was the wart-afflicted Fabius, whom the historians later dubbed "Maximus." Unfortunately, many modern military commentators echo these ancient prejudices, perhaps because many of them are high-ranking military officers or associates of such officers and think of themselves as aristocrats.

What made Varro so bad in the eyes of the aristocratic writers was that he not only questioned the judgment of Fabius, he actually ridiculed the august chief of the Fabian clan. He, the son of a meat-packer—"the butcher," his opponents called him—made fun of the noblest Roman of them all. He asked if Camillus spent his time aimlessly wandering in the hills after the Gauls sacked Rome. But Varro and Fabius saw Hannibal from entirely different points of view. Fabius was sure that the longer Hannibal stayed in Italy, cut off from his own country, the weaker he would get. He was a nuisance, to be sure, but he could never capture Rome or any other major city. He couldn't hurt anyone but peasants and slaves. But to Varro, Hannibal was death and famine incarnate. He was roving the countryside, burning farms, plundering towns, and slaughtering farmers. Hannibal was killing his people, and Fabius was just following him around observing the carnage. How, Varro asked, could the Romans expect to keep their allies, people Rome promised to protect in return for obedience, if it couldn't protect its own people? And even Varro didn't say it, but Hannibal was indirectly enriching Fabius and his fellow senators. Small farmers were fleeing the land, crowding into Rome, and selling their farms for a pittance. The senators were buying up the farms, incorporating them into their already vast estates, and working them with slaves.

At the next election, Varro was elected consul, along with Lucius Aemilius Paulus, a conservative aristocrat who had considerable military experience. Rome raised an enormous army, and instead of dividing it between the consuls, kept it together. The consuls would command on alternate days.

Hannibal's masterpiece

Finally, the Roman and Carthaginian armies were facing each other, and it was Varro's day to command. There were 86,000 Roman troops, 80,000 infantry and 6,000 cavalry. This was more than double the size of Hannibal's army on August 3, 216, although Hannibal had 10,000 cavalry. The size of the Roman force presented a problem. In the legions' usual checkerboard formation (*quincunx*, the Romans called it) the Roman line would be two miles long. That would be almost impossible to control with a system that relied on trumpets to convey the commander's orders. To shorten the line, Varro ordered the maniples to close up. That turned the army into something like three phalanxes. The plain around the village of Cannae, however, was good ground for a phalanx. Still, the line was more than a mile long. Varro had to rely on subordinate commanders. Lucius Aemilius Paulus would command the heavy cavalry on the Roman right; the two previous consuls, Marcus Atilius and Gnaeus Servilius, would lead the infantry; and Varro would take the light cavalry on the left.

Hannibal had chosen the ground. He let the Romans come to him. The wind was at his back, so the dust of battle would blow in the faces of the Romans, and the morning sun would be in their eyes. On his left flank, between the infantry and a river, were his heavy cavalry, Spaniards and Gauls. On the right flank was a cloud of Numidian horsemen. Just inside the cavalry on each side were the African heavy infantry, wearing Roman armor they had gained in previous battles. Each infantry wing was perched on an end of a V-shaped range of hills that ran back from the Carthaginian front. The center of the infantry, mostly Gauls, did not hold the rest of the hills. Instead, their line bent forward, making a bow with the center facing the Romans. The bare-chest Gauls, with their horned helmets and long swords, looked exactly the same as the barbarian's Roman legions had recently crushed. They weren't the same. Two years of campaigning under Hannibal had turned them into disciplined soldiers, among the most experienced infantry to be found in the Mediterranean.

The Romans shouted their war cry and clashed their shields and spears together. *Velites*, the light infantry javelin men, and Sicilian archers ran forward. Hannibal countered with his Balearian slingers. The Balearic Islanders carried three slings, for long, medium, and short ranges, draped on their bodies. They swung their long slings, weapons that could outrange most bows, and showered the Romans with a hail of lead sling bullets. Then the cavalry charged. The Roman heavy cavalry, perhaps fearing a flank attack by the Carthaginians, was tightly crammed between the infantry and the river. Hannibal's horsemen threw their heavy javelins at the Romans, turned away, then returned and threw more javelins. The big, pilum-like spears penetrated shields and scale corselets. Horses hit by the javelins fell or went mad, bucking and rearing in the cramped Roman ranks. The Roman heavy cavalry had lances instead of javelins. Desperately trying to stay on their mounts, they could seldom manage a powerful lance thrust. Between cavalry charges, the Carthaginian slingers hit them with barrages of sling bullets. One bullet hit Aemilius Paulus, inflicting a compound fracture. Weak from loss of blood, the consul fell off his horse and died in the midst of the melee. The Roman heavy cavalry became so disorganized they got off their horses and tried to fight as infantry. But they were not legionary infantry. They were a disorganized mob. The Celtic cavalry dismounted, too. A confused, sword-swinging brawl was the kind of fighting they were born to, and there were far more of them than there were of the Romans. The Roman heavy cavalry was annihilated.

The cavalry action was different on the other flank.

Varro's lightly armored contingent, mostly allies rather than Roman citizens, had javelins, but they couldn't concentrate their fire. The swirling mass of Numidians attacked them from all directions. The Roman light cavalry were involved in a kind of mounted dance, with the African nomads leading. Then a party of 500 Numidians surrendered. The Romans disarmed them and started to lead them to the rear. But as they were passing through the heart of the Roman cavalry, the Numidians drew hidden swords and cut down their "captors."

Just then, the Carthaginian heavy cavalry, having finished their opponents on the Roman right, rode completely around the legions and attacked Varro's troops from the rear. The Roman light cavalry panicked and fled to the rear, carrying Varro with it.

In the center, the Roman infantry was unaware of all that. They struck the center of the Carthaginian line, crowding in to get a chance to cut down the hated Gauls.

Slowly the Gauls gave ground. Hannibal was leading them in person, along with his brother, Mago. The Carthaginian line became flatter until it was straight. As the Gauls retreated, their ranks became thicker. The African phalanxes on the hills didn't retreat at all. The Romans pushed on, and the Gauls retreated farther. Then they were backing up the slopes of the hills in the rear. Resistance got stronger. Companies of African phalangites appeared from behind the hills. And the African phalangites on the flanks began to push toward the center. The Roman infantry had crowded into a sack, which was now closing. The hastati and principes were packed so tightly together they couldn't throw their pila. The triarii couldn't even lower their pikes.

Then the Carthaginian cavalry charged from the rear. Hannibal's riders jumped off their horses, drew their swords, and cut the knee tendons of the legionaries from the rear.

By afternoon, it was all over. Some 70,000 Romans were dead. Roman troops had suffered the worst defeat they ever had or ever would.

The end of the dream

With Cannae, the most overwhelming defeat Roman arms had ever suffered, Hannibal expected to trigger a general revolt of Rome's subject peoples. He waited for new allies to appear. None did. The Greek city of Capua invited him to come there, but the Capuans did not join his army. He was actually getting fewer recruits than had before. Hannibal was puzzled. So were many others.

One man was not: Gaius Tarentius Varro. The Roman army had stopped following Hannibal around as it had under Fabius. Rome had sacrificed the flower of its manhood to rid Italy of the destroyer. It failed, but Rome's allies knew the Romans would not abandon them. The allies had regained their trust in the city on the seven hills.

Hannibal stayed in Italy. He destroyed four more Roman armies and killed five more Roman commanders. But he couldn't provoke a revolt and eventually got weaker. Finally recalled to Africa, he was defeated by a Roman army under a new Cornelius Publius Scipio, son of Hannibal's one-time opponent. The young Scipio had learned much from the tactics of Hannibal, and he greatly excelled the Carthaginian as an intriguer. He managed to win over a Numidian king and with him, a huge force of the magnificent Numidian cavalry. In 202, near the town of Zama in North Africa, Scipio defeated Hannibal in the last battle of the war. Hannibal escaped to fight another day, but the Hannibalic War was over.

Most modern historians say the Battle of the Metaurus in 207 BC, where Caius Claudius Nero defeated the reinforcing army of Hannibal's brother, Hasdrubal, was the decisive battle of the Hannibalic War. But Hasdrubal's force still wouldn't have added enough men to besiege Rome. And Cannae had cemented the loyalty of Rome's allies. There would be no revolt.

Cannae was decisive in another way. For 14 more years, Hannibal continued to ravage Italy. For 14 more years, Latin farmers abandoned their land and sold it to the great landholders of the senatorial class. They crowded into Rome. The rootless refugees destabilized what had been the ultra-stable Roman commonwealth. Military adventurers, like Marius, Sulla, Pompey, and Julius Caesar, recruited them for what amounted to private armies. The Roman Republic, a state governed by its citizens, disappeared. Under Augustus Caesar it became the Roman Empire.

Battle 24

Malplaquet, 1709 AD
The Sun King

Who fought: French (Claude-Louis-Hector Villars) vs. British, Dutch, and Germans (Duke of Marlborough).

What was at stake: In the short term, who would sit on the Spanish throne. Actually, it marked the beginning of the end of absolute monarchy. Louis XIV had to call on his people for help.

"My dominant passion is certainly love of glory," Louis XIV wrote in 1666. The glory that appealed most to Louis was military glory. Other kinds of glory took unusual personal talent, but to gain military glory, the King could call on the resources of the whole country. France was a large country, and it had an excellent army. The French army would win wars, and the French King would gain personal glory. Louis saw nothing odd in this. Although he never said, "L'etat c'est moi," he could have. To Louis, he was France; Charles II was Britain; William of Orange was the United Provinces of the Netherlands. All were engaged in a great game. The object of the game was glory. To gain glory, the rulers of France, Britain, the Netherlands, Austria, and Spain engaged in a seemingly endless series of wars. Nations changed sides, but France was always opposed by the Netherlands and usually opposed by Austria and Britain. Spain, a shell of its former glory, tried unsuccessfully to stay out of things. Sweden and the German states joined in when it seemed appropriate.

Louis's concept of *gloire* was definitely not "blood and glory." Neither blood nor mud appealed to him. He first went campaigning with a silk headquarters tent, staffed

135

by beautiful young noblewomen. He was shocked at the way some of his generals wasted men's lives. In his next war, he left the ladies behind but brought along an artist to record scenes of his triumphs. The painter was forbidden, however, to show any violence. The Sun King was no coward. In the Third Dutch War, in 1673, Louis personally led the final assault on the powerful fortress of Maastricht. But Louis was averse to unnecessary bloodshed. And that helped establish a new trend in warfare.

The new trend was partly a reaction to the excesses of the Thirty Years War, when rampaging armies spent a generation trying to depopulate Germany. As a boy king, Louis had seen that kind of warfare close up. He was a fugitive while French factions ravaged the countryside in the ferocious War of the Fronde. Louis was a leader in the movement to replace the undisciplined mobs of previous wars with small, highly trained national armies. He promoted generals like the Viscount of Turenne, a master of maneuver who usually had his opponents half-beaten before any shots were fired. Louis's greatest find was Sebastien le Prestre, a commoner's son who had enlisted as a sapper. The young King recognized the young soldier's talent as a military engineer and heaped promotions upon him. As Sieur de Vauban, le Prestre is now recognized as the greatest military engineer in history.

Instead of pillaging the countryside, the new armies depended on supplies stored in forti-fied magazines. That made sieges a key strategy in late 17th-and early 18th-century warfare. In seigecraft, Vauban was king. His techniques were so infallible that when his approach trenches to a fortress's walls reached a certain point, it was universally agreed that the garrison could sur-render without the slightest loss of honor. In the field, Turenne and his disciples maneuvered the enemy out of contact with his magazines resulting in, if not surrender, a hasty retreat. Warfare was not exactly bloodless, but it was a far cry from the endless massacres that character-ized the recently ended wars of religion.

Louis was so successful that he became the "Sun King," the center of the European solar system, around whom all the other rulers revolved. But the other rulers got tired of spinning around the lord of Versailles. Louis's aid to the Muslim Turks, at war with his Austrian rivals, the Hapsburgs, gave them an excuse to form the League of Augs-burg.

The War of the League of Augsburg—all Europe except Turkey at war with France—was the first "world war" of modern times. It was fought in Europe, the Americas, India, and on the high seas. Turenne had died. So had the Marquis of Louvois, Louis's great minister of war. But the Duke of Luxembourg proved to be a master tactician, and Louis still had Vauban. But the King was old and tired, and the war was exhausting his resources. He was happy to sign a peace treaty that let him keep most of his conquests.

The Spanish succession

Louis had finally decided to stop disturbing the peace of Europe. Then the King of Spain, Don Carlos II, died. He had no children. His closest heirs were the son of the Emperor of Austria and the grandson of Louis XIV. In his will, Carlos stated that he wanted his throne to go to Louis's grandson, the Duke of Anjou. War immediately broke out with Austria. Britain and the Netherlands felt threatened by the combina-tion of French power and Spanish gold. They joined Austria. So did Denmark and all of the German states but Bavaria.

To compound Louis's troubles, his resources were limited. Years of high living by his court had drained the treasury. And all of the great Frenchmen of the past—all but Louis himself—were gone. Luxembourg had died. Louis had quarreled with Vauban over the King's treatment of French Protestants, and the great engineer had retired.

His ancient enemies were gone, too. That was not a good thing for France. His greatest enemy, William of Orange, who forged alliance after alliance against him, first as leader of the United Provinces of the Netherlands and later as King of the United Kingdom of Great Britain and Ireland, was dead. William was a talented diplomat, but a grossly incompetent general who nevertheless loved battle with an unholy fervor and demanded leadership of the anti-French armies. Replacing William was John Churchill, the Duke of Marlborough, one of the most talented generals who ever wore a British uniform. The Austrians found another star—a Frenchman, Prince Eugene of Savoy, who had left his native country vowing never to return except at the head of an army.

For a short time, it looked as if Louis's luck would save him again. While Marlborough was beating the French in Flanders, Claude-Louis-Hector Villars trounced the Austrians and their allies at Hochstett in 1703. Villars lost 1,000 men, and the Imperialists lost 11,000. But Villars became so disgusted at the dawdling of his ally, Elector Maximilian of Bavaria, that he resigned. Few in the French court were sorry to see him go. They considered Villars to be a loud, boastful, uncouth lout. He was, but he had talent, something none of his successors could claim.

Marlborough took his army of Dutch and British south to join the Austrians, moving in a way that completely baffled the French, who hoped to cut him off. He met Eugene and led the Allies to a crushing victory over the French and Bavarians at Blenheim. Marlborough, it turned out, was a most atypical 18th-century general. The casualties on both sides were enormous. The English, and especially the Dutch, were shocked. They kept Marlborough on a tight leash for a while. Villars, with a new command, had some success campaigning in the Rhineland, but in 1706, Marlborough had a chance to work his magic again and routed the French at Ramillies and drove them out of the Spanish Netherlands (more or less modern Belgium). Again casualties were high, and again the Dutch politicians "chained" Marlborough.

The Allies invaded Spain, but that expedition quickly bogged down. The Duke of Berwick, an English Catholic fighting for the French in Spain, defeated the Earl of Galway, a French Protestant with an Irish title fighting for the English in support of the Austrians. The Spanish themselves detested the invaders and began guerilla fighting.

But in 1708, Eugene took his army down the Rhine and joined Marlborough. They routed the main French army in Flanders and invaded France. The winter that followed was the coldest in a century. In France, wheat seed died in the ground and half the livestock froze to death. France had been defeated, foreign invaders were ruling part of the country, and famine was killing the population. Louis XIV, the world's proudest monarch, was humbled. He sued for peace.

"My enemies, not my children"

Led by the Dutch, the Allies gave Louis 40 conditions for peace. He would have to give up all his conquests, he would have to cease all aid to his grandson in Spain, and so on. But the last demand shocked the old King: He would have to drive his grandson from the Spanish throne.

When he saw the last demand, Louis said, "If I must have war, I will fight my enemies, not my children."

Then Louis XIV, the epitome of the absolute monarch in this age of absolute monarchy, did something revolutionary.

He went to the people of France. He wrote a broadside addressed to the people at large:

> "I can say that I have done violence to my character...to procure promptly a peace for my subjects even at the expense of my personal satisfaction and perhaps even my honor....I can no longer see any alternative to take, other than to prepare to defend ourselves. To make sure that a

united France is greater than all the powers assembled by force and artifice to overwhelm it....I have come to ask...your aid in this encounter that involves your safety. By the efforts that we shall make together, our foes will understand that we are not to be put upon."

Money poured into the treasury. Volunteers rushed to the recruiting offices. Louis gave command of the army to Villars the only general who seemed capable of winning battles. Winning battles with these rawest of recruits would not be easy, but Villars threw himself into the task of turning them into an army. But hard as he worked, the recruits worked harder.

"I am humble," the braggart general said, "when I see the backbreaking labor men perform without food."

Few of Villars's men had ever seen a musket before they responded to their king's appeal. Marlborough had drilled his men incessantly in musketry. They fired by platoons instead of by lines, giving the commander more flexibility. Marlborough spent even more time training his cavalry, and the British cavalry was considered the best in Europe. His second in command was the brilliant Prince Eugene. Villars' second was Louis Francois, Duke of Boufflers, a brave but sick and cautious old man.

When spring began to thaw the tundra that France had become, Marborough set out to besiege Mons. An ordinary general, outnumbered like Villars, would have prepared for a siege. Instead Villars moved to block Marlborough in the field.

"That very murdering battle"

Villars fortified a line that stretched between two expanses of woodland. Eighteenth century infantry tactics in Europe were based on maintaining perfectly dressed lines of bayonet-armed footmen when the enemies closed with each other. Woods played hell with such tactics.

Marlborough, as he had already shown, was no more typical of the 18th-century than Villars was. The usual commander in that era would have tried to flank the French and cut them off from their supplies. Marlborough craved a battle. His plan was to hit both ends of the French line, forcing Villars to thin his center to reinforce his flanks. Then he would smash through the French center.

Marlborough sent 20,000 Germans, in 40 battalions against the middle of the French line. Suddenly, they turned and marched against the Wood of Taisiers, the anchor of the French left. Then 40 Allied guns, a huge number at that time, opened up on the woods. The Germans advanced in three lines, bayoneted muskets on their shoulders, marching at the stately pace of 80 steps a minute in time with beating drums. They were marching over 800 yards of open ground against an enemy hidden in the woods.

Before they got near the woods, the French opened fire. Cannon balls from the woods took out whole files with one shot. Other cannons from the French center knocked down rows of infantrymen. In the stolid manner of 18th century infantry, the Germans closed the gaps in their lines and continued marching. They outnumbered the French in the woods four to one. The French gunners changed to grapeshot and knocked bunches of Germans down with each shot. When the attackers got to the edge of the woods, the French blasted them with a volley of musket-fire and charged with bayonets. Two of the three major generals and all of the colonels in the first German line were killed. The first line went crashing back against the second. The second wave stopped the French, and the third wave came up to join the fight. The French sent their reserves into the battle.

On the other flank, Dutch and Scottish troops launched their attack 20 minutes after the Germans. Once again, the French fired from the front and the flank carpeted the ground with allied bodies. A French counterattack drove back the Dutch and Scots, but a charge of the Hessian cavalry saved the Allied infantry—for the moment. Marlborough had to take English troops from his center to prevent a rout on his flank.

But on the French side, Villars had practically denuded his center to stop the flank attacks. He was forming up troops for a counterattack when he was hit. He fell from his horse but refused to be taken from the field. He sat on a chair directing the battle until he lost consciousness. Boufflers took over.

Marlborough rode up to the center of the line and observed that French trenches were unoccupied. He sent his cavalry to break through. The cavalry crossed what had been the center of the French line, but the horses were exhausted. The French cavalry met them and the two bodies of horse staggered through an indecisive fight. Boufflers withdrew his army in good order.

It was all over—the bloodiest battle since the invention of gunpowder. Marlborough himself referred to the fight as "that very murdering battle."

Backlash

The French had lost 10,000 men and the Allies almost three times that. Of 80 Dutch battalions engaged, there were not enough men to make 18.

"If it please God to give Your Majesty's enemies another such victory," Villars wrote to Louis, "they are ruined."

Louis wasn't so sure. His best general was seriously wounded, his enemies were still in France, and the new winter looked as if it would be as ferocious as the last. "I am infinitely miserable," he told his surgeon.

But he was scarcely less happy than the rulers of Britain and the Netherlands. Marlborough's "butcher's bill" was too high.

And Villars recovered. In Spain, the Spanish people had united behind Louis's grandson, Philip V, and were driving the invaders out. In France, the fires of patriotism were still burning. More and more Frenchmen volunteered for the army. Villars took the offensive, and Marlborough and Eugene tried to avoid battle. Then the British made sure there would never be another Malplaquet. They recalled Marlborough and the British troops and made a separate peace. Villars stepped up his offensive. With a series of maneuvers worthy of Turenne or Marlborough himself, he drove Eugene and the Dutch out of France and Flanders. In six weeks, Eugene lost 53 battalions and strongholds it had taken years to capture.

First glimmer of a new dawn

The end of the war lifted Louis from his misery, but Malplaquet was even more important to his country and to Western civilization. For the first time, a monarch "by divine right," and of all monarchs, Louis XIV, the proudest of them all, had to go to the people. The common people of France had saved their country. They had shown that supreme power resides not in a divinely inspired king, but in the people. It was a lesson that would be taken up by the philosophers and demonstrated twice more in the century, first across the Atlantic, then a few years later in France.

Battle 25

Parthian cavalry.

Carrhae, 53 BC
A New Alexander?

Who fought: Romans (Crassus) vs. Parthians (Surena).

What was at stake: The survival of Eastern civilization.

Marcus Licinius Crassus, the richest man in Rome, was on his way to join his army and perform great deeds in the East. But not all Romans were looking forward to that.

The seemingly interminable unrest and civil war in Italy, a legacy of Hannibal's invasion, had ended up with three men the most important figures in the Roman world. Crassus was one, a former lieutenant of the late dictator, Sulla. He had used his position on the winning faction to make a fortune from the estates of his enemies. Pompey, Sulla's chief assistant, was the second. Pompey had since made a name for himself by eliminating pirates in the Mediterranean and knocking down bumptious kings in the East. The third kingpin was the leader of the popular party formerly led by Sulla's enemy, Marius. His name was Julius Caesar.

Crassus and Pompey managed to get themselves elected consuls in defiance of the Senate. Neither cared for the other, and both feared the increasingly powerful Caesar. To avoid another round of civil wars, the three got together and, in effect, divided the Roman Empire among themselves. Pompey's domain would be Spain;

Caesar's, Gaul, and Crassus's, Syria. Each hoped to rule his portion in a way that would let him outshine the other two and become the sole ruler of Rome.

Crassus was delighted with his portion. Pompey got Spain, which had silver mines and controlled all trade with the mysterious lands beyond the Pillars of Hercules. But Spain was entirely surrounded by water or by Caesar's fiefdom of Gaul. There was no place for a soldier to go. All three were soldiers. Crassus had the least experience, but it was he who broke the back of the Spartacus Revolt. Caesar, in Gaul, had plenty of chance to demonstrate his military skill. But the Gauls were almost barbarians—there were no great riches to be had in their lands.

Syria was different. East of Syria was Babylon and the ancient land between the rivers. East of that was Persia, now held by the Parthians, and beyond that were the mysterious empires of the East.

Crassus, quiet and amiable before he joined the triumvirate, according to Plutarch, was "strangely puffed up, and his head heated...he proposed to himself in his hopes to pass as far as Bactria and India, and the utmost ocean."

In other words, he saw himself as a new Alexander—greater Alexander. He would go beyond India and conquer the legendary empire of China. He would return to Rome leading most of the world in his triumphal parade, and his two rivals would have no choice but to defer to him.

Not all Romans were delighted by the idea that one rich man would be able to use the men and resources of Rome to make war on a friendly nation for his personal benefit. One such was Ateius, the tribune of the people. Ateius raised a mob of people to stop Crassus on his way out of the city. Pompey, however, appeared and calmed the crowd so that Crassus was able to pass. Ateius dashed ahead and was waiting for Crassus at the city gate. When Crassus appeared, Ateius threw incense on a fire, poured wine on the ground, and "cursed him with dreadful imprecations, calling upon and naming several strange and horrible deities."

But Crassus's mind was on the gold of the East and the glory of his return to Rome. He gave little thought to "strange and horrible deities," or even to his prospective enemies, the Parthians.

The Parthians

The Parthians were related to the Scythians—or Sakas, as they called themselves. They spoke a language similar to that of the Persians and Medes. For centuries, they had roamed the plains of Central Asia, including the eastern part of the Persian Empire. When Alexander and his Greeks marched across Persia on their way to India, the Parthians found themselves part of the Macedonian Empire, and later part of the Greek Seleucid Kingdom. About 250 BC, Arsaces, the chief of the Parthians, declared his independence and made an alliance with Greek-led Bactria, a Central Asian kingdom covering much of the area of modern Kazakhstan, Kyrgysrtan, and Tajikistan.

Antiochus III, father of Judas Maccabeus's foe (see Emmaus, pg. 113), forced the Parthians to acknowledge his sovereignty after a campaign lasting seven years. But the Parthians didn't stay conquered. Under Mithradates I, the Parthians rose again and drove the Greeks out of Persia and Media. In 145 BC, Mithradates captured Seleucia on the Tigris (in modern Iraq) and made it his capital. Then events in far-off China stopped the Parthian march of conquest. Emperor Wu Ti launched a major attack on the Huns. The khan of the Western Huns was beheaded and his people scattered. Chinese troops pushed into Central Asia. Another group of nomads, the Caucasian barbarians that the Chinese called Yue Chi, were displaced. The Yue Chi moved west, almost destroying Bactria and the neighboring Greek kingdom of Menander and menacing the Parthians' eastern frontier. The Yue Chi pushed the Saka tribes outside the Parthian domain into Mithradates's empire. It was another replay of the Central Asia domino game that was to continue periodically until the time of Tamerlane. The Armenians, who had been conquered by the Parthians, took advantage of the confusion and declared their independence.

But the Parthians rallied under the second Mithradates and subdued the Saka invaders and the Armenians. Like the Great King of Persia before him, the Parthian leader was a king of kings. Besides Parthia itself, he ruled the kings of Armenia, Elmais (Elam), and Persis (Persia) and the ruler of the Suren kingdom, a mostly Saka state acting as a buffer between Parthia and the wild Sakas and Yue Chi of the steppes. When Crassus moved into Syria, the Parthians were across the border. They had reached an understanding with the Romans, and relations were peaceful. That was a good thing for both nations, considering their respective military establishments

Horse archers and legionaries

The Parthian army was just a slight modification of the ancient military system of all Eurasian nomads. The system had been used by the Cimmerians and the Sakas and would be used later by the Sarmatians, the Huns, the Turks, and the Mongols. It was based on the horse and the bow. Both were absolute necessities for herdsmen who had to guard their livestock against wolves, bears, leopards, and human enemies. The horses were small animals with enormous endurance. The bows were composed of layers of horn, wood, and sinew—weapons far more powerful than anything seen in the settled lands. The Parthian organization was as ancient and traditional as its weapons. The horsemen were divided into units of tens, hundreds, thousands, and, occasionally, ten thousands. Their leaders signaled them by waving standards and beating kettledrums mounted on horses.

The wild nomads fought under their clan leaders, and the Parthians under officers appointed by the king, but those officers were almost always clan leaders. The army Crassus would face was led by one of the greatest of the clan leaders, the head of the Suren clan, called Surena by the Romans. Surena was only 30 years old, about half the age of Crassus. He was tall, handsome, and famous for his valor, but he painted his face and brought along dozens of concubines to entertain him on the march.

The modification the Parthians had introduced into the ancient steppe military system was the use of armored lancers, something they had picked up from the Persians. The richest Parthians wore lamellar armor—armor composed of thin metal plates laced together—which covered them from head to foot. They rode huge horses and carried long lances. All of the Parthians, horse archers and lancers alike, had spent their lives on horseback. A millennium of trial and error had developed the Parthian military system. Nothing was better adapted to warfare on the arid plains of Asia.

It was not, however, well adapted to fighting in forests and mountains. Mithradates II had no easy task getting the Armenian mountaineers to acknowledge his sovereignty, and the Romans had given them serious trouble in the mountains of Syria.

The army Crassus was leading was far different from the one Gaius Tarentius Varro took to Cannae. The Roman army was no longer a peasant militia called up to render service in an emergency. Marius had begun the practice of recruiting the landless proletariat of Rome. Soldiering was the only work Crassus's troopers knew.

Their weapons would have been familiar to Varro's men, but the checkerboard formation of 120-man maniples was gone. There was still a checkerboard formation, but the maniples had been grouped into cohorts of some 600 men each. Ten cohorts made a legion. Crassus had seven legions—all infantry of course, and about 4,000 cavalry. The King of Armenia, not really happy with Parthian rule, sent Crassus 600 cavalrymen and some advice: Don't try to fight the Parthians on the plains; lure them into the mountains, where their cavalry will have trouble. He urged Crassus to invade Parthia from Armenia. Crassus, thinking the Armenian was just trying to improve his own situation, said he would go through Mesopotamia.

Into the trap

Crassus crossed the Euphrates, entering Parthian territory, and marched along the river. Parthian horse archers appeared, but they fled when Roman cavalry tried to engage them. An old Arab approached the camp and asked to speak with the general. Some of the troops who had been in Syria recognized him. He had given the Romans valuable information in the past, they said. Crassus allowed the Arab to come in.

"If you meant to fight," the Arab said, "you should have made all possible haste, before the king (of the Parthians) should recover courage and collect his forces together." He said King Hyrodes of Parthia was planning to seek refuge among the Sakas of the steppe and had sent Surena with a small force to divert the Romans.

It was basically a lie, although there was some truth in the Arab's tale. Surena had a smaller force than Crassus. He had 10,000 horsemen, including 1,000 heavily armed cavalrymen in his personal bodyguard, while Crassus had 40,000 infantrymen and 4,000 cavalrymen. Surena was not leading the main Parthian army, which was invading Armenia. It seems that Hyrodes wanted his powerful vassal (and potential rival) to take the brunt of the Roman attack. Even if Crassus triumphed, he would still have to face the main Parthian force in a weakened condition. To make sure the Romans took the bait, Hyrodes had sent the Arab to them.

The Arab told Crassus that his best course was to quickly crush Surena then turn on Hyrodes before he could disappear into the endless steppes. He offered to show the Romans how to cut off Surena, whose light-armed cavalry had been continually retreating from them.

So Crassus and his men left the river and the rolling hills along its banks and "into vast plains, by a way that at first was pleasant and easy but afterwards very troublesome by reason of the depth of the sand, no tree, nor any water, nor any end to be seen; so that they were not only spent with thirst, and the difficulty of the passage, but were dismayed with the uncomfortable prospect of not a bough, not a stream, not a hillock, not a green herb, but in fact a sea of sand, which encompassed the army with its waves." The Arab left, telling Crassus that he was going to contrive a way to disorder the enemy.

The Romans finally reached a small stream near the village of Carrhae. A short distance away, they saw Surena's army. It looked even smaller than they had expected. The Parthian general had hid most of his troops behind the dunes. They covered their armor with skins so the glitter of the sun on the naked iron would not give them away. Suddenly the rolling thunder of hundreds of kettledrums exploded. Parthian horsemen in gleaming armor seemed to rise out of the ground. Their heavy cavalry charged the Romans with leveled lances. The Roman ranks remained firm, and the Parthians fled, with the horse archers shooting over their shoulders. The Parthians ran in all directions. Then the Romans realized that the steppe warriors had surrounded them.

Crassus ordered his light-armed soldiers to counterattack, but a storm of arrows forced them back. The Parthian arrows were able to pierce Roman shields and body armor. The Parthian horse archers rode around the Roman army, shooting down the ranks of infantry. The Roman cavalry couldn't come to blows: The Parthians ran away, shooting behind them all the time. The Romans waited for their enemies to run out of arrows, but Surena had a thousand camels loaded down with extra arrows.

Crassus's son, Publius, organized a major counterattack with 1,300 horsemen, 500 archers, and eight cohorts. The Parthians made a show of resistance, then fled. Young Crassus pursued. When he was too far from the main army to receive support, the Parthian heavy cavalry charged the Roman horse. The Roman retreated and set up a defensive position. The Parthian lancers stayed in place, but the horse archers surrounded the Romans and shot them down. Publius was killed. The Parthians cut off his head, stuck it on a lance, and took it to the main Roman army to taunt Crassus.

When night fell, the Romans retreated. The troops became separated in the dark. The units Crassus was commanding personally were surrounded. Some Arabs approached them with the message that Surena desired a conference. Crassus accepted, knowing that death was the only alternative to surrender. During negotiations, a dispute between the Romans and Parthians came to blows. Crassus was killed, and the surviving Romans enslaved.

East and West

The death of Crassus left Caesar and Pompey sole rivals for power in Rome. In the civil war that followed, Caesar vanquished Pompey and established one-man rule. When Caesar was assassinated, his heir, Octavius, became Augustus Caesar, the first Emperor of Rome. Roman emperors would rule in western Europe for almost half a millennium and in Eastern Europe for a millennium and a half. Moreover, Western Europe would be haunted by a series of ghosts of the Roman Empire, beginning with Charlemagne and ending with Napoleon.

Even more important, Carrhae established that there would never be another Alexander. The young Macedonian had carried Greek culture to India and to the borders of China. There, cut off by the horse archers of the steppes, it had withered and died. Centuries before, Darius the Great had failed to conquer Greece. Centuries later, the armies of Genghis Khan would fail to conquer Europe. Europe would try again to conquer the East during the Crusades and again would be foiled by the deadly combination of desert and horse archer.

East met West repeatedly, but never the twain did join. The world's civilizations did not become homogenized, and the conflict of West and East would be a recurrent theme in world history.

Battle 26

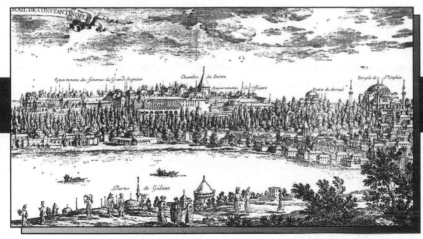

Constantinople, Part II, 1453 AD
The Drinker of Blood

Who fought: East Romans (Giovanni Giustiani) vs. Turks (Mohammed the Conqueror).

What was at stake: The survival of Islam in Europe.

Mohammed II was irritated every time he looked at the walls of Constantinople. In 1446, his father, Murad II, fighting a coalition of Christian states, had to pay the Eastern Roman Emperor a toll of one ducat for each man in his army in order to ferry his troops across the Bosphorus.

Constantinople was often called the eastern rampart of Christendom. Its importance was not merely symbolic. The walled metropolis controlled the Bosphorus, the only good way to get from Anatolia to the Balkan Peninsula, as well as the sea route from the fertile lands around the Black Sea to the Mediterranean. The city had not blocked the Turkish advance into Europe—the profits from ferrying Turks across the strait were too good. It was, however, a mighty pain for expansion-minded Ottoman sultans.

Now the sultan himself, the 22-year-old Mohammed, was going to remedy that situation. Mohammed was not a man given to shilly shallying. His first act on becoming sultan in 1451 was to send an assassin to drown his baby half-brother, who might

145

grow up to be a rival for the throne. His next act was to execute the assassin. His third act was to marry the baby's mother to a slave. His soldiers called him "the Drinker of Blood." He didn't mind. One of the few people he admired was a Transylvanian nobleman called Vlad the Impaler, also nicknamed Dracula (the little Devil). When Turkish envoys refused to remove their turbans in Dracula's presence, he had the turbans nailed to their heads. Mohammed thought that was such a noble notion he adopted it himself. There were, of course, skirmishes between Mohammed's men and Dracula's. But when Dracula impaled thousands of Turkish prisoners, Mohammed said, "It is impossible to drive out of his country a prince who does such grand things as that."

Mohammed was well educated. He spoke Turkish, Greek, Latin, Arabic, Chaldean, and Slavonic. He studied the lives of great leaders and had sound ideas on strategy. He demonstrated that soon after his coronation by making a landing on the European shore of the Bosphorus north of Constantinople. His troops built a fort, called Roumelia Hisar, and filled it with cannons. Now he could cut Constantinople off from the Black Sea.

Constantinople

Ever since Constantine the Great moved his capital from Rome to the old Greek city of Byzantium and named it after himself, Constantinople had been coveted by enemies. Russians and Arabs, Magyars and Bulgars, Vikings and Seljuk Turks had all besieged it. It had resisted them all, but in 1203, an army of misdirected crusaders took it, and repeated the feat in 1204 (see Constantinople, Part I, pg. 46). But that happened more than three centuries before this. The walls had been rebuilt.

On the north of the city a wall studded with towers ran along the shore of the Golden Horn, then around the point and down along the Sea of Marmara, south of the town. To the west of the city, on dry land, were Constantinople's famous double walls. Actually, there were three walls, because the inner face of the water ditch in front of the walls—a moat 60 feet wide and 15 feet deep—was built high enough above the surface of the ground to act as a breastwork. Behind the moat was a 25-foot wall with towers less than a bowshot apart. Twenty yards behind that wall was a 45-foot wall with 112 towers, each 60 feet high. In 1203, Enrico Dandolo, the Doge of Venice who actually commanded the crusader expedition, chose to attack the sea wall because there was only one barrier. But Dandolo commanded a powerful fleet. Mohammed's navy was pitiable by comparison.

Although the physical damage done by the crusaders had long since been repaired, the psychological damage was still serious. The native Greeks (Greek Orthodox) hated the "Latins" (Roman Catholics). The Latins returned the feeling. The town of Galata, across the Golden Horn, had been settled by Genoese, who declared their neutrality in the coming battle with the Turks. To gain help from the West, Emperor John VI, the predecessor of Constantine XI, agreed to accept the leadership of the Pope. This outraged his own people. When Constantine accepted Latin help, an Orthodox priest named Gennadius roused a mob, which rioted outside the Emperor's palace shouting "Death to the excommunicated!" (the Latins).

Of 25,000 men of military age in the city, Constantine could find only 5,000 willing to fight the Turks. The Pope sent 200 men under a Cardinal Isidore, and a number of Latin (mostly Italian) volunteers and mercenaries joined the defenders. In response, the Orthodox priests announced that they would refuse absolution to anyone who had any dealings with the Latins. Altogether, Constantine could oppose Mohammed's 200,000 men with about 8,000.

Mohammed's army, however, looked more formidable than it was. Of the 200,000, according to a Florentine soldier named Tedaldi, only 140,000 were effective soldiers. The rest were "thieves, plunderers, hawkers, and others following the army for gain and booty." But 12,000 of the soldiers were Janissaries, the best infantry of any European nation. The Janissaries had been children of Christian parents, taken in the Turkish "blood tax" and raised in Islam. They trained to be soldiers from childhood and were brought up in a strict, almost monastic, discipline. The rest were Bashi-bazouks, Turkish feudal cavalry, and peasant militia from Anatolia.

The most impressive part of the Turkish army was its artillery. Mohammed had more guns and bigger guns than any prince in Europe or Asia. He has been called "the world's first great artilleryman."

If cannons were Mohammed's greatest asset, Constantine's greatest asset was two men, both foreigners and Latins: Giovanni Giustiani of Genoa, a famous commander who arrived with 700 soldiers in two large galleys, and Johann Grant, a German military engineer. Constantine appointed Giustiani commander-in-chief of his forces.

Mohammed took a few Byzantine outposts, in one case, driving out the garrison with a gas attack, using burning sulfur. He then impaled the garrisons. Next, he brought up his heavy guns. The guns moved at a snail's pace. To drag one of these guns took 50 yoke of oxen and 450 men. It took about two hours to load each gun, and the guns could fire only seven or eight shots a day. Constantine and Giustiani had plenty of warning about where the attack would take place. That was a good thing, because Constantine had only one man for each 18-foot section of wall if he spread them evenly. As it was, in the sections of the wall not directly threatened, Giustiani reduced the defenders of the towers to squads of three or four men.

The assault

On April 12, Mohammed began the world's first organized artillery bombardment. There were a dozen great bombards, enormous cannons that fired stone balls weighing more than 1,400 pounds and 56 smaller guns. Firing went on night and day, but at first without noticeable effect. Then the Turkish gunners concentrated on a single spot on the wall. Eventually, the outer wall crumbled, but the Turks found that their enemies had built a new wall behind it.

On April 18, the impatient Mohammed ordered a general attack. Giustiani had no artillery like Mohammed's, but he defended the wall with small cannons, catapults, muskets, crossbows, and "wall guns," small, portable cannons that fired five lead balls with each shot. He mowed the Turks down in heaps. Mohammed was so enraged by the failure of his infantry, he thought about loading their bodies into the bombards and shooting them over the walls of Constantinople.

At the same time the Turkish fleet tried to break the chain across the Golden Horn, as the Venetians had done three centuries before. But the chain remained unbroken. The Turkish navy was not the Venetian navy. It proved that two days later.

Three Genoese warships loaded with soldiers and munitions approached the harbor, escorting an East Roman grain ship. The Turkish admiral, a renegade Bulgarian named Baltoglu, led 145 Turkish galleys out to capture the Christian ships. The Genoese smashed through the Turkish fleet, ramming some galleys and snapping banks of oars off others. The Constantinople garrison lowered the chain to let the Christian ships in, then raised it again. Mohammed again flew into a rage and ordered Baltoglu to be impaled. His officers, fearing the precedent that executing a commanding officer would set, talked him out of that. So Mohammed had four slaves spread-eagle Baltoglu on the ground while he beat the unfortunate admiral with a heavy stick.

The sultan sent an envoy to the Emperor with a proposal: that Constantine move to the Pelopennesus in Greece and rule from there but let Mohammed have the city. Constantine refused.

Because he could not break the chain across the Golden Horn, Mohammed decided to go around it. He sent workers to level the mile of dry land between the Bosphorus and a stream called The Springs. They built a wooden runway, greased it, and dragged 70 ships over it. Next, he built a floating bridge over the Golden Horn. Now he could concentrate his forces anywhere he wanted.

On May 7, Mohammed launched another assault on the walls. Giustiani and his men beat it back with heavy losses. Mohammed tried again May 12 and suffered even heavier losses. The sultan, however, was constantly getting reinforcements. The East Romans were not.

The Turks on May 18 rolled a siege tower up to the moat. Gunners on its top could shoot down on the walls to clear them of defenders. As the attackers attempted to get the tower across the moat, Giustiani rolled barrels of gunpowder into the ditch and blew it up.

"What I would not give to win that man over to my side," Mohammed said. He attempted to bribe the Genoese, but Giustiani would not be tempted.

Above-ground assaults having failed, Mohammed tried mining. Johann Grant half-buried drums behind the walls. The vibrations of the drums showed him where the enemy was digging. Then he dug counter mines. He blew up some Turkish tunnels and filled others with poisonous sulfur dioxide from fire pots. He flooded other tunnels or sent infantry through his countermines to kill the Turkish diggers.

Mohammed was growing worried. He feared that if he didn't take Constantinople soon, the Christian nations would unite and send relief. He ordered an assault on all of the walls to begin May 29. It would continue night and day until the city was taken. The defenders had to extend themselves to the breaking point, but they continued to beat off the waves of Turkish attackers.

At the north end of the land walls, where they joined the wall along the Golden Horn, the Turks got a break. From ancient times there had been a tiny postern gate in the ditch. Emperor Isaac Angelus had blocked it up during the crusader troubles in 1204, but it had recently been reopened—and forgotten. Some Janissaries found the undefended gate and rushed in. Their greed almost destroyed this golden opportunity. They were plundering the palaces when defenders led by the Bocchiardi brothers, who were Latin volunteers, closed the postern passage and cut off their retreat. Driven out of the palace, the Turks ran south, inside the inner wall.

Meanwhile, Giustiani was fatally wounded, causing some confusion among his troops. Then, the Turkish fugitives hit them in the flank. The main Turkish army got over the wall, Constantine led a countercharge and was killed, and Constantinople became a Turkish city.

There was a massacre, of course, but Mohammed stopped it. He had no wish to rule a desert. He gave the Christians in the city freedom to worship in their own way and appointed the Latin-hating Gennadius patriarch. Constantinople has been a Turkish city ever since.

The end of the ancient world

The fall of Constantinople was really the end of the Roman Empire. Constantine had founded the city when the Empire ruled lands from Britain to Mesopotamia. The Empire had lost much territory since, but it was still the Roman Empire. There were Western attempts to re-create the Roman Empire, beginning with Charlemagne, but Constantine's city and territory was the real thing. Now it was gone, and with it the last vestige of the classical world which had begun in this same area almost 3,000 years before.

It was also the birth of a new European power. The Ottoman Empire established its capital in Constantinople and spread out from there to dominate the Balkans and much of Eastern Europe.

It was the birth of a new world. The medieval world, which had grown up outside the Roman Empire, would die as surely as the Empire itself. A new interest in classical civilization had been slowly growing in Italy, the beginnings of what we call the Renaissance. Now scholars steeped in classical learning fled west, to Italy. The Renaissance ("rebirth") got a jump-start.

Turkish victory in the eastern Mediterranean provoked a Christian reaction. At the other end of the inland sea, little more than a generation later, the Spanish drove the last Muslims out of the Iberian Peninsula. And the Western nations took to the sea (see Diu, pg. 36). The same year as Spain's final triumph over the Moors, a Genoese captain, sailing under the Spanish flag, discovered a new world.

Battle 27

The Armada, 1588 AD
Reluctant Antagonists

Who fought: Spanish (Duke of Medina Sidonia) vs. English (Lord Howard of Effingham and Francis Drake).

What was at stake: England's aspirations of great power status.

The monarchs didn't want war. There was little love between Elizabeth I of England and her brother-in-law, Philip II of Spain, but there was little hate either. Their relationship was quite professional. Early in her career, Philip had supported Elizabeth, not because he had been married to her half-sister, Mary, but because England would be a most helpful ally against France. The French were supporting Elizabeth's rival, Mary Stuart of Scotland. Philip saw a French plot to take over England and Scotland and wipe out Spain's connection with the Netherlands. Elizabeth also looked on Spain as an ally. She had good reason to fear France.

To the rest of the world, Spain looked like Europe's greatest power. She had conquered immense areas in the Americas, including the rich and civilized kingdoms of Mexico, Central America, and Peru. Philip had just annexed Portugal and now had the extensive Portuguese holdings in Africa and Asia. His infantry was generally conceded to be the best in Europe, and now Spain's armies were led by Alessandro Farnese, Duke of Parma, who was the greatest general of his time.

But Philip knew the other side of the story. Spain's population was small compared with that of France, and her resources were even smaller. The biggest part of the peninsula was arid plains, such as those of North Africa. Most of the rest was mountains. Philip's country was no cornucopia like that of his rival across the Pyrenees. His greatest resource was the gold and silver of the Americas, which he used to pay his superb army. But an army like that was expensive, and sometimes the soldiers went unpaid. When that happened, they were likely to riot and massacre civilians without any reason. Such behavior made the already difficult task of putting down a revolt in the Netherlands almost impossible. Besides open revolt in the Low Countries, there was dissension in the peninsula itself. Spain was a collection of kingdoms with long local memories that had been united for less than a century. And the Portuguese never considered themselves Spanish. Philip had the best legal claim to the crown of Portugal, but he wasn't the popular choice. He had to fight his way to the throne.

In the Netherlands, Parma won battle after battle, but the rebels would not give up. It was a religious war. The rebels were Calvinists and Philip's troops were Catholics. The war featured the ugliness that characterized all the European religious wars of the 16th and 17th centuries. Churches were burned, cities were sacked, and people, especially clergy, were massacred by both sides. The lowlanders could not match Philip's infantry, but they had a navy of shallow draft ships that could outmaneuver the Spanish on the high seas and traverse estuaries and rivers where Philip's ships could not follow. Philip had his hands full in the Netherlands. He could not afford a new war.

Neither could Elizabeth. Or she said she couldn't. In the war that followed, her admirals were continually begging for victuals for their men. Parliament was reluctant to vote for new taxes to support a war. Elizabeth was, her apologists say, forced to rely on her household budget. But she could easily have supported her navy in style for what she spent annually on her wardrobe. Further, this thrifty queen missed no opportunity to make money on the side. She made herself a partner with John Hawkins in Hawkins's slave trading business. That, in fact, was one cause of the friction between England and Spain. Slave-trading in the Spanish territories was a government monopoly. Hawkins and Elizabeth were cutting into Philip's profits. As relations with Spain became more strained, Elizabeth made herself a silent partner of the pirate admirals, Francis Drake, Martin Frobisher, and Hawkins, who preyed on the Spanish treasure ships. Drake and the others didn't confine their operations to the "Spanish Main." They seized Spanish ship in the Bay of Biscay and the English Channel, playing hell with Spain's efforts to supply its troops in the Low Countries. Spanish authorities in the Netherlands repeatedly called on Philip to invade England and put an end to these attacks on their supplies. Philip repeatedly refused.

Elizabeth, too, had to contend with war hawks. "Military and seafaring men all over England fretted and desired war with Spain. But the Queen shut her ears against them," the historian Camden wrote. The pirates and slavers wanted legal cover for their activities, and they wanted the additional support of a national effort. The Calvinists in England were another pro-war group. England at the time was divided among Calvinists, Anglo-Catholics, and Roman Catholics. The Calvinists wanted to help all Continental Calvinists, especially the Dutch rebels and the French Huguenots. But the religious division of her country was another reason Elizabeth wanted to avoid war.

A change of policy

Parma's victories in the Netherlands aroused a new fear in Elizabeth. She feared, with reason, that the rebels were about to offer sovereignty of the Low Countries to the King of France. Although a Catholic, the French monarch was an ancient enemy of Spain, and his dynasty had long coveted the Low Countries, where the French had ties of blood and language. Therefore, Elizabeth did her best to keep the rebellion alive. That so incensed Philip that he encouraged a Catholic plot to overthrow the Queen. Elizabeth now saw her main enemy to be not France, but Spain. She entered a defensive alliance with that other formidable woman across the Channel, Catherine de'Medici. The French went to war. Catherine sent a fleet under Filippo Strozzi carrying Dom Antonio, the pretender to the throne of Portugal, to seize the Azores. A Spanish fleet, under the Marquis of Santa Cruz, routed it in 1582. The next year, another French fleet, under Aymard de Chaste, again took Dom Antonio into battle. This time Santa Cruz's ships practically annihilated the French.

The victories gave Santa Cruz such confidence that he wrote to Philip urging an invasion of England.

Philip again refused, but relations with England were going from bad to worse. Elizabeth sent Drake and his pirate navy to ravage the Spanish West Indies. Then she sent 5,000 soldiers under the Earl of Leicester to help the Dutch rebels.

Philip took another look at the Santa Cruz plan. The Marquis had suggested a huge fleet of ships embarking with an army from Lisbon and invading England directly. Philip finally consented, but he modified the plan. The Spanish fleet was to clear the channel so that Parma and most of the army that was already in the Netherlands could cross the channel and invade England. While Philip was gathering ships, Elizabeth took care of a potential fifth column: She had Mary of Scotland beheaded.

The non-invasion of England

On January 30, 1588, the Marquis of Santa Cruz, Spain's most talented admiral, suddenly died. For some reason known only to himself, Philip appointed the Duke of Medina Sidonia to replace him. Medina Sidonia had never served in either the navy or the army.

Elizabeth had 34 ships in her private navy, but Drake had almost as many in his. The Queen called up Drake and the other pirates as well as all armed merchantmen. She appointed Lord Howard of Effingham commander-in-chief of the fleet. The largest English ships were as large as the largest Spanish ships, but they were lower above the water. Altogether, the English were able to send out 172 ships to the Spanish 130. The Spanish had more big-bore, short-range guns—489 to 98—but the English had more long-range light guns—1,874 to 635. The Spanish fleet included galleys and galleons, equipped with beaks for ramming, and a large complement of infantrymen. Spain was, after all, a Mediterranean power and had recently helped win that last galley fight, the Battle of Lepanto. It had not learned the lessons of Diu (see pg. 36) as well as the English had, although the victors at Diu were Portuguese. The English had never been strong in the ram-and-board tactics of galley warfare; the rough seas around their island made that type of fighting impractical. And English sailors had undoubtedly heard how Portuguese gunners destroyed the Turkish/Egyptian galleys off the Indian coast.

The Spanish fleet, known as "the Armada," got off to a bad start. After he went to sea, Medina Sidonia discovered that much of his food was putrid and his water casks leaking. Many of his men were sick. He asked Philip to postpone the expedition a year. Philip refused, but sent new supplies. On July 19, an English scout ship sighted the Armada entering the Channel. The Spanish saw the picket ship, but not the English fleet. Alonzo de Leyva, Medina Sidonia's second-in-command, recommended that they head directly for Plymouth, where the English were based, and attack them before they could reach the open sea. Spanish strength was in ramming and boarding, operations best suited to narrow waterways. But Medina Sidonia said the King had ordered them to go through the Channel and meet Parma.

The fighting began the next day. The English ships seized the "weather gauge," which meant they caught the wind before the Spanish did, giving them an advantage in maneuvering. The Spanish ships were massed in three divisions: the van, the main battle, and the rear division. The English were in a line. The English swept by the Spanish, firing broadsides at long range. The Spanish replied with their heavy guns but did little damage because the English were out of effective range.

The English didn't do as much damage as might have been expected, because the long-range guns were light. They had, however, thoroughly outmaneuvered the Spanish. They were deployed in line, giving them maximum use of their guns, while the Spanish were bunched up, with the guns of most of their ships blocked by their own fleet. Further, the heaviest Spanish guns pointed straight ahead, the most effective way for the galley tactics of head-on charge. The English guns lined the sides of their ships allowing broadsides. The English were able to sweep around the Spanish array and attack the ships in the rear division. To meet them, the whole Spanish fleet had to reverse direction, something not easily accomplished from the formation they had.

The English concentrated their fire on one ship at a time. *San Salvador,* the ship carrying the paymaster of the Armada and his money, caught fire and blew up. Two more Spanish ships were disabled. The loss of his sailors' pay was serious for Medina Sidonia, but not as serious as the loss of powder and shot wasted firing at out-of-range English ships. He'd have to put into a friendly port to resupply.

Howard realized that, too, and ordered a hot pursuit of the Spanish as night fell. Drake was to lead the pursuit, so he lighted a huge lantern on the stern of his flagship, *Revenge,* and set out. Suddenly the light disappeared, and the English pursuers were thrown into confusion. What happened was that Drake came upon one of the disabled Spanish ships. His piratical instincts got the better of him, and he stopped to loot the ship. He doused the lantern so he wouldn't have to share the booty with the other captains.

"He thinketh to cozzen us of our shares of 15,000 ducats;" wrote Martin Frobisher, "but we will have our shares, or I will make him spend the best blood in his belly."

The English confusion gave Medina Sidonia time to reorganize his fleet. He checked on his supplies and decided he still had enough ammunition to engage the English, but the next day both fleets were becalmed. The following day, the wind resumed, and this time the Spanish had the weather gauge. According to Howard's report, "it may well be said that for the time there never was seen a more terrible value of great shot, nor a more hot fight than this was." But little damage was done to either side. There was enough firing, though, to make the English send boats to shore to get more ammunition while armed merchantmen kept the Spanish busy. The Spanish fleet was still near the south entrance to the English Channel, with no friendly port in reach. Medina Sidonia sent a courier boat to Parma, telling him he would soon arrive. Then the Spanish fleet, with no shot left, fled up the Channel with the English in pursuit. Medina Sidonia still had 124 ships. Howard's fleet had scattered somewhat during the battle and resupply operations, but he still had 136 ships. Medina Sidonia had the Armada anchor in narrow waters off Calais. He wanted the English to close with him so he could begin ramming and boarding. The English, however, selected eight of their ships, set them afire, and sent them sailing directly at the Spanish fleet.

At about the same time, a courier arrived from Parma saying he wouldn't be able to meet the Armada with his troop ships and landing craft for at least two weeks. What happened was that the Dutch rebels' fleet had bottled up Parma's force in the harbor of Bruges.

When they saw the fire ships approaching, the Spanish panicked. They cut their anchor cables and put to sea. One Spanish galleasse, *Capitana*, was stranded on the beach. Howard then proved that a Queen's admiral could be as tempted by loot as any pirate. He led an attack on *Capitana* and took it after a stiff fight. Meanwhile, the rest of the Armada had sailed out of sight to the north, pushed by a strong wind from the south. The English finally caught up with the Armada, and there was more fighting, but there was no longer a chance of an invasion.

The end of the Armada

Even the weather had turned against the Armada. A tremendous wind from the south made it impossible for the Spanish to reverse course and try to reach Parma. To get back to Spain, the ships of the Armada had to sail around the north end of Scotland. And they were not only out of ammunition, they were running short of food and water. The weather turned worse. Many of the sailors became sick; others were weakened by the lack of food. They were not up to handling ships in heavy weather. Altogether, 63 of Medina Sidonia's ships were lost, mostly wrecked on the coasts of Scotland and Ireland.

The fate of most of the lost ships is simply unknown. Winston Churchill and a number of other authors have stated that they were driven aground in Ireland where the "wild Irish" slaughtered their crews—giving the impression that Ireland at that time was inhabited by naked cannibals who routinely killed all strangers. Some Spaniards shipwrecked in Ireland fell into the hands of English soldiers who indeed killed them. Others probably suffered the fate of those found by the O'Flahertys, the feudal lords of the Connemara area of Ireland. The "ferocious O'Flahertys" controlled 11 castles in western Ireland, but they wanted to curry favor with the English. They hanged the shipwrecked sailors. Irish folklore, however, has always maintained that most of the Armada survivors met a different fate. Like the Picts, the Gaels, the Welsh, the Normans, and all the other nationalities that found themselves on that island, they became Irish, and their descendants live in Ireland today.

Philip II accepted the defeat as God's will. Instead of blaming Medina Sidonia, he reinstated him as governor of Cadiz. Elizabeth celebrated the end of the Spanish peril by cutting off revenues to her sailors. On August 8, a week after the Armada moved out of contact, Howard wrote to the Queen's ministers, "I pray to God we may hear of victuals, for we are in great want." Two days later, he wrote, "Sickness and mortality begins wonderfully to grow amongst us; and it is a most pitiful sight to see, here at Margate, how men, having no place to receive them into here, die in the streets." And on August 29, "It were too pitiful to have men starve after such service...Therefore, I would rather open the Queen Majesty's purse something to relieve them, then they should be in that extremity."

The fruits of victory

The defeat of the Armada has become a milestone in English folklore. That's surprising if you look only at the physical results. There was an extended naval battle.

The English, with a superior fleet, had much the better of it, but the most remarkable thing about the battle was the small amount of damage either side inflicted over the course of a week. Like the *Kamikaze*, or divine wind, that destroyed Kublai Khan's fleet off Japan, the weather caused the greatest harm to the Spanish. England was not invaded, of course. But credit for that should go as much to the Dutch rebels as the English sailors.

The battle did have an effect on naval strategy. Alfred Thayer Mahan, arguing for the importance of coaling stations in the age of steam, pointed out that when navies were under sail, they could go anywhere, but modern ships needed bases where they could refuel. But if sailing ships did not need fuel, they did need ammunition if they were to fight. The Armada battle proved the need for friendly bases near the site of a fight. Henceforth, English grand strategy always aimed to ensure friendly coasts near the home islands.

The most important result of the defeat of the Armada was the boost it gave to English confidence. The inhabitants of an unimpressive island in the North Sea decided that they were a Great Power and proceeded to act accordingly. They built up an empire that lasted almost 400 years, and put to shame those of Alexander, the Romans, and even Genghis Khan.

Battle 28

Captured Germans going to the rear.

The Marne, 1914 AD
The Best Laid Plans...

Who fought: French (Joseph Joffre) and British (John French) vs. Germans (Helmut von Moltke the younger.)

What was at stake: The German domination of Europe and the spread of imperial autocracy.

"It is the 35th day," said the little man with the withered left arm. "We are besieging Rheims; we are 30 miles from Paris." The little man, Kaiser Wilhelm II of Germany, was happy. He thought everything was on schedule, as planned by Field Marshal Alfred von Schlieffen.

The Schlieffen Plan had German forces capturing Paris within 40 days. Schlieffen had calculated that it would take 40 days for the massive, but slow-moving, Russian military machine to mobilize enough to attack Germany. Under Schlieffen's plan, the French army would have been surrounded and defeated by the time Paris had fallen. Germany could then shift its army east and deal with the Russians. It could do that because of its excellent railroad net and meticulous planning by the Great General Staff. Since the elder Moltke had demonstrated how railroads could win wars in 1870, all European general staffs had become railroad experts. The German Great General Staff was the most expert of all.

The French Revolution and Napoleon had shown the power of mass armies, as opposed to the small bands of highly trained automatons that had characterized 18th-century warfare. Prussia had instituted compulsory military service for all men, who, after a period of active duty, would be in reserve forces. Reserve troops would get annual refresher training and be recalled to military service in case of war. All Continental European powers copied the Prussian system.

That left the problem of getting these potentially huge armies to the battlefield. Railroads solved that problem. The prime duty of the Prussian general staff was making plans for countering various potential enemies and scheduling trains to get men and munitions to the right places at the right times. In the middle of the 19th century, Prussia used its mobilization plans to defeat a succession of enemies, most memorably France in the Franco-Prussian War of 1870. That war resulted in the creation of the new German Empire. The King of Prussia became Kaiser (from Caesar), or Emperor, and the united Germany developed Europe's most powerful army.

Helmuth von Moltke the elder was the Prussian chief of staff who orchestrated the concentration of German forces against France. Alfred von Schlieffen, who faced a new problem, succeeded him. A revenge-seeking France had allied itself with Russia and was making friendly gestures toward its ancient enemy, Britain. France was less populous and economically weaker than Germany, but France combined with the other two nations could overwhelm Germany. Germany had allies, too, of course. But each was, in a sense, "a broken reed that pierceth the hand of him who leans on it." Austria-Hungary, its chief ally, was belligerent but had serious internal weaknesses. Italy, the third member of the Triple Alliance, did not want to go to war.

In the event of a two-front war, Schlieffen planned to immediately knock out the French army and any troops the British might send, and then face the Russians. He predicted that in the event of war, the French would thrust directly into Alsace and Lorraine, territories they had lost to Germany after the Franco-Prussian War. Schlieffen planned to create a new Cannae (see page 127).

Most people who remember Cannae at all think Hannibal's double envelopment of the Roman army was the key to the Carthaginian victory. Schlieffen knew better. The Romans lost because they were unbalanced: They were directing their force in the wrong direction. When they were exerting all their efforts against the yielding Carthaginian center, the Carthaginians attacked their flanks and rear.

Schlieffen's plan called for a massive German right wing to wheel through Belgium, cross the thinly defended Belgian-French border, and attack the French army's left flank and rear. At the same time, the French, he predicted, would be driving into Germany, where a weak left wing would fall back to draw the French into a trap. Schlieffen continued to refine the plan until his death. One touch was to mass troops on the Belgian-German border to induce the French to enter Belgium, thus putting the onus for violating the small country's neutrality on France, not Germany. His last words were reportedly, "Keep the right wing strong."

The war everyone was expecting finally broke out. Helmuth von Moltke the younger was chief of the German Great General Staff. When Serbian-backed assassins killed Archduke Franz Ferdinand of Austria-Hungary, Austria-Hungary issued an ultimatum to Serbia. Russia had assured Serbia of its backing. So far, Germany was not involved, although it was supporting Austria-Hungary. Russia began mobilizing its army. If it had mobilized only on the Austria-Hungary border, there was a chance a world war would not have begun. But all European mobilization plans were so intricate they were almost impossible to change—absolutely impossible at the last minute. Time was of the essence. The country that mobilized first could strike first. The country that struck first would probably win. So the Russian army was mobilized against Germany as well as Austria-Hungary. Germany declared war on Russia.

For a brief time, there was a chance that France might not join Russia in the war. The Kaiser tried to stop execution of the Schlieffen Plan. "That is impossible," Moltke told him. And that was that. Kaiser Wilhelm was later demonized by much of the world as an incarnate fiend, stained with the blood of innocents. In reality, he was a faintly ridiculous little man who liked to dress up in military uniforms and entertain visitors sitting on a wooden horse, an amiable blowhard who had a penchant for putting his foot in his mouth. He would have made a wonderful character in a musical comedy. Instead, an unkind fate had made him the unchallenged leader of a large and powerful nation.

...Oft gang agly

France did not remain undecided for long. She declared war on Germany, and Britain followed by also declaring war on Germany a short time later. France did not, however, oblige Germany by moving into Belgium first. But as Schlieffen predicted, she launched an attack into Lorraine.

The German invasion of Belgium was not the cakewalk Moltke & Co. expected. The Belgians resisted strongly, but their modern forts around Liege and Namur could not stand up to the Germans' enormous 42-centimeter and 30.5-centimeter howitzers. And the masses of German troops simply overwhelmed the Belgian army. French intelligence had predicted that the Germans would use both their active duty army and first line reserves in the attack. The Germans, however, had dipped much deeper into their reserves. They had called up twice as many men as the French expected.

British and French dispatches filled the newspapers of neutral countries with horror stories of German atrocities in Belgium. In the postwar revulsion against war, these stories were discounted as mere propaganda. But they weren't all propaganda. German soldiers did not throw babies up in the air and catch them on their bayonets. They did, however, take hostages, and shoot or bayonet hundreds of them after false reports of Belgian sniping. They killed 212 civilians at Andenne, 384 at Tamines, and 612 at Dinant. They shot scores of priests, saying they were inciting civilian resistance. In fact, there was no civilian resistance in Belgium. The Belgian government, fearing the sort of reprisals the Germans had taken against *franc tireurs* in the Franco-Prussian War, had collected civilian-owned guns before the invasion began. The killing of priests was mostly done by members of Max von Hausen's Third Army, who came from Saxony and had not completely recovered from the bigotry of the Thirty Years War period. The most notorious German atrocity occurred in the university town of Louvain. German troops killed 209 civilians, then burned the university and the town, leaving 42,000 people homeless. All this killing and burning was not done by battle-maddened infantrymen but by reservists who hadn't yet seen combat and were acting under orders.

The "rape of Belgium" was real, and it was not only immoral but also a serious mistake. It turned the neutral world against Germany, especially the big neutral across the Atlantic. The United States, determined at first to remain utterly aloof from the war in Europe, suddenly turned pro-Allies in spite of the fact that a huge proportion of its population had roots in Germany. The serious consequences of the "rape of Belgium" would come home to Germany in another three years.

The Belgian atrocities could not be blamed on Moltke and the Great General Staff. But Moltke made another mistake that would have consequences in weeks, not years.

When the German Empire was formed, its constituent states kept their own royalty and royal governments. These lesser kings, princes, and dukes were men to reckon with. Moltke did a lot of reckoning. Rupprecht, the Crown Prince of Bavaria, Germany's second largest state, commanded one of the two armies in the "weak left wing." Rupprecht did not like the idea of retreating and allowing the French on German soil. Pressured by princely pique, Moltke doubled the strength Schlieffen had planned for the left wing.

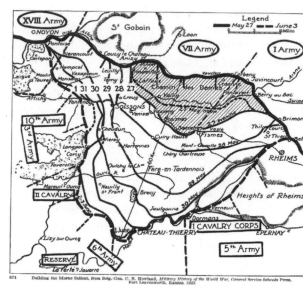

A map of the Marne.

When fighting began, the Germans were able to stop cold the French attack in the eastern section of the line. The French, therefore, never had a chance to dig themselves into a hole. Joseph Joffre, the French commander-in-chief, was able to deploy troops to meet the Germans coming through Belgium. He wasn't able to stop them. There were too many Germans. But surrounding the French Army and the British Expeditionary Force was going to be very difficult indeed. Rupprecht compounded the German trouble by launching his own invasion of France. That fared no better than the French invasion of Germany. And on August 20, the Russians invaded East Prussia, far ahead of von Schlieffen's schedule. They routed three German corps and collected 7,000 prisoners. Moltke hurriedly detached two corps from the offensive in the west and sent them to East Prussia.

Meanwhile, the French managed to collect enough troops to organize a new army, the Sixth, in Paris. It looked as if that would be desperately needed, because Sir John French, the British commander, was considering pulling out of the fight. The French Fifth Army under Charles Lanrezac had left his force unsupported at Mons and again at Le Cateau. Lord Kitchener, the British Minister of War, had to come to France and order Sir John back into battle.

The Marne

The German right wing was still advancing, but it may have been advancing too fast. As the German wing drove through Belgium and northeastern France, it had to detach units to garrison captured cities. At its extreme right was the First Army, under irascible, 68 year old Alexander von Kluck. Kluck was supposed to swing around Paris and head back east to surround the French and British and take them in the rear. Kluck was known as a hard driver, but it's easy to do your hard driving from a seat in an automobile. Since they'd left the German railheads on the Belgian border, his troops had been moving on their feet. The heat was ferocious—one of the warmest summers of the century. Most of Kluck's troops were reservists—clerks, machinists, teamsters, not professional soldiers. They weren't used to marching 20 miles every day. They were tired. They were also hungry. Bringing supplies across country was a real problem, and looting the farmland they passed through didn't entirely solve it.

The Germans had lost contact with the British. Instead of marching off into the void west of Paris, which would only exacerbate their troubles, they turned southeast to close with Lanzerac's Fifth Army. A British reconnaissance pilot noticed that the German First Army had changed direction. It was marching in front of Paris instead of enveloping it.

The French Sixth Army moved out of Paris to strike the German flank. The German general commanding the corps on the extreme right of the line, Hans von Gronau, struck first. His counterattack halted the French temporarily, but it also increased the danger to the German forces. Kluck's army had not been in contact with Karl von Bulow's Second Army. Gronau's advance against the French opened the gap.

The French and British now outnumbered the Germans on the end of the German right wing. Joffre ordered all French units to counterattack. Kitchener had already ordered Sir John French (who was not subject to Joffre's orders) to counterattack. Sir John, however, moved as if he were wearing lead shoes.

But even that was enough. A German reconnaissance pilot reported seeing four long columns of enemy troops moving into the gap between the German First and Second Armies. Moltke ordered a general withdrawal, and the Battle of the Marne was over.

Miracle of the Marne?

The Marne fight decided that 1914 was not going to be another 1870. There would be no quick German victory. If the Schlieffen Plan had succeeded, it's probable that the German army, especially if led by such emerging officers as Erich Ludendorff and Max Hoffmann, would have disposed of the Russians rather handily. Germany would have picked up more French territory, probably extended its boundaries into Russian Poland, and acquired some colonies from Britain. And the world might have gone on as it had most of the time since the fall of Napoleon.

But there was no quick victory for anyone. Instead, the Western Front settled into the massive meat grinder known as trench warfare. The Eastern Front was slightly more mobile but no less bloody. More combatants (though not civilians) were killed in World War I than in any other—even World War II. As the war went on, more countries became involved—Bulgaria, Turkey, Italy, Japan, and the United States. The war ended with the virtual exhaustion of the European powers and was followed by a tremendous depression and a wave of revolutions. Josef Stalin, Benito Mussolini, and Adolf Hitler, plus a crop of bush-league tyrants, emerged to lead the world into a new world war—a more terrible one, because whole populations, not merely armies, were the targets.

Battle 29

Rhodes and Malta, 1522 and 1565 AD
The Hellhounds

Who fought: Knights of St. John (Philippe Villiers de l'Isle Adam) vs. Turks (Suleiman the Magnificent).

What was at stake: The Turkish domination of Europe and the dominance of Islam and Eastern Civilization.

They had known it would be coming. On June 22, 1522, Gabriele Tadini di Martinego had arrived from Crete, where he had been building fortifications for the Republic of Venice. The famous engineer from Crema had told his hosts, the Knights of St. John, that the Grand Turk was on his way to assault their fortress, and he couldn't bear to miss that fight. Philippe Villiers de l'Isle Adam, grand master of the order, welcomed the Italian soldier heartily. Martinego was one of the foremost artillerymen of the age.

Now, at daybreak on June 26, the defenders of Rhodes saw 300 Turkish ships outside the great chain they had stretched across the entrance to their harbor. There were 10,000 of them in the first wave. Before long, there would be 100,000. L'Isle Adam had 600 knights and about 5,000 other soldiers, no mobile artillery, and only seven warships. The Knights had no way to oppose the landing. A month later, the Grand Turk himself—Suleiman the Magnificent—appeared with more troops and more artillery. The Turkish guns included 40 large bombards and 12 enormous basilisks. When the sultan arrived, they opened fire using a new weapon. For the first time in history, a city was bombarded with explosive shells. A single shot from one of these guns could knock down a house even if it missed.

The Turks might have expected that this first use of such a weapon would break the spirit of defending troops. But the Knights were no ordinary troops.

The Order of the Knights of the Hospital of Saint John the Baptist of Jerusalem was a ghost of the past. It was an order of monks that had been founded before the Crusades. The monks' original purpose was to operate a hospital for the benefit of Christian pilgrims in the Holy Land. The order grew and was organized by languages or "langues." There were the langues of Provence, Auvergne, France, Italy, Spain, England, and Germany, each with its own superior. When the First Crusade ushered in an era of virtually continuous war with the Muslim powers, the Hospitalers added fighting to their duties. They took vows of poverty, chastity, and obedience and cared for the sick and injured. But they also wore mail, rode chargers, and fought the enemies of Christendom with lance and sword.

Eventually driven out of the Holy Land, the Knights ended up on Rhodes. They never gave up fighting the Turks. Rhodes is a bare 10 miles from the shore of Anatolia, the heart of the Ottoman Empire.

While the Knights were watching the Turks set up their siege lines, Hernan Cortes was completing the conquest of Mexico; Portuguese envoys were being entertained in the imperial court at Peking; and the last Crusader stronghold had fallen more than three centuries before. A new day had dawned, but the Knights of St. John, now generally called the Knights of Rhodes, had not changed their objectives.

They had changed their techniques, though. The Knights relied on cannons and muskets more than lances and swords. They replaced their mail with the heavy plate armor worn by the most advanced European warriors. And these one-time desert-dwellers had become seamen. Their small fleet of galleys—seven, one for each langue—sallied out to capture Turkish merchant ships. Most important, they had fortified Rhodes in the most modern way. Thick, low walls, surrounded by dry ditches and partially hidden by an earth glacis, were able to defy cannons. Bastions and a variety of outworks made it possible to sweep the ditches with musket and artillery fire. Solid shot and even explosive shells could not breach underground shelters.

The Muslims called the Knights "the Religion," a term they had for their own orders of dervishes. They respected the soldier-monks for their military skill and their utter fearlessness. But they found their piracy intolerable. They called Rhodes "the Stronghold of the Hellhounds."

The first test

Mohammed the Conqueror, who had taken mighty Constantinople, decided to blot out the nest of pirates just off his coast. He sent an army and a fleet of 160 ships under Meshid Pasha. It arrived on May 23, 1480 and immediately tried to storm the west wall of the city. That bloody failure convinced Meshid Pasha that the Hellhounds were made of sterner stuff than most of his enemies.

Meshid shifted his attention to the Tower of St. Nicholas, an isolated fort on a peninsula north of the city. The Mediterranean galley of that time was, like its ancient namesake, a shallow draft ship capable of sailing, but rowed in battle. The difference was that its bow was covered by a wide deck on which cannons were mounted.

The Turkish commander sent his galleys charging the tower from the sea, while his infantry tried to storm it from the land. The bow guns belched, and the Janissaries clambered ashore while their comrades kept up heavy fire on the opposite side of the tower. The Knights replied with cannons and muskets. Galleys were wrecked on the beach and sunk in the water. Janissaries were shot down in heaps. Meshid Pasha withdrew his forces to try another tactic.

This time, he concentrated on the southeast wall of the city. The Turks aimed their heavy guns at the most vulnerable spots on the wall and began digging mines beneath them. They made two breaches in the wall, but when they charged into them, they found that the Knights had built new walls behind them and mounted cannons on those emergency barriers. The Turks were slaughtered. Before they could recover, the Knights charged out and smashed all the siege works.

Meshid moved back to the St. Nicholas Tower. This time, he built a floating bridge so his troops could go ashore *en massé* instead of in dribs and drabs. An English knight named Rogers swam underwater and cut the bridge's anchor cables so the current could carry it out to sea.

Meshid ordered two consecutive storms from the land against the tower. Turkish bodies piled up, but the Pasha couldn't get a foothold.

Meshid ordered an artillery bombardment all around the city to confuse the defenders about where he would strike next. While that was going on, his engineers secretly tunneled into the dry ditch. They began building an earth mound that would let attackers run over the top of the wall. The Knights met this threat with their trebuchet.

The trebuchet was a pre-gunpowder artillery piece invented about the time of the Crusades. Instead of relying on the torsion of twisted ropes, it used gravity. An enormous counterweight was mounted on the short arm of a pivoted beam with a missile carried in a sling at the end of the long arm. When the counterweight dropped, the long arm flew up and released the missile. The Knights' trebuchet could sling a missile up to 500 yards. Range could be adjusted by sliding the counterweight up and down on the short arm. Range also depended, of course, on the weight of the missile.

For this target, the Knights didn't need long range. The stones they threw were enormously heavy. They not only killed the mound builders and flattened the mound, but they also caved in the mining tunnels. The Knights followed up the trebuchet bombardment with another sortie. Meshid was back to ground zero.

The Pasha set up sharpened stakes outside the walls and sent word to the Knights that if they didn't surrender, they'd end up impaled on those stakes. The Knights laughed at him. Meshid redoubled his artillery and mining operations. The Turks made another breach in the wall, and the Pasha sent in his troops. This time, they included a suicide squad with orders to kill the Grand Master at all costs. The Grand Master, a Frenchman named Aubusson, was wounded, but the Turks who got into the city were annihilated. Meshid decided to cut his losses, which were enormous, and sailed back to the mainland.

Sultan Mohammed ignored Rhodes after that. So did his successors, Bayazid and Selim the Grim. But in 1520, Turkey got a new sultan, a new man with new ideas.

The Lawgiver

The Christian powers called him Suleiman the Magnificent, the man who expanded the Ottoman Empire to its greatest extent and who developed its greatest power. His own people, who saw him as a kind of reincarnation of his Biblical namesake, called him Suleiman the Lawgiver. Both nicknames were justified.

Suleiman had inherited an empire that had been conquered by nomads—his ancestors, the Osmanli (Ottoman to the Westerners) Turks—who were greatly outnumbered by settled peoples. The laws of the empire still reflected the mores of nomads. The Osmanlis were no longer wandering herdsmen, but they had not adapted to such innovations as urban living, schools, and guns. Suleiman tried to not merely bring his country up to date, but to get ahead of his European rivals.

He had almost the only regular army in Europe, but it was not large. The army's greatest strength was in its feudal cavalry. Suleiman modernized and expanded the army by greatly expanding the regular artillery to include 3,000 gunners. This was at a time when civilian contractors manned much of Europe's artillery. The Sultan wrote new regulations for the Janissaries, a Western corruption of *yenicheri,* or young troops. The regulations were sound enough to govern the conduct of sieges until the 19th century.

The Janissaries were slaves. So were government officials, who, like the Janissaries, had been taken in the "blood tax." Suleiman did not institute this system. What he did was promote the slave officials to the highest rank. Whereas Turkish nobles had headed the various branches of government, under Suleiman these posts went to the brightest graduates of the slave schools—the "organization." His friend and vizier, Ibrahim, to whom Suleiman gave the greatest power any Turkish vizier ever exercised, was a Greek, born of Christian parents.

Continual war upon unbelievers was expected of any Ottoman sultan. Suleiman was not so sure that additional conquest was best for his country. Turkey controlled the overland trade routes between Europe, India, and China. Trade, which thrives in peace, brought more wealth to the empire than war. But the Janissaries and the Spahis (regular cavalry) depended on loot for their income. If there were no campaigning, they could cause trouble. So when his courtiers told him the King of the Hungarians had killed his envoy, Suleiman ordered the Drum of Conquest to be sounded, and the army marched against Belgrade, a Serbian city held by the Hungarians.

After a siege of a week, the garrison surrendered. In his diary, Suleiman noted: "Suleiman [he always referred to himself in the third person] crosses the bridge and enters Belgrade, where he goes to Friday prayer in a church in the outer city, changed over into a mosque." The Hungarian captives were allowed to go home. The Serbs were sent to Constantinople, where they would serve their conquerors. It was a short and easy siege, so the Turks were merciful. Besides, the young sultan was still an idealist who believed in the brotherhood of man.

Back in Constantinople, Suleiman devoted himself to increasing trade with the West. There was only one thing interfering with Turkish trade: the Stronghold of the Hellhounds. That, Suleiman decided, had to be eliminated.

The great siege

The sultan would have liked the coming siege to be as easy as the siege of Belgrade. He hoped, in fact, that it might be easier. The tall, thin, gray-eyed, young sultan sent a messenger to the powerful white-bearded ancient who commanded the Knights. If the Knights of St. John surrendered, they would be transported to Crete or anywhere else they chose with all their relics and treasures, and any of the Christian Rhodians who desired it could be transported with them. If the Christian townspeople stayed, they would not be molested or robbed and could freely practice their religion. If they did not surrender, all would be killed.

As any of their old enemies from the Crusades could have foretold, the Knights would not surrender.

Suleiman was getting his first taste of real war. At first, he was optimistic.

"The Sultan changes the position of his camp," an early entry in Suleiman's diary reads. "Heavy bombardment silences the guns of the city."

Then the Turks let their guns cool and the Knights climbed out of their bomb-proof shelters and returned fire.

The diary recorded the mounting casualties, and the Turks had nothing to show for them. But Suleiman drove his men to greater efforts.

Turkish siege methods were not as sophisticated as those of the Italian masters who were peddling their services all over western Europe. The Turks, for example, drove their approach trenches, technically called "saps," directly at the walls of a besieged fortress. The Italians dug zigzag saps so a cannon ball could not traverse the length of the sap, killing everyone in it. To provide shelter for their sappers, as well as positions for their guns, the Turks dug parallel trenches at right angles to the sap every few yards. The difference in technique seldom made much difference. Few gunners could shoot accurately enough to enfilade a long length of trench.

But the Turks had fought few artillerymen like Martinego. The engineer/gunner was a master of what were then called the "mysteries" of artillery. He could use plumb lines to determine the center of a gun's muzzle and double plumb lines on a ruler to locate the center of the breech so a cannon could be aimed accurately. He most likely used the "gunner's quadrant," first described by his countryman, Niccolo Tartaglia, as an instrument to determine the angle of elevation. Certainly, Martinego used the few days he had before the invasion to pace off distances from the walls to various parts of the outlying area. He knew the amount of powder and the angle of elevation needed to achieve any range. The impact of Martinego's genius landed heavily on the Turks.

"The commander of the cannons is killed," reads a later entry in Suleiman's diary. "The chiefs of the firelock men and the cannoneers, wounded."

Stymied in their saps, the Turks turned to tunnels. They could dig under the walls and blow them up with gunpowder. Martinego had an answer for that, too. Like Giustiani at Constantinople (see **Constantinople, Part II, page 145**) Martinego planted the upper half of drums all along the inside of the walls, each covered with a few dry peas. The peas' dancing indicated where digging was underway. The Knights met mines with countermines.

"The miners meet the enemy, who use a great quantity of flaming naphtha," Suleiman wrote in his diary.

The defenders couldn't stop all the mines. The Turks dug no less than 54 tunnels. The walls were breached in some places. But there were always barriers behind the breaches, and ferocious Hellhounds behind the barriers.

"The troops penetrate inside the fortress, but are driven out with heavy loss by the use the infidels make of a new kind of catapult," Suleiman recorded.

Frustrated, the Sultan ordered a storm. Then another, and another. None brought lasting success. Suleiman began recording insignificant events as victories: "Some Circassians break in, carrying off four or five banners and a great plank that the enemy had filled with metal hooks to tear the feet of the besiegers."

The siege dragged on for weeks, then months. Suleiman tried surprise attacks. He tried carefully prepared assaults. Nothing worked. There were temporary successes. The troops broke through a section of wall held by the Langue of England. The old Grand Master himself led the counterattack that drove them out.

The Sultan began to grow desperate. He wanted to end the siege before winter.

"The earth and the stonework above the ground only will be the Sultan's," he proclaimed to his troops. "The blood of the people inside and the plunder will be yours." On September 24, he ordered an attack on all points. The Turks lost 15,000 men. The Knights lost 200.

The fruitless attacks went on. The weather grew colder. Suleiman ordered the ruined buildings of ancient Rhodes repaired to serve as winter quarters. Even the Janissaries began to grumble. Suleiman ordered the fleet to return to the mainland to seek shelter from the winter storms. That way, none of the troops could desert. At the end of October, he ordered no more general attacks.

On the first day of December, Suleiman sent word (indirectly, through a Rhodian civilian) that if the Knights surrendered, they could have the same terms he offered at the beginning of the siege. L'Isle Adam had sent envoys to the Holy Roman Emperor, the Pope, and the King of France begging for aid. The Christian powers, though, were too busy with their own feuds. The Grand Master weighed the possibilities. If the Turks took the city by storm, all his knights and soldiers, as well as all the Greek Christian civilians on the island, would be massacred. He asked for a truce of three days. Suleiman willingly granted it.

A wine ship from Crete carrying 200 volunteers landed on Rhodes in the dead of night. The Turks discovered it and considered the truce broken. A crowd of Janissaries gathered in front of the walls. A French artilleryman fired at them. The Turks replied with a wild attack on the whole circumference of the city. The Knights cut them down in droves.

In the Turkish camp, Suleiman totaled up his losses. In the six months of fighting, his forces had suffered 60,000 dead and uncounted wounded.

In the city, L'Isle Adam asked Martinego about the state of the defense. He considered the information and, on December 21, sent word to Suleiman that he would surrender on the terms that had originally been offered.

The Sultan accepted. He did not know that there were only 180 knights and 1,500 soldiers able to stand and that they had only enough gunpowder for 12 more hours of fighting.

L'Isle Adam left the city to call on the Sultan.

"You are worthy of praise, because you vanquished Rhodes and showed mercy," said the old soldier-monk.

Suleiman gave the Grand Master a robe of honor. He turned to his friend, Ibrahim, and remarked, "It is a pity that this fine old man should be turned out of his home." When the Grand Master went back to Rhodes, Suleiman returned the visit. He rode into the ruined city with only a couple of companions and told the knights outside the Grand Master's residence that he had come to inquire after the health of their master. The knights were amazed that the Grand Turk, sometimes called the Unspeakable Turk, was a good-looking, young man who could have been any of the Western soldiers they knew.

Suleiman was as good as his word. The Knights and their soldiers, as well as hundreds of Rhodians, were transported to Crete in Turkish ships. The wounded knights and soldiers left behind were taken to Crete as soon as they had recovered enough to be moved.

The Legacy of Rhodes

Suleiman never forgot the mud, the blood, the bodies, and the stink of death on Rhodes. For the next four years, the Drum of Conquest remained silent.

Then during the winter, while the sultan and his Pashas were hunting in the Balkans, the 12,000 Janissaries in Constantinople rioted. They wanted action, and they wanted loot. Suleiman returned and had the ringleaders executed, but he knew he'd have to take the campaign trail again. He followed the suggestion of his ally, King Francis of France, and attacked Hungary, a part of the Holy Roman Empire.

The Empire and France were at war, and the Empire was also at war with itself, as the Catholics battled the Lutherans. A purely Hungarian army gathered to defend Europe as the Turks advanced. For Suleiman, it was almost too easy. Near Mohacs, the Hungarian calvary charged the Turks. They cut through the first line of lightly armed Turkish feudal cavalry. They broke through the second line. Then the immovable Janissaries stopped them. Before they could recover, the Spahis and the feudal cavalry, who had deliberately let the Christians through their lines, closed in from their flanks and rear. For centuries after that, no matter what disaster overcame them, Hungarians would say, "But more was lost on Mohacs Field."

Suleiman recorded that victory in his diary. The experiences of Rhodes had made war even more disagreeable to the Sultan, but they had not made him more compassionate. At Rhodes, the naive young Sultan had a life-altering experience. He would never be the same. His diary records how the bright young man began to change to something much darker.

On August 30 he wrote: "The Sultan rides out. Order to the troops to bring in all prisoners to the council tent."

On August 31: "The Sultan seated on a throne of gold received the salutations of the viziers and officers; massacre of prisoners. Rain falls in torrents."

On September 2: "Rest at Mohacs. 20,000 foot soldiers and 4000 mailed riders of the Hungarian army are buried."

Suleiman put a Turkish garrison in Buda, the Hungarian capital, and established Janos Zapolya as a client king of Hungary. Then, as defender of the Sunni Muslims, he turned east to deal with the Shiite Shah of Persia.

Meanwhile, Ferdinand, brother of Emperor Charles, had himself proclaimed King of Hungary by the remnant of the Hungarian nobility. Ferdinand was already Archduke of Austria and King of Bohemia.

In 1529, Suleiman gathered between 125,000 and 200,000 soldiers and marched toward Vienna.

Vienna was nothing like Rhodes. Its crumbling walls were no more than six feet thick and seven feet high. Their outdated gun ports were too small for modern artillery pieces. Suleiman probably hoped to lure Ferdinand into meeting him with his field army. His army was strong in cavalry, and horses aren't much good at climbing city walls.

The first Austrians the Turks saw, however, were 5,000 old men, women, and children who had been expelled from Vienna because they were "useless mouths." The Turkish cavalry killed most of them. The horsemen then ranged far and wide around Vienna, killing peasants and burning houses. They, instead of a circumference of trenches, would keep help from reaching the city. During these operations, they slaughtered about 100,000 civilians.

Suleiman's siege forces occupied only the area south of the city. Their heaviest artillery had bogged down on muddy roads, following one of the rainiest summers in memory, but they didn't need it against the flimsy walls of Vienna. The defenders had supplemented their walls with earthworks, but Vienna was still nothing like Rhodes. The Turks began digging their usual saps and tunnels. They exploded mines, opening several breaches in the wall, one of them wide enough for 24 men abreast. Each time, though, they were blocked by emergency barricades manned by stern German and Spanish (Emperor Charles V was also King of Spain) infantry.

It was becoming obvious that Rhodes had changed more men than Suleiman. The Janissaries had lost their taste for siege work. Suleiman promised the Janissaries 1,000 aspers per man and 30,000 aspers plus promotion to the highest rank to the first man inside the city. On October 14, three enormous mines went off, opening a breach 130 feet wide. The Sultan ordered an attack. Nobody moved.

From the walls, Vienna's defenders saw Turkish officers flailing their men with whips and sword flats. For the first time in history, a Turkish army refused to attack when ordered. That night, the Turks began burning everything they didn't need and killing all their prisoners. Some they threw into the fires. Then they marched back to Constantinople. The Turkish army's threat to Western Europe had died at Rhodes. But the Turks had a navy, too.

War at sea

After Vienna, Suleiman turned his back on Europe to continue his feud with the Shah of Persia. To keep the Empire busy, he relied on sea power. His first admiral was an Albanian potter named Khair ed Din, who had acquired a ship and become a pirate. He was such a successful pirate that he soon had an entire fleet, mostly ships captured from the Christians. Suleiman built him a new fleet and recruited sailors to man it.

For several years after being expelled from Rhodes, old L'Isle Adam had visited the courts of Europe, looking for a home for his order. Finally, Charles V gave him Malta, a rocky spot between Sicily and Tunis the Emperor could find no use for. The Knights were delighted. From Malta, they could pretty well deny the western Mediterranean to Turkish shipping. The red-bearded Khair ed Din, nicknamed Barbarossa by the Christians, and his enormous battle fleet could raid far and wide, of course. The Knights couldn't stop him with their seven red galleys. But Barbarossa was never rash enough to attack the new stronghold of the Hellhounds.

On Malta, the Knights fortified two rocky peninsulas in the harbor and built a dockyard between them. At the end of the harbor, they built a detached fort called St. Elmo.

For years, the war ebbed and flowed. At one point, the Empire's navy, under Andrea Doria, captured Torgut himself—Barbarossa's most trusted lieutenant, the man the Christians called Dragut. Jean Parisot de la Vallette, one of the Knights who had helped defend Rhodes, saw Torgut chained to an oar in one of Doria's galleys.

"*Senor Dragut, usanza de guerra*," de la Vallette said in Lingua Franca. ("Mr. Dragut, it's the way of war.")

"*Y mudanza de fortuna*," Torgut replied cheerfully. ("And a change of luck.")

De la Vallette hastened to Doria and urged him to accept the ransom Barbarossa had offered for Torgut. De la Vallette, too, had once been a galley slave on a Muslim ship.

De la Vallette and Torgut were to meet again, years later. At that time, de la Vallette was Grand Master of the Knights of Malta, as the order was now called. Torgut was commander of all Turkish naval forces, Barbarossa having died. Torgut was the only commanding admiral in that seesaw war between Muslims and Christians who had never been defeated. And Suleiman was a bitter old man who had executed his best friend and his two oldest sons and was dying of cancer. The sultan now had one passion: to even the score with the Religion, the Hellhounds, who had frustrated him so long ago and were now raiding right up to the Dardanelles. He ordered an attack on Malta.

On May 18, 1565, a Turkish force under Piali Pasha and Mustafa Pasha landed on Malta. It consisted of 30,000 men, including 7,000 Janissaries and 6,000 Spahis. Opposed to them were 500 Knights, 1,300 Spanish soldiers, and 4,000 sailors and Maltese. The Turkish artillery had been especially cast for this expedition. One gun weighed 40 tons and threw 200-pound balls. Two more weighed 20 tons and threw 90-pound shot. For their artillery, the Turks brought 100,000 iron cannon balls and for both guns and mines, 170 tons of gunpowder.

The siege turned into a Turkish disaster long before its conclusion. Torgut was killed. With Torgut died Turkish chances of securing mastery of the Mediterranean.

Turkish attacks continued. The Turks eventually took an outpost, Fort St. Elmo, at a cost of 4,000 men.

For the next 73 days, the Turks assaulted the citadel. They tried to cut the chain across the harbor, but Maltese swimmers with knives in their teeth did in the Turkish engineers. The Turks dragged galleys overland to attack the citadel. They lost all the ships and all the crews. They made a breach in the wall of Castle St. Michael, the fortification on one of the peninsulas of the citadel. Mustafa ordered a continuous storm of the breach. The Knights and their men at arms stood in the breach and cut down a continuous stream of Turks. Mustafa finally stopped the slaughter by calling off the attack. He would try a new plan. His army would attack the citadel at all points. Somewhere the thin line of Knights and men at arms would have to break.

Then the Turkish lookouts saw a Spanish fleet bearing down on Malta. The Turks launched their own galleys and sailed away.

The old soldier fades away

Suleiman was furious. He was convinced that the army could accomplish nothing unless he were there to lead it. He ordered the Drum of Conquest sounded. The army would invade Austria. Unable to sit on a horse, he was carried in a litter. The army was heading for Erlau in the Carpathians, where he expected to find the Austrian army. On the way, Suleiman heard that a Hungarian fort called Sziget was holding out. Sziget was a minor fort, not a Vienna, not even Malta. But the Sultan wanted to wipe away the stain of unsuccessful sieges. He ordered a detour.

The Turkish force attacked Sziget furiously on August 5, 1566. The officers wanted to be able to tell the sultan it had fallen before nightfall. It didn't. The attacks went on. On August 29, the sultan offered the lord of Sziget, Count Miklos Zriny, a kingdom if he would surrender. He wouldn't. Suleiman told his Janissaries to fill in the moat. If they didn't do it quickly, he said, he would fill it with their testicles.

On September 4, the sultan died. His vizier, afraid that the army would run away if they learned Suleiman was dead, had his body secretly embalmed and propped up on a throne. The attacks continued. With his castle crumbling around him, Count Zriny put on his best armor and led his followers in a counterattack. All were killed. The sultan's death could not be concealed any longer. The Turkish army forgot about the Austrian army and returned to Constantinople.

His son, aptly called Selim the Sot, succeeded Suleiman. Turkey was now launched on the course that would lead to its being "the Sick Man of Europe." The Ottoman Empire had reached the height of its power under Suleiman the Magnificent. But under Suleiman, at the sieges of Rhodes and Malta, it began a long but steady decline into what we now call the Third World.

Battle 30

The Moors attacking the Franks.

Tours, 732 AD
The Sweep of the Crescent

Who fought: Franks (Charles Martel) vs. Moors (Abd ar Rahman).

What was at stake: The survival of Christianity and Western civilization.

In 100 years, the Sons of the Prophet had conquered most of the known world. From Arabia, an arid, barren land of few resources, they had swept over Syria, Mesopotamia, and Persia, right up to the borders of China. In the other direction, they had conquered Egypt and the rest of North Africa, crossed the Straits of Gibraltar, and then conquered Spain in a single year. The huge and powerful Empire of China had checked the Arab advance. So had the highly organized Eastern Roman Empire. But Islam continued to expand. Moorish Muslims pushed ever deeper into Africa. Other Moors eyed the fertile fields of what once was Roman Gaul. Muslim conquests had already proved that God was with them, they thought. And across the Pyrenees to Gaul looked like the direction He had chosen for them.

Gaul was anything but organized. The Visigoths had defeated the Romans and had taken their province, but they had been routed by the Franks and driven into Spain, only to be conquered by the Moors. The Frankish Merovingian kings, descended from one of the chiefs who helped defeat Attila **(see Chalons, page 180)**, had degenerated into a line of feckless playboys who frittered away their power. Now Gaul and the adjacent area of Germany were a welter of warring baronies. The Franks were the dominant people. They

170

had gained their power two ways. First, they became Catholic, instead of Arian, Christians, adopting the religion of the Gaulish population. Second, they kept up their ancient infantry tradition. The other German invaders of Rome's empire had been mainly horsemen. The Frankish foot formations had defeated cavalry again and again. Only the original Huns and the Byzantines under Narses (see **Busta Gallorum, page 94**) had found an answer to Frankish tactics. But though the Franks were a single people, they were not a single state. They had many jealous lords. And the other German peoples had not disappeared. There were Visigoths in the south and Swabians and Bavarians in the East. Just outside any lands claimed by the Merovingians, there were pagan Saxons and Danes in the north who loved to raid over the border. Gaul, in short, looked even riper for conquest than Spain had been.

The Muslim conquest began the usual way: with plundering raids. The Moors, descendants of Hannibal's Numidians, had always been interested in plunder. The raids also served another purpose: They weakened the enemy leadership and terrorized the enemy population. Musa, conqueror of Spain, began raiding Gaul in 711, immediately after destroying the Visigoth kingdom. Raiding was followed by conquest. In 719, the Moors occupied Narbonne; in 725, they took Carcassonne and Nimes. In 726, the Moors raided up the Rhone Valley as far as the Vosge Mountains. They besieged Bordeaux but were defeated by Duke Eudo of Acquitaine.

The mayor of the palace

While the Spanish Visigoths were falling before the Muslims, the Franks, Visigoths, and other tribes in Gaul were experiencing different kinds of trouble. It began long before Tarik the Moor landed the first Muslims at the rock that bears his name, Gibraltar (Gebel al Tarik—the Mountain of Tarik). Germanic chiefs made themselves little sovereigns, and the king of Frankland stopped ruling. Power passed to his chief minister, called the mayor of the palace.

The title has nothing to do with mayors as we know them, and precious little to do with palaces. It comes from the ancient Roman title *major domus*, which has nothing to do with restaurants. The *major domus* was the chief servant in a rich man's house, literally the most important in the house. The mayor of the palace was the most important of the king's men. His duties were those of the Roman Empire's Master of Soldiers.

In 687, Pepin II, mayor of the palace, made himself master of the three major provinces of Gaul: Austrasia, Neustria, and Acquitaine. But when Pepin died in 714, Gaul again plunged into anarchy. In the confusing struggle that followed Pepin's death, his illegitimate son, Charles, succeeded him as mayor of the palace, and Duke Eudo of Acquitaine declared his independence. Charles called up his troops. Under Frankish law, all free men could be called to military service, although usually only some of them had to serve. Charles had Neustria to begin with, and he soon conquered Austrasia. Then he turned on Acquitaine and forced Duke Eudo to submit. Charles was campaigning against the Saxons and Swabians when he learned of the Moorish raid up the Rhone. The Moors were gone before he could do anything about them. But they would be back.

The road to Tours

The Moors usually came around the eastern end of the Pyrenees. The Mediterranean coast of Gaul was slowly being eaten up by the Spanish Muslims, who moved east and north from Narbonne. In 732, however, the threat came from the western Pyrenees. A Moorish chieftain, Othman ben abi Neza, became the ally and son-in-law of Duke Eudo. Othman's domain was in southern Gaul, on the north side of the Pyrenees. The alliance with the powerful Christian duke and the mountains between him and Spain gave Othman a false sense of security. He declared his independence.

Emir Abd ar Rahman of Spain crossed the mountains to deal with the rebel, apparently at the pass of Roncevalles, later the site of Roland's last battle. Othman fled into the mountains, where he committed suicide rather than face capture. Abd ar Rahman, now north of the Pyrenees, decided to move into the heart of Gaul. According to Muslim sources, he was a general who made careful plans, so it probably was not a spur-of-the-moment decision.

Abd ar Rahman led his main army due north, along the Atlantic coast, but sent a second column east, toward Arles, to distract the Christians. Eudo called up his levies and met the main Moorish army at Bordeaux. The second battle at Bordeaux was quite different from the first. The Moorish cavalry, mostly unarmored and mounted on agile horses, swarmed all around Eudo's men, throwing javelins, charging with lances, and swiftly retreating to strike a new point. Eudo's army was routed. Abd ar Rahman sacked and burned Bordeaux, then continued north.

Charles, the strongman of the Franks, was ready this time. He called up his levies, all infantry, of course, and was joined by what was left of Eudo's forces. Eudo again pledged his fealty to Charles. Charles then marched to Tours to intercept the Muslims. Tours is far north of Bordeaux, but Charles's army was necessarily much slower than Abd ar Rahman's. By the time he reached Tours, the Moors had already looted the city. Abd ar Rahman had, in fact, turned south toward Poitiers. The Moors had by-passed Poitiers in their haste to loot the rich abbey at Tours. Now they planned to besiege Poitiers.

Charles's footmen came panting after the Moors. Abd ar Rahman was not in a hurry. He was not fleeing. He had dispatched columns far and wide to loot, massacre, and devastate a wide belt of this infidel land. When he heard that the Franks were approaching, he called back his columns.

The men of the north

The two armies met near Poitiers. Few details survive, and information about the numbers of the antagonists are wildly exaggerated by both Christian and Muslim writers. It seems clear that both armies were very large for those times. Apparently they spent a week in minor skirmishing, feeling each other out. Then Abd ar Rahman sent his horsemen charging the densely packed mass of Frankish footmen. The Arabs and Berbers hurled javelins as they approached, but all the Franks had large shields. Most of them wore metal helmets and those in the front ranks had mail shirts. The Franks answered the javelin attack with their national weapon, the *francisca*, a short-handled throwing axe. A francisca thrown by an experienced axe-man could split a shield or cleave most mail. Few of the Moors had either shields or armor.

The Muslims scattered and charged again. Some threw javelins, others attacked with short lances. Few horses, though, can be made to charge a line of spears. The Moors tried, but the Frankish line remained unbroken.

"The men of the north stood as motionless as a wall," reported a monkish chronicler. "They were like a belt of ice frozen together, and not to be dissolved as they slew the Arab with the sword."

A Muslim chronicler reported, "The hearts of Abd ar Rahman and his captains were filled with wrath and pride, and they were the first to begin the fight. The Moslem horsemen dashed fierce and frequent forward against the battalions of the Franks, who resisted manfully, and many fell dead on either side until the going down of the sun. Night parted the two armies, but in the gray of the morning the Moslems returned to the battle. Their cavaliers had soon hewn their way into the center of the Christian host."

If they did, they didn't stay long. Christian sources deny that there even was a second day. On the second day, they say, the Franks again lined up to do battle, but there were no Muslims in sight. Charles sent out scouts who reported that the Moorish camp had been abandoned. The Muslims had not even taken the plunder they'd accumulated.

What's certain is that Abd ar Rahman did not return with them. According to a Christian writer, "The Austrasians, vast of limb and iron of hand, hewed on bravely in the thick of the fight; it was they who found and cut down the Saracen king."

When they found their emir dead, the Moors fled south precipitously. They did not return. The tide of Muslim conquest was again stopped. And this time the check was not administered by a powerful empire, but by a normally disorganized crowd of semi-barbarous tribesmen.

For years, historians pooh-poohed the contention of Gibbons and others that Tours saved Western civilization. They held that Abd ar Rahman's expedition was nothing but a raid for plunder. But currently the consensus is that the "merely-a-raid" theory is going to the opposite extreme.

To anyone observing conditions in Gaul as Abd ar Rahman undoubtedly did, that country looked like an even better prospect for conquest than Spain. And if the Emir of Spain planned no more than a giant raid, raiding, as pointed out above, was a normal Arab preliminary to conquest. After Tours, there was never another Muslim raid on a scale that even approached Abd ar Rahman's expedition. Most of the raiding went in the other direction, with Franks raiding into Spain.

As for Charles, after Tours, his countrymen called him "Charles Martel," Charles the Hammer, the same nickname the Hebrews had given Judas Maccabeus (**see Emmaus, page 113**). Charles Martel initiated a reform of the Frankish military system. He concluded that although infantry was effective in a set-piece battle, it was too slow to deal with the many threats to his kingdom—Moors, Saxons, Danes, Swabians, Lombards, and others who could attack from every direction. He organized a cavalry unit to be his personal bodyguard which slowly developed into a requirement that all Franks who could afford it must appear mounted when called out to fight. Charles's encouragement of cavalry was one of the principal factors creating European chivalry, an institution that would be a major influence on Western history for the next 700 years. Charles followed his victory at Tours by driving all of the Moors out of Aquitaine.

Charles Martel pushed his religion as vigorously as his Muslim counterparts, but he used different methods. He sent Irish and Anglo-Saxon monks east and north to convert the heathen Germans. Charles decided to become king in name as well as in fact, and he founded the Carolingian Dynasty. His grandson, known as Charles the Great, or Charlemagne, founded an empire he declared to be a restoration of the Western Roman Empire and was, in fact, the political base of Western Civilization.

Battle 31

Tanga, 1914 AD
Doves

Who fought: German colonial troops (von Lettow Vorbeck) vs. British colonial troops (Insert commander here).

What was at stake: In the short-term, control of East Africa. In the long-term, proving the equality of the races on the battlefield.

"I wish to take this opportunity to make it abundantly clear," said Sir Conway Belfield several months after World War I had broken out, "that this colony has no interest in the present war except in so far as its unfortunate geographical position places it in such close proximity to German East Africa." Sir Conway Belfield was the governor of British East Africa, later named Kenya.

His German counterpart, Dr. Heinrich Schnee, could not have agreed more. As colonial governors went in 1914, Heinrich Schnee was one of the most enlightened. The colony had 1,000 schools for blacks. Literacy in German East Africa was higher than in any country on the continent. Schnee developed an institute of tropical biology and agriculture. Coffee plantations flourished. So did the native farmers, who were pretty much left alone. German colonists still lorded it over the Africans, but not the extent the British did in neighboring British East Africa.

"Where the natives are concerned, the English are remarkably narrow-minded; it never occurs to them to regard them as human beings," wrote Karen Blixen, a

Danish woman who had just settled in British East Africa. Blixen would later become famous as the writer Isak Dinesen. Most English colonists assumed that Africans were an inferior race, capable of only the most menial tasks. The colonists thought they would always need Europeans to guide them.

Schnee, on the other hand, saw Africans as people with the potential to develop their talents to the same extent as Europeans. Among white people in Africa, Europe, or North America, Schnee was, in this regard, very much in the minority in 1914. One of the few whites in Africa who agreed with him was the military commandant of German East Africa, Lt. Col. Paul Emil von Lettow Vorbeck.

But Schnee and von Lettow Vorbeck disagreed completely on another fundamental matter.

Schnee wanted to keep East Africa neutral. He believed it was his duty to do whatever is best for the colony. He could not see how involving his people in a European war over matters of absolutely no interest to them could benefit them. Besides, there was no way German East Africa could be saved if war came there. The British Royal Navy controlled the seas, so no reinforcements could come from Germany. Britain could drown German East Africa in men from its colonies, as it had drowned the Afrikaners in the Boer War a few years before.

Von Lettow Vorbeck agreed that the odds were heavily against Germany in a colonial war. But he believed that he had a duty to draw as many enemy troops away from Europe as possible. He told Schnee war was coming, whether he liked it or not, and he had better prepare for it.

Schnee, in turn, pointed to the General Act of Berlin of 1885, an international conference at which all African colonial powers declared that in case of war in Europe, all African colonies would remain neutral, if everyone agreed. Schnee saw that the only two who had to agree were the Germans and the British. The French did not border his colony and the Belgians and Portuguese were unlikely to initiate any fighting. Schnee held a number of consultations with Norman King, the British consul. London was encouraging but non-committal. Finally, after conferring with his superiors in Britain, Consul King said although London would put nothing in writing, it was inclined to honor German East Africa's neutrality if the German colony remained strictly neutral.

Hawks

Neither Schnee nor von Lettow Vorbeck hoped there would be a war. Others did. One was an Englishman named Richard Meinertzhagen. Meinertzhagen was on duty with the Indian Army as an intelligence officer. A big game hunter and an ornithologist, he had previously commanded native troops in East Africa. He wanted action, preferably in Africa.

Meinertzhagen was an Englishman with a German name. Another hawk was a German with an English name. Thomas Prince, now Thomas von Prinz, was the son of an English father and a German mother. He had gone to British schools until he was 15. Then his parents died, and he went to live with relatives in Germany. After he graduated from Germany's Ritter Akademie he tried to get a commission in the British Army. He was turned down. So he attended the German military academy at Kassel, where he met von Lettow Vorbeck. He took part in Germany's colonial wars in Africa, where the Africans gave him a nickname—Bwana Sakharani, "the Gentleman Who is Drunk with Fighting" or "Lord Berserker"—and the Germans gave him a von. He Germanized his name to Prinz and became a super-patriot. Although retired from the army, he raised a black and white volunteer force and placed it at von Lettow Vorbeck's disposal. He needed the help.

Von Lettow Vorbeck 's regular army was a few hundred black *askaris* (from *askar*, Arabic for soldier) with white officers. The troops were armed with ancient Mauser 1871 rifles—a single shot, black powder weapon that left an enormous cloud of white smoke after each shot. The old Mauser was good enough for keeping order among spear-armed tribesmen but was totally obsolete for modern war. Lettow sent dispatch after dispatch to Berlin begging for better equipment, especially newer rifles. He got some uniforms, but few rifles. Berlin knew it would soon need all the modern rifles it had in Europe.

In British East Africa, the regular military was no better off than in its German neighbor. Its equipment was nearly as obsolete, and its askaris were not so well trained. The British settlers did not want the King's African Rifles to be too effective. As Judith Thurman, a biographer of Isak Dinesen, puts it, "They were afraid to arm the natives with weapons that could be turned against them; and they were afraid that the Africans—who were soldiers of great prowess, stamina, and courage—would lose respect for their white superiors." When the settlers organized a militia, it was as much to guard against a black revolt as against a German invasion. Karen Blixen wrote to her mother that "in the event of a native uprising it [her farm house] has been chosen as headquarters and assembly point for all the farmers in the district."

The settlers were not, in fact, worried about the war. As soon as war was declared, there was a rush of war fever. "Bands of settlers," wrote a witness, "cantered into Nairobi on horses and mules, and formed themselves into mini-regiments of irregular cavalry. Their weapons were fowling pieces and elephant guns, their uniforms tattered bush jackets and broad-brimmed tera hats with fish-eagle feathers protruding from leopard-skin puggarrees." But the war fever soon wore off, and the "troops" went back to their farms.

The settlers knew the Germans could not win. They knew that an army would come from India that would squash the German army like a bug. Their complacency annoyed the new settler, Karen Blixen. "One cannot help—despite ancient hatred of the Germans— reacting against the incredible boastfulness of the English," she wrote to her mother.

War

That summer, Gavrilo Princip fired the shot that killed the Austrian archduke and tens of millions of others. "The lights began going out all over Europe," as a British politician said. But in Africa, the lights stayed on for a while.

The German cruiser *Konigsberg* undid Schnee's plan for a neutral German East Africa. Just before war was declared, *Konigsberg* left Dar es Salaam to go commerce raiding in the Indian Ocean. On August 6, less than a week after the opening of the war, *Konigsberg* captured the British steamer *City of Winchester*. The British began seriously hunting *Konigsberg*. Somehow, the British Foreign Office had not told the navy about King's discussions with Schnee. Two British cruisers entered Dar es Salaam harbor. When they couldn't find the German cruiser, they shelled the radio tower. The governor fled inland to Morogoro. In spite of his efforts, war had come to German East Africa.

Von Lettow Vorbeck now took over. He ordered Tom von Prinz to take his troops to the Kilimanjaro area and raid British outposts and cut all telegraph and telephone lines and the Uganda Railway. That would induce the British to send troops to East Africa. Von Prinz immediately took the British railroad station at Taveta, driving off the British troops stationed at the town. Then he began mining the railroad, tearing up track, and cutting communications wires.

The British were coming, but it took them a while. Meanwhile, the Germans were raiding in all directions. This was a good trick, considering that von Lettow Vorbeck had only 216 German officers and 2,540 black askaris at the beginning of the war. He sent German officers and askari NCOs around the colony to recruit new askaris. He enlisted large numbers of civilian settlers as auxiliaries, called on reserves and latched on to any volunteer talent like Tom von Prinz.

Von Lettow Vorbeck's highest-ranking volunteer was Kurt Wahle, a retired major general in the army of Saxony. Wahle was in Africa visiting his son when the war broke out. He came to von Lettow Vorbeck, and although he greatly outranked the lieutenant colonel, offered to serve under him. Von Lettow Vorbeck put him in charge of transportation. In a few weeks, the general vastly improved the efficiency and security of the German supply routes. Next, von Lettow Vorbeck gave Wahle 600 men and launched him at Kisumu, a port city on Lake Victoria, which was the terminus of Britain's Uganda Railway. The British sent a steamboat full of troops to stop Wahle, but the German armed tug *Muanza* drove it off. The British then attacked overland with the South African Mounted Rifles. The Afrikaner mounted infantry had repeating rifles using smokeless powder. The German askaris' single-shot black powder Mausers were definitely outclassed. Wahle lost a quarter of his officers in that battle. Lettow's main aim, though, was not to win battles but to siphon enemy strength from France.

In London, Lord Kitchener, although one of the most overrated soldiers in English history, was not foolish enough to take troops from France to deal with a minor annoyance in East Africa. But the settlers in Africa were complaining, and the newspapers told of the threat to the colony by the "ruthless" and "ferocious" von Lettow Vorbeck. Kitchener agreed to transfer a partially-trained battalion of the North Lancashire Regiment and 10,000 distinctly third-rate troops from India to East Africa.

"They constitute the worst in India," Richard Meinertzhagen wrote in his diary, "and I tremble to think what may happen if we meet with serious opposition." Captain Meinertzhagen was intelligence officer for the Indian expedition.

Von Lettow Vorbeck's intelligence service, based on a network of black agents who regularly crossed the border, was pretty good. He knew the Indians were coming. He knew about when they'd arrive. But he didn't know where they'd strike. The British plan was for one army to hit the Germans in the Kilimanjaro area, where Lettow's strength was concentrated. The second army would make an amphibious landing at Tanga in northern German East Africa, the colony's second largest port. Tanga was the Indian Ocean terminus of one of the colony's two east-west railroads. The other terminus on that road was Moshi, Lettow's headquarters near Kilimanjaro. The British knew most of the German troops would be found between those two points. They were to be crushed in the Indian nutcracker.

Tanga

British intelligence officers in Africa had assured the commander of the Tanga landing force that Tanga was unoccupied. Meinertzhagen pointed out, however, that because of the railroad, von Lettow Vorbeck could have troops there in short order. He was ignored. The commander of the King's African Rifles offered his unit as pre-landing scouts because they were African and knew the territory. Major General

Arthur Aitken, commander of the landing force, said the service of the KAR would be unnecessary. His "magnificent" Indian troops would have no trouble beating a bunch of blacks. He said he intended to "thrash the Germans before Christmas."

Captain F.W. Caulfield, commander of the landing force's naval escort, heard about the agreement between Schnee and King, but he didn't hear that it had ended. He insisted in sending a ship into Tanga harbor with a white flag to inform the Germans that all deals were off. So von Lettow Vorbeck learned that Tanga was a target. There was a further delay while the British swept the harbor for non-existent mines. Although they didn't find any, Caulfield remained suspicious. He persuaded Aitken to land about a mile from the town, out of sight behind a headland. It was 9:30 p.m. on November 2—almost 24 hours after they first appeared—before the first British troops, a mere two companies, landed. They found themselves in a swamp swarming with crocodiles and poisonous snakes. They had landed in the worst possible spot.

The British landed troops all through the night. At dawn, they attacked, reaching the outskirts of Tanga. Lettow was still moving troops down the rickety railroad from Moshi, but his handful of askaris brought the Indians to a standstill.

More British troops landed and tried to outflank the German askaris, but the brush was too thick for them to see anything. The German askaris didn't have to see anything—they just hosed down the brush with machine guns. Some British attempted to rush the machine guns, but they were all wiped out. British officers tried to get the Indians to resume their advance, but they refused to move. The German askaris counterattacked. The Indians couldn't see them in the dense brush, but they could hear them. So they broke and ran. Brigadier Michael Tighe reported to Aitken that his 2,000 Indians were outnumbered by "2,500 German rifles." Meinertzhagen, who had been present through all the action, said, "From what I saw it was more like 250 with four machine guns." Meinertzhagen was right. The British force lost 300, mostly officers and NCOs.

Von Lettow Vorbeck got his last troops into Tanga at 3 a.m. on November 4. He bicycled into town to look over the situation and even passed through the British-held sector. At the telegraph office he found a message from Schnee forbidding him to fight in Tanga. He ignored it, and from that point on, he, not Schnee, would be the top German authority in German East Africa. He had about 1,000 men in Tanga, askaris and von Prinz's settlers. Aitken had about 8,000.

The British didn't resume the attack until noon. By that time, most of the Indians had already emptied their canteens. By 3 p.m., they had advanced only 600 yards. British troops were dropping from heat exhaustion.

The German machine gunners had set up interlocking fields of fire. Members of the one company of askaris with the modern Mauser 98 rifles were sniping from treetops.

The fighting was house-to-house. The German askaris began to push back the fading Indians. The English of the Lancashire battalion were also forced back. During their retreat, the Lancs passed through a grove full of wild beehives. Annoyed by the commotion, the bees—the "African killer bees" of modern horror stories—attacked them. The English soldiers were convinced that the Germans had wired the beehives to trigger the attack. They hadn't; attacking the troops was the bees' own idea.

By dawn on November 6, von Lettow Vorbeck was in firm control of Tanga. The British evacuated after sending Meinertzhagen to the Germans with a white flag to arrange a truce. The attackers had 800 killed, 500 wounded, and hundreds more missing. Lettow captured 16 machine guns, hundreds of rifles, and 6,000 rounds of ammunition, along with other supplies. His own losses were trifling, except for the death of his old friend, Tom von Prinz.

When the British appeared off Tanga, von Lettow Vorbeck had sent messages to all his units in the Kilimanjaro area to come to Tanga as soon as possible. The message didn't reach the troops at Longido, commanded by a major named Kraut. (A little later, von Lettow Vorbeck's enemies would field a general named Brits.) That was a lucky break for von Lettow Vorbeck. The second prong of the British offensive ran right into Kraut's force while Aitken's men were landing at Tanga. Kraut had one company of settlers and three companies of askaris—86 Germans and 600 Africans. The British, more of the Indian Army, had 1,500 men. The Indians fought bravely, charging the German machine guns, but the firing stampeded the mules that were carrying their supplies. With the mules gone, the soldiers had only the water in their canteens. That night, the Indians withdrew, and the first British offensive was dead.

The British generals, of course, greatly overestimated the size of the forces opposing them. Kitchener accepted their figures, but he wasn't mollified. He sacked Aitken and replaced him with Brigadier Richard Wapshare. With his new assignment, he gave Wapshare a new order: no more offensives. Wapshare didn't object. In his diary, Meinertzhagen wrote that the mention of von Lettow Vorbeck's name "sends him [Wapshare] off into a shivering fit of apprehension."

A new view

Tanga set the tone for the rest of the war in German East Africa. Von Lettow Vorbeck, leading a tiny army of askaris, tied up hundreds of thousands of South Africans, British, Indians, and assorted colonial troops all through the war. Usually retreating, but never cornered, he inflicted casualties on the enemy that were many times the size of his entire army. When the war ended—he learned of the end by capturing an enemy dispatch rider—he was invading British territory.

Tanga seldom makes any list of the world's decisive battles. The East African campaign itself is barely a footnote in most histories of World War I.

Tanga and the East African campaign proved that black soldiers could fight as well as white soldiers. Earlier, Admiral Togo had proved that Asians could beat Europeans, but this wasn't quite the same thing. Europeans didn't really think that Japanese and Chinese were inferior—just somewhat backward, mechanically. Tsushima drastically revised that idea. But the prevailing white view of blacks was that they *were* inferior, perhaps even subhuman.

As most whites weren't even aware of the war in East Africa, white opinion didn't change much. Black opinion did. African natives had been beaten so often, that they had come to believe the whites were invincible. When peace returned to Africa, they knew that idea was false. It took a while for the native Africans to decide what to do about it. Finally, they followed the example of the Irish (see **Dublin, page 104**). At the beginning of World War II, Liberia was the only independent country in Africa. Today, there are no colonies.

Battle 32

Aetius and family.

Chalons, 451 AD
Attila

Who fought: Romans (Aetius) vs. Huns (Attila).

What was at stake: The old order.   Chalons marked the real beginning of the Middle Ages.

The King of the Huns was going to his wedding. His part of the wedding party was unusually large, even for a king. With King Attila rode thousands upon thousands of horsemen. They didn't wear wedding garments. They wore armor and swords. They carried lances and bows. They came from many nations—Huns, the Iranian Alans, the German Ostrogoths, Gepids, Heruls, Lombards, and other German tribes plus some Slavic clans.

Attila expected to fight for his bride. Her brother didn't approve of the wedding. Her brother was the Emperor of Rome.

This affair started when the Emperor, Valentinian, found that his sister, Honoria, was having an affair. More specifically, he found her in bed with her chief steward, a lad named Eugenius. Valentinian worried continually about whom the beautiful Honoria might marry, because if anything should happen to him, that man would be the next Emperor of the West. If she married a ruthless, ambitious man, his new brother-in-law might arrange for his demise. If she married a weak, bedazzled man, like Eugenius, Honoria herself might do the arranging so that she could rule through her new husband.

Valentinian had Eugenius executed and betrothed his sister to a safe and stolid senator, Flavius Bassus Herculanus. Honoria sent an SOS to the only non-Roman monarch in Europe strong enough to help her: Attila the Hun.

She sent her message by a slave who also gave Attila her signet ring as a sign of the message's authenticity. Attila chose to take the ring as Honoria's pledge to marry him. He knew the Roman princess was beautiful, and, being a Roman princess, she was, of course, rich. But neither beauty nor gold interested him much. He could get all the beautiful women he wanted. As for gold and the trappings of wealth, a Roman who was once his guest wrote:

> "While sumptuous food had been prepared—served on silver plates—for all the other barbarians and us, for Attila there was nothing but meat on a wooden trencher. He showed himself temperate in other ways, too, for gold and silver goblets were offered to the men at the feast, but his mug was of wood. His dress, too, was plain, having care for nothing other than it be clean, nor was the sword by his side, or the clasps of his barbarian boots, nor the bridle of his horse, like those of the other Scythians, adorned with gold or gems or anything of high price."

For Attila, there was only one objective: power. And only one way to power: control of fighting men. To him, the best fighting men were nomads like his own Huns, or the Alans or the Goths and the other East Germans in his horde. He had most of the nomads in Europe in his kingdom, but he wanted those who had fled from the Huns and entered the Roman Empire. Most of them were now in Gaul.

Gaul, Attila said, would make an excellent dowry for Honoria. He called for his secretary, Orestes, a Roman who had long before joined the Huns and was now a Hunnish noble. He had Orestes write a note to Valentinian, telling the Emperor that the Khakhan of the Huns was coming to claim his bride.

Attila was truly a *khakhan* (king of kings). After his people had been driven west by the Avars (see Adrianople, page 63), they had incorporated first the Alans, then the various German tribes in their empire. Attila was able to field an army as large as anything the Roman Empire could come up with. His army and that of the Romans were, in fact, remarkably similar. Both were predominantly German and cavalry, and the Roman commander was an old friend of Attila.

Aetius

Flavius Aetius was the son of a Roman general. As a child, he had been sent as a hostage to the court of the Khakhan of the Huns. There he struck up a friendship with Attila. In the stew of anarchy called the Western Roman Empire, this proved to be a fortunate friendship. Aetius was able to hire Hunnish mercenaries from Attila to enforce his will against Roman generals and the barbarian kings who were roaming around in the Empire. Although Roman armies had more cavalry than they did before Adrianople, Roman generals still thought like infantrymen. The German barbarians were mostly mounted, but they couldn't shoot from horseback, and what archers they had were footmen. Aetius, leading his Hunnish horse archers, had little trouble keeping them in line.

When he heard of his sister's dealings with Attila, Valentinian's first thought was to execute her. Marcian, the Eastern Roman Emperor, and Valentinian's mother, Placidia, forbade that. Placidia had been by turns a Roman princess, a Gothic queen, a Roman empress, and the sole ruler of the West as regent for the underage Valentinian.

Beautiful, brainy, and with a will of iron, she was no woman to ignore. So Valentinian resigned himself to Honoria's continued existence and called on Aetius to raise an army.

Aetius has been sainted by historians as "the last of the Romans," while Attila is usually depicted as some kind of monster. But Attila was described by a man who knew him, the Roman diplomat, Priscus, as "a lover of war, he was personally most restrained in action, most impressive in counsel, gracious to suppliants, and generous to those to whom he had once given his trust." Aetius, in contrast, once told a friend and fellow general, Boniface, the Roman Master of Soldiers, that Placidia was planning to kill him. If summoned to the Empress, he advised Boniface, that the only way to stay alive would be to refuse to come. He then told Placidia that Boniface was planning to revolt. Placidia summoned Boniface. He refused to come. Aetius, with the aid of Hunnish mercenaries, then made himself Master of Soldiers. Placidia finally understood what Aetius had done and let Boniface know that all was forgiven. Boniface returned and defeated Aetius, who fled to his friend, Attila. Then, it was said, Boniface died of natural causes and Aetius again became Master of Soldiers.

One of Aetius's problems was the Visigoths. The Visigothic king tried to ally himself with the powerful kingdom of the Vandals in Africa. He proposed a marriage between his daughter and the Vandal king's son. That alliance would make the barbarians in the west far too powerful for Aetius. The Roman general wrote to the Vandal king, Gaiseric, accusing the Visigothic girl of all kinds of vices and saying she was unworthy of Gaiseric's family. As he expected, the Vandal king had the girl's ears and nose cut off and then sent back to her father.

The Visigoths most likely did not know of Aetius's correspondence with Gaiseric. In any event, their fear of the Huns was great enough to make them enlist in Aetius's army. Visigoths and the remnant of the Ostrogoths who had entered the Roman Empire some 70 years before made up one-third of his army. They served under Theodoric, the King of the Visigoths. In addition to them there was a contingent of the ubiquitous Alans and a mass of Frankish footmen. There was also, of course, the regular Roman army, which was composed almost entirely of German mercenaries.

Chalons

Although the meeting of the two armies has been called the Battle of Chalons, it actually took place closer to Troyes. Aetius posted his troops on a U-shaped range of hills, a topographic feature reminiscent of the Cannae **(see page 127)**. Aetius seems to have been thinking of Cannae. He put his strongest forces, the Visigoths and the Romans, on opposite flanks. In the center, he placed the Alans and the Franks. The Romans didn't trust the Alans, who were more like the Huns than the familiar Germans. As for the Franks, they were West Germans from the Rhine area, living in a land of dense forests and small farms, completely different from the prairies inhabited by the East Germans. The Franks fought on foot, and every Roman knew that infantry could not compare with cavalry in battle. Hannibal had put his least reliable troops, his Gauls, in the center of his line, relying on his African heavy infantry and cavalry to crush the Romans' flanks and attack their rear. But Hannibal's Gauls were able to retreat before the Roman infantry was, and draw them into a trap. The Frankish foot soldiers weren't mobile enough to retreat before Attila's cavalry. The Franks nailed the Roman line in place.

The Roman array must have looked impressive. Attila set up a wagon-fort and built a funeral pyre in the middle of it. If routed, he said, he would meet his end there, which does indicate that the "King of the World," as he called himself, felt less than supremely confident.

Attila's opinion of the Alans was quite different from that of Aetius. He put them in the center of his line, along with his own Huns. The center of the Roman line was where the Khakhan planned to strike his heaviest blow. The Roman Alans were there, but so were the Franks. The Franks were not nomads—they were farmers who had no cavalry and very little archery. One charge in the center would most likely rout the Franks and shatter the Roman line.

"Seek victory in that spot," he told the Hunnish khans and German kings, "for when the sinews are cut, the limbs soon relax. "

The Hunnish kettledrums thundered, and a cloud of arrows whistled toward the Roman line from Attila's Huns and Alans. Then Attila's whole army galloped forward. Because only the Huns and Alans were horse archers, Attila would have to fight in the East German manner—a wild, bull-like charge with lances. Huns and Alans could charge as well as any Germans. Attila's Huns had much heavier armor than their ancestors did, and the Alans had invented this kind of charge. On Attila's right were the Ostrogoths and Slavs, on his left, the Gepids, Heruls, Lombards, and minor East German tribes.

As Attila's men neared the Roman center, a shower of short, razor-sharp axes that cut through armor and shields and split the skulls of horses hit them. The Franks had thrown their national weapon, the *francisca*. The Franks then charged the Hunnish cavalry, striking down men and horses with spears and swords. The Huns had never seen infantry charge cavalry before. The Roman Alans, big men in heavy armor, also charged. It made no difference that some of their opponents were also Alans, because the Alans were always fighting other Alans anyway. On the Hunnish left, Roman discipline and higher ground gave the Germans in the Roman regular army an advantage over the minor German tribes in Attila's army.

On the Hunnish right, the Ostrogoths and Slavs were gaining ground against the Ostrogoth's western kinsmen, the Visigoths. Attila deftly shifted his Huns and Alans to the right and pressed forward. In the melee, old King Theodoric fell off his horse and was trampled to death.

"They have killed the King!" a Visigoth yelled. "Revenge the King!" others shouted. A berserker fury filled the Visigoths. They, too, pushed forward. Attila had his drummers signal retreat. The Hunnish army galloped back to the wagon fort, while Huns and Alans dropped back to delay pursuit with arrows.

But there was no pursuit. The Visigoths had lost their leader, and the Franks were unable to pursue cavalry. Most importantly, Aetius couldn't afford to destroy Attila's army because the Huns were the only force Aetius could call on to coerce the German tribes. He'd been lucky: He'd beaten the Huns but left their army intact and his friend, Attila, alive. He would still be able to hire Hunnish mercenaries. Right now, he wanted to get the Visigoths dispersed. He suggested to Theodoric's son, Thorismund, that he hurry home before some usurper could grab his throne. Thorismund, knowing his people's addiction to usurpation, agreed and took his army away. The Romans watched Attila for a while, then both armies went home.

Unexpected decisions

At first, it looked as if Chalons had decided nothing. Attila did not consider himself beaten. He didn't light his funeral pyre, and he was not ready to loan Aetius any more troops. Instead, he invaded Italy the next year, still seeking Honoria and her dowry. Aetius couldn't stop him. The Germans in Gaul and Spain were too busy with their own affairs to save a neighboring country. Attila ravaged Italy right down the gates of Rome. Then he turned back. Modern historians, seeking a reason, say the Huns were suffering from sickness and hunger. But Attila's contemporaries said Pope Leo I confronted Atilla and convinced him to go home. Whether or not Leo awed Attila is irrelevant. The important thing is that people believed that he was. Emperors, kings, and generals, by their cruelty and indifference to the sufferings of their people, had begun to lose the confidence of the masses. Aetius had stood by while the Huns ravaged Italy. Leo stayed with his people, and instead of fleeing, had confronted the barbarian king. The barbarian had gone home. Secular leaders—gods in the old pagan order—were now just untrustworthy tyrants. People put their confidence in clerics, believing that even they could perform miracles. The Middle Ages had begun, and the Roman Empire of the West was finished.

The year after his invasion of Italy, Attila married a new wife, a beautiful German girl named Idilco, or Hilda. The usually-temperate Attila drank heavily. That night, he had a violent nosebleed while asleep and drowned in his own blood. Fearing robbers, the Huns buried Attila and his treasure in an unmarked grave. They left no monument to the great khakhan; all that survived were the legends about him in the folklore of Central Europe.

With the great khakhan gone, the Germans in his empire wondered why they had deferred to the Huns. Chalons had proved that Germans could beat Huns, and there were many more Germans than Huns. At the Battle of Nedao, a year after Attila's death, the East Germans ended the Empire of the Huns forever. With it went the threat Aetius had used to cow the barbarians.

Valentinian decided he didn't need Aetius. One day, while going over accounts, Valentinian drew his sword and killed the Master of Soldiers with his own hand. A few days later, two of Aetius's Hunnish bodyguards assassinated Valentinian. The Western Roman Empire plunged into complete anarchy. Finally Orestes, once Attila's secretary, led an army of East Germans into Italy and captured Rome. He made his son, Romulus Augustulus, Emperor, but Orestes's troops mutinied and killed him. They deposed Romulus Augustulus, who achieved a kind of fame as the last Roman Emperor of the West. Historians call this the fall of the Western Empire. Actually, the Western Empire had already fallen about as low as it could get, and the process began with the defeat of the Huns at Chalons.

Battle 33

El Cid, Spanish Christian hero who occasionally fought for Muslim rulers.

Las Navas de Toloso, 1212 AD
Trouble in Dar es Islam

Who fought: Spanish (Alfonso of Castille, Pedro of Aragon, and Sancho the Strong) vs. Moors (Mohammed al Nazir).

What was at stake: The fate of Islam in Spain and Spanish aspirations to great power status.

The crushing defeat of Muslim forces at Tours **(see page 170)** in 732 was one of the first of a whole string of disasters for the followers of Mohammed. Chinese-led Uighur Turks had defeated the Arabs in 730 at Samarkand and again in 736 at Kashgar. At the same time (731–732), Khazar Turks invaded Arab lands through the Caucasus and got as far as Mesopotamia before being pushed back. And in spite of years of trying, the Muslim Arabs could make no more headway against the Eastern Roman Empire.

In a century, the Arabs had conquered the largest empire the world had ever seen. Now, internal stresses as well as external enemies had stopped the empire's explosive growth.

In spite of what they professed—the brotherhood of all believers—the empire was an Arab, not a Muslim, empire. Arabs held the highest positions in both civil and military affairs. In the middle of the eighth century, descendants of Mohammed's uncle,

185

Al Abbas, led a revolt in Central Asia. Mainly ethnic Persians, the rebels overthrew the Omayyad Caliph, who claimed descent from Mohammed's son-in-law, Omar. They founded a new, Abbasid, Caliphate.

In Spain and North Africa (west of Egypt), in the area known as el Maghrib (the West) the natives were also restless. The Libyan Desert separated el Maghrib from the rest of Dar es Islam. The Muslims in el Maghrib, mostly African Berbers, had no more use for the Persians than they had for the Arabs. They didn't recognize the Abbasid Caliph. Instead, various Berber chieftains ruled small sections of the countryside independently, while Arab leaders, who had settled in the cities, ruled city-states. Eventually the Berbers found another descendant of Omar and proclaimed a new Omayyad Caliphate. The Omayyads adopted the Spanish city of Cordoba as their capital.

The new Caliphs at first attempted to revive the holy war against the Christians in northern Spain, but soon found other things to interest them. Spain, long ruled by the Romans, was a more urban—and urbane—place than Africa. The Arabs had brought their own poetry to the country, along with the art and architecture they had picked up from the Persians, and the science and mathematics they learned from the Greeks, the Mesopotamians, and the Indians. The Visigoths had a literature of their own and had adopted the old culture of Rome. Under the Muslims, Christians and Jews had freedom to practice their religions and were able to engage in the learned professions. Many Jews came to Spain from less tolerant countries in northern Europe. Before long, Muslim Spain was a center of civilization, not only in Europe but in the whole Muslim world as well. Writing, painting, architecture, science, and philosophy flourished in Omayyad Spain.

In the other Spain, the tiny principalities of the North, there was less civilization and a good deal less religious tolerance, especially for Muslims who had stolen Christian land.

The other Spain

The Muslims had never conquered all of Spain. The northwest corner, Galicia, was inhabited by dour Celts (called *Gallegos* by the Spanish), who enjoyed dour Celtic weather. The climate in foggy, rainy Galicia, on the shore of the Bay of Biscay, would have seemed perfectly normal to any Irishman or Scotsman, but it was not inviting to the sun-baked sons of the desert. Just east of the dour Gallegos were the dourer Basques. The Basques spoke the same language their ancestors spoke in the Stone Age. They had defied any attempts to assimilate them by Gauls, Romans, Visigoths, and Franks. They were not going to let the Arabs and Berbers be the first to conquer them.

There has long been a notion in the non-Spanish world that Christians from France gradually pushed the Muslims back. The notion was probably started and spread by the Franks. Any reader of Cervantes's masterpiece, *Don Quixote*, knows that Charlemagne and his Franks were never pure heroes to Spanish Christians. The Basques proved it by ambushing and wiping out the rear guard of Charlemagne's army as it retreated through the pass at Roncevalles. East of the Basques were the incipient kingdoms of Castile and Aragon. And everywhere in that Christian fringe were dukes, counts, and other warlords in more castles than you can count.

For a long time, there was no organized *reconquista*. There was no organized anything in Christian Spain. The Spanish lords were not only jealous of each other, but they contributed to the fragmentation of Christian Spain by dividing their kingdoms up among their sons.

That situation might have resulted in further Muslim conquests if the Omyyad Caliphate itself had not quickly fragmented into *taifas*, independent Berber tribal states. In 1031, a council of taifa kings formally abolished the caliphate. There was a lot of raiding back and forth. Stealing from someone of the other religion was not considered a sin by either the Christians or the Muslims.

All warfare in Spain, however, was not Christians versus Muslims. Berber chiefs attacked by other Berber chiefs enlisted Christians to help them. Christian lords, in turn, had no qualms about seeking help from Muslims when facing Christian enemies. The great Spanish hero of this age was Rodrigo Diaz de Vivar, known as el Cid Campeador. His title is instructive. "Cid" is a corruption of the Arabic "sidi," meaning lord. "Campeador," is champion, a title Christians gave their heroes. A jealous Castilian king had exiled the Cid, so he offered his sword to the Muslims. He deserved his fame as a fighting man, triumphing on field after field. But nevertheless, the Christians were gradually pushing back the increasingly fragmented Muslims. In 1085, the Castilians took Toledo, the old Visigoth capital, now a major taifa capital.

Then, the taifa kings did something dangerous. They sought help from Africa, which lost them the services of the Cid. Even worse from their point of view, they lost their independence and the good life.

The Almoravids

The Maghrib, and a good part of West Africa south of the Sahara, was under the control of the Almoravids. While the Muslim rulers of Spain were sipping wine, watching dancing girls, and discussing philosophy, a Tuareg in the Sahara was getting religion. Tuaregs are Berber nomads, people whose hardscrabble life defies comparison. "Tuareg" is an Arabic name (singular: Targui). It means "the forsaken of God," as "Berber," which is Arabic from Greek, means "barbarian." Tuaregs ran the caravans that crossed the desert. One of them, Yana ibn Omar, saw how different life in the Arab cities was from his own existence, in which a pool of clear water was an almost unimaginable luxury. The Muslims of his time, he concluded, were corrupting Islam. Luxury was turning them from God. To set things right, he led an army of Tuaregs against the west African oases, then against the cities of the north. He then founded a dynasty, called the Almoravids.

The Almoravids quickly conquered all the Maghrib and extended their dominion to the black empires of the Sudan. When the Spanish Muslims called on it, the Almoravid Empire was the most powerful Muslim state in the world.

These African puritans took one look at what life was like in Spain and saw that they had a double task: They must not only drive back the infidels, but they must reform their erring brethren as well. An Almoravid Spain had no attraction for the Cid, who went back to fight for the Christians. With him went thousands of Mozarabs, as Christians in the Muslim area were called, and Jews. Barbarians, like the Tuaregs, and later the Turks, had no idea why the Prophet made exceptions for the "people of the Book." The Castilian king again exiled the Cid, but this time Rodrigo did not return to the Muslim lands. He raised a private army of both Christians and Muslims and carved out a kingdom for himself. For the rest of his life, he was King of Valencia.

When the Cid died, the Almoravids retook Valencia and quite a bit more. But the warriors from the Sahara quickly succumbed to the fleshpots of Al Andulus, as the Muslims called Spain. Once again the back-and-forth raiding resumed and, thanks to the emigration from Muslim Spain, Christian Spain gained manpower, civilization, and even an approach to unity. *Reconquista* was now a definite Christian aim

The Almohades

Once again, a Muslim prophet appeared in the backwoods. This time it was Abu Mohammed ibn Tumari, a lamplighter's son in the Atlas Mountains. He began preaching against luxury and soon converted a man who had a natural talent for military leadership, Abd el Mumin. Abd el Mumin raised an army and took over leadership of the movement. By 1149, he had made himself Emir of Morocco. He founded a new dynasty, the Almohades, and when he died in 1163, he was emperor of a larger territory than the Almoravids held. Apparently unable to learn from experience, once again, a taifa king invited the African reformers to come to Spain and save his people. They came; they saw; they conquered. By 1172, they controlled all of Al Andulus, and their first order of business was to wipe out the licentiousness of their co-religionists. The Almohades did not succumb to the fleshpots. They kept their capital in the Atlas Mountains. But by 1195 they were ready to take on the infidels. The Almohades' Emperor Ya'cub gathered an army of Islamic troops from all over Africa and Spain to march against Castile, the largest and most aggressive of the Christian Spanish states.

Alfonso the Lucky

At the time Castile was ruled by Alfonso VIII, nicknamed the Lucky. After his first meeting with Ya'cub's army, he was lucky to be alive. The Muslims routed the Christians, and Alfonso made a humiliating peace with Ya'cub. He was lucky to be able to sign a peace treaty. One lucky break was that the old Almohade emperor knew he was dying and wanted to go back to his beloved mountains to die. The other was the result of an earlier stroke of luck, when Alfonso of Castile was able to marry his daughter to Alfonso of Aragon. The King of Aragon died near the time of the battle. His crown went to his son, Pedro II, grandson of Alfonso of Castile. Aragon, on the Mediterranean shore, was a relatively powerful Spanish state, and Pedro was famed as a knight-errant. Continuing the campaign against both Castile and Aragon would take more energy that old Ya'cub wanted to expend.

About this time, an idea originating in the Holy Land came to Spain. The military monks founded in Outremer, the Knights of St. John and the Knights Templars (**see Rhodes and Malta, page 161**), inspired three orders of Spanish monks: the Knights of Calatrava, the Knights of Alcantara, and the Knights of St. James. Like their crusader counterparts, the Spanish orders were brave, disciplined, and very professional soldiers. Spain had not seen a disciplined military force since the Corps of Slaves, mameluks maintained by the Caliphs, had been disbanded.

Ya'cub finally died in 1199. His son, Mohammed al Nazir, never liked the peace with the Christians and he saw with apprehension that Castile was growing stronger. Alfonso, on his part, felt ready to challenge the Muslims again. He denounced the treaty, and Mohammed al Nazir declared a holy war. The Spanish Christians countered with a holy war of their own. The Archbishop of Toledo persuaded the Pope to declare a crusade against the Muslims in Spain. Both sides began recruiting wildly.

At that moment the Muslim world was relatively peaceful. Mohammed al Nazir was able to recruit unemployed soldiers from as far east as Persia and Turkestan and as far south as Nubia, on the upper Nile. Alfonso's agents toured the courts of Europe and picked up a horde of knights and men at arms. Most of both armies were cavalry. The Christian strength, as always, was heavy cavalry—mailed horsemen expert with the lance and sword. Muslim strength was in light cavalry—horse archers and javelin men wearing less armor than their enemies but more mobile.

Sancho cuts the chain

Al Nazir's plan was to draw his enemies away from their bases and confront them with a strong position they couldn't break through. Soon, their supplies would run out. Logistics were not well developed in the Middle Ages. They'd have to retreat, which would mean they'd scatter, making them an easy prey for his agile horsemen. He fortified the passes of the Sierra Morena Mountains, a little north of the Guadalquivir River and Cordova, and waited. When Alfonso's allies, his grandson, King Pedro of Aragon, and King Sancho the Strong of Navarre, saw the situation, they advised Alfonso to retreat, but Alfonso wanted to go on.

Then a shepherd appeared and showed the Christians an unguarded path around the passes. The knights made their way over the path and suddenly appeared on the heights above the Muslim army. Al Nazir's main body was located on some small plains in the midst of hills, a geographical feature called "navas" in Spanish.

Mohammed al Nazir's luring of the Christian army far away from its bases was a smart strategy, as was confronting it with the fortified passes, but keeping the bulk of his forces on the navas was not. The small plains didn't provide enough room for his light horse to operate effectively. But the navas were perfect ground for the bone-crushing charges and hand-to-hand melees that were the Christians' most effective tactics. Even so, the size of the Muslim army was so great the Christians spent two days in prayer before they even moved.

The Muslim army was a great mass. In the center was Mohammed al Nazir. The Emperor stood under a large parasol that served as a standard and behind a stockade of logs bound together with a chain. He held a sword in one hand and a Koran in the other. Around him on all sides was a bodyguard of picked troops. El Nazir was no Alexander the Great, riding at the head of his cavalry striking force. On the other hand, he was in the line of battle—a position no modern head of state or even commanding general would ever find himself in.

The Christian army was divided into the customary three "battles." Alfonso commanded the center; Pedro of Aragon commanded the left; Sancho the Strong commanded the right. The Christians charged. It was their kind of battle: a wild, hand-to-hand brawl. But there were so many Muslims. It was the largest Muslim army ever seen in Europe, the largest Muslim army that would ever be seen in Europe for centuries hence. The wings commanded by Pedro and Sancho slowly pushed the Muslims into the rocky, wooded hills behind them, where they would lose all their mobility. But in the center, the Muslims, fighting under the eye of the Emperor, drove back the Christians. The Knights of Calatrava were almost wiped out.

"Archbishop, it is here that we ought to die!" Alfonso yelled to the Archbishop of Toledo as he rushed forward.

"No, sire, it is here that we should live and conquer," the churchman replied. He pointed out that the Muslim horsemen had been stopped by Alfonso's infantry spearmen, and the Knights of St. James were slashing into their flank.

Alfonso's standard, following the King, pressed forward. The Muslims slowly fell back. But it was Sancho the Strong, not Alfonso, who reached the stockade first. Sancho demonstrated why he had his nickname. He chopped through the chain stockade and burst into Al Nazir's bodyguard. The royal parasol, sheltering the Emperor from the sun, went down.

"Shah mat," Persian chess players used to say, the origin of our "checkmate." "The king is dead," meaning the game is over. At the Navas of Toloso, the game was over. The Muslim army panicked and tried to flee. Most of them didn't get far. The slaughter was terrific. It almost wiped out the warrior aristocracy not only of Muslim Spain but also of North Africa. The losses hurt Egypt and Arabia and were felt as far as Central Asia.

On to America

The aftermath of such a horrendous battle seemed incongruous. The Christian army took a few towns and castles and went home. Pedro of Aragon was killed in battle the next year, Alfonso of Castile died a year later, and Christian Spain went back to its intracommunal feuding.

The Muslim threat was over. The Almohade Empire in both Spain and Africa began to fall apart immediately. It was extinct 50 years after the battle. The Muslim taifa states paid tribute to the Christian kings. Most importantly, the Christians held the central plateau of Spain, containing the headwaters of all the Spanish rivers and the intersections of all the roads. Geography had always been a strong force against centralization in Spain. That obstacle was now removed.

The Muslim states slowly were wiped out until only Grenada, in the far south, remained. Less than three centuries after the fight on the Navas of Toloso, Isabella of Castile married Ferdinand of Aragon, and Spanish unity was almost achieved. Ferdinand and Isabella then invaded Grenada and drove the last Muslim ruler out of Spain. That was in 1492. The Spanish then looked for new worlds to conquer. They found them across the Atlantic.

Battle 34

Ghengis Kahn.

Gupta, 1180 AD
The Encroaching Gobi

Who fought: Mongols (Temujin) vs. Keraits (Wang Khan) and their allies.

What was at stake: The rise of Temujin, later Genghis Khan, and ultimately the Mongol conquest of Eurasia and the interchange of ideas between East and West.

They didn't know why, but their world was drying up. Every year the sands of the Gobi inched farther north. Every year, there were fewer water holes. Every year, the grass was drier and sparser. To feed their animals, they had to find new pastures. And in the new pastures, they collided with other clans who were also being driven off their ancestral land by the advancing desert. There was war. Defeated clans, in fleeing the battlefield, pressed on other clans. There was more war, and the fugitives either occupied new land or fled farther.

The growth of the desert and the wars it caused created a human avalanche. That was an old story in High Asia. Earlier, the Huns, the Avars, the Bulgars, and the Magyars had been driven to new lands. This time, many of the Turkish tribes—The Seljuks, the Khazars, the Pechenegs, the Kankalis, the Kipchaks, and others—were driven west. Some of the fugitives prospered in their new homes. The Seljuks developed a mighty empire. But not all of the Turks were driven from their pastures. Fighting for the best land went on in High Asia. The struggle involved more than Turks. Mongols, Tibetans, and Tungusi all fought for living space. The Turks were the strongest. The Shah of

191

Mongols fighting.

Kwaresm carved out an empire that covered all of what was later called Turkestan, and the Uighurs took over the ancient Tocharian cities of the Tarim Basin. Among the weakest of the steppe people were the Mongols, scattered clans of nomads related to the once-mighty Avars.

The Mongols lived close to the borders of China—too close. The Chinese subsidized a neighboring nomad people, the Tatars, to keep their borders free of potential enemies. The Tatars attacked the Mongols and beat them so badly that many of the Mongol clans began calling themselves Tatars. Not all the Mongols were willing to accept second place in their corner of the world. Yesukai the Strong, Khan of the Yakka Mongols, raided the Tatar camps continually. On one raid, he captured a beautiful Tatar girl, named Houlon, on her wedding night. A year later, he returned from another raid to learn that Houlon had borne him a son. He named the boy Temujin, the name of a Tatar khan he had brought back as a captive.

When Temujin was a small boy, Yesukai was invited to a Tatar feast. On his way home, he felt sick. He had been poisoned, and when he reached home, he died.

With the strong khan dead, enemies—Tatars and others—attacked from all sides. A certain Targutai, Khan of the Taidjut Mongols and a former vassal of Yesukai, persuaded most of Yesukai's clansmen to join him. Yesukai's family was outlawed and hunted like animals. One time Temujin was captured and clamped in a wooden yoke. He escaped only because a Taidjut clansman took pity on the boy, freed him from the yoke, and hid him in a cart loaded with wool. Taidjut warriors thrust spears into the cart, but missed Temujin.

"The smoke of my house would have vanished and my fire would have died out forever if they had found you," the Taidjut told the young Mongol. "Go now to your brothers and mother."

Temujin did. Then he went to the clans who once followed his father. During the unequal struggle with the Taidjuts, he had been gaining a reputation as a warrior. Many men wanted to follow such a leader. Among the Mongols and other peoples of the pastures around the Gobi, ethnicity got little consideration. Descent from famous warriors did help one gain leadership—Temujin was descended from the legendary Bour-chikoun, the Gray-Eyed Men, probably the ancient Yue Chi (see **Adrianople, page 63**). But the warriors of the steppes, like the ancient Celts, chose their own leaders.

When Temujin's horde (from *ordu*, an army or camp) numbered several thousand warriors, he took the bride Yesukai had picked out for him years before. After the wedding, he called on Toghrul Khan, chief of the Keraits, a mostly Turkish tribe who were mostly Nestorian Christians. Both Toghrul Khan and the Emperor of Ethiopia have been identified as the inspiration for the medieval European legend of "Prester John" (see **Diu, page 36**). Toghrul Khan had been a longtime friend of Yesukai. Toghrul took the young Mongol as his adopted son. Soon after that, Temujin's bride, Bourtei, was kidnapped by the Merkits, as his own mother had been kidnapped from the Tatars. Temujin secured the help of the Keraits, one of the strongest tribes in the Gobi area, and got his bride back. The Yakka Mongols, backed by the powerful Keraits, had become a force to be reckoned with on the eastern steppes.

Temujin used the newfound peace to build his warriors into an army. From ancient times the steppe nomad society was a military society. All the men, of necessity, could ride and shoot arrows from horseback. Every male from 14 to 70 years of age was expected to fight for the clan. At times, the women, who could also ride and shoot, took part in the fighting. In battle, each man belonged to a squad of 10—nine men and a leader. He would remain a member of that squad until his fighting days were over. Each squad of 10 was part of a company of 100. The companies usually fought in squadrons of 500, although they were sometimes grouped into regiments of 1,000.

Temujin used this military organization as the basis of his civil administration. Each squad leader now was the chief of 10 tents and so on. More importantly, Temujin drilled his warriors in times of peace and imposed strict discipline on them at all times. Every unit, from regiment to squad, stayed together at all times. There would be no dispersing to loot until the khan allowed the troops to do so. Temujin's army maneuvered in response to signals he sent with his standard of nine yak tails; the smaller units responded to orders given by kettle drums and hand signals.

The Battle of the Wagons

One day, when his ordu numbered 13,000 warriors, Temujin was leading his whole clan to new pastures. The scouts he sent ahead came galloping back with the news that an enormous army of Taidjuts in battle formation was just ahead of them.

Temujin's old enemy, Targutai, had persuaded a number of other clans to join him in order to eliminate the aggressive new leader of the Yakkas. He had 30,000 men organized in squadrons of 500. Each squadron was five ranks deep, with men in the first two lines wearing iron armor. The last three ranks wore leather armor.

Temujin's clan was strung out in a long file, but he immediately ordered his men into battle formation. As they had practiced before, they lined up in regiments of 1,000, each regiment 10 ranks deep. Normally, in Mongol warfare, the women, children, and livestock were far to the rear. This time, Temujin formed a wagon laager at one end of his line. There were no warriors in it. Instead, the women and boys under 14 were given bows and arrows and told to defend the wagons.

Both sides charged, volleying arrows as they rode. Temujin's denser formations hit the center of the Taidjut line and knifed through it. But the Taidjuts, seeing the undefended wagons thought of loot, and they forgot about the Yakka warriors and charged the wagons. A hail of arrows from the wagons stopped them. Then Temujin's warriors, responding to signals from the nine yak tails, hit them from the rear. The clans Targutai had persuaded to join him fled. The Taidjuts soon followed. Targutai's huge army, more than twice the size of Temujin's, left 6,000 dead on the field.

After this battle, the Mongols formally elected Temujin khan. The decision was practically unanimous, but several others thought that they were more entitled to the position, and they left in a huff.

Wang Khan

The new khan ordered his vassals to inform him of any unusual occurrence in their neighborhoods. One messenger reported that the Chinese had sent an envoy to Toghrul Khan, probably to ask him for help against the Tatars, who were raiding China. Temujin sent a messenger to the Chinese, asking them to visit his clan. The Chinese came and the Mongol Khan learned that they were, indeed, asking for help against the Tatars. Temujin proposed that he join Toghrul Khan in a campaign against the people who had murdered his father. Toghrul and the Chinese agreed. The Mongols and Keraits routed the Tatars and kept the loot the nomads had stolen from China. The Chinese were delighted anyway. They gave Toghrul Khan a title: Wang Khan, Emperor of Khans. They made Temujin Warden of the Marches.

For the next six years, the two khans were partners in all the wars on the steppes. When they took prisoners, Wang Khan, as he liked to call himself, made them slaves. Temujin incorporated them into his army. Temujin grew steadily stronger, and the son of Wang Khan, Sengun, grew steadily more jealous. He conspired with some of Temujin's disaffected relatives and finally persuaded old Wang Khan that the Mongol was planning to take over his kingdom. The old man eventually let Sengun have his way.

The Kerait prince invited Temujin to come to the Kerait ordu to discuss weddings that would link the two peoples. Once there, Temujin would, like his father, be poisoned. At the last minute, Temujin suspected foul play and sent envoys to stall the Keraits. Then two herdsmen told Temujin that a Kerait army was on the way to attack him.

When the standard stood on Gupta

Temujin's warriors were spread over miles of prairie. He didn't have time to get reinforcements from the scattered ordus. He put the women and children on camels and in light camel carts and sent them away. He drove the horses and cows out across the steppe. He left a few men to light the campfires and keep them going until the enemies appeared. Then he led all his warriors to a range of mountains about a half-day's march away. All the tents and their household furnishings were left in place.

The Keraits burst into the Mongol ordu and shot the khan's tent full of arrows. Then they learned that the camp was deserted. Looking around, they decided the Mongols had fled in panic. They took up the trail and were strung out in a long line when they approached Temujin's position. Temujin's men charged out of their hiding places and routed the Kerait vanguard. But when Wang Khan's main body came up, they were forced back. Desperately trying to hold the high ground against overwhelming numbers, Temujin called for his standard bearer. He told the officer to take a few troops and sweep around the Kerait army and plant the standard on a hill in their rear. He was to execute the *tulughma*, the "standard sweep." It was a common nomad attack—but not by a vastly outnumbered army.

"Oh Khan, my brother, I will break through all who oppose me," said Guildar, the standard bearer. "I will plant the standard on Gupta. I will show you my valor. If I fall, nourish and rear my children. It is all one to me when my end comes."

Guildar planted the standard on Gupta, and the Keraits could not capture it. Sengun was wounded. Threatened in the rear, and with night falling, Wang Khan withdrew.

"We have fought a man with whom we should never have quarreled," he said.

For years afterwards, Mongol bards would tell of the day "when the standard stood on Gupta." The warriors of the steppes considered it an act of unparalleled audacity, a move only an unconquerable leader would make.

It took a while for that lesson to sink in, though. It even took a while for Temujin's own Mongols to come to his aid. Then a chieftain named Daaritai brought his warriors up to join Temujin. Daaritai was Temujin's uncle, but he was also a leading retainer of Wang Khan. Other eastern clans joined the Yakka Mongol army. Wang Khan, his son, and his son's henchmen, now over-confident, had grown arrogant, alienating even their followers. The Gobi clans compared the achievements of the two leaders, Wang Khan and Temujin, especially their conduct at Gupta. They decided to throw in their lot with Temujin.

Stealthily, Temujin took his army across the steppe, attacked the Keraits in their camp, surrounded them, and forced them to surrender. He took the Kerait warriors into his army. Wang Khan, Sensun, and the disaffected Mongols who had joined them fled. Hostile tribesmen in the west soon killed the Kerait khan and his son.

Temujin sent messengers to the leaders of all the Gobi clans calling for a general council, a *Kurultai*. Turks, Mongols, and Tungus came. The object was to name one supreme leader of the nomad peoples. To no one's surprise, the council elected Temujin.

A shaman at the council went into a trance. When he came to, he announced that the new leader must have a new name. He would be Genghis Khan, Emperor of all Men.

After half a century, much of it as a fugitive, most of it as an underdog, the Mongol khan was about to begin a career of conquest that would make Alexander's pale in comparison. When he died, his empire stretched from the Pacific Ocean to the Black Sea. Unlike Alexander's, his empire did not break up with his death. His sons and grandsons kept it together and expanded it. The Mongols ruled China for a century and a half. Not until the 16th century did Russia become free of the Mongols. The Moghuls of India were originally Mongols.

The Mongol Empire was more than just a wide expanse of territory. The Khan's Peace facilitated travel between East and West. Not for centuries after the end of Mongol rule did trade between China and the West reach the level it had under the Khans. Ideas traveled between the Far East and the West as never before. The trebouchet, which replaced the catapult as a siege engine, came from China, as did gunpowder, which uses what the Arabs called "the snow from China": potassium nitrate. Roger Bacon, an English monk, wrote the first formula for gunpowder in 1259, 44 years after Genghis Khan sacked Peking. Even more importantly, Europe learned to make cheap paper, which made the mass production of books possible. The Greeks had invented the astrolabe, which made navigation of the ocean possible, but it was lost to Western Europe. The Persians and Chinese had it as well, but it was not until the Mongol conquest that the astrolabe reached Europe.

Battle 35

Chickamauga, 1863 AD
The Chess Masters

Who fought: Federals (William Rosecrans) vs. Confederates (Braxton Bragg).

What was at stake: The fate of the Union.

Few generals were more unlike than Braxton Bragg, a black-browed, morose martinet of a professional soldier, and William Rosecrans, a cheerful, hot-tempered, and profane industrialist-turned-general. Bragg led the Confederate Army of Tennessee; Rosecrans led the Union Army of the Cumberland. (The Confederates named their armies after states, the Federals after rivers.) The two generals had one thing in common: If wars were chess games and soldiers chessmen—pieces that always moved where they were supposed to and never bled and died—both men would have been masters.

At the end of 1862, neither side in the American Civil War had much to celebrate. Yankees had been occupying northern Virginia almost continuously since the outbreak of war. They were less than a day's ride from the Confederate capital, Richmond. Lee had managed to invade the North once. He had been defeated at Antietam Creek in Maryland, the bloodiest day of the war. On the other hand, the Union army, which almost always outnumbered the Confederates, just couldn't make headway against the Army of Northern Virginia. McClellan had been frightened off the Peninsula, and Burnside had sent his troops into a death trap on the slopes of Fredericksburg.

In the West, Union forces had been moving east from Shiloh toward Chattanooga, which was a key rail center and the gateway to eastern Tennessee and northern Georgia—two Unionist islands floating in the Confederate sea. There was a lot of ineffectual maneuvering before Braxton Bragg got command of the Army of Tennessee. Bragg invaded Kentucky, forcing Union troops to backtrack to defend that border state.

The trouble was that the Kentuckians, by and large, didn't want to be "liberated" by the Confederacy. Instead of joining the Confederate army, they sniped at Bragg's campfires. Union troops in Kentucky outnumbered Bragg's. Disheartened, Bragg retreated to Tennessee. There was a small fight at Perryville, followed by a much bigger one at Stones River. There, Bragg outflanked the Union army, now under Rosecrans, while the Yankees outflanked him. Before long, the two armies were facing each other in opposite directions from their original positions. After the first day, Bragg telegraphed Richmond that he had won a great victory. Then the Federals took a hill threatening Bragg's rear and could not be dislodged. Each army suffered more than 30 percent casualties, making Stones River the bloodiest battle of the war in proportion to the men engaged. Most of Rosecrans's generals thought they should retreat. Rosecrans, literally soaked with the blood

Snodgrass House, occupied by Brannan's troops.

of men he had fought beside that day, thought otherwise. On January 3, Bragg saw that Rosecrans was getting reinforcements. He retreated.

Bragg was perfectly willing to trade almost uninhabited real estate for a chance to trap his enemies. Confederate politicians denounced the retreats as a blot on Southern honor, but Bragg was a warrior, not a politician.

Bragg's new line blocked the railroad and the only good road between Murphreesboro, Rosecrans's position, and Chattanooga. On each side of Bragg's line was an expanse of mountains and pine barrens without a single decent road. Rosecrans would have to make a frontal assault, which in this war, because of the universal use of rifles, was practically mass suicide. Rosecrans seemed to be stalled. He had been at Murphreesboro for months.

Rosecrans was building up supplies for his next advance. He never got enough horses to match the enemy's cavalry, but he outnumbered Bragg's infantry—especially because Bragg needed to send troops to Vicksburg, where Grant was conducting a siege. Washington had more than enough delay and ordered Rosecrans to move on. So on June 26, he did.

Rosecrans sent cavalry and reserve troops into the barrens around Bragg's left flank. Bragg was not deceived. He knew the Yankee move was a feint. He easily repulsed it and a subsequent attack on the middle of his line. He braced for a renewal of the assault. A major Confederate victory in the West could end the current stalemate and change the course of the war. Then the heavens opened up and a blinding rain began. It continued for 15 days, turning the whole area into a morass. Bragg waited.

On June 30, mud-caked Federal troops appeared out of the barrens at Manchester in the right rear of Bragg's army. Rosecrans had taken them on a wide sweep through the "impassable" pine barrens. Bragg hurriedly evacuated his line and fell back on Chattanooga. During that move, the army's chief surgeon saw a side of Bragg that few others ever did. The stern martinet broke down and cried. He cried because he had no choice but to leave a hospital full of sick and wounded to the mercies of the advancing Yankees.

"The crisis is upon us," the *Chattanooga Rebel* warned, as Bragg's men streamed through the city. In Chattanooga, the Confederate general's popularity rating was about as high as Abraham Lincoln's. Newspapers compared him unfavorably with Rosecrans, "one of the western men," not a typical Yankee.

Meanwhile, Grant had taken Vicksburg. Rosecrans deduced, correctly, that Confederate troops who had escaped would be joining Bragg. He again halted and waited. Washington again screamed at him to move. On August 16, Rosecrans resumed the big chess game with a knight's gambit.

The knight was John T. Wilder's mounted infantry, known as the Lightning Brigade. Wilder's men had been ordinary infantry until they voted to provide their own horses so they could match the mobility of the Rebels's mounted guerrillas. Then Wilder bought Spencer repeating rifles for the whole brigade.

Wilder's men worked their way through the mountains around Chattanooga and surprised Bragg's outposts on the mountaintops. Artillery Captain Eli Lilly laid his guns on two steamers tied up at the Chattanooga waterfront and destroyed them both. Confederate guns, 19 of them, opened fire on Lilly's four guns. Lilly returned their fire. By the end of the day, all Confederate guns had been silenced.

Other Lightning Brigade troopers, plus infantry from two more brigades, occupied the riverbank north of town. They seized boats, chopped down trees, and made as much noise as they could. Bragg, deciding that Rosecrans planned a river crossing north of town, pulled in his outposts south of Chattanooga and sent the troops to reinforce those in the north.

Rosecrans sent his whole army across the river south of Chattanooga. Because Lilly's gunner continued to pound Chattanooga, Bragg didn't learn of the crossing until a week after it happened, and he hastily evacuated Chattanooga.

The fox sets a trap

Rosecrans, surrounding Chattanooga, thought he had trapped the Confederate fox. But Bragg was setting a trap of his own. He called for volunteers who were both brave and intelligent. Brave, because they would no doubt end up in a Federal POW camp, where the chances of death were greater than in the hottest infantry fight. Intelligent, because their job was to convince Union intelligence officers that they were deserters and that Bragg's army was stampeding in panic.

The "deserters" found a receptive audience. Washington had nagged Rosecrans unmercifully about his delays. He was eager to show the brass how fast and decisively he could move. His army advanced in three widely separated corps, each cut off from the others by rows of mountains. Rosecrans didn't have enough cavalry to screen the advance of each corps. Dan McCook's corps got all the cavalry, and Thomas Crittenden's got the Lightning Brigade. George Thomas had to use James Negley's infantry division as an advance guard for his corps. There was a reason for using horsemen in that role. The advance guard had to be far enough in advance so that the enemy it detected could not immediately fall on the main body. When it did find an enemy, it had to be mobile enough to quickly get back to the main body, if necessary. Infantry didn't have that mobility.

Rosecrans was offering his army for Bragg to destroy piecemeal. Of course, he didn't see it that way. He thought he was chasing a panic-stricken rabble.

It was Bragg's move in the big chess game. He moved his bishop. He was a real bishop—Leonidas Polk had traded the mitre and crozier of an Episcopal bishop for the sabre and braid of a Confederate lieutenant general. As a bishop, Polk's only superior had been God. He was reluctant to render to Braxton Bragg that which had been the Almighty's. Previously, Polk and another of Bragg's corps commanders, William J. Hardee, had asked President Jefferson Davis to replace Bragg with Joseph E. Johnston. Davis asked Johnston to investigate the situation. Joe Johnston found that morale among the enlisted men was high, although many of the officers were hostile to Bragg. Davis did nothing, and Bragg replaced Hardee with D.H. Hill, from the Army of Northern Virginia.

Bragg ordered Polk to send Thomas Hindman's division to hold Negley. He ordered D.H. Hill to send Cleburne's division to finish off the Yankees. Hindman arrived but did nothing except watch while he waited for Cleburne. It was a long wait. Bragg sent a courier to Hill to ask where Cleburne was. Hill replied that the Irish-born general was sick. He had not sent another division or even the same division under another commander. Bragg ordered Simon Bolivar Buckner to take his two divisions and join Hindman. Then he jumped on his horse and spurred over to Cleburne's area. Pat Cleburne was perfectly healthy, said he had received no orders to move, and was amazed that anyone had reported him sick.

William Rosecrans.

Bragg tried to have Hill removed from command. The Confederate government, however, refused to side with the "cowardly" Bragg, who had abandoned Chattanooga without a fight, against a veteran of the "glorious" army of Northern Virginia. It did, however, transfer James Longstreet, Rosecrans's roommate at West Point, and his corps from the Army of Northern Virginia to the Army of Tennessee. Because the Federals occupied the most direct rail route, the transfer was not to be completed before the battle. When the showdown came, Bragg did, however, have a rough parity with Rosecrans. The Confederates numbered 47,500 infantry and 14,500 cavalry. The Federals had 56,000 infantry and 9,000 cavalry.

Meanwhile, Hindman and Buckner decided they had a better plan than the commanding general's. They sent a courier back to get Bragg's approval, and sensibly, Negley withdrew.

Opportunity knocked again. Crittenden, still under the impression he was pursuing a panicked mob, sent two divisions to Ringgold and one to Lee and Gordon's

Mill, separating his forces. Bragg moved his bishop again. Polk was to take his entire corps to Lee and Gordon's Mill and attack the one Federal division. Polk reported that he had arrived and taken up a strong *defensive* position. Believing the Yankees had begun to concentrate against the bishop, Bragg led Buckner's corps up to reinforce him. He found Polk still holding his defensive position. The Federals had disappeared.

The River of Death

It dawned on the Union leaders that they were not rounding up a panicked mob. Bragg's army was hiding in the mountains like an Indian war party, seeking to ambush them. They concentrated their corps and moved closer together. The Federals were strung out on the west side of Chickamauga Creek, named by the Cherokees "the River of Death" after a terrible smallpox epidemic.

Bragg planned to cross the creek between Crittenden's corps, the Yankee left flank, and Gordon Granger's reserve corps, then swing around Crittenden. Then his own right wing, under Polk, which was north of the Yankee position, would use the more difficult northern crossings, protected by the troops already on the west bank. After that, his right wing would drive back the Yankee left. The Union army would then swing to the south like a hinged gate and end up in McLemore's Cove, a loop in the creek where Confederates would surround it. It was a good, sophisticated plan—if Bragg had been using chessmen instead of unpredictable humans.

Robert H.G. Minty's cavalry brigade was holding Reed's Bridge, one of the two key crossings. At 7:30 in the morning, a mass of horsemen burst out of the woods and dashed for the bridge firing revolvers and sawed-off shotguns. Minty's dismounted troopers blasted them back with their breech-loading carbines. The one brigade was facing the entire corps of the famous Nathan B. "get there first with the most" Forest. Minty's men were not impressed. Forest certainly had the most, but he wasn't getting anywhere for a while. Forest's men dismounted and brought up their artillery. Minty's troopers held on. By noon, the Con-

Braxton Bragg.

federate infantry had reinforced Forest. The Yankee cavalry made a fighting withdrawal.

Meanwhile, Wilder's Lightning Brigade had been holding off two Confederate infantry divisions at Alexander's Bridge, the second key crossing. Forest, having driven back Minty's brigade, rode south to help the Rebels at Alexander's Bridge. Wilder's skirmishers withdrew across the bridge. The Confederate column dashed toward the bridge. Wilder's men opened a drum-roll of fire with their repeating Spencers. A witness said the Confederates rushed forward in a continuous stream, but when they reached a certain point, the whole column seemed to sink into the ground. The Civil War saw the first large-scale use of repeating rifles. Against weapons like the Spencer, the tactics of Bunker Hill just didn't work.

However, the sheer volume of overwhelming numbers did. By the time darkness fell, Wilder's men were forced to move back. But one mounted infantry brigade had held up two infantry and two cavalry divisions for a full day, completely ruining Bragg's plan. The Confederates tried to reorganize in the dark and move up the creek bank, but Bragg's blitzkrieg was now impossible.

In chess, there's a move called castling, in which a player moves his castle next to the king and puts the king on the other side of the castle. The delay gave Rosecrans a chance to perform the military equivalent. He ordered George Thomas, his most steadfast corps commander, to pull out of line and take up a position on the left of Crittenden. At the same time, McCook's corps would move north to close the gap. Bragg's men would not be going around the end of the Yankee line. They would be walking into the middle of the best Federal troops.

Some of the Confederates, blundering through the darkening woods, got into the diminishing gap between Crittenden and McCook. Confronted by the Lightning Brigade, they tried to charge across a clearing. The repeating Spencers cut them down in heaps. They ducked into a drainage ditch. The Federals brought up two cannons double-shotted with cannister, cans filled with iron balls. After these two enormous shotguns raked the ditch, Wilder later said, "One could have walked 200 yards down that ditch on dead Rebels without touching the ground."

Old Pete's lucky break

Bragg had reorganized his army before the battle. He couldn't remove the insubordinate Hill, but he could lessen his influence. Although he had three corps, Bragg divided his army into two wings—in effect, two giant corps, commanded by Polk and Longstreet. He put the insufferable Hill in Polk's wing. The Bishop was to deliver the decisive stroke under the original plan. Polk had been almost as unreliable as Hill, but Bragg knew him. He didn't know Longstreet. "Old Pete" Longstreet had a great reputation in the East, but all Bragg knew about eastern generals was that Daniel Harvey Hill was one of them.

In spite of all the evidence he'd seen, Bragg never seemed to believe that a soldier could willfully disobey orders. Each new case surprised him. Bragg's god was Duty. Once, he was both a post quartermaster and a battery commander. As a battery commander, he put in for certain supplies. As a quartermaster, he disapproved the requisition. Nobody, not even himself, could keep him from doing his duty. By this time, he recognized that his generals were not Napoleon's marshals. He devised a plan so simple that the most simple-minded could follow it. Polk was to open the attack with John Breckenridge's division of Hill's corps striking the extreme left of the Federal line. As soon as it heard firing, the next division was to go into action, and so on.

The attacks were to begin with the first light. Nothing happened. At 10 p.m., Bragg rode to Polk's headquarters to learn what happened. The Bishop-General was reading a newspaper waiting for his breakfast. He'd commence things after breakfast. Bragg responded with a torrent of the kind of language the clergy seldom hear, and the attack got under way. Breckenridge's men advanced through what they thought were empty woods in a pea-soup fog. Suddenly the fog lifted and they found themselves looking at Yankee infantry behind log breastworks. They were slaughtered.

The next division attacked as soon as it heard the firing. If fared no better. Bragg was sending his army one division at a time against entrenched riflemen. It was a recipe for disaster. Finally, he gave up this plan and issued an order for all divisions to attack at once.

Longstreet had already decided he would not fight one division at a time. That would be worse than Pickett's charge, which had crippled his corps at Gettysburg. Longstreet, like Pickett, never forgave Lee for that fiasco. Longstreet formed his corps into a deep column, an enormous human battering ram that he hoped to punch right through the Union line. A column cut down the number of men exposed to an enemy's fire at one time. Only when they formed a column were the British successful at Bunker

Hill. Columns repeatedly let Napoleon breach enemy lines. But the enemies of the Redcoats and Napoleon had smoothbore muskets. Smoothbores were effective at 80, not 800, yards. The rate of fire of the slowest of the Federals' muzzle-loading rifles was as fast as the fastest smoothbores. And the firepower of the Yankee breech-loaders and repeaters was unimaginable in previous wars. Generals educated in smoothbore tactics still seemed unable to comprehend it. It looked as if Longstreet was preparing a bloodbath that would make even him forget Pickett's charge.

Then fate, riding with a Yankee staff officer, breezed into Rosecrans's headquarters. The officer had passed the position held by John Brannan's division. The troops were hidden by woods, and the officer thought there was a gap between the divisions of Thomas Wood and Joseph Reynolds. He reported that to Rosecrans.

Rosecrans, busy shifting troops to meet the attacks all along his line, spoke without considering the matter: "Tell General Wood to close upon General Reynolds."

Wood knew the order was absurd, but earlier that day, he had been the target of ferocious invective from Rosecrans, who could teach the average mule skinner something about cursing and obscenity. He followed orders to the letter and moved his division behind that of Reynolds, creating a real gap, but Longstreet's battering ram came right through the gap.

Seeing Confederate troops all around them, the Yankees panicked. Rosecrans saw his entire right wing melting away. Unable to stop them, he joined them. With the Federals on the run, the Confederates paused for lunch. John Wilder saw an opportunity and opened fire on the Confederates. He was preparing to charge the startled lunch-breakers when an assistant secretary of war appeared and ordered him to the rear. The assistant secretary, Charles A. Dana, the New York newspaper man, was in a gibbering panic, but Wilder didn't think he could ignore such a high-ranking member of the government, so he retreated.

Dana had been sent to the Army of the Cumberland to spy on Rosecrans, whom Secretary of War Edmund Stanton deemed insufficiently radical. Another spy in Rosecrans' headquarters was his chief of staff, James A. Garfield, who reported to Salmon P. Chase, the secretary of the treasury. At Rossville, where the retreating Yankees had paused, Rosecrans learned that George Thomas's corps was still in the field. He prepared to return and join Thomas, but Garfield talked him out of it. The place for the commanding general, he said, was in Chattanooga, where he could reorganize the troops and prepare to resume the fight. The chief of staff could represent him in Thomas's corp. He persuaded Rosecrans. Later, Garfield was elected president, partly because, he said, he stayed on the firing line when Rosecrans fled to the rear.

The Rock of Chickamauga

George Thomas, the Virginia aristocrat known to his men as Old Slow Trot or Old Pap, never got excited. Longstreet ordered charge after charge on Thomas's position, but openly marching against riflemen hidden by breastworks and trenches is a losing proposition unless the entrenched enemy panics. Thomas's men contracted calmness from their commander. They just continued loading and shooting.

They got some help, though. John Brannan collected fragments of the routed Union forces and joined Thomas, occupying Snodgrass Hill, a high point on Thomas's southern flank. Gordon Granger, commanding the reserve corps, brought his troops up the sound of the guns.

The barrels of Thomas's rifles grew searing hot. Some men ran out of ammunition.

"Fix bayonets," said Old Pap. They did, and threw back another Confederate wave. It was growing dark and Longstreet was growing desperate. He called for reserves and was told that there were no reserves. Polk's men were all shot out, and they were unable to help. The Confederate attacks stopped.

Thomas began to move to the rear. He moved out one division at a time. Confederate officers, Breckenridge and Cleburne among them, reported how they had attacked the "fleeing" Yankees and how the enemy was in a panic. The facts tell a different story. The Federals marched back, a division at a time, through the entire Confederate army. They kept their order and organization. The few Rebel attacks that there were, were less than half-hearted.

The Confederates won the battle, but Thomas's retreat showed that they had lost something more important. In the second half of the battle, the Confederates had every advantage: numbers, position, and the elation that comes from having achieved a great victory. But they couldn't dislodge a third of the Yankee army. They had exhausted their energy and their morale. They couldn't stop Thomas's corps— one piece at a time—from marching right through them.

Bragg's generals, of course, put the blame on Bragg. Forest urged Bragg to immediately pursue the Yankees. But Bragg had lost one-third of his army, and the rest of his troops were almost too exhausted to move. He knew he could not pursue. Forest did not understand that. The cavalry leader, a former slave dealer and future founder of the Ku Klux Klan, was not noted for his sensitivity.

The Confederates surrounded the Federals in Chattanooga, and it soon became apparent that Bragg's army had suffered irreparable psychological damage. A Union supply column started over the mountains to reach the men in Chattanooga. The Confederates tried to stop it. They were routed, not by Federal troops, but by stampeding mules. Thereafter, supplies and reinforcements came steadily over the "cracker line."

"Here's your mule!"

Federal reinforcements poured into the theoretically beleaguered city of Chattanooga. Ulysses S. Grant was placed in charge of all western operations. He relieved Rosecrans and promoted Thomas in his place. With Grant came his right-hand man, William T. Sherman, leading the Army of the Tennessee, and "Fighting Joe" Hooker with part of the Army of the Potomac.

Grant planned to break out of Chattanooga with the new troops. Hooker would attack on the Union right and Sherman on the left. The Army of the Cumberland, Grant decided, was too dispirited to attack. (Grant's reading of Dana's report on Chickamauga led to this conclusion and to his sacking of Rosecrans.) The Army of the Cumberland would hold the center and demonstrate against the Confederates on Missionary Ridge.

This best-laid plan went seriously agley. After an initial success on Lookout Mountain, Hooker was stalled when Bragg burned the bridges over Chickamauga Creek. Sherman ran into unmapped territory held by the Confederacy's fighting Irishman, Pat Cleburne, and his reinforced division, and he stopped, too.

Meanwhile, the Army of the Cumberland, demonstrating at the foot of Missionary Ridge, got tired of taking fire. Some soldiers, on their own initiative, began crawling up the precipitous slope. Phil Sheridan, the Union's fighting Irishman, raised a whiskey flask to toast his Confederate enemies. A shell exploding nearby almost finished Sheridan before he could finish the toast.

"Now that was damned ungenerous," he called. "Just for that, I'll take those guns." He started up the hill and the whole Army of the Cumberland followed him.

The Rebels fired a couple of volleys then threw down their rifles and ran.

Bragg came out and called to his men, "Stop men! Here's your general!"

The men replied with what had been a deadly insult in the Old Army: "Here's your mule!" After that insult from the men he loved in secret, Bragg was a broken man.

Sheridan clambered up the slope as fast as his short legs would take him. He ran to the nearest gun and straddled it like a horse.

The lost cause

Chattanooga was nothing like Chickamauga. At Chickamauga, Bragg had 20,950 casualties, one-third of his army. Rosecrans suffered 16,179. It was a bloody, hard-fought battle. At Chattanooga, there were 56,359 Federals and 64,165 Confederates actually engaged, with the Confederates holding the high ground. Federal casualties came to 753, and the Confederate count came to only 359. The Rebels ran like rabbits.

D.H. Hill explained what his side lost at Chickamauga: "The elan of the Southern soldier was never seen after Chickamauga." Or as a Confederate veteran put it many years later at a reunion of Chickamauga veterans, "You Yanks got into our inwards."

In the West, the Federal army was not merely an enemy to the Army of Tennessee, it was an elemental force. It could not be beaten, even after a third of it had been routed. The Confederate forces in the West lost heart.

George Thomas.

Except for Sherman's foolish attack on an entrenched position at Kenesaw Mountain, the Confederacy never won another battle in the West. Sherman drove through to the sea and was moving north toward Virginia when Lee surrendered.

Gettysburg, usually called the turning point of the war, proved only what Lee had already demonstrated at Antietam: that he couldn't conquer the North. Grant's capture of Vicksburg gave the Union control of the Mississippi. But the Union already controlled 99 percent of the great river. The Confederate victory at Chickamauga guaranteed that the United States would be "one nation, undivided, with liberty, and justice for all."

Or justice for almost all. Rosecrans, until he issued one thoughtless order, was the only Federal commanding general who never lost a battle. Chickamauga ruined his military career. Still, he was able resume his business and even get elected to Congress. Garfield, his double-crossing subordinate, was elected president. But a little later, he was assassinated. Braxton Bragg, who had experienced the most consistent bad luck throughout the war, continued to have it. He served as a military advisor to President Davis, and just before the last shot, he led a ragtag rabble in a hopeless attempt to stop Sherman, leading the finest army ever fielded in North America. After the war, he wandered through the South. He tried engineering, selling real estate, and selling insurance. He failed at all three. When he fell dead on a Galveston street in 1880, he owned little but his inflexible integrity.

Battle 36

Lepanto, 1571 AD
Selim the Sot

Who fought: Spanish, Venetians, and allies (Don Juan of Austria) vs. Turks (Ali Pasha).

What was at stake: Turkish domination of the Mediterranean.

S elim the Sot, the unworthy son of Suleiman the Magnificent, **(see Rhodes and Malta, page 161)** wanted a conquest of his own. The last thing he wanted was to ride at the head of an army, but if his target was an island, he could send a fleet while he remained safe in Constantinople. He was thinking of Cyprus. Centuries before, Muslims had taken the island and expelled the Knights of St. John. But more recently, the expanding sea empire of Venice had taken it back.

Venice and the Ottoman Empire had a peculiar relationship. The Italian republic occasionally warred with Turkey, but it was the Turks' main trading partner in Christendom. Venice depended on the Oriental goods it bought from Turkey and then sold in Europe. It had urged the sultan to destroy the Portuguese who were taking over the trade with India and China. Turkey tried and failed (**see Diu, page 36**). The effects of the Muslim defeat of Diu were starting to have an effect on the European power structure. They weren't strong enough yet to have affected Selim's father, who brought the Ottoman Empire to the height of its power, but they were weakening Venice.

Mohammed Sokolli, once Suleiman's top vizier and now a vizier for Selim, opposed the project. Venice and the distant kingdom of France were the only Christian powers

205

at all friendly to Turkey. The Ottomans' natural enemy was the Holy Roman Empire of the German People. The Empire's Kingdom of Austria confronted Turkey at its western boundary. At the other end of Europe, the Hapsburg Kingdom of Spain, ruled by the Emperor's nephew, was trying to cope with a Muslim revolt. Helping these rebels would be a worthy enterprise. Turkey didn't need Cyprus, Sokolli said. If it tried to take Cyprus by force, it might unite all the Christian powers against it.

Selim was a moral degenerate, but there was nothing wrong with his mind. He asked his mufti, Ibn Sa'ud, "When a Muslim country has been conquered by infidels, is it not the duty of a pious prince to recover it for Islam?"

The theologian said it was indeed.

As for the Christians uniting, the Sultan told Sokolli, there was no chance of that. They were not only divided, but subdivided.

Venice had no friends in Christian Europe because of its long-term relationship with Turkey. The kings and princes also hated it because it was a republic. And as the Oriental trade declined, it had expanded its land boundaries to get agricultural land. (It had previously existed solely by commerce.) That expansion put Venice in conflict with both the Empire and the Papal States. Spain's only interests were in its new empire across the Atlantic and trade in the western Mediterranean. It certainly had no interest in Venice's trade with trade the East. In fact, the Spanish King, Philip II, was about to press his claim to Portugal, which was taking the Oriental trade away from Venice and its Turkish partners. Spain, Venice, and the Papal States all belonged to one branch of Christianity, the Catholics, which was in deadly conflict with another branch, the Protestants. The Holy Roman Empire was divided between these two branches and appeared to be heading toward a cataclysmic civil war. Spain, too, was fighting Protestant rebels in its Netherlands provinces. Catholics didn't even help Catholics. The powerful Kingdom of France was a mortal enemy of all Hapsburgs, in both Spain and the Empire.

If Turkey invaded Cyprus, Selim said, it would have to deal only with Venice.

Il papa

The Muslims had been defeated in the Indian Ocean, but events in India did not loom large in European consciousness. The Turks had failed to take Vienna, but they were still the greatest military power in Europe, and they still looked as if they wanted to conquer the world. Turkish fleets had never stopped taking Christian ships and raiding Christian shores. Turkish cruelty toward their enemies had, if anything, grown even worse. The ordinary people of Europe, particularly in Central Europe and on the Mediterranean shore, lived in terror of the Turks.

This was not the case for their leaders. The Emperor worried about the Protestants, not the Muslims. The King of France worried about the Hapsburgs, both the Spanish and the German branches. The King of Spain worried about the King of France, particularly about his plans for further expansion in Italy. The Pope worried about them all—the Spanish, the French, and the Germans.

In 1566, a new Pope, Pius V, was elected. He was quite different from the stereotype of the Renaissance Pope. An ascetic with an utterly blameless personal life, he had more general worries. He was afraid the Muslim Turks would swallow all Europe. Sultan Selim ruled an empire that stretched from Central Asia in the north to the southern frontier of Egypt and Yemen in the south, from Mesopotamia in the east to Morocco in the west. The Turks were still moving forward, and now they were threatening Venice. Pius began trying to form a Christian league to oppose them. But the princes of Europe resisted.

On September 13, 1569, a gunpowder factory in the Venetian Arsenal exploded. The blast set off a roaring conflagration. The Arsenal was the heart of Venetian military power—the place where powder was compounded, guns were cast, ships were built, and weapons of all kinds were stored.

The explosion was bad enough, but reports of the damage grew as they passed from mouth to mouth. When Selim heard about it, it seemed that Venice was now defenseless. Selim sent 280 galleys and other warships with 85 troop ships to Cyprus. The fleet was commanded by Piali Pasha, who had failed to conquer Malta (see **Rhodes and Malta, page 161**). The army was under Lala Mustafa Pasha. Lala Mustafa was Selim's kind of commander. The sultan's tutor, he had connived with Selim to frame his brother, Bayazid, and cause Suleiman to execute him. In June, Lala Mustafa laid siege to Nicosia.

Nicosia was hardly a fortress city, but the 10,000-man Venetian garrison threw up earthworks and refused to surrender. Early in August, they sallied out and drove back the enormous Turkish army, capturing some booty before being driven back behind their trenches.

Meanwhile, the Pope had gotten Spain and Venice to reluctantly agree to cooperate. Genoa joined them and the Papal States in his "Christian League," as did some smaller Italian states and the Knights of St. John. France turned a stone-deaf ear to the Pope. The Empire also refused to join, although it did allow Philip of Spain to recruit some German soldiers. The allies formed a combined fleet. There was so much bickering among them, however, that nothing was accomplished.

On Cyprus, in spite of their overwhelming numbers, the Turkish soldiers were demonstrating that they still hadn't recovered from Rhodes. Lala Mustafa ordered Piali Pasha to send troops from the fleet. With this huge addition, he was able to storm Nicosia. He then massacred the garrison and the citizens and moved on to Famagusta. Selim sent Lala Mustafa reinforcements and expanded the fleet, which he put under the command of Ali Pasha.

Famagusta's garrison numbered only 7,000, but it held off the Turks until winter set in. Marco Quirini, a Venetian admiral, smashed the Turkish blockading fleet and took supplies to Famagusta, a coup which caused Selim to lop off a number of Turkish heads. Lala Mustafa resumed his attacks on the city in the spring. By August, the city was still holding out, and Lala Mustafa began to worry about his own head. Finally, he offered the Famagusta garrison the same terms Suleiman had offered the Knights of Rhodes: If they surrendered, they and the citizens would be unharmed and would be transported to the Christian land of their choice. They surrendered.

Lala Mustafa was no Suleiman. After the Venetians had laid down their arms, he enslaved the defenseless troops and had his men cut their leaders to pieces—all except the Venetian governor, Antonio Bragadino. Lala Mustafa had Bragadino's ears and nose cut off. Then, after marching him around the city, he had Bragadino flayed alive.

Don Juan

Selim was not going to stop with the conquest of Cyprus. Because Venice wanted war, he'd give it war. He ordered Ali Pasha to carry the war to Venice. Ali sailed up the Adriatic and, seeing no Venetian ships, raided every Venetian post along the shore, with Bragadino's stuffed skin hanging from the yardarm of his flagship.

Ali didn't see any Venetian ships because they were all in Sicily, where they were to join the Spanish and other allies. The fall of Famagusta seemed to energize the

Christian League. They were really uniting. Their Doge, Sebastiano Veniero, commanded the Venetians in person. Venicro was a worthy successor to Enrico Dandolo, who, centuries before, led the crusaders against Constantinople (**see Constantinople, Part I, page 46**) at the age of 80. Veniero was 75. He had hoped to command the combined fleet, but Philip of Spain, who was paying half the cost of the operation, wanted to appoint the commander. He chose his half-brother, Don Juan of Austria. The new commander was 26.

Juan was the illegitimate son of Charles V and the daughter of a German merchant, who had been living in relative obscurity until Philip became king and appointed him to lead the war against the Moriscos. Don Juan was handsome, charismatic, full of energy, and had a decent amount of military skill. More important, he had common sense, which seemed to be lacking among the leaders of the allies.

As soon as he took command, Don Juan changed the composition of the fleet. No longer would each nationality have its own ships. He mixed Spaniards, Neapolitans, Venetians, Germans, and Sicilians in each of the three divisions of his fleet. In what was to be the last great galley battle in history, the galleys would, as usual, go into the fight as if they were armies. Agustino Barbarigo of Venice would command the left wing; Giovanni Andrea Doria of Genoa would command the right. Don Juan took the center division. His ship was flanked on the left by the flagship of Doge Sabastiano Veniero and on the right by Marco Antonio Colonna, the papal admiral.

Don Juan, unlike most Mediterranean admirals, seemed to think there was something to be learned from the Portuguese Indian campaigns. In front of each division, he posted two *galleasses*, sailing ships lacking oars but bristling with guns. They were to blast the Turks with gunfire and disrupt their formations. Because of their high sides, they were difficult to board. The galleys of both sides had their main batteries firing over the bow. The Turks had more warships, 273 to the League's 231, but the League had more guns on each ship. The Turkish galleys had three guns firing over their bows; Don Juan's had four. To make the guns more effective, Juan had his crews saw off the rams on their ships. The ram of a Renaissance galley was more like a bowsprit than the bronze beak that cleaved the waves on a classical galley. The Renaissance ram was designed to smash the oars of an enemy rather than hole its hull, so cutting off the rams made it easier for the Christians to use their guns effectively.

The League fleet heard that Ali Pasha had retired to the Gulf of Corinth, a long fjord running deep into Turk-occupied Greece. The Christian ships set out for the gulf.

Lepanto

Ali Pasha heard that the Christians were on the way and prepared to meet them near the town of Lepanto. He, too, divided his fleet into three divisions. Both sides cleared their decks and piled bedding along the sides as protection from missiles. They loaded the detachable chambers of their cannons, then fitted them to the guns. The Turks uncased their bows, and the Christians loaded their arquebuses. Men in the rigging held fire pots to throw on enemy decks and other had grappling irons to pull enemy ships close for boarding. On each ship, soldiers in armor prepared for close combat with spears and swords.

Because the Turks had more ships, their line would overlap the Christian right. Doria, commanding the right division, advanced obliquely to the right to avoid being flanked. His division, then, did not close with the Muslims as fast as the others. The Christian left wing and the Muslim right came into contact first. Mohammed Sirocco Pasha planned to flank Barbarigo's division by sailing close to shore. The Venetian, unfamiliar with the shallows, had stayed well away from shore. But when he saw the Turks rowing close to shore, Barbarigo knew it was safe for his ships, too. He turned and charged, catching the Turks in the flank. Marco Quirini, who commanded Barbarigo's right wing, swung around and took the Turks in the rear. Barbarigo was killed in the fighting, and his nephew, who succeeded him, was killed almost immediately afterwards, throwing the Christian left into some confusion. But Frederigo Nani and Quirini restored order, drove the Turks ashore, and killed or captured them all.

In the center, Don Juan and Ali Pasha exchanged salutes and closed with each other. Don Juan's gallcasses poured such effective fire on the Turks that the Muslim ships rowed furiously away, breaking up the formation. Juan's galleys maintained a slow stroke and straight line while they demonstrated superior gunnery. Ali Pasha steered

Galleass.

straight for Don Juan's galley. The soldiers on each ship boarded the other twice, only to be pushed back. Veniero brought his ship into the melee. On the other side of *Real*, Don Juan's flagship, Colonna burned a Turkish galley then joined the struggle between the flagships. Ali was killed and the whole Turkish center routed.

Meanwhile, on the Muslim left, Uluch Ali, who had been trying to flank Doria, suddenly reversed course and drove into the gap between Doria's division and Don Juan's. He got into the Christian rear and defeated several galleys. Doria turned about to follow the Turks, but the Marquis of Santa Cruz, the Spanish admiral commanding the reserves, got there first. Don Juan, who had been towing away captured Turkish galleys, cut his prizes loose and headed for Uluch Ali. Uluch Ali fled and reached a Turkish harbor before the Christians could get him.

A matter of morale

Although Lepanto did not strike nearly as heavy a blow to Islam as Diu, it was more celebrated at the time—and far better remembered now. The Turk, who appeared invincible at sea, had been beaten. It was not merely a case of failing to take a city: The Turkish navy had been almost annihilated.

Selim tried to put a brave face on it. "They have merely singed my beard," he said. He ordered a new fleet to be built and put to sea as early as possible. It was done. But the new fleet was built of green wood. It leaked badly, and its crews were as green as the wood. Most of the experienced Turkish sailors were at the bottom of the sea. Selim's new fleet made no attempt to further carry the war to the Christians. It avoided battle.

Lepanto did not break the power of the Ottoman Empire. But it did end the fear of the Turks that had been growing in Europe for centuries. From then on, Turkey was just another power to the people of Europe—one that they saw growing weaker and weaker.

Battle 37

Jackson at New Orleans.

New Orleans, 1814 AD
Old Hickory

Who fought: Americans (Andrew Jackson) vs. British (Edward Packenham).

What was at stake: The reaffirmation of U.S. independence.

It seemed to Major General Andrew Jackson that the British would never stop trying to take away American freedom. Once again, they'd been inciting the Indians to raid and massacre frontier settlements. Jackson was a product of the frontier. Born and raised in North Carolina, he had crossed the Appalachians and set up a law practice in the cluster of log huts called Nashville, Tennessee. He had little love for Indians, who he felt were savage brutes who killed women and children and tortured captives to death. But he actively hated the British, and he had his reasons.

During the Revolution, Jackson had joined the Patriot militia at 13, years before he theoretically would have been allowed to serve. He fought in the bitter, fratricidal war the Revolution had become in the South. He was captured. An arrogant British lieutenant ordered the boy to clean his boots. Young Jackson refused and demanded to be treated as a prisoner of war. The officer swung at him with his saber. Jackson would have been beheaded if he hadn't instinctively thrown up his arm. As it was, his arm was cut to the bone and his face was slashed. Then he and other prisoners were marched 40 miles without food or water to a prison camp where there were no beds, no blankets, and no medical attention. Young Andy and his brother, Robert, captured with him, caught smallpox, and Robert died.

After the war, Jackson started his law practice, bought an estate, went into politics, became a judge, and was elected a U.S. senator. Later the Tennessee militia soldiers elected him major general. The British were still meddling in American affairs. The Napoleonic wars were in full swing, and British agents in the United States were recruiting Americans for a planned expedition against French and Spanish possessions in the West Indies. They had even begun negotiations with Alexander Hamilton, the U.S. secretary of the treasury, for such an expedition. The plan called for an all-British fleet, with some American sailors serving on British ships and taking orders from British officers. In effect, the British were still treating the United States as if she were a colony. President John Adams squelched that plan as soon as he learned of it. The British did, however, stop American ships on the high seas and impress American sailors on those ships into the Royal Navy.

This led to war. American troops unsuccessfully attempted to invade Canada. British troops from Canada were equally unsuccessful in attempts to invade the United States. In the South, British agents were paying the Indians to take the warpath against the American settlers. They were successful with the Creeks, but that was more due to the pleadings of Tecumseh, the Shawnee advocate of Indian resistance, than to the British.

Jackson, commander of the Tennessee militia, begged the governor to let him fight. He was ordered to take the militia to New Orleans and put himself and his troops under the command of Brigadier General James Wilkinson.

Wilkinson was perhaps the sleaziest official in American history. Jackson hated him and had once called him a "double traitor," which he actually was. After the war, it was discovered that Wilkinson was a secret agent of the Spanish government. Wilkinson hated Jackson as much as Jackson hated him, and he was afraid of Jackson, because the ex-judge might expose him. To prevent that from happening, he pulled strings and had Jackson's army disbanded in the wilderness about 800 miles from home. The idea being that, to prevent starvation, Jackson's men would enlist under Wilkinson, and the troublesome militia general would have to return to Tennessee. Jackson foiled the scheme by paying his men and providing their rations from his own funds while he marched them home.

The general was stewing in Nashville because he'd been deprived of action. Then he got the sort of action he didn't want: He became involved in a barroom brawl with Thomas Hart Benton, the future senator from Missouri, and his brother. Jesse Benton shot Jackson, then Tom Benton shot him again. Jackson almost lost an arm for the second time and was near death for several days.

Meanwhile, the Creek War was getting worse and worse. An army of Creeks under William Weatherford, also known as Red Eagle, a Creek chief who led the faction known as the Red Sticks, sneaked up on Fort Mims in Mississippi Territory (present-day Alabama), and suddenly dashed through the open gate. They massacred more than 500 people—soldiers, civilians, men, women, and children. As soon as he had strength to get out of bed, Jackson led his militia against the Indians. With his wound throbbing and his body racked with dysentery, Jackson led them on forced marches that outran their supplies. For days, his men had nothing to eat but berries they picked along the way.

"He's tough as hickory," they said, and for the rest of his life, Jackson was known as "Old Hickory."

Jackson, leading his militia and friendly Indians, beat the Creeks in battle after battle. Finally he attacked the main Creek stronghold, Tohopeka, a heavily fortified village in the bend of a river. Jackson delayed the attack until the Creeks could move their women and children across the river. Then his infantry charged after fire from his two cannons. Jackson lost 47 men, but 900 Indians were killed. Among Jackson's soldiers was a young officer named Sam Houston and a private named Davy Crockett.

With the Indian troubles settled for the moment, Jackson went back to his estate, the Hermitage. Jackson learned from spies that British ships and troops were seen in Florida, which was Spanish territory. Spain, once a French ally, was officially neutral, but Jackson was convinced she was secretly helping Britain. He wanted to invade Florida, but the government didn't want war with Spain. He was advised to stay out of Florida. Jackson didn't consider advice an order. He wrote to the Spanish governor of Florida, advising the governor that he, Jackson, could not permit the use of Florida as a British base. He received a contemptuous reply. The Spanish thought they knew which way the war was going.

The British

Napoleon had been defeated. London was ready to deal with the Americans. It would transfer Wellington's troops and Nelson's ships to the new world and crush the insolent "rebels." The Royal Navy would raid the American seacoast cities, including the new capital, Washington. An army of 14,000 veterans of the wars against Napoleon would drive down the historic Richelieu-Lake Champlain-Hudson invasion route. British seaborne forces would shut down the American ports on the Gulf of Mexico and close the mouth of the Mississippi. Without access to the Gulf, the economy of the American states and territories in the Mississippi Valley would be paralyzed. Those areas might well be detached from the Union.

At first, the plan seemed to be working smoothly. The Royal Navy, led by Vice Admiral Sir Alexander Cochrane and his subordinate, Rear Admiral Sir George Cockburn, blockaded all ports on the Atlantic and raided the American coast with impunity. In the North, Lieutenant General Sir George Prevost asked Cochrane to step up his raiding to create a diversion for his invasion down the Hudson. Prevost was leading the largest army yet assembled in America during this war, but he still wanted more help from the navy. An army of 14,000 men would seem piddling compared to the numbers that had recently fought in Europe, but communications in North America made it almost impossible to field more. Opposing Prevost were 4,500 Americans, mostly militia. In Jamaica, the British were assembling another large army, including both veterans of the European wars and free West Indian blacks.

On August 19, 1814, a British force from Bermuda and Jamaica landed on the shore of the Chesapeake, drove away an unprepared American militia force, and, on the night of August 24–25, burned Washington. The U.S. government fled. Then the British plan hit a rough spot. The burning of Washington alerted the militia in nearby Baltimore. A British attempt to take Baltimore on September 12–14 only resulted in a lot of casualties, including the death of Major General Robert Ross, who led the land forces there and at Washington. The British army and navy returned to the islands for what Cochrane expected to be the masterstroke of the war: the closing of the Gulf.

What London once believed would be the masterstroke had already been smashed. Prevost's 14,000 men had to be supplied by water. No roads in that area, most of them no more than footpaths, could support an army that size. To protect Prevost's communications, the British launched a fleet on Lake Champlain. It attacked a somewhat smaller American flotilla under Captain Thomas Macdonough. Macdonough's ships were anchored. British fire wiped out all the guns on the starboard side of Macdonough's flagship, *Saratoga*, but he pivoted around his anchor cable and blasted the British with broadsides from his port guns. Another of his ships, *Eagle*, cut its cables and reversed position so it could use its port guns. The action was short and violent. It ended with one of the American ships disabled and all four of the British ships disabled and captured.

Prevost's line of communications had disappeared, and the British went back to Canada.

Everything now depended on Cochrane's plan. There were British troops in Florida, and British ships were using Florida harbors. The British had agents operating out of Florida to stir up the Indians—an incredible bit of optimism after Jackson had crushed the Creeks.

Cochrane knew that peace negotiations were already under way in France. A victory on the Gulf Coast now would make all the difference in the outcome of the war.

Negotiations

Britain had the preponderance of military power in North America, but the situation was reversed in Ghent, where peace talks were being held. Representing the United States were John Quincy Adams, the future president; Henry Clay, later one of the triumvirate of Clay, Webster, and Calhoun that dominated the Senate; Albert Gallatin, who had served as secretary of the treasury for 13 years; James Ashton Bayard, a distinguished senator; and Jonathan Russell, an experienced diplomat. The British delegates were not their country's brightest stars. Vice Admiral Lord Gambier had seldom been on a ship, William Adams was an admiralty lawyer, and Henry Golburn's principal qualification seemed to be that he hated America and all things American. The British wanted much of the western United States to be attached to Canada, and the prevention of settlers moving into a large area set aside for the Indians in what was left of the United States. The impressment of sailors the British considered deserters from the Royal Navy would continue, and the right of Americans to fish in Canadian waters would be revoked.

With Napoleon confined on the Isle of Elba, British officials considered sending Wellington to America to finish the job. The "Iron Duke" didn't like the idea. What was the use of his going to America, he asked, until Britain controlled the Great Lakes and Lake Champlain? As the Americans controlled all those bodies of water, everything depended on Cochrane's plan. To command the land forces in the Gulf expedition, London sent his brother-in-law, Sir Edward Pakenham, not Wellington.

New Orleans

Meanwhile, Jackson invaded Florida and captured Pensacola with little effort. There was no one to oppose him but a tiny and bedraggled Spanish force. The British had boarded their ships, blown up their fort, and sailed away as soon as the Americans appeared.

Jackson knew that the ultimate British goal was New Orleans, which was the only real city in the western wilderness and the key to the Mississippi. But he knew enough about the country surrounding the city to doubt that the British would land there. New Orleans was 105 miles from the mouths of the Mississippi, built on the silt of the Mississippi Delta. The Delta, someone said, is not really land—not land as most people know it. It's an expanse of extremely boggy soil broken up by innumerable lakes, bays, bayous, and creeks and filled with impassable swamps. The logical approach to New Orleans,

Jackson thought, would be to land at Mobile, the only good harbor west of Pensacola, and march overland to New Orleans. He fortified Mobile heavily and left most of his regulars there. He then moved on to New Orleans, which was a good move. The British had made an attempt to take Fort Bowyer in Mobile and had been driven off. The temporary British army commander, Major General John Keane, thought Jackson was waiting for them in Mobile, and decided to surprise Old Hickory by landing at New Orleans. With no opposition but the New Orleans militia, Keane expected a repeat of the Washington expedition. The British officers brought their wives along, and the wives brought their best dresses, looking forward to the social whirl of New Orleans.

Jackson's situation in New Orleans was not encouraging. The forts around the city were run-down. Some of the militia were excellent troops, like Brigadier General John Coffee's mounted rifles, but the New Orleans companies were an unknown quantity. A reinforcement consisting of militia from Kentucky didn't have enough guns to go around.

One exotic component of Jackson's army was a detachment of pirates from Lake Barataria (really a narrow-mouthed bay). Urged by prominent New Orleans citizens to incorporate the pirates in his army, Jackson swore he'd have nothing to do with the "hellish banditti." Then he met the pirate leader, Jean Lafitte, who resembled Blackbeard the way the Marquis de Lafayette resembled Captain Kidd. Lafitte, a polished Frenchman, had served in both the French and British navies. He had many close friends among the New Orleans aristocracy. He raided only Spanish ships, because he had some sort of grudge against Spain. But he evaded customs bringing in his booty, which put him at odds with the American authorities. The British had already asked for his help, but he had rejected them. Jackson was charmed and remembered that the pirates certainly must be experienced in handling cannons. He added the "hellish banditti" to his army.

Another exotic component was the regiment of free blacks, most of them Haitians who had fled the revolution there. Chockataw Indians, led by Chief Push-Ma-Ta-Ha, were also ready to fight the British. A paymaster who tried to withhold some pay to the non-white troops felt the rough edge of Jackson's tongue. Wages were to be paid immediately, the general said, "without inquiring whether the troops are black, white, or tea." And, of course, there were the frontier riflemen. According to Vincent Nolte, who was there, the riflemen knew nothing of military drill but were most serious about "the more important part of their calling, which was quietly to pick out their man and 'bring him down.'"

Jackson repaired the forts, then sent wood-chopping teams into the creeks and bayous to block them by felling trees across them. Waterways were the highways of the Mississippi Delta.

The Rodriguez Canal

The British forces landed on some uninhabited islands off the Louisiana coast. The rest of the expeditionary force soon reinforced Keane's advance party. On December 23, Keane took a group of 1,800 men in a fleet of shallow draft boats across Lake Borgne to set up a beachhead.

Somehow, Jackson's tree choppers neglected to block one waterway, the Bayou Bienvenue. The British, after driving off the gunboats Jackson had stationed as pickets on Lake Borgne, discovered the bayou. Keane's men rowed up the bayou and found themselves in the sugar plantation of Major General Jacques Phillippe de Villere, commander of the Louisiana militia. They crept up on the plantation house and surprised the general's son, Major Rene Phillippe Gabriel Villere. Keane posted a guard, sent back a courier and waited for Pakenham and the rest of the army to come up. They were only two hours from New Orleans, and Jackson didn't know they had landed.

Suddenly Major Villere broke away from his guards. He ran across the yard, leaped over a fence and mounted a horse. In a short time, he was in Jackson's headquarters with the news.

Jackson poured a glass of wine for each of his aides and said, "Gentlemen, the British are below us. Tonight we must fight." Then as the officers left to spread the news, he ground his fist into a palm and mumbled, "I will smash them, so help me God!"

He sent the schooner *Carolina* down the river to fire on the British camp. The British had just begun to sleep when a voice from the river yelled, "Now give it to them for the honor of America!" *Carolina* fired a broadside into the camp, then another, and another. Jackson waited half an hour, then sent his infantry charging into the camp. The ship ceased fire at the same time so no Americans would be hit by "friendly fire." The militia fired a volley and charged the stunned British, thrusting with bayonets and hacking with scalping knives and tomahawks. Coffee's mounted rifles rode around the camp and charged from the rear. The disciplined British units soon regained their cohesion and began to fight back. Some even had the wit to try deception. Captain John Donelson, having killed a number of the enemy and made prisoners of others, saw troops coming up on the rear of his men. They shouted that "they were General Coffee's men, having by some means learned the general's name. They advanced within about 10 steps, ordered us for d--d rebels to lay down our arms...I answered them, they be d--d and ordered my men to open fire."

Jackson withdrew his troops from the confused melee and ordered them to construct breastworks behind the Rodriguez Canal, a shallow waterway that crossed the only road to New Orleans. Some of the breastworks were built of cotton bales, but most were mud, an unglamorous substance, but one even better for stopping bullets and cannon balls. Jackson had 24 dead, 115 wounded, and 74 prisoners in the night attack. Keane's losses were 46 killed, 167 wounded, and 64 prisoners.

Pakenham arrived with the main body on Christmas day. He saw that something must be done about the two American ships, *Carolina* and *Louisiana*. He lined the river bank with light cannons and constructed ovens to turn cannon balls into "red hot shot." At the next appearance of the ships, the British gunners and their hot shot set *Carolina* ablaze. *Louisiana* tried to move away, but there was no wind. The sailors lowered rowboats and towed her away.

Jackson made breaches in the levee to flood the ground in front of his line, but the Mississippi was dropping and all he succeeded in doing was making the already muddy ground muddier. He sent out foraging parties to collect all the shovels in the area. His men were digging and piling up dirt around the clock. When they were finished, they had a parapet five feet high with a ditch (the canal) four feet deep and 10 feet wide in front of it. The line ran 1,500 yards between the Mississippi and a cypress swamp. Behind the parapet were a 32 pounder cannon, three 24-pounders, and an 18 pounder, as well as a number of smaller guns. Across the Mississippi, with Jackson's right flank, the general had built a small fort containing a 24-pounder and two 12-pounders.

Pakenham launched his first attack on December 28. The British Congreve rockets, which had spooked the American militia at Washington, had no effect on Jackson's men. Neither did the British cannons, fired from long range. *Louisiana* spotted columns of British infantry moving up and peppered them with grapeshot. American cannons behind the canal and across the Mississippi joined in. So did the riflemen, and Pakenham called off his assault.

At night, Pakenham's men dragged their own guns over the muddy flat to positions about 700 to 800 yards of the American line and emplaced them behind dirt filled sugar barrels. Because the gunners had to work at night to prevent them from being targets for the American artillery, the gun platforms were uneven.

On New Year's Day, the British guns opened fire. The American guns replied. Because of their uneven platforms, the British fire was inaccurate. The American fire was not. American cannon balls and shells penetrated the sugar barrels and silenced the British guns. Pakenham again cancelled an infantry assault. That night, the British artillerymen dragged their guns back over the muddy field in a driving rain. More British reinforcements were coming. Jackson sent riflemen to snipe at the British camp and keep them from having a restful night.

Many of Pakenham's troops would not have had a restful night in any case. They were digging through the levee so that British rowboats, dragged laboriously over-land, could be launched on the river. British marines and sailors, plus light infantry from a regular infantry regiment and a West Indian regiment, were to cross the river and attack Jackson's detached battery. They would capture the guns and turn them on the Americans. Meanwhile, the rest of the army would attack Jackson's line.

The attack began on January 8. The long columns of red-coated soldiers could be seen a mile from the American line, as they marched over the open mud flats. Not seen were the West Indians who filtered through the cypress swamp. They could not concentrate because of the terrain. Their role was to fire and distract the American left. Another West Indian regiment, with three regular infantry companies, moved along the outside of the levee toward a battery Jackson had established across the canal from his line. They, too, were not seen.

Major General Sir Samuel Gibbs led 2,200 men against the left-center of Jackson's line, held by an 18-pounder and Tennessee and Kentucky militia under Major General William Carroll. Major General Keane led a second column of 1,200 men. This was to attack the right of Jackson's line. Troubles began immediately.

The 44th Regiment of Foot, at the head of Gibbs's column, was to bring fascines (bundles of sticks) to fill in the canal and ladders to climb over the combined canal bank and breastwork. The 44th had morale problems. They had shipped out to America the day before they were to be mustered out of the army. At the last minute, Gibbs discovered that they had forgotten the ladders and fascines. He sent men back to get them. As it turned out, hardly any of his men got close enough to the American rampart to use the ladders even if they had been available.

The force that was sent across the river to attack Jackson's detached battery was eight hours late. Moving up the boats took longer than Packenham expected. By the time the troops, under Colonel William Thornton, had formed up across the Mississippi, the battle had already begun. Guns in the detached battery were enfilading the British assault columns.

One part of the plan that went perfectly was the surprise attack by the West Indians and others on the battery in advance of the canal. But once the British had taken the battery, they were exposed to fire from both the American main line and the battery across the river. They were driven back or killed.

Keane's column was supposed to attack the American right, but seeing Gibbs's troops faltering under the American fire, it marched obliquely to converge with the other column. That increased the troops' exposure to both the American artillery and the American riflemen. Jackson's army had a high proportion of riflemen for those times, and the rifle's effective range was five to 10 times that of the smoothbore musket.

The crowning British mistake was that the whole attack began too late. The advance was supposed to take place in darkness to eliminate the American advantage of aimed rifle fire. The sun was up before any movement began.

Not to be left out of things, the Royal Navy sailed up the Mississippi, perhaps to support Pakenham. They were stopped at Fort St. Phillip, far below the battlefield.

The British troops advanced with great bravery. None were braver than their leaders. Keane, Gibbs, and Pakenham were actually leading their troops, and leading them from horseback. They made perfect targets for Jackson's riflemen. All three generals were quickly cut down. The American cannons fired first exploding shells, then grape shot, then cannister. The balls in cannister shot were smaller and more numerous than those in grape. Each shot knocked down batches of men. The riflemen had begun firing when the Redcoats were about a quarter of a mile away—a range incredible to those who knew only smoothbore muskets. The American musketeers, who were more numerous than the riflemen, joined in when the British were less than 100 yards away. Jackson reported that his men fired "with a briskness of which there have been but few instances, perhaps, in any country."

"Never before," wrote a British lieutenant, "had British veterans quailed. But it would be silly to deny that they did so now…That leaden torrent no man on earth could face. I had seen battlefields in Spain and in the East…but nowhere…such a scene as this."

The British retreated. Then the men threw off their knapsacks, reformed, and advanced again. The American fire never ceased. About 70 Britons reached the canal, some 20 climbed the breastworks, and all were either captured or killed.

"I had never had so grand and awful an idea of the resurrection," Jackson wrote later, "as when I saw 500 Britons emerging from the heaps of their dead comrades, all over the plain rising up." They were surrendering.

The only British success was Thornton's boat-borne brigade, which finally captured Jackson's detached battery, held by only 450 men. But by the time they captured it, the British army was in full retreat. Thornton's men joined them.

The British losses, according to the official record, were 291 dead, 1,262 wounded and 484 captured of the 4,000 troops engaged in the battle. Many of the wounded, like Pakenham and Gibbs, never lived to get to the ships. Most of them never saw England again.

Jackson's losses, of the troops on his main line, were eight killed and 13 wounded. Five more had been killed and 26 more wounded at the detached battery across the river. New Orleans was probably the most lopsided defeat the British Army suffered in its entire history.

A wasted victory?

It has become customary to say that New Orleans was a useless battle, because the peace treaty had been signed before it was fought. Because news could travel only as fast as a sailing ship, nobody knew the war was over.

The peace treaty left everything exactly as it had been before the war. Wellington had pointed out to the British government that its forces had not earned the right to claim any new territory. That, the repulse at Baltimore, and, especially, the defeat on Lake Champlain, convinced them to forget all their extravagant demands. The American delegates realistically compared U.S. military strength with that of Britain and were happy to settle for antebellum status. The Napoleonic Wars were over, and impressment was no longer an immediate problem.

Although the war was over, New Orleans was a major shock to the British government. Impressment was never, ever tried again. Never again did Britain dare to treat the United States as a colony.

In 1829, during a debate in Parliament on a boundary dispute with the United States, one MP said, "We had better yield a point or two rather than go to war with the Americans."

"Yes," said another MP, "We shall get nothing but hard knocks there."

New Orleans had established once and for all the independence of the United States of America.

Battle 38

Revolutionary crowd overthrows the Duma.

Petrograd, 1917
The Perils of Prosperity

Who fought: Russian mobs (later V.I. Lenin) vs. Russian governments (the Tsar's, then Kerenskii's).

What was at stake: The creation of a large Communist state and later the spread of Communism over the world.

In a way, Russia never had it so good. When World War I began, that vast country was just starting to emerge from an agricultural economy. The government went into a crash program of industrial mobilization. Factories expanded enormously, creating a tremendous demand for labor. Peasants left the land to take jobs in mines, railroads, and factories. The economy was booming.

That boom created a shortage of agricultural products, especially food.

To finance the expansion, the government issued tons of paper money, unsecured by gold or anything else. Prices skyrocketed. Wages went up, too, but not as fast as prices. Large landowners took vast tracts of farmland out of production because they couldn't afford to pay farm workers. (Serfdom had been eliminated in Russia around the same time that slavery had been eliminated in the United States.)

Although the number of workers on the railroads almost doubled between 1914 and 1917, the railroads were unable to deliver as much food. Most of that was because

218

of the demands placed on them by the army, but some of it was because the new, unskilled labor wasn't able to maintain the roads and rolling stock as well.

So, as a result of the booming economy, more people in Russia were starving than ever before.

The meat grinder

Then there was the war, a curse that was common to all the belligerents. Young men had gone off to the battlefields, fired with patriotic fervor and a desire to perform heroic deeds. But heroic deeds were passé. Machine guns and barbed wire had replaced valor. Men died in heaps without even seeing the enemy, slain by invisible artillery. Great swords like Excaliber and Durandel belonged to another age—now there was poison gas.

Three years of this had affected all the troops. Before the end of 1917, the Italian Army panicked at Caporetto; the French Army had a massive mutiny; the British Army some smaller ones. The German Army was on the verge of another, but it was saved by a decisive victory on the Russian front. It didn't matter that the Germans were not entirely responsible for their victory. Russia had collapsed from within. The Russian army suffered from morale problems greater than those of any other belligerent, and so did the Russian people.

Intellectuals in Russia were largely skipped by mobilization. So were essential workers in transportation, mining, and factories. The peasants, the lowest rung on the social ladder, went to war. The peasants had always fought Russia's wars, but in other wars, there weren't so many non-peasants. Never before had so many Russians been exempt from military service. The Russian peasant-soldier had been famous for his dogged bravery. But in this war, he was not fighting Swedish musketeers, French cuirassiers, or other soldiers. He was fighting a vast, impersonal killing machine. And as 1917 began, to top his troubles, the peasant in the trenches was getting letters from home telling him his family couldn't get bread.

Petrograd

The city of Peter the Great, in the early years of the 20th century, resembled Paris at the end of the 18th century, except that the monarchy was in even worse shape. Revolution had been in the air since the beginning of the century. One week after Port Arthur surrendered to the Japanese (see **Tsushima, page 51**), troops fired on unarmed demonstrators in front of the Winter Palace, killing and wounding hundreds. Demonstrations around the country turned into mutinies in the armed forces. Tsar Nicholas II had to promise reforms, including a constitutional monarchy that included a legislative body, the Duma. That took the fire out of most of the rebels, and the army was able to put down the rest.

There remained, however, an enormous disparity of wealth between the nobility and the peasants, with only a minuscule middle class in between. Then there was the Tsar himself, a weak man who couldn't say no to his Tsarina, the strong-willed but somewhat nutty Alexandra.

"We're heading for revolution," Aleksei Putilov, a Petrograd industrialist, told the French ambassador, Maurice Paleologue, early in 1917. Paleologue was not sure that would be a bad thing. "Anything is preferable to the state of anarchy that characterizes

Russian troops who joined the rebel, ready for anything.

the present situation," he reported to Paris. "I am obliged to report that at the present moment, the Russian Empire is run by lunatics."

Tsarina Alexandra believed she literally had a direct line to God, who told her which officials should be appointed. Her communications from the Almighty came through a self-appointed holy man, the monk Grigorii Yefimovich Rasputin. Rasputin has to be one of the strangest characters in modern history. He seemed somehow to be able to stop the bleeding of the hemophiliac Tsarevich, Alexis. After a long line of incompetents and thieves had been appointed at the suggestion of Rasputin and his disciples, other "holy men," some Russian nobles decided to get rid of Rasputin. They poisoned his food, but the poison didn't affect him. They shot him in the head, but he didn't die. They carried him out and pushed him under the ice on a frozen river. After several hours of immersion, the "holy man" finally gave up the ghost. He didn't die soon enough to save the government.

"We want bread!"

On the morning of February 23, 7,000 women workers walked out of a textile mill and demonstrated for higher pay and lower prices. By nightfall, the crowd of demonstrators, chanting, "We want bread," had swelled to more than 70,000. The next day, there were 150,000 demonstrators. By the third day, there was a quarter of a million. The police tried in vain to keep the mob in check. On the fourth day, the troops of the Petrograd garrison joined the protestors.

The mob, now supported by soldiers with armored cars and machine guns, opened the city's prisons. Socialist politicians began organizing them. The mob elected the first Soviet of Workers' and Soldiers' Deputies. On March 2, Nicholas II abdicated.

Some members of the Duma organized a provisional government, but it had to work with the Petrograd Soviet. Other soviets sprang up all over the country. In this governmental chaos, an obscure provincial lawyer, Aleksandr Kerenskii, appeared. Kerenskii was a spellbinding orator and was able to keep both the "Revolutionary Provisional Government," as the Duma members called themselves, and the Petrograd Soviet, happy. "Russia must stay in the war," he told both the "soldiers and workers" and the politicians, "and it must drive the wicked capitalist out of Mother Russia and preserve socialist ideals." They cheered him wildly.

Germany got ready to oppose the "Kerenskii offensive" with conventional and unconventional weapons. The conventional weapons featured the rolling artillery barrage ahead of infantry called "von Mackensen's phalanx," developed on the Eastern Front by hard-eyed General August von Mackensen. The unconventional weapons were a couple of Russian radicals, Lev D. Trotskii and Vladimir I. Lenin. German agents found them in Switzerland, where they had been living in exile, and smuggled them back into Russia.

Kerenskii's oratory was able to inflame the soldiers, but when they got to the front, they found the war was just as bad as ever. Conditions in the rear were, if anything, worse. They began to desert in droves. Karenskii's offensive died so quickly it was practically stillborn.

Moscow again lapsed into total chaos, and the Germans again began to advance. Trotskii organized the Red Guards, a private army of the Bolsheviks, the majority faction of the Social Democrat Party. Their mission was not to fight the Germans but to implement the will of the Bolsheviks' leader, V.I. Lenin. Lenin, who had been preaching "peace and land" to the masses of Russia, was able to overthrow Kerenskii with a coup the night of October 24–25. He announced a new government on October 26, and offered to make peace with the Germans. He repeated the offer on November 15, and the Germans accepted.

Results: long-range and short-range

Germany occupied a vast amount of Russian territory as a result of the peace, but much more important, it was able to shift hundreds of thousands of troops to the Western Front. There, Erich Ludendorff, who by this time was acting generalissimo of the German forces, prepared to knock France and Britain out of the war (**see France, page 222**).

The real importance of the rebellion in Petrograd, however, is that it set the stage for the creation of the Soviet Union. The Soviet Union was to become a major factor, and at times *the* major factor, in international relations for most of the 20th century.

Battle 39

France, 1918 AD
The Coming Climax

Who fought: French, British, and Americans (Ferdinand Foch) vs. Germans (Erich Ludendorff).

What was at stake: The renewed possibility that Germany—a Germany run by the mad Ludendorff—would dominate Europe.

For three gruesome years the armies of Britain, France, and Germany had struggled on the Western Front. Germany had been fighting on two fronts, so the Allies had numerical superiority, although they had no unity of command. They had slowly, at the cost of millions of lives, pushed the Germans back—but not far. The Germans still occupied part of France and most of Belgium.

Across the Atlantic, the United States, which had turned sharply against Germany after the invasion of Belgium **(see The Marne, page 156)**, was growing closer to the Allies as a result of Germany's unrestricted submarine warfare. On February 3, 1917, the United States broke off diplomatic relations with Germany. The United States was an enormous country—almost as populous as Russia—and an industrial power greater than even Germany. Its developed natural resources were far greater than any European country's. It seemed certain that the United States would enter the war on the Allied side. That was cause for rejoicing in Britain and France, but not for despair in Germany.

In spite of its size and economy, the United States was not able to immediately make its weight felt in Europe. It had a large and powerful navy, but its army was minuscule and, except for rifles, lacked modern weapons. Its production of the weapons of modern war—machine guns, artillery, tanks, and airplanes—was almost nil.

Before April 3, when President Woodrow Wilson of the United States asked Congress to declare war on Germany, the food riots began in Petrograd, and the Tsar abdicated (**see Petrograd, page 218**). In October, Lenin overthrew the provisional Russian government, and the Russian front collapsed. The Italian rout at Caporetto drew Allied troops from France, while Germany was able to transfer its troops from the East to the West.

Erich Ludendorff, who had made his reputation in the capture of the Belgian forts and as Paul von Hindenburg's chief of staff in East Prussia, saw a chance to knock the French and British out of the war before the Americans could influence the outcome. For the ambitious Ludendorff, it was like a gift from heaven.

The man on horseback

Ludendorff looked like a caricature of a German general: a thick-necked, burly man who never smiled, had neither friends nor sense of humor and had no interests but work. He differed from the traditional model in that he meddled in politics. His intelligence and energy had won him a position on the general staff, but his lobbying for an increase in the size of the army bounced him off to an unimportant regiment.

Ludendorff was, in his own way, a political philosopher. After the war, he would become an ardent supporter of Adolf Hitler. In his book on "totalitarian warfare," Ludendorff was to declare that war was the highest expression of a nation's "will to live;" therefore politics must be subservient to the needs of the military. In war, a nation should place everything at the service of the military. In peace, the national aim must be preparedness for the next war. He preached a religion of nationalism. All women should accept that their highest calling was to bear children who would "bear the burden of the totalitarian war." All men should eagerly prepare to fight the next war. Anyone who might express, or even entertain, views critical of the High Command should be ruthlessly liquidated. Such views were too insane even for Hitler. He pensioned off the old soldier as soon as possible.

When World War I began, Ludendorff returned to the staff. As a sightseer from the general staff, he took command of a brigade whose commander had been killed and led it through the ring of forts around Liege and occupied the city. He became an instant hero. When danger threatened in the east, he was sent to East Prussia in time to meet the Russian invasion. The German commander, Hindenburg, was a superannuated Junker who got the command on the strength of his position as an East Prussian aristocrat. He wisely followed Ludendorff's suggestions.

Ludendorff, in turn, wisely followed the suggestions of Max Hoffmann. But although both Hindenburg and Ludendorff became popular heroes as a result of Tannenberg, Hoffmann did not. Hoffmann didn't fit the German Army's image of a hero. He was a tall, fat man who hated exercise and loved food. He was considered the worst fencer in the army and was such a poor horseman he once fell off his mount while parading in front of the Kaiser. Before the war, according to historian Barbara Tuchman, "He drank wine and consumed sausages all night at the officers' club until 7 a.m., when he took his company out on parade and returned for a snack of more sausages and two quarts of Moselle before breakfast." Unlike Ludendorff, he was amiable, quick-witted, and respected no one. Most importantly, the fat around his waist did not extend to his brain.

In late 1916, the firm of Hindenburg and Ludendorff was moved out of the Eastern Front to replace Erich von Falkenhayn as chief of the general staff. Hoffmann stayed behind as chief of staff on the Eastern Front. Hindenburg, never distinguished for his brilliance, was 70 years old and increasingly dependent on Ludendorff. The pushy Ludendorff quickly made himself, in effect, the military dictator of Germany, even deciding who should be in the Kaiser's cabinet. The first thing "Ludenburg-Hindendorff" did was construct a permanent defense line across France and Belgium. It was named the Siegfried Line, although the British called it the Hindenburg Line. But that defense line was just insurance. With the Russian war over, Ludendorff put together a plan for a "peace offensive" in the West. It would depend on new tactics—tactics the German Army had been evolving over the previous three years.

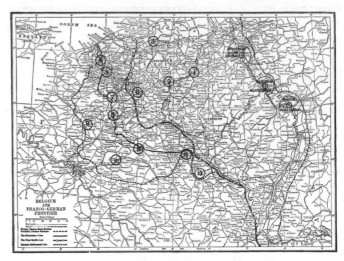

Hindenburg Line battle map.

Storm troopers

In 1914, the German Army's tactics were among the most conservative of the world's major armies. In spite of the slaughter caused by breech-loading and repeating rifles in the American Civil War and the two Anglo-Boer wars, German infantry practiced attacking in columns of platoons. The company commander marched in front of his company and each platoon, lined up almost shoulder-to-shoulder, followed, one behind the other. Platoon leaders marched on the right of each line and NCOs marched behind their platoons to keep the privates from dropping back.

The British, never famed as military innovators, had adopted an open order advance, with plenty of room between each man. They knew something was needed after losing several battles to sharpshooting Afrikaners. They had already changed their red coats for khaki so they'd make less inviting targets for Pathan marksmen on India's Northwest Frontier. The Germans, to their credit, did adopt uniforms of "field gray," a color well adapted to campaigning in northern Europe. France went into the war with its soldiers wearing red trousers. After a few thousand Frenchmen had been killed, that item of uniform was changed. Still, outraged conservatives cried, "But red pants are France!"

German authorities believed that advancing in open order would encourage riflemen to hide to avoid combat—showing what the aristocratic officer class thought of the "other ranks."

"They evidently intend to handle their infantry in close lines in the next war," an American officer wrote after observing German maneuvers in 1893. "The average German soldier is not a person to be turned loose in a skirmish line and left to a certain degree to his own devices…They prefer to lose men than to lose control of the officers over them."

German authorities believed that each platoon should be within the sound of the platoon leader's voice, which, in the noise of battle, did not carry far. The troops fired volleys on command. Volleys were supposed to establish "fire superiority," which would cause the enemy to keep his head down. The troops would then charge with bayonets. The authorities thought that this *Furor Teutonicus* would cow the enemy. It didn't. The highly trained British regulars cut them down in heaps at Mons.

The Germans began to change their infantry doctrine rapidly after that and the trench warfare that followed. First, special assault teams were formed to lead attacks on trenches. The "storm troops" carried a shorter, lighter version of the standard Mauser 1898 rifle and a large number of hand grenades. Supporting them were machine guns and a variety of trench mortars. Flame-throwers and more machine guns were added to the assault units. Then Germany adopted a light machine gun, like the Lewis gun, which was already used by the British, the Belgians, and the Chauchat of the French. The German gun, the Maxim 08/15, was heavier than the Allied guns, but much more reliable.

With the new weapons went a new organization. In the old army, nobody below company commander could exercise any initiative. In the evolving German infantry, platoon leaders, then even squad leaders, were expected to adapt to the circumstances. Platoons and squads were often widely separated during an attack, and the men took advantage of available cover, such as the numerous shell craters. Small units by-passed strong points and tried to get on the flanks or rear of centers of resistance.

Allied infantry also evolved during the years of trench warfare, although it hadn't changed as much as the German infantry. The Allies, however, had a brand-new weapon, the tank, invented by the British. Ludendorff was not impressed with tanks, however. Owing to mishandling, the tanks had not managed to break the dug-in deadlock.

Ludendorff thought he saw another way to break the deadlock. During the winter of 1917–18, all German infantry were trained in the new storm troop tactics. The younger and more active men were grouped into storm troop battalions, with one battalion to a division. With storm troops leading the way, the German infantry were to attack the Allied lines. They'd bypass strong points, using cover and operating in small, semi-autonomous units. They would follow the lines of least resistance, and above all, they would keep pushing forward. Ludendorff, in other words, was planning to use the tactics the Germans had developed for small operations—tactics the French called "infiltration"—and expand them to a giant scale. Instead of limited objectives, he was seeking complete victory.

Ludendorff planned to strike where the French and British armies joined. His troops would break through, then swing north, surrounding the British and pushing them against the channel ports. The sea and the Royal Navy protected Britain itself, so his attack couldn't knock Britain out. However, it could knock it out of France, and that might end the war. The French Army was much larger than the British, and the German general feared that he didn't have enough troops to strike a decisive blow against the French in a short time. He had to gain a quick decision, because...

..."The Yanks are coming"

A few months before, the need for a knockout blow didn't seem so urgent to the Germans.

"They will not even come, because our submarines will sink them," Admiral Eduard von Capelle, secretary of state for the navy, assured a committee of the Reichstag. "Thus America from a military point of view means nothing, and again nothing and for a third time nothing." Ludendorff agreed and approved an intensification of unrestricted submarine warfare.

But at their best, the German U-boats were never able to shut down shipping to France and Britain. Three months after Capelle's statement, convoys, minefields, and air patrols had turned the tide against the U-boats. The first elements of a projected American army of four million were in France. If they didn't have enough artillery, machine guns, tanks, and planes, the Allies had plenty to give them. The Americans got busy in other ways. American naval ships tightened the Allied blockade of Germany to the point where literal starvation became a distinct possibility for the German population. The French and British officers still had not gotten over the notion that Americans were colonials in need of guidance from the wise Europeans. They wanted to integrate the American troops into their armies. General John

A British tank.

J. Pershing, the American commander, disabused them. He told Marshal Ferdinand Foch, who had become the Allied commander, that the U.S. Army was an organic unit, and it would fight as a unit. Pershing did, in a few emergencies, lend American troops to the Allies, but the doughboys never became replacements.

The peace offensive

The Germans struck near Arras. Ludendorff massed his troops in the darkness and opened with a violent bombardment from hundreds of artillery pieces. The shelling began suddenly: The Germans had not first sighted in their guns. They used both high explosive and gas shells, and then the infantry came forward under the cover of a pea-soup fog.

The main thrust was to be delivered toward Arras by the German 17th Army, with the 18th Army acting as a flank guard south of the 17th. The 17th army was held up in front of Arras, but the 18th went charging through the weakly held line in front of it. If Ludendorff were following his own principles, he would have shifted his reserves to the 18th and told it to keep on going. The 18th had broken the Allied main line of resistance and was in the enemy's rear. With a little extra push it would have been able to swing north, cutting the British off from the French completely and forcing them back to the channel.

Instead, Ludendorff told the 18th Army to halt. It was getting too far ahead—farther than his plan called for. He sent his reserves to the 17th Army. The 17 didn't take Arras, but it took a lot of casualties. After two days, Ludendorff let the 18th resume its advance toward Amiens. But by that time the Allies had brought up reserves to block the Germans, and on April 4, Ludendorff called off the attack.

The Germans did get close enough to Paris to shell it. But three specially constructed, fabulously expensive guns did the shelling. The shelling may have been good propaganda, but militarily, it was worthless.

Ludendorff made another try to the north on April 9. It was conceived as a diversion, but it made surprising gains. Instead of shifting masses of troops to the area, Ludendorff dribbled in divisions a few at a time. Eventually, it became a full-scale offensive. But by that time, the British had reorganized their defense. As before, when the defense hardened, Ludendorff threw in more troops. However, he got nothing but more casualties.

Although he insisted that he was going to bypass centers of resistance to "punch a hole in the line," Ludendorff was not following the line of least resistance. He was butting his head against the areas of most resistance. This was not the way things went on the Eastern Front. Something was missing.

That something was Max Hoffmann. The gluttonous general would certainly have persuaded his chief not to throw away his numerical superiority in fruitless attacks on strongly fortified areas. But Hoffmann was now overseeing things on the now peaceful (for Germany) Russian front.

Ludendorff attacked again, this time south of the bulge he had created in the Allied line. The attack was a month later than scheduled because the Germans had wasted so much time in the north. American intelligence had warned the Allies the attack was coming, but the warning was ignored until captured prisoners confirmed it. The commander of the French 6th Army had foolishly massed his troops in the front line, where they were slaughtered by the first German bombardment, instead of holding a large reserve to counterattack. The Germans quickly reached the Marne, but by that time, the French had their reserves in place. American troops were now holding positions on the Western Front. German numerical superiority was rapidly going down the drain. The Germans did manage to get across the Marne, but an Allied counterattack drove them back.

Collapse

The tide had turned, Ludendorff had run out of time, and he no longer had numerical superiority. American troops were taking an increasing part in the counterattacks. The counterattacks were conducted the way Ludendorff's peace offensive should have been. They were a series of attacks, each broken off before its impetus was spent, each paving the way for the next. On August 7, the Allies secretly massed 456 British and French tanks. They attacked the next day, closely followed by infantry.

Ludendorff lost his nerve. "August 8 was the black day of the German army in the history of the war...It put the decline of our fighting power beyond all doubt....The war must be ended."

When the retreating Germans had straightened their line, Ludendorff felt better, and he wanted to continue the war. But nobody else, except the Kaiser, did.

The German population had had enough—enough of food and fuel shortages and enough of casualty lists. Revolution was brewing. Then Bulgaria, attacked by French and British troops based in Greece, surrendered. The Turks, driven back in Palestine and Mesopotamia, also surrendered. The Italians broke through on the Alpine front, and Austria was out of the war. Ludendorff was forced to resign. The Kaiser was asked to abdicate. Instead, Wilhelm went to army headquarters on the Western Front and talked about using the army to quell the revolution at home. He was advised that the troops would not fight for him, and he fled to Holland.

The "war to end war?"

World War I was over. The war had killed more soldiers in less time than any war in history. Four empires were destroyed. Monarchy, except for a handful of royal figureheads, had disappeared in Europe. Central and Eastern Europe were consumed by chaos. Out of chaos arose a generation of savage dictators, with Adolf Hitler and Josef Stalin the greatest and most savage. An almost unbroken stream of small wars, followed by a second Great War, followed the "Great War." The Second World War killed as many soldiers as the first and twice as many civilians as soldiers.

What would have happened had Ludendorff's offensive succeeded? That's hard to say. All of Europe was exhausted. Russia was in a civil war that would have ended in a Red victory no matter what happened elsewhere. The Ottoman Empire was gone for good, and nothing could have restored it. Austria-Hungary was already fragmented. Of all the major belligerents, only the United States and Japan were relatively untouched.

The world would have been different if Germany had won, but considering all the damage that had been done, it wouldn't have been any better. With Ludendorff as the unchallenged master of continental Europe, it could only have been worse—much worse.

Battle 40

Bowie fights to the end at the Alamo.

The Alamo and San Jacinto, 1836 AD
No Quarter

Who fought: Texans (William Travis) vs. Mexicans (Antonio Lopez de Santa Anna).

What was at stake: The Texas struggle for independence, which led to the U.S.-Mexican War and an enormous increase in the United States's size.

A blood-red flag fluttered from the bell tower of the church of San Fernando. It stood for "no quarter." So did the tune the band was playing, *el Deguello*, and the slow, deceptively sweet melody that dated from Spain's wars with the Moors and had introduced a million bullfights. In the pale light of early dawn, four columns of Mexican soldiers moved through the trenches surrounding the old mission-turned-fort. They filed into the saps that led to the fort's walls.

Young Colonel William Barret Travis had just completed his watch on the walls when he heard a volley of cannon fire. He snatched up his shotgun and returned to the walls. Outside, Travis saw his men firing their cannons and their long "Kentucky" rifles. Each rifleman had three or four loaded rifles beside him so he could keep up rapid fire when the Mexicans tried to charge. Mexican bodies were spread out on the fields around the fort. Mexican troops were huddled at the base of the walls. Travis fired both barrels of his shotgun at the mass of Mexicans, reloaded, and fired again.

"Our columns left along their path a wide trail of blood, of wounded, and of dead," wrote Lieutenant Colonel Juan Enrique de la Pena of the Mexican Army. "It could be observed that a single cannon volley did away with half the company of chasseurs from Toluca."

The Mexicans planned to bring up ladders to scale the walls of the fort, but most of the ladder carriers had been killed. Only one ladder was apparent to Pena.

Travis knew the army of President-General Antonio Lopez de Santa Anna was going to pay heavily for this day. But he also knew that they would win. There were too many Mexicans and too few Texans—5,000 to 182. But as Travis wrote at the beginning of the siege, "I am determined to sustain myself as long as possible and die like a soldier who never forgets what is due his own honor and that of his country."

Santa Anna

Tall, handsome Antonio Lopez de Santa Anna had only one political principle. "If I were made God," he once said, "I should wish to be something more."

Santa Anna had been an officer in the Spanish Army when another Spanish officer, Augustin de Iturbide, joined the rebels who had been sporadically fighting Spain for 20 years. Santa Anna joined Iturbide. Iturbide beat the Spanish decisively and made himself Emperor of Mexico and what is now Central America. Santa Anna, now an imperial officer, revolted and overthrew Iturbide. Mexico became a republic and adopted a liberal constitution, giving its states (modeled on the states of its northern neighbor) considerable autonomy. But in the capital, one would-be strongman succeeded another.

Spain saw an opportunity to retake its most prized colony: the land it had called "New Spain." But Santa Anna led the Mexican Army against the former colonial masters. He thoroughly outmaneuvered the Spanish at Tampico and drove them into the sea. The victor of Tampico, the republican hero, returned in triumph and made himself president. For the next 30 years, Santa Anna would dominate Mexican politics. He would become chief executive seven times and be deposed seven times. One time, fleeing from his enemies, he was captured by cannibal Indians. Fortunately for him, his enemies found him before the Indians could prepare dinner.

Originally an advocate of liberal, decentralized government, Santa Anna as president resolved to remake the government into a centralized dictatorship. Politicians in the northern states objected. Santa Anna led his army against the state governments in Zacatecas and Coahuila. He sent his brother-in-law, General Martin Perfecto de Cos, against a third state: Texas.

Sparsely settled, Texas had once been kept by Spain as a buffer area between New Spain and the French of Louisiana and later the Americans of the young republic that had purchased Louisiana. Moses Austin, a Connecticut native who had lived in Louisiana when it was Spanish territory, convinced the Spanish governor to let him bring in American settlers. They would become Spanish citizens, he said, and would protect the frontier state from Indians and other enemies. Austin died before he could complete his project. His son, Stephen, took up the job. Stephen was joined by other American *empresarios*.

When Mexico gained its independence, the *Tejanos* drew up a democratic constitution for the state of Texas. Stephen Austin took it to the capital. To his surprise, he was imprisoned as a revolutionist. Released by mistake while Santa Anna was campaigning in the north, he returned to Texas and denounced the president as "a base, unprincipled, bloody monster." He said, "War is our only recourse. No halfway measures, but war in full."

The Texas Revolt

Even before he dispatched Cos, Santa Anna had reopened a military post at Anahuac to make Texas aware of the power of the federal government. Travis, a lawyer and an ardent nationalist, collected 25 men and a cannon and marched on Anahuac. They fired one cannon ball at the Mexican fort, and the commander and his 44 men surrendered.

At the headquarters he had established at San Antonio de Bejar, Cos heard that the *Tejanos* had another cannon at Gonzales. He sent 100 dragoons to fetch it. The dragoons saw the cannon, surrounded by 160 rifle-armed Texans. Hung over the cannon was a sign reading "Come and take it." The Texans fired the cannon, loaded with scrap iron and pieces of chain, and the dragoons galloped back to San Antonio.

By this time, settlers from all over Texas had begun to converge on Gonzales. Many others came from the United States. Part of the Louisiana Grays, a volunteer militia company, arrived. Colonel Benjamin Miliam took 300 men from this embryo army and attacked the Mexicans in San Antonio. In December of 1835, after five days of fighting, Cos, and what was left of his 1,400-man force, surrendered. The Texans allowed them to go home after they promised they would never return under arms.

The Texans left a garrison in the San Antonio fort, a converted mission called "the Alamo" because it had been occupied for years by a Mexican unit from a town named Los Alamos. The mission complex was never intended to be a fort. Its walls were a quarter of a mile long and had neither bastions nor parapets. The San Antonio garrison was far too small to hold a place that size.

Most of the Texans didn't worry about that. They thought the war was over and went home. Sam Houston, a veteran of Andrew Jackson's campaigns (see **New Orleans, page 210**), and newly appointed commander of the Texas Army, was not so optimistic. He knew Santa Anna was preparing to return and that his first stop would be San Antonio. He ordered Colonel James Neil, commander of the Alamo, to destroy the Alamo's walls and retire.

Houston had trouble with the Texas politicians. First, they adopted the Matamoros Plan, an alliance with liberal elements in other northern Mexico states to detach the mineral-rich north and form a new nation, including Texas, which would stand between the United States and Mexico. To effect this, Texas was to send a body of troops to the Mexican city of Matamoros. The government gave command of the Matamoros expedition to an inexperienced officer named James Fanin. Then the government sent Travis to the Alamo with reinforcements. Houston wanted Travis to aid in the evacuation. The politicians knew, however, that Travis, a nationalist firebrand, would never retreat, and they were right.

Colonel Neil had to leave San Antonio. He turned the command over to Travis. The garrison, however, wanted to take orders from Colonel James Bowic, a famous adventurer and knife-fighter who was now a resident of San Antonio. Bowie's late wife belonged to an important San Antonio clan. Bowie, however, was dying of tuberculosis and was increasingly confined to bed. He and Travis agreed to share the command.

Another celebrity in the garrison wanted no command. Davy Crockett, also a veteran of Jackson's campaigns, who arrived leading a dozen "Tennessee Mounted Volunteers," said he wanted to be considered only a "high private." Crockett and his troops were among the many volunteers who made their way to the old mission as danger threatened. Among the honored defenders of the Alamo were James Nowlin of Ireland, James Northcross of Virginia and Andres Nava of San Antonio.

Santa Anna set out for San Antonio with a winter march across the mountains and the high plateau of central Mexico. Military experts said such a march was impossible, but Santa Anna performed it—after a fashion. For a soldier of his reputation, his march discipline was abominable. He simply set out across the desert, expecting his troops to follow as best they could.

Some couldn't. Some troops from the tropical Yucatan froze to death in the ferocious blizzards that blasted the Mexican army. There was no grazing for the horses, and few of Santa Anna's troops carried fodder. The President-General left a trail of dead animals and more than a few dead men long before he arrived at San Antonio de Bejar on February 23, 1836. He had only part of his army. Mexican units arrived a bit at a time, but most of the artillery never made it.

Fanin, still in Goliad, heard that Santa Anna had arrived in San Antonio. He started to march toward the besieged garrison, then changed his mind and went back.

Santa Anna had little concern for any human life but his own. He was also impatient. Neither were particularly good traits for a military leader, and the combination was deadly. Santa Anna also seemed to have been unreasonably optimistic. When Bowie asked about terms, Santa Anna sent a note that there could be no terms but unconditional surrender. Rebel troops who had surrendered unconditionally at Zacatecas had been massacred. But still, Santa Anna expected a quick surrender. He expected it even after he'd run up the no quarter flag.

Instead, the siege dragged on. Mexican troops dug saps, trenches approaching the walls, but they couldn't establish airtight siege lines. Messengers left the Alamo and reinforcements came in. The Mexicans' smooth-bore muskets—surplus British Brown Besses—couldn't match the range and accuracy of the Texans' long rifles. Mexican Captain Rafael Soldana noticed one rifleman particularly:

> "He was a tall man with flowing hair. He wore a buckskin suit with a cap all of a pattern entirely different from those worn by his comrades. This man would rest his long gun and fire, and we all learned to keep a good distance when he was seen to make ready to shoot. He rarely missed his mark, and when he fired, he always rose to his feet and calmly reloaded his gun, seemingly indifferent to the shots fired at him by our men. He had a strong, resonant voice and often railed at us. This man I later learned was known as Kwockey [Crockett]."

The longer the siege went on, the more impatient Santa Anna became. In early March, he decided to wait no longer for the artillery. He'd have his men storm the walls without artillery preparation.

Remember the Alamo!

On March 6, the attack began with Cos, the parole-breaker, leading one of the four Mexican columns. He directed his attack at a palisade covering a gap in the walls. His troops crowded up to the palisade but couldn't get through it. One colonel was trampled to death by his own men as troops from the rear pushed forward, crushing front-line troops against the barrier. The Texans directed a stream of fire against the struggling crowd.

Other Mexicans flowed along the base of the walls. This way they were more difficult targets than in the open field. They reached a timber and earth redoubt where the timbers had collapsed. Mexican General Juan Amador clambered up the fallen barrier. His men swarmed after him. Crockett and the Tennessee volunteers fought furiously, but the Mexicans broke through. Travis stood on the wall. Pena noticed him:

> "He would take a few steps and stop, turning his proud face toward us to discharge his shots. He fought like a true soldier. Finally he died, but he died after trading his life very dearly."

A single bullet in the forehead dropped Travis into the courtyard. The Texas gun crews were forced away from their cannons and, with the rest of the garrison, withdrew to the stone barracks and the ruins of the church. The Mexicans turned the cannons around and fired into the barracks. Then the Mexican infantry burst in, and Bowie, confined to his bed, fired at them with his pistol. The soldiers thrust their bayonets into him and lifted him up "until his blood covered their clothes and died them red," in the horrified words of Bowie's sister-in-law, Juana Veramendi de Alsbury. The Mexican infantry, in an insane fury, bayoneted everyone in sight, even some of their comrades. The Mexican officers, with great difficulty, managed to save most of the women and children.

Seven Texas soldiers were captured, Pena reported. One of them was "the naturalist, David Crockett, well known in North America for his unusual adventures." They were brought before Santa Anna "under the protection of General Castrillon." Santa Anna was enraged that Castrillon had spared anyone. He ordered their execution. "The commanders and officers were outraged at this action and did not support the order," Pena wrote, but several other officers of the President's bodyguard, who had not been in the fighting, drew their swords and hacked the Texans to death.

Santa Anna took the Alamo. He lost an estimated 600 dead—a high price to pay for the capture of a crumbling ruin held by 182 men.

Meanwhile, the Matamoros Plan had died. The Mexicans attacked Goliad, and Fanin decided to retreat. He took his 400 men from his fortifications and attempted to march through 1,400 Mexicans. After two days of fighting, the Texans surrendered on the condition that they would be paroled to the United States. General Jose Urrea reported his victory to Santa Anna. Santa Anna ordered him to kill all the prisoners, and only a handful managed to escape.

Goliad joined the Alamo as two incidents that Texans would always remember. They vowed revenge, and they did not have long to wait.

The Alamo remembered

Sam Houston would have agreed with George S. Patton that fixed fortifications are "a monument to the stupidity of man." He would counter Santa Anna with empty space, which Texas had an abundance. The last time the Mexican generalissimo confronted empty space, he let his army string out all across northern Mexico. Houston retreated before the Mexican Army, and Santa Anna detached unit after unit for garrison duty, to guard his supply lines and to bring up supplies. Burning towns as he advanced, he was sure the Texans were routed.

On April 20, he thought he had Houston and his army bottled up in the maze of bayous along the San Jacinto River. He had only 750 men by this time, but Cos arrived with 500 more. Supremely confident, Santa Anna and his whole army took a siesta before the attack that would annihilate the rebels.

Houston had 800 men and two cannons. At 3:30 p.m. the Texans crept silently through the woods and across an open field in front of the sleeping Mexicans. Suddenly, the two cannons belched double loads of grapeshot, and two fifes and a drum broke into "Come to My Bower," a slightly bawdy popular song. Screaming "Remember the Alamo," Texas troops charged, cutting down Mexicans with rifle, musket, bayonet, and sword. The Mexicans tried to flee, but at Houston's orders, his chief scout, Erastus "Deaf" Smith, had destroyed the bridge that was the only exit from the battlefield. The Mexicans dropped their arms and ran into the water. There, "between hell and high water," they were trapped. The Texans lined up and shot them down like ducks in a shooting gallery. Colonel John Wharton of the Texas Army tried to stop the massacre. A soldier told him, "Colonel Wharton, if Jesus Christ were to come down from heaven and tell me to stop killing Santanistas, I wouldn't do it, sir."

Santa Anna escaped into the woods but was captured two days later. He signed a document recognizing the independence of Texas. A few years later, the Republic of Texas was, at the request of the Texans, annexed to the United States. Shortly after, Santa Anna, once again in power, got into war with the United States.

Because of that war, the United States gained what became the states of Texas, Oklahoma, New Mexico, Colorado, Utah, Arizona, Nevada, and California. She had taken a major step toward becoming a world power.

Battle 41

Chinese standard bearer.

Wu-sung, 1862 AD
God's Younger Son

Who fought: The Ever-Victorious Army (the Ward Corps led by Fred Ward) vs. the Taiping Rebels (the Chung Wang).

What was at stake: The fate of China. (Ward demonstrated that Chinese with Western equipment could fight as well as Westerners.)

Hong Huoxiu had failed the examination. In Imperial China in 1836, everything depended on success in examinations. Only by passing examinations could one rise in the government bureaucracy. The 22-year-old schoolteacher sank into depression. He lost his appetite and seemed to lose all his energy. He went back to studying the Confucian classics so he'd do better when he took the examinations again. But he studied another book as well. The book, *Good Words for Exhorting the Age*, was by Liang Afa, a Chinese man who had been converted by an American Protestant missionary.

The book concerned a strange Supreme God of Heaven and how his worship could bring heavenly peace (Taiping). Hong saw many parallels between the beliefs of the Christians and traditional Chinese teachings, and as he looked at the life around him, he saw much that was opposed to both. There were violent crimes, sadistic executions, corrupt rulers, and oppressive landlords. Big-nosed barbarians were ravaging China, the Middle Kingdom—the heart of civilization. (The First Opium War had begun.) Foreign usurpers (the Manchus) ruled it.

With this disturbed state of mind, Hong took the examination a second time. Not surprisingly, he failed. When he returned home, his depression became so extreme that he got sick and then he lost consciousness.

Eventually Hong came out of his coma, and told his family a strange tale. While his body was unconscious, he said, his soul had been taken up to heaven, where he met the Supreme God and his Son, Jesus. He learned that he was God's second son, the younger brother of Jesus. God told him that China had been taken over by devils and he must return to earth and fight them. He would no longer be Hong Huoxiu but Hong Xiuquon. (Xiu-quon means "Complete Fire.")

Hong lived up to his new name. He began preaching the message he had received from heaven, going from village to village. He made many converts, especially among those alienated from the Manchu-dominated society—pirates, bandits, and members of anti-government secret societies. The powers-that-be reacted by arresting and executing Hong's followers. Hong responded by organizing his church like an army. Every four men and their families were commanded by a corporal, and every four corporals by a sergeant. Four sergeants reported to a lieutenant and four lieutenants to a captain, and so on, up to general. Generals commanded divisions of 13,155 men each. The top generals, known as kings ("wang" in Chinese), were Hong's closest associates. Hong was called Tien Wang (Heavenly King).

Hong's church was not just organized like an army—it was an army. It fought back against the persecutors. The Taiping army fought so well that it captured Nanking, the old Imperial capital. Hong sent his armies out in all directions to drive the devils out of China. At about that time, the Second Opium War began, distracting Imperial troops. It began to look as if the Taipings would take over all of China.

It also began to look as if Hong was mentally unbalanced. Until the Heavenly Kingdom was achieved, the Taipings were forbidden to drink alcohol, smoke opium, or have sex. Even married couples who slept together were beheaded. The rules applied to everyone but the Tien Wang. Hong's palace was filled with mistresses and he was usually intoxicated with drugs or drink.

The Taipings, however, no longer depended on Hong for leadership. The movement had developed a number of talented generals, such as Li Xiucheng, known as the Chung Wang (Faithful King), who was leading the army pressing toward Shanghai.

Warfare in Imperial China was often derided by Westerners: Much of it was based on bluff and bluster. But it had a nasty side: Victory was often followed by massacre. The Taipings were particularly nasty. Before it was over, the Taiping Rebellion would end more than 20 million human lives: It was the bloodiest war between the time of Genghis Khan and World War II.

The filibuster

Because the Chung Wang was bearing down on his city in 1860, Wu Hsu, the *taotai* (mayor) of Shanghai, was willing to listen to the young barbarian. So was the governor of Kiangsu Province, Hsueh Huan. The barbarian, a 28-year-old American named Frederick Townsend Ward, was the son of a Massachusetts ship owner. He had experience as an officer on clipper ships, but he preferred the life of a mercenary soldier. He had been what was called, in the 19th century, a filibuster (from the Spanish *filibustero*, a freebooter). He had served under the greatest American filibuster, William Walker, who had conquered Nicaragua. Leaving Walker, he had fought with the French Army in the Crimean War. Then he returned to the sea and shipped out to China as first mate on a clipper.

Fred Ward had left his ship in China and become an officer in the Shanghai Pirate Suppression Bureau. Wu had organized the SPSB, which used armed steamboats to patrol the Yangtse and fight the river pirates. The pirates were a byproduct of the first Opium War. When the British took Hong Kong, they drove the pirates out of that part of the sea. The pirates now plied their trade on China's great rivers. They threatened to wipe out Shanghai's thriving trade with the interior. Ward, Wu learned, had proven to be a most competent fighting man in service against the pirates.

The young man told the mandarin that he had seen the Taipings in action, and he knew that he could recruit an army of foreigners, armed in the Western manner, that could beat them on the battlefield or drive them out of their strongholds. If the Shanghai authorities would buy the weapons and pay the troops' salaries, Ward promised victory over the Taipings. His force would retake cities from the Taipings if the government would pay a bounty for each city.

The project would not be cheap. The salaries were $50 a month for enlisted men, $200 a month for officers, and $500 a month for Ward. Bounties for the cities would depend on the importance of each. Ward would negotiate the bounties before attacking. In addition to the bounties, Ward's troops would be entitled to all the precious metals, jewels, and other items of value they could loot from the cities.

Wu and Hsueh did some quick calculations. Ward's proposition was expensive. On the other hand, the Chung Wang had never been defeated. Neither official relished the prospect of being dead. They accepted Ward's offer.

The Ward Corps

Shanghai was a weapons bazaar, with everything from cannons to daggers on sale. Foreign arms merchants, trying to capitalize on the strife in China, were offering everything from the most modern weapons to the uttermost junk. Most of the buyers didn't know the difference. Ward did. He purchased Sharps breech-loading rifles, probably the best military rifle of the time, and Colt's Model 1851 revolver, the famous "Navy Colt." For soldiers, he recruited Western adventurers he found in the bars of Shanghai's Western "concessions," areas the government had been forced to relinquish to foreign control. Ward picked an old friend, Henry Burgevine of South Carolina, as second in command and hired 100 Westerners. Most were American, but the "Ward Corps" also included Danes, Frenchmen, Englishmen, Prussians, and Swiss.

In its first battle, the Ward Corps helped the Imperial troops counterattack the Taipings. The attack was so successful that Wu ordered Ward to recapture the city of Sung-chiang. Ward had no artillery, so he tried surprise. Unfortunately, his army of bar flies began celebrating their victory before they attacked. They made so much noise approaching the city they woke up the Taipings, who blasted them with everything they had. The Ward Corps ran away. Ward paid off most of the survivors and began recruiting a new army.

This time, he recruited in Shanghai's Filipino community. "Manilamen" served on the crews of western ships all over the Far East. Captains vied to sign them up, because they were intelligent, hard working, and brave. Best of all, from Ward's point of view, they all spoke Spanish, a language in which he was fluent. Ward quickly signed up 80 Filipinos, including 23-year-old Vicente Macanaya, who, with Burgevine, became his chief lieutenant. Word of the good pay Ward was offering spread through the Filipino community. More and more joined the Ward Corps.

As the Ward Corps grew, Wu pressed the filibuster to take the field. This time, Ward would not be rushed. He bought artillery. To teach the Filipinos how to handle cannons, he hired deserters from the British Army, the main Western military presence in China. He bought more rifles and revolvers for his men, but armed himself with nothing but a rattan walking stick.

For his second attack on Sung-chiang, Ward left the Westerners who remained from his first army at home. He took 200 Filipinos on a steamer going away from Sung-chiang. After dark, Ward and his men left the boat and marched back to Sung-chiang, where they were to lead an attack by the Imperial Army. Ward's men sneaked right up to the city's moat. They blew down the east gate with their cannons, and Ward led the charge. But a second gate blocked the entrance. Ward exploded 1,000 pounds of gunpowder against the second gate, but the explosion made a hole only big enough for one man to crawl through.

"Come on, boys, we're going through!" Ward yelled and dived through the hole. Macanaya, Burgevine, and the rest followed. The Ward Corps fought its way to the top of the wall and turned the Taipings' cannons against them. They shot up a rocket to signal the Imperial troops outside, but the government army did nothing. Ward's 200 Filipinos, firing Sharps rifles and cannister shot from the cannons, routed the Taiping defenders—more than 1,000 men.

The victory was costly. Sixty-two of Ward's men were killed and another 100 wounded, including Ward. (Ward would be wounded 15 times in China.) But the loot—gold, gems, guns, and gunpowder—was enormous.

Wu and Hsueh were delighted, but the Western merchants in Shanghai, especially the British, were livid. This American filibuster would bring the wrath of the Taipings on them. This would end the good life they had built for themselves on the China Coast. Further, Ward was luring British soldiers and sailors into his army.

Ward's success also shocked the Chung Wang and his Taiping troops. They had never before seen such a demonstration of the superiority of Western weapons and tactics. The Chung Wang deduced that Ward's next objective would be the city of Ch'ing-p'u. He sent one of his best units there. All the soldiers had guns, and their commander was an English mercenary named Savage.

Once again, Ward tried a surprise attack. His men silently put scaling ladders against the walls and climbed up. As they were assembling on the wall, fire exploded from Taiping positions all over the city. Five bullets hit Ward in a matter of seconds. The Ward Corps was literally blasted off the wall. Unable to speak, Ward wrote out orders and gave them to Macanaya. Vicente led the fighting retreat.

The British *North China Herald* reported: "This notorious man (Ward) has been brought down to Shanghai, not as hoped, dead, but severely wounded."

Ward was taken to Paris for treatment. The Chung Wang entered Shanghai but was soon called away by the Tien Wang to help stop an Imperial army driving east from Hunan. Meanwhile, the British and French won the Second Opium War and sacked the Emperor's palace in Peking.

The rebirth of Ward

When Ward returned to China, the British arrested him. They learned that he was now a Chinese citizen. Unable to turn him over to American authorities, they confined him on a warship. But Vicente Macanaya got a message to his general. One dark night, Ward slipped through a porthole and was picked up by the Filipino officer on a small boat. The British were unable to find him. They were having a new set of troubles. Now that they were no longer fighting the Imperial forces, they found the Taipings much less friendly.

Ward had begun recruiting a third army. When he first came to China, he believed, like most Westerners, that Chinese could not be trained to fight in the Western manner. The performance of Savage's Taipings helped convince him he was wrong. If Filipinos, who had no military experience, could become first-class soldiers, why couldn't Chinese? And there were far more Chinese in China than Filipinos, Americans, or Europeans.

Wu was delighted with the idea. It was much cheaper because Chinese soldiers could be paid less than foreigners, and it satisfied his nationalism because China had too long been oppressed by foreigners. And Ward was about to become his son-in-law. He had already become the *taotai*'s partner in a number of business enterprises, and he used his profits to buy war materials. Wu and Hsueh got Ward a commission as a colonel in the Imperial Army.

The Ward Corps grew to 7,000 men. Ward retained a bodyguard of 200 Filipinos commanded, of course, by Macanaya. At first the officers were American, European, or Filipino, but Ward began promoting Chinese to officers as they got experience. The men wore Western-style uniforms and drilled in the Western manner. Ward purchased large amounts of artillery and built up a small navy of river steamers. In swampy Kiangsu Province, crisscrossed by rivers and canals, water was the fastest way to travel. Ward's boats were more than transportation: He used them as floating batteries.

Ward devised a new strategy to go with his new army and the changed environment. The British and French no longer saw the Taipings as co-belligerents. The rebels were now a threat to Shanghai and its foreign concessions. Ward proposed to use the Ward Corps as a mobile strike force. With the backing of European troops, it could clear all the Taipings out of all territory within 30 miles of Shanghai and keep them out. The British and French were not yet ready to commit their forces to the defense of Shanghai, but they no longer saw Ward as an outlaw who must be neutralized.

Wu-sung

The Chung Wang had improved his army. They had many more guns and more Western mercenaries to lead them, and the Faithful King was again advancing on Shanghai. He aimed to capture the "treaty ports"—the ports where Westerners had concessions—and cripple the government's trade with the outside world. His troops took a position near Wu-sung, where they could cut off access to Shanghai's harbor. The Taipings had just settled into their trenches when they saw a new enemy approaching. It looked like a Western army: It wore Western uniforms, marched in the Western manner, and had Western equipment. But in front of the marching men, a color guard bore a banner with a single Chinese character, "Hua." Hua (pronounced Wah) was the Chinese pronunciation of Ward.

When they got within rifle range, the Ward Corps lay down and opened a blistering rifle fire with Western breech-loaders like the American Sharps and the Prussian Dreyse. Artillery and mortar shells exploded in the Taiping trenches. Although they were entrenched and outnumbered Ward's men, the Taipings were overwhelmed by the firepower of the troops they termed "imitation foreign devils." They climbed out of their trenches and dashed away.

Wu-sung established a pattern. A week later, Ward and 500 men took the city of Kwang-fu-lin in a surprise attack, panicking a garrison reported to number 20,000. Imperial authorities gave the Ward Corps a new name: "The Ever-Victorious Army," and promoted Ward to general and to increasingly higher grades of mandarin. He married Wu's daughter and bloodily repulsed the Chung Wang's whole army at Sung-chiang. His army killed 2,300 Taipings in the first few minutes of the battle. Ward finally gained the support of British and French troops—although the Ever-Victorious Army continued to do most of the fighting.

The Chung Wang devised a new system of field fortifications in depth. A British officer named Stavely was convinced that the Taipings would flee in panic when they saw British regulars advancing. The Taipings didn't flee. The British regulars did, after the fire from the entrenched Chinese cut down rows of them. Ward countered the new development by using his share in the loot from captured cities to buy more cannons and steamboats. He smothered the Chung Wang's men with shellfire before leading up his infantry.

The Chung Wang struck back with a well-equipped army of 50,000. He took several towns and surrounded two of Ward's strongholds. Ward finally broke the siege of Sung-chiang, his headquarters, and drove the Taipings away from Ch'ing-p'u, where another part of the Ever-Victorious Army was holding out.

Chinese government officials continued to heap honors on Ward. He was showing them that they did not need foreign help to put down rebels and that Chinese could fight as well as Westerners. But although Ward was a Chinese citizen, they didn't completely trust a big-nosed barbarian who refused to wear a queue. The Europeans were even less happy with Ward. He was saving their treaty ports for them, but he was showing the Chinese how to fight. The more astute of the Westerners recognized that the role of cock-of-the-walk that Europeans and Americans were playing in China was coming to an end.

There was not universal mourning, then, on September 20, 1862, when Ward received his 15th wound—the fatal one—outside Ningpo, in Chekiang Province.

Ward's veterans wanted Vicente Macanaya to take command, but the Chinese authorities were not ready to give such authority to a "Manilaman." Burgevine, a less competent commander but, like Ward, a Chinese citizen, got the post. A short time later, Burgevine tried to rob Wu Hsu and had to flee for his life. The Chinese government hired a British officer, John Holland, who hated Americans and was totally incompetent. The Ever-Victorious Army was routed and almost destroyed after he took command. Finally, the command went to Charles George Gordon. Gordon adopted Ward's tactics, but didn't have Ward's inspiration. He was competent, but that was all. He did, however, have inspired publicists, who credited him with all of Ward's victories and even with ending the Taiping Rebellion, which, of course, he did not do. The Chinese government disbanded the Ever-Victorious Army a year and a half before the end of the rebellion.

Historians, chiefly British ones, still perpetuate the myth of "Chinese" Gordon and the Taiping Rebellion. But in China, the Chinese built a temple to honor Hua, who had been Frederick Townsend Ward and who became a Confucian demigod. He was revered as the man who brought the new ways of war to his people so they were able to resist being carved up by Europeans the way Africa had been carved up.

Because Ward died two months before he reached 31, and because China is such an enormous country, he hadn't been able impart his lessons thoroughly. He made a start, but it was China's neighbor, Japan, that first took Ward's teachings to heart. **(See Tsushima, page 51)**

Wu-sung, which began the Ever Victorious Army's string of victories, has importance that goes beyond China and Japan. It was the first to show that non-Caucasians could fight as well as whites. Tsushima **(see page 51)** showed they could decisively beat whites. Tanga **(see page 174)** and the campaigns of von Lettow Vorbeck showed that blacks could fight as well as Occidentals and Asians, but Wu-sung was the first.

Battle 42

Waterloo, 1815 AD
He's Back!

Who fought: French (Napoleon I) vs. British and Prussians (Duke of Wellington).

What was at stake: Whether Napoleon's dictatorial "republicanism" or reactionary monarchy would dominate Europe.

Napoleon had returned, and no single news item had ever so shaken the governments of Europe. The Corsican adventurer that all the crowned heads had believed to be safely confined on the Isle of Elba had landed in France. Louis XVIII sent Marshal Michel Ney to capture the deposed emperor as soon as he heard of the landing. Ney set out, vowing to bring his one-time commander back in an iron cage. But as soon as Ney saw Napoleon, he exclaimed, "My emperor!" and fell at his feet.

For more than 20 years, Napoleon had dominated Europe. The French adored him. So did the common people in many other European countries—even in England, his most steadfast and relentless foe, there were people who saw Napoleon as a potential liberator from aristocratic oppression. When he invaded Russia, besides Frenchmen, his army included Dutchmen, Germans, Italians, and Poles. Thousands of Europeans eagerly followed this complete autocrat, believing that he would spread the ideals of the French Revolution: liberty, equality, and fraternity. Even more amazing, Napoleon himself believed that he was an apostle of the Revolution. He aimed to remake Europe, sweeping away all the medieval institutions that he believed had been grinding down the human spirit for generations.

Napoleon dreamed of uniting the European nations into a confederation bound together by "a unity of codes, principles, feelings, and interests." He would head the confederation, of course, but under him would be an assembly modelled on "the American Congress or the Amphictyons of Greece." He would form independent republics in England and Ireland, liberate Spain from superstition, and reestablish the Kingdom of Poland as a buffer against "the barbarians of the north," as he called the Russians. He would also break up Austria's polyglot empire, liberate Hungary, and drive the Turks out of Europe.

To do all this—and he almost succeeded—Napoleon had used the revolutionary army developed by the French Revolution. The Revolution brought universal conscription and mass armies. To control these huge masses of men, the revolutionary generals invented the division system—small units including all branches and capable of acting independently. They jettisoned the "thin-line" tactics of the Old Regime, which required turning soldiers into automatons. Instead they took advantage of the native intelligence of their troops. French tactics were based on swarms of skirmishers who moved and took cover as they saw fit. The skirmishers masked columns of infantry who were less vulnerable to volleys by the enemy and capable of punching through the thin lines in bayonet charges. Napoleon, originally an artillery officer, added massed cannons.

Napoleon's forte was strategy. The French army was more mobile than its enemies, partly because it lived off the land instead of depending on wagon-borne supplies. Napoleon spread his divisions widely so his enemies never knew his real objective, and quickly concentrated them where and when it seemed most appropriate. In battle, his favorite method was to drive a wedge between enemy forces (he usually faced more than one army), concentrate on one part, destroy it, and then attack the second part.

Napoleon prided himself on being the champion of the common people against aristocratic oppressors, but in Spain and Russia he had turned the common people against himself. Guerrilla ("little war" in Spanish) warfare supplemented by regular armies in opposite ends of Europe led to Napoleon's downfall. But now he was back in France, and the common people of France again rallied around him.

The 100 days

Back in Paris, and again Emperor of France, Napoleon had to raise a new army. There was no dearth of volunteers, but he had trouble picking subordinate commanders. Many, like Ney, had become royalist officers, but some, unlike Ney, would not switch again. His former chief of staff, Louis-Alexandre Berthier, was eager to rejoin his old chief, but Berthier had a fatal accident before he could resume his post. To replace him, Napoleon chose Nicolas Soult, an excellent field commander, but one who had never been chief of staff of an army or even a corps. Napoleon would not take back Joachim Murat, who had joined the Emperor's enemies in order to keep his Napoleon-granted title of King of Naples. Murat had been his best cavalry leader. To replace him as cavalry commander, Napoleon chose Emmanuel Grouchy, a brave horse-soldier who had commanded the cavalry defending France in 1814. But when the campaign began, Napoleon put Grouchy in command of the entire left wing. Grouchy had never been tested in such an important and independent command. To command the right wing, Napoleon appointed Ney. Ney, called "the bravest of the brave," had the courage of a lion and the loyalty of a dog. He also had, at times, the mental flexibility of a rhino. Napoleon put his most competent commander, Louis-Nicolas Davout, in command of Paris. He said he would not feel safe with anyone else in the position. Davout, who longed to be in the battle, protested fruitlessly. "But Sire," he said, "if you are the victor, Paris will be yours, and if you are beaten, neither I nor anyone else can do anything for you." Napoleon would later regret all his choices.

Napoleon had landed in France while the Congress of Vienna, intent on bringing Europe back to its pre-Napoleon look, was still in session. It immediately began devising an all-Europe campaign to end the Napoleonic threat once and for all. An Anglo-Dutch-German army of 93,000 would join a Prussian army of 117,000 in Belgium; an Austrian army of 210,000 would mass on the upper Rhine; a Russian army of 150,000 would march across Germany to the middle Rhine; and an Austrian-Italian army of 75,000 would concentrate in northern Italy. The army in Italy would drive for Lyons, and the others would converge on Paris. The attack would begin between June 27 and July 1, 1815.

Napoleon, leading 124,588 men, moved first. Early in June, he invaded Belgium, planning to beat the English under Wellington and the Prussians under Blucher, before they could unite. He would then take on the Austrians and the Russians.

Napoleon moved into a position between the scattered armies of Wellington and Blucher. Ney was to keep Wellington busy while Grouchy engaged the Prussians. The Allies belatedly began to concentrate. The Emperor decided to dispose of the Prussians first. He would pin down Blucher's left (the side away from Wellington), then annihilate his right and center. He ordered Grouchy to attack, most heavily on the Prussian center and right. Then Ney was to shift some troops to envelop Blucher's right and fall on his rear.

Unfortunately for Napoleon, Ney's troops who were to hit the Prussian rear got lost. When they finally began to move against the Prussians, they were coming from an unexpected direction, which led the French to think they were Prussian reinforcements. By the time they were correctly identified, it was too late for Napoleon's masterstroke. As it turned out, the badly beaten Prussians were able to disengage under cover of night.

Grouchy was to pursue the Prussians, but what his scouts reported to be the Prussian army was really a crowd of fugitives who were deserting Blucher. Grouchy moved in the wrong direction, giving the Prussians time to reorganize.

Ney, meanwhile, was moving against the English with uncharacteristic caution. He knew Wellington had the knack of hiding his troops until he was ready to attack. But the position Wellington eventually occupied, at Quatre-Bras, had no Allied troops. If Ney had moved with his usual speed, Wellington would have had to establish a defensive position well to the rear. As it was, Wellington first made contact with Ney in front of Quatre-Bras. When he saw the enemy, Ney reacted like a bull seeing a waving red flag. He tried to recall the corps he had sent against the Prussians, then he sent Francois Kellermann to charge the English infantry with a single brigade of heavy cavalry. Kellermann's overmatched troops nevertheless scattered two English regiments and penetrated Wellington's line deeply until they were repulsed. The day ended in a draw, with both Ney and Wellington still bringing up their troops.

Napoleon told Ney to continue the attack at first light and sent some of Grouchy's troops to support him. Grouchy was to keep the Prussians moving away from Wellington.

Ney did not attack at first light. He did not move until 11 a.m., when the Emperor himself stormed into Ney's camp. By that time, Wellington had been able to retreat peacefully. Further, the troops of d'Erlon's corps, who had been sent from Ney to attack the Prussian rear, and then recalled, didn't arrive until 2 p.m. Napoleon himself led the French against the still-retreating English, who were saved by a tremendous cloudburst which turned the fields into an impassible sea of mud.

The rain continued through the night. At 1 a.m. Napoleon rode through the storm to visit his outposts. When he returned, he found a message from Grouchy reporting that the Prussians were retreating and he would follow them. Napoleon dictated a message to Grouchy telling him to keep after the Prussians, but also that the rest of the army was about to attack the English, therefore he should move closer to Ney's position to guard against Prussian support for Wellington. Napoleon's order, which was not dispatched until 10 a.m., confused Grouchy. He let the Prussians escape. Some of the responsibility for the foul-up may belong to Soult, the inexperienced chief of staff. Soult, however, later suggested that Grouchy be recalled to support the attack. Napoleon, convinced that Grouchy was driving the Prussians in full retreat, if not rout, rejected the idea.

Waterloo

Napoleon usually opened a battle with a heavy bombardment of the point to be attacked. Infantry were the least vulnerable to cannon balls, the missile most effective at long range, when standing in line. They were most vulnerable when standing in columns or squares: A single cannon ball could kill an entire file of troops standing one behind the other.

Troops in columns, on the other hand, could move far more easily, in either attack or retreat. Squares, with a line of bayonets facing in all four directions, were needed to meet cavalry, which could attack from all sides.

The object of the bombardment, therefore, was to keep the enemy in line so the cavalry could attack them while the French infantry, marching in columns, closed in. If the enemy infantry formed squares to meet the cavalry, they would be more vulnerable to the artillery. When the French infantry reached musket range, they would deploy into line to use the fire of its muskets most effectively. Troops in either columns or squares could fire only a small proportion of their muskets at one time.

Wellington was familiar with French tactics. He kept his troops lying on their bellies behind a rise in the ground. The French cannon balls screamed harmlessly over their heads. When the French reached the crest of the hill, the English infantry rose and fired a volley that smashed the head of the French column. This scene was repeated over and over. The French cavalry should have made mincemeat of the prone English lines, but lack of coordination between the infantry and cavalry was one of the most glaring French errors at what became known as the Battle of Waterloo.

As the battle was beginning, French troopers learned that the Prussians were not retreating. They were advancing to help Wellington. Napoleon, however, believed he could drive Wellington from the field before Blucher arrived in strength. He sent an order to Grouchy to come back immediately. But there was no way Grouchy, now engaged with a Prussian rear guard, could come quickly.

Wellington had begun the battle with 67,661 men, not much less than Napoleon's 71,947, and he was holding a strong defensive line. Even so, by the end of the day, he was in a desperate situation—but so were the French. Ney, frustrated by repeated repulses, ordered a giant cavalry attack. He was attacking infantry in fortified positions, which was something like trying to knock down a brick wall with your head. Napoleon, desperate, threw virtually all of his troops into the offensive.

Then the Prussians appeared, the Allies counterattacked, and France's First Empire was finished.

A new era

The object of the Congress of Vienna was to restore Europe to the state it had been in before the French Revolution, and even to provide a king for France. But marooning Napoleon on the island of St. Helena in the South Atlantic could not turn back the clock. The Allies had to be satisfied. Russia acquired Finland and almost all of Poland. The German states formed a confederation, which in two generations would become an empire—replacing the empire of Napoleon as the prime power on the continent of Europe. Britain, triumphant over France, became the world's only superpower, a position it held for most of the rest of the century. And the ideals of the French Revolution—liberty, equality, and fraternity—continued to pop up and gain ground for more than a century. Even today, at least a form of democracy is the norm virtually everywhere in the world outside the Middle East.

Battle 43

Medieval Persian warriors.

Kadisiyah, 637 AD
Kaffirs

Who fought: Arabs (Sa'ad ibn abu Wakkas and Kakaa ibn Amru) vs. Persians (Rustam).

What was at stake: Islamic expansion into non-Semitic and pagan lands—how, if they triumphed, the primitive Muslims would control the conquered people. The course they took was to foster religious hatred between Muslims and Christians for 1,000 years.

To the newly converted Muslim Arabs who poured out of Arabia in the early 17th century, the world they had vowed to conquer didn't look so strange. The people in Palestine, Syria, and Mesopotamia spoke Arabic or similar languages such as Aramaic and Hebrew. They were "People of the Book"—Christians or Jews. They believed in one God, and they honored the same prophets as the Muslims. Many of them looked back to the same ancestor, the wandering Aramean (Abraham).

To the east, though, was another world. The peoples of the Persian Empire, Persians, Parthians, Sakae, and others, all spoke strange languages. Neither the words nor the grammar of those Indo-European tongues resembled the Semitic languages of the Arabs, Jews, and Arameans. The Semites had been governed by patriarchs, or in the Roman Empire, patriarchs overseen by Roman bureaucrats. The Persians had an intricate system of feudalism with a crowd of kings, nobles, and knights, all of whom controlled some piece of territory, and all of whom were directly responsible to a "King of Kings." But the biggest difference was that the Persians didn't know God or His prophets. They worshipped two gods, representing the principles of good and evil. The good god, Ahura Mazda, manifested himself in light, the sun and fire. To the Muslim Arabs, the Persians were "fire worshippers" and *kaffirs*, pagans.

To the Persians, the Arabs were barbarians—bandits and raiders, but not a military power like the Romans. The Roman war had been a disaster **(see The Yarmuk Valley, page 117)**. The armies of Heraclius had swept over the Empire and chased the Shah, Chosroes II, briefly called Chosroes the Conqueror, into his capital, Ctesiphon. Heraclius offered peace, but Chosroes refused the offer. That was too much for his people. They killed the Shah. The peace they accepted stripped Persia of all Chosroes's conquests and spoils and left the Persians exhausted.

The Romans were exhausted, too, but the Persians were in worse shape. The Persian Empire was always hovering on the brink of anarchy because of the rules of succession—or more accurately, the lack of rules— to the throne of the King of Kings. The Shah's son did not automatically succeed him. Chosroes' son died of the plague and his son was an infant, so the crowd of lesser kings and greater nobles immediately began a series of wars of succession. In the next four years, 12 nobles claimed the crown, and all were deposed. Eventually, the Persians settled on a child, who was given the name Yezdigert III, with a general named Rustam as regent.

Rustam led an army that resembled the Parthian army that defeated Crassus at Carrhae back in the days when Rome was the capital of the Roman Empire **(see Cannae, page 127)**. Like the Parthian, it was an army that had developed from the ancient horse-archer horde of the Eurasian nomads, but it was even more sophisticated than the Parthian Army. The Persian nobles were the core of the army. They aspired to an idealized concept of the soldiers of Cyrus the Great. Cyrus's troops, they believed, had to learn only how to ride, shoot, and tell the truth. The Persian noble had to learn a great deal more, but nothing that would make him resemble an intellectual. The Persian noble fought from the back of a horse wearing a helmet and lamellar armor that covered him from neck to ankles. He had to learn to use the bow, the lance, the sword, the axe, the mace, and the dagger. He even had to learn, after a fashion, to take orders. Men who couldn't afford much armor—poor nobles and any who were not slaves or serfs—made up the light cavalry (horse archers). Infantry were neither numerous nor important in a Persian army.

Rustam heard that the tribes of the Arabian desert were getting restless and that they had made some attacks on settled lands. He had no worries, though, even when he heard that the followers of some desert madman were concentrating near the Arab satellite state of Hira.

The people of the Prophet

Arabia is a harsh land. There is little water, and agriculture is possible only with intense irrigation. Trade, with camel caravans across the desert and in ships on the Red Sea, provided employment for many. Some adventurous souls, real-life versions of Sindbad the Sailor, took ships across the Indian Ocean and even to China and back. But there were always more people than the land could support. For centuries, Arabs emigrated to Egypt, Syria, and Mesopotamia. Others, living on the brink of starvation, killed their infant daughters.

In the thriving commercial city of Mecca, a certain caravan owner began inveighing against the immorality he saw. Mohammed preached against drunkenness and promiscuity, infanticide, and idol worship. He made such a nuisance of himself he was driven out of Mecca. He fled to Medina in 622, where he made converts. Mohammed made a virtue of things necessary for life in the desert, such as hospitality and abstemiousness. He forbade wine, but he compromised on sex, limiting each man to no more than four wives. He roundly condemned the killing of babies. If his followers had to kill, they should kill the enemies of God. Thus, he proposed a new solution to the overpopulation of the Arabian peninsula.

Soon Mohammed had gathered a sizable army of believers. He took Mecca from the idol-worshippers and united the tribes of Arabia. Even before the Muslims took Mecca, they had been raiding Roman and Persian lands. Mohammed died, however, before he could mount a major campaign outside of Arabia. But the Muslim campaigning produced two extraordinary generals: Khalid ibn al Walid and Amr ibn al As. Both knew that their lightly armed forces could not stand up to the Roman and Persian armies in the kind of knock-down-drag-out fight the imperial troops liked to wage. They developed strategy and tactics based on the Arabs' strength, hit-and-run raiding. In 636 (see **The Yarmuk Valley, page 117**) Khalid concentrated a swarm of Arab armies and routed a Roman army in the Battle of the Yarmuk.

Kadisiyah

A Bedouin sheik named Muthanna proposed to Khalid that the Muslim armies should join his pagan clan, the Bakr, in a raid on Hira. Khalid agreed, and the two armies raided Hira in 633. That annoyed Rustam, who gathered the Persian Army to teach the Arabs a lesson. Muthanna appealed to Omar, Mohammed's successor as head of Islam, hinting that he might accept the new religion. Caliph Omar, bracing for a showdown with the Romans, sent some help, but not much. At what became known as the Battle of the Bridge, Rustam unleashed a weapon new to the Arabs: elephants. The Arab horses panicked, and the Arabs were crushingly defeated. That, Rustam concluded, would take care of the Arab problem.

But two years later, the Arabs, under Khalid, had skirmished a Roman army to annihilation on the Yarmuk, and the Muslims now held Palestine and Syria. Rustam again mobilized his army.

Omar saw that the Persians were threatening the communications between Syria and Arabia. Conquering that sprawling empire of fire-worshippers had not been one of his higher priorities, but he had to do something. He began concentrating Arab armies and gave command of them to Sa'ad ibn abu Wakkas, an old companion of the Prophet. He sent ambassadors to Shah Yezdigert, demanding that the Shah convert to Islam or pay the head tax levied on unbelievers. Yezdigert, now a teenager, said that if the Muslims wanted his land, he'd give them his land. He gave each ambassador a bag of dirt and sent them home, noting that if they weren't ambassadors he'd have beheaded them.

The Arabs crossed the Euphrates, and Rustam marched to meet them. The Persians had a larger army, and Sa'ad was in no hurry to fight. But Arab foragers ran into Persian cavalry, and battle became inevitable.

The Persians opened it in their customary fashion, with Persian knights riding out between the armies and challenging champions from the other side. The Arabs accepted eagerly, but the better-armed Persians usually prevailed in single combat. Little by little, the fight became a typical Arab battle. Small groups of Arabs rode toward parts of the Persian line, loosed their arrows, and rode away. The retreating Arabs scattered in all directions, and, not weighed down by armor, were faster than the Persian cavalry. Frustrated by his inability to close with the Arabs, Rustam sent in the elephants. Again, the Arab horses panicked. Arab foot archers, however, stood their ground and shot down the mahouts and killed some of the elephants. Still, the Arab army was driven back in disorder, being saved only by darkness.

The next day was a reenactment of the first, minus the elephants. Rustam was reluctant to use elephants against any kind of determined opposition. When panicked, the big animals were a greater a danger to their side than to the enemy. As at the Yarmuk, the Arabs were starting to skirmish their enemies to death. Reinforcements were arriving from Syria, but Sa'ad the next day was so afflicted with boils he was unable to sit on his horse. He turned over command to Kakaa ibn Amru, leader of the Syrians.

Fighting Arabs, Rustam found, was like trying to gather smoke. They never stood still, their horses were fleeter, and they had no camp to destroy. He brought up more elephants. But the troops he was facing now were not merely raw desert tribesmen. The Syrian reinforcements had fought in Roman armies, so they knew how to handle elephants. Their horses were trained not to panic. They rode up to the elephants and shot their drivers and the troops on the beasts' backs. Their infantry attacked the big animals with spears, arrows, and swords. The elephants were routed. The stampeding elephants tore gaps in the Persian line and Kakaa sent his troops charging through the holes. The Persians ran, and the Arabs attacked in small groups like a swarm of bees.

At daybreak, a sandstorm began. The wind blew into the faces of the Persians, who stood with their backs to a canal. Rustam tried to swim to safety, but an Arab named Hillal ibn Alkama caught him by the foot, dragged him back, and beheaded him. What was left of the Persian army fled.

New directions for Islam

Arab armies swarmed across Persia. Yezdigerd fled to the towering Hindu Kush Mountains, where he died in obscurity 16 years later. The Arabs pushed into Afghanistan and the Turkish lands of Central Asia. And *Dar es Islam* had swallowed a new and barely digestible meal. Persia was a pagan land, a land where the language, customs, and institutions were all strange. This was true of the Turks, also, but they were unsophisticated barbarians. The Persians were heirs to millennia of civilization and as humble about it as their neighbors to the east, the Chinese. And there were more Persians than Arabs. The Arabs could see only one way to control this vast conquest: religion.

The Koran demanded tolerance of the People of the Book. Fire worshippers were not People of the Book. The Arabs began a long and violent persecution of the Mazdaists. Some fled to India, where today they are called Parsees. Others converted, but being such a large and civilized block in Islam, they brought new values, customs, and outlooks to their adopted religion. Persian poetry enhanced the already highly developed poetry of the Arabs. Persian painting was utterly new to Muslims, who avoided making "graven images." Persian architecture, Persian mathematics, and Persian philosophy all contributed to what was to become the glorious Islamic civilization of the Middle Ages. But the Persians also brought the hierarchical organization of their native feudalism and the ferocious intolerance of their Mazdaist heritage.

That last added fuel to the persecution begun by the Arabs. The Persians passed it on to the Turks, who were to apply it in the Near East—a major factor in inciting the Crusades. Conversion by the sword was hardly a new concept, but it was seldom so uncompromising—or successful—as the Muslim project in Persia. In fact, it was so successful that it created imitators. European Christians adopted it and applied it first to Muslims in the Crusades, then to other Europeans, and finally to the nations they colonized.

In the short run, its adoption by Islam led to a bitter conflict between *Dar es Islam* and Christendom for 1,000 years.

Battle 44

Ivan the Terrible.

Kazan, 1552 AD
The Land of Mystery

Who fought: Russians (Ivan the Terrible) vs. Mongols (Shah Ali).

What was at stake: Whether Russia could finally end Mongol domination and become fully independent?

At the beginning of the 16th century, Russia was more unknown to western Europeans than China. This was strange, because until the 13th century she had developed along the same lines as other countries of northern Europe.

Russia began as a number of trading posts built by Swedish Vikings. The Swedes allied themselves with the Slavic, Finnic, and Alanic inhabitants of the forests and steppes and founded independent states. Russians from those states had been among the waves of barbarians who pounded in vain on the gates of Constantinople, and Russians had been among the barbarians who learned Christianity from missionaries sent from Constantinople. When Constantinople was under siege by the Muslims, the Russian principalities had been the bulwarks of Christianity in Eastern Europe.

The Russian states came to recognize the Prince of Kiev as first among equals, but they never united as a single nation. Outside pressure prevented that. First, it was the Germans who, blocked by the French in the west, began expanding eastward, spearheaded by the Teutonic Knights. The Knights had shifted their focus from the Muslims of the Near East, to the Cuman Turks of the steppe, and the pagan Prussians of the Baltic. Then they changed the motive of their crusading from religion to nationalism. They fought the Catholic Poles and the Orthodox Bulgarians and Russians. The Russians reacted by not only fighting back, but by turning away from contact with the West. Hatred of the "Latins" grew rapidly and became a permanent feature of Russian thought. At the same time, the Russian states began quarreling among themselves, which left them in poor condition to resist a really horrendous threat: the Mongols of Genghis Khan.

Emperor of all men

The Mongols of the 13th century had inherited a superb military machine, using the ancient organization and tactics of the Eurasian horse archer. Scores of generations before them had the same thing, but the Mongols suddenly acquired the people to use that machine to its utmost (see Gupta, page 191). Genghis Khan and two of his subordinates, Subotai Bahadur and Chepe Noyon, are unquestionably three of the greatest generals in history. And by a stunning stroke of fortune, all three of them were able to work together. Further, the supreme Mongol commander, Genghis Khan, who called himself Emperor of All Men, had the vaulting ambition to take full advantage of his good fortune. "One God in heaven and one khan on earth," he liked to proclaim.

In 1218, Genghis Khan led his armies against Mohammed Shah of Kwarezm. Kwarezm was an enormous empire including all of Persia and Turkestan. It hardly appears in the pages of history because Genghis and his troops snuffed out its existence, along with "Mohammed the Conqueror," almost before it began to exist. Mohammed fled to an island in the Caspian Sea, but he died there before the Mongols could get him.

Subotai and Chepe, who had led two divisions (20,000 cavalry) in pursuit of the Shah, asked the khan's permission to return through the unknown territory north of the sea. He agreed and sent some reinforcements. The Mongols devastated Armenia, routed an army of Cumans, Alans, and Circassians, annihilated the army of the Prince of Kiev, and laid waste to the Crimea before returning to the Gobi. Chepe died en route, but Subotai brought back a huge quantity of loot and a detailed report on the lands that he had visited. Genghis died four years later, but before he died, he sent Subotai west to hold the lands he had conquered.

In 1235, the new khan, Ogotai, ordered a new wave of conquest. Mongol armies struck east, south, and west. Subotai, this time accompanied by Batu, grandson of Genghis Khan, again devastated eastern and central Europe. The Mongols crossed the Volga, destroyed Russian armies, burned Cracow (shooting the bugler as he tried to give the alarm) and other Polish cities, and wiped out the armies of Boleslas of Poland, Bela of Hungary, Henry the Pious of Germany, and the Teutonic Knights. The Mongols ravaged Silesia, burned Pest, and penetrated Austria. Then a messenger arrived telling Subotai and Batu that Ogotai had died and they were all needed at the great council to be held in the Gobi. Most of Europe was saved. All of Russia, except the principality of Novgorod, had been conquered.

The Golden Horde

Subotai next commanded a Mongol army against the Merkit nomads of eastern Siberia, but Batu returned to the west to rule the western steppes. He established what came to be known as the Golden Horde. He founded Serai, a tent city on the Volga, as his capital and levied tribute on what remained of the Russian states.

For three centuries the states of Russia had to accept Mongol overlordship. The Mongols held their vassals tightly, even deposing princes who displeased them. The Russian princes could still wage war, but only with the permission of the Khan of the Golden Horde. Prince Alexander Nevsky of Vladimir became a Russian hero by defeating the Swedes, but he still had to touch the ground with his forehead before Batu's successor. The Prince of Moscow gained power by punishing other Russian principalities for disobeying the Mongols.

Russian feeling against the "Latins" (who were Germans and Swedes) contributed to their isolation. So did the Mongol overlordship. The domains of the Golden Horde stretched from the western boundaries of Russia deep into Central Asia. Batu was not the Great Khan, but he was actually the most powerful of the descendants of Genghis Khan, having made his cousin, Mangu, the Great Khan. The Mongols in China became Chinese, and the Mongols in Persia adopted Persian civilization, but the Mongols in Russia, having one foot in Russia and another in Turkestan, did not accept Slavic civilization. For a while, it seemed that they might. Batu's son was a Nestorian Christian and was sympathetic toward the Orthodox Christians of Russia. But he died before he could succeed his father. Gradually, the people of the Golden Horde became Muslim. They did not, however, adopt the civilization of the Arabs or the Persians. They remained nomadic Turks (ethnic Mongols were a small ruling class). The main cultural result of their conversion was to turn them against all Christians, and especially western Christians.

The descendants of Genghis Khan, like the generals of Alexander, waged war among themselves for primacy in the Mongol Empire. By the late 14th century, these civil wars had so weakened the Golden Horde that the Russian princes began to withhold tribute. The Mongols sent a punitive expedition against Moscow, which was becoming the most powerful of the Russian principalities. Prince Dimitrii Donskoi of Moscow repulsed the Mongols in 1373. A little later, he invaded the territory of the Golden Horde. He beat the Mongol general Mamai in 1378 and again in 1380.

The Golden Horde seemed like it was about to collapse. Then help came from the east. Toqtamish, Khan of the White Horde, a Central Asian power, and an ally of a new Turkish potentate, Timur i Lenk (Timur the Lame, known in the West as Tamerlane) came to the aid of the western Mongol horde. Toqtamish invaded Russia and sacked a number of Russian cities. He demolished Moscow. The Lithuanians tried to intervene, and Toqtamish wiped out their army. Toqtamish next decided to reconquer the portion of Central Asia Tamerlane had taken from the Mongols. This was hardly his best idea, but Tamerlane, who had built towers of skulls outside other cities, was merciful to the Golden Horde. He returned the prisoners he had taken, and although he deposed Toqtamish, he did not kill the former khan.

The Golden Horde continued in power for another half century, but in 1459, it broke up into two khanates, that of Crimea and of Kazan. The Khanate of Crimea was not limited to that peninsula: it also included much of southern Russia. The Khanate of Kazan, which claimed to be the Khanate of the Golden Horde, included the rest. Prince Ivan III of Moscow, also known as Ivan the Great, owed tribute to Kazan. He made alliances with the Khan of Crimea and with the Shah of Persia, then refused to send tribute. The Khan of Kazan led his army against Moscow. Ivan led his out to meet the Mongol leader. Neither wanted to begin a battle. The Mongol was afraid of being attacked in the rear by the Crimeans, the Persians, or both. After facing each other for weeks in 1480, the Khan took his troops back to Kazan. In 1502, the Khan of Crimea, nominally subject to the Khan of Kazan, attacked and destroyed Serai, the old capital of the Golden Horde and the Khan of Kazan. This was the end of the Golden Horde. In its place were three totally independent khanates—Kazan, Crimea, and Astrakhan.

The roles of the Russians and the Mongols began to reverse. Now the Russians became the aggressors. The Prince of Moscow interfered with the internal affairs of Kazan, even supporting his own candidates for khan. Kazan and Crimea united and invaded Russia again, but Russian artillery stopped them before they got to Moscow.

In spite of their preoccupation with affairs to the east, ideas from the West had begun to reach Russia. The biggest idea was gunpowder. Artillery became an important part of Russian armies. The Mongol khanates had a few cannons they obtained from their co-religionists, the Ottoman Turks, but nothing compared to what the Russians had. Russian armies, like Mongol armies, were once primarily horse archers. Now the most important Russian fighting men were infantry musketeers, and they began to supplement their bows with wheel lock pistols. Russian soldiers, mounted and foot, started wearing western-style plate armor. Even more important than improved weaponry was the fact that Russia was no longer a conglomerate of independent principalities. The Prince of Moscow, by enforcing the Mongols' will, had enlarged his own domain to the extent that he could field a Russian, not merely a Muscovite, army. There were a lot more Russians than members of the former Golden Horde.

Ivan the Terrible

For a while, there was a confusing welter of warfare among the three khanates and the principality of Moscow. Sometimes the Muscovites seemed to have the advantage, other times it was the Mongols.

Then, the Muscovites got a new prince, Ivan IV. Raised in a court remarkable even in 16th-century Russia for intrigue, treachery, and cruelty, Ivan was a man of contrasts. Pious, who was devoted to his people and generous to those in need, was also deceitful, egotistical, and cruel. He earned his nickname not so much for his ruthlessness, which was considerable, but for the power he acquired by destroying the power of the Russian nobility. Ivan truly believed that he was the successor to the East Roman emperors who had disappeared when Constantinople fell in 1452. He had himself crowned *tsar* (Caesar) of all the Russians.

At the time, the Mongols of Kazan were giving all the Russians trouble. Mongol raiding parties were destroying crops, killing peasants, and burning villages all over Russia. The teenage Ivan led an army against Kazan, but torrential rains turned the land into a sea of mud, bogging down the artillery. Some cannons broke through the ice of the Volga. Ivan saw this as a bad omen and returned to Moscow, but his troops did approach Kazan, where they defeated a Mongol force.

Khan of Crimea then invaded Astrakhan and united that khanate with his land. He wrote to Ivan: "You are young, but now you are grown up. Let me know what you want: my affection or bloodshed? If you want my affection, do not send us trifles. Indeed, like the King of Poland, who sends us 15,000 gold pieces annually, you should send us substantial gifts. If you desire war, I am prepared to march on Moscow and your land will lie under the hooves of my horses."

Then the Russians captured a courier carrying a message from the Khan of Kazan to the Khan of Crimea asking for military aid. Ivan knew it was time to break the power of the Mongols once and for all. He believed God had chosen him for the task.

He chose Kazan as his first target. Kazan was the weakest of the three khanates, its khan was a child, and the regent, Ulan Korshchak, was unpopular. Ivan was sheltering a pretender to the khan's throne, Shah Ali, who had a Mongol army of his own, and many of the Mongols in Kazan favored him over Ulan Korshchak.

On November 24, 1549, Ivan led 60,000 men against Kazan. Dissension among the nobles in the army delayed him, but he eventually reached Kazan. Then the weather changed. The icy fields soon became mud during the unseasonably warm spell. As a result, the artillery officers feared that they would not be able to move their guns. On February 25, Ivan raised the siege, but to make another strike easier, he established a fortress, which became a city, Sviazhsk, only 20 miles from Kazan. He also secured the allegiance of some of the nomad tribes in the area. Ulan Korshchak saw that there was no hope of victory. He fled from Kazan with some Crimean troops, but the Russians captured him and cut off his head. Kazan agreed to accept Shah Ali as khan.

The final blow

As soon as he sat on the throne, Shah Ali began squabbling with Ivan over the territory that the Russians had annexed. Eventually, Ivan had enough. He deposed Shah Ali as Mongol khans in the past had deposed Russian princes. He sent a viceroy to rule Kazan.

The people of Kazan, though, closed their gates to the viceroy. Ivan again called up his army. This time, he took about 140,000 men. They had just begun to march when Ivan stopped. He was worried that the powerful Crimean khanate might attack. Scouts brought the word that the Crimean Khan's men were besieging Tula, a town south of Moscow. Ivan began to march towards Tula, but the Crimean Khan lifted the siege and fled southward, raiding villages and capturing villagers to be sold as slaves to the Venetians. In spite of his imperious letter to Ivan, the Crimean Khan was afraid of the Russians. Ivan again marched on Kazan.

The Mongols in Kazan were made of sterner stuff than the Crimean Khan. There were about 35,000 of them, including nomads in the surrounding countryside. The Russians dragged up their cannons and hid them behind wickerwork gabions filled with earth. The Mongols frequently sallied out, but they weren't able to capture the Russian guns. Nomads hiding in a nearby forest caused more damage, striking the Russian lines with pinprick raids, often at night. The raids were usually coordinated with sallies from the city. The garrison would signal the nomads when and where to strike with flags from the wall. The forest was vast, and the Russian scouts had no idea where the enemy's base was. Eventually, Ivan hid a large part of his army, so it could respond instantly to the next nomad raid. The Russian ambush worked as planned, and when the nomads dashed back to the forest, Russian cavalry and mounted musketeers followed them closely. The nomad fort was on a hill surrounded by swamps. The Russians dismounted and while one group attacked from the front, another group, circling unseen through the woods, climbed over the wall.

While this was going on, the Russians were filling up the moat around the city with tree trunks and earth. The walls of Kazan were made of wood and stone and were 25 feet thick. There was no way the Russian artillery could batter them down. Ivan ordered his men to start digging under two of the city's towers. Digging was slow, and food was getting scarce for the besiegers. It was hard to bring up enough food for the huge Russian host. To speed things up, the Russians built a movable wooden tower, an enormous thing 42 feet high, with 10 heavy and 50 light cannons in its upper stories. Moving this engine up to the walls, however, was also a slow process. It took two weeks. When it was finally in position, its cannons caused great destruction in the city, but the Mongol soldiers had created earthworks behind the threatened portion of the wall and went on fighting.

Ivan was worried. It looked as if the siege would last into the winter, a most unpleasant prospect. And the force he had sent into the forest had not yet reappeared.

Then, Prince Gorbaty-Shuisky, commander of the force that took the nomad fort, and his men came out of the forest. They arrived with a huge amount of loot, including wagons loaded with grain and herds of cattle. The Russians no longer faced a food shortage. After taking the fort, Gorbaty-Shuisky's men had ranged over the countryside raiding Mongol villages. They also freed thousands of Russians who had been held as slaves by the Mongols. The constant Mongol raids on Russian territory were mainly expeditions to capture slaves. They kept some of the slaves themselves; others they traded to the Crimeans, who sold many of the captives to Venetian and Ottoman slave traders. Those raids were why Ivan was determined to destroy the Mongol power.

On October 1, Ivan could feel winter in the air. Everything depended on the sappers. On October 2, a plume of smoke and dirt erupted under one of the towers. Men, timbers, and rocks went hurtling through the air. To Ivan, the sight was followed by a noise like a thousand thunder claps. Then there was a second explosion. The Russian miners had planted dozens of barrels of gunpowder under two of Kazan's towers and opened wide breaches in the walls. Ivan's troops dashed in. Cornered in another tower, the Khan surrendered. Some of his troops fought on; others tried to escape by climbing over the walls, and all who had not surrendered were killed.

The end of an era

The destruction of Kazan ended the Mongol raids into Russia. It also marked the beginning of the end of Mongol power in Europe. Two years later, Ivan invaded the khanate of Astrakhan. It was Kazan all over again. Ivan installed a client khan named Dervish, but Dervish revolted. Ivan marched again. Dervish fled and Ivan annexed the khanate to Russia. The Crimean khanate survived—greatly reduced in territory—only by allowing itself to be annexed to the Ottoman Empire.

The end of Mongol domination allowed Russia to enter the European milieu more fully. Ivan even entered trade relations with far-off England, a country about as familiar to Russians as the dark side of the moon. The reentry process was slow, though, because the Russians still spent much of their time looking east. But now they were concerned with conquering the East—Siberia, and Turkestan—not worrying about the threat by Eurasian nomads.

Battle 45

Lutzen, 1632 AD
Defenestration

Who fought: Imperialist forces of the Holy Roman Empire (Count Wallenstein) vs. Swedish Army and Protestant German forces (King Gustavus Adolphus).

What was at stake: Theoretically, whether Catholicism or Protestantism would dominate Germany; actually, whether Germany could achieve any kind of unity.

By his Letter of Majesty, King Matthias of Bohemia had guaranteed religious freedom to his subjects living on royal land. But years later, Matthias, who was also Holy Roman Emperor, began ceding royal lands to Catholic bishops, who did not allow the building of Protestant churches on their lands.

In Bohemia, the nobles elected the king. Matthias was old and near death. It was time to elect a new king. The king they elected was Archduke Ferdinand—like Matthias, a Hapsburg. The Protestant nobles of Bohemia tried to get Ferdinand to endorse the Letter of Majesty. He didn't say no, but he didn't say yes, either. On May 22, 1618 in the Hradcany Palace in Prague, a Protestant mob gathered to demand that the Emperor stop ceding royal lands and that the king-elect endorse the Letter of Majesty. Matthias, in Vienna being Emperor, told his royal governors to resist the mob. They did. The mob grabbed two of the governors, Jaroslav Martinitz and William Slavata, and dragged them to a window of the audience hall.

"Jesu, Maria, help!" Martinitz screamed as he hurtled through the window. Slavata clawed at the window frame as he called on the Blessed Virgin to help him.

Someone knocked him senseless and pushed him through. The crowd then threw their secretary out for good measure.

"We'll see if your Mary can help you," one of the rebels jeered, looking through the window. A moment later, he pulled his head back in with a look of amazement. "By God, his Mary has helped!"

Martinitz staggered to his feet and climbed a ladder protruding from another window. The secretary followed. Some of Slavata's servants dashed into the courtyard and carried their master to safety.

This incident, known as the First Defenestration of Prague (throwing people out of windows became something of a Czech tradition as a way of answering political problems) resulted in no immediate deaths. In the long run, it caused a very conservatively estimated eight million deaths—seven million of them civilians—in a horror show called the Thirty Years War.

The Bohemian nobles took back the election and gave the crown to Frederick, the Elector of Palatinate. Frederick was neither a Catholic nor a Lutheran, although the vast majority of Bohemians were one or the other. He was a Calvinist, but as he was neither a Catholic nor a Hapsburg, that seemed to be enough. It might seem that whoever was the King of Bohemia was nobody's business but the Bohemians', but the King of Bohemia was one of the seven electors of the Holy Roman Empire. Three of the electors were Catholic bishops; three were Protestant princes. Bohemia was the swing vote. The Holy Roman Empire divided into two factions: the Catholic League and the Evangelical Union of Protestant Princes.

In Bohemia, Heinrich Matthias von Thurn, who had led the defenestration mob, took command of the army. The Letter of Majesty became a dead letter. Religious toleration went out the window like the governors, but it didn't revive. The Jesuits were expelled on June 9, and then the Bohemians rejected an offer by Emperor Matthias for peace talks. Thurn's army, helped by Protestant troops from Saxony and Savoy and the first of the great mercenaries, Peter Ernst von Mansfeld, invaded Austria. The most devastating war in European history up to that time had begun.

The Four Horsemen of the Apocalypse

The war was so devastating because there were no decent national armies in Central Europe and no effective feudal armies anywhere. No feudal lords could afford enough of the new weapons (muskets and cannons). They could afford to give their serfs time for training to use those weapons effectively even less. Only full time, professional troops could effectively use the combination of muskets, pikes, and cannons required in a modern war. And because no monarch in Central Europe had a system of regular taxation, princes and kings couldn't raise national armies, like those of Spain and Sweden, either.

Troops were supplied by private contractors—mercenaries. The generals of the age, Mansfeld, Tilly, Pappenheim, Piccolomini, and others, would fight for whoever paid them. When the pay stopped, they "lived off the land." The main difference between a brigand band and a mercenary army was that the brigands had more compassion for their victims. For the next 30 years, mercenaries would ride across Germany like the Four Horsemen of the Apocalypse. Later, some national armies would join the fray—French, Spanish, and Swedish—but they were no improvement on the mercenaries.

The war had not been on long when Matthias died. Ferdinand, the deposed king-elect, replaced him as Emperor, having secured the needed vote from the wavering Frederick. The kingship of Bohemia would no longer have a bearing on who was Emperor, but hostilities had already begun. Fueled by religious fanaticism and dynastic ambitions, they would continue.

On November 8, 1620, the Catholic forces of Maximilian of Bavaria, under Johan Tzerclaes Tilly, decisively defeated the army of Frederick of Bohemia. Frederick had made the mistake of stopping payments to Ernst von Mansfeld. Mansfeld had stopped fighting. Without Mansfeld, Thurn's troops could not withstand Tilly's. Frederick, a popular choice for king who had quickly made himself unpopular, fled. Prague was sacked, and Ferdinand auctioned off the estates of the Protestant Bohemian nobles. The high bidder for many of the estates was a tall, dark, craggy-faced Czech, a Moravian noble named Albrecht Eusebius Wenseclaus von Waldstein. Waldstein had been born to a Protestant Bohemian family, but was orphaned and raised by Catholic relatives. He converted to Catholicism and aspired to a military career in the service of Archduke, later Emperor, Matthias. He showed both talent and valor fighting the Turks and quickly became a company commander. He learned, however, that without a title and money he would never advance much further. He quit the army and married a very old and very rich widow. The lady was so happy that she gave him a love potion that nearly killed him. Fortunately for the young Czech, her age did her in before her love potions did him in. At the age of 23, Waldstein found himself one of the richest men in Moravia. He introduced scientific agriculture on his estates. He built storehouses for surplus crops and established schools and manufacturing in his villages. He organized medical services, poor relief, and provision for times of famine for the peasants. Such things were almost unheard of in Central Europe in the 17th century. Waldstein was no humanitarian, but he knew that happy and educated people are more productive than ignorant and sullen ones. He sold the products of his estates far and wide and became much richer.

When the Thirty Years War began, he raised troops for Archduke, later Emperor, Ferdinand. Ferdinand made him Count Wallenstein, the name by which he is usually remembered. Wallenstein lavished the same care on the equipment and training of his troops as he did on his estates. Bethlen Gabor, King of Transylvania and pretender to the throne of Hungary, defeated two imperial armies and was threatening Vienna. Wallenstein defeated him twice. After the last battle, Gabor renounced his claim to Hungary and made peace. Two years later, Gabor revolted again, and again Wallenstein saved the Empire. Ferdinand rewarded Wallenstein by making him Duke of Friedland and giving him the power to coin money and create nobles.

Then, Denmark entered the war on the Protestant side. Denmark was larger and more powerful than most of the German states in the Empire, and it was subsidized by England. And Mansfeld found a new employer, Duke Christian of Brunswick. Ferdinand, at the same time, was running out of money to raise a new army. He approached Wallenstein, who, by this time, owned most of Bohemia, for a loan. Wallenstein, instead, offered the Emperor an army—50,000 men, trained, equipped, and led by himself.

It was an offer Ferdinand couldn't refuse. As far as he knew, Wallenstein's only genius was in making money. But 50,000 men was 50,000 men, and all they'd cost would be their monthly pay.

Tilly was engaging—none too successfully—the Danes. Wallenstein confronted

Mansfeld. The clash between Wallenstein's raw farm boys and Mansfeld's seasoned troopers was a disaster for the old mercenary. Wallenstein all but annihilated Mansfeld's army and then chased its remnants across Europe to Dalmatia, where Mansfeld died. Wallenstein marched north, annexed Tilly's army, and drove the Danes out of Germany and most of Denmark. King Christian fled to the Danish islands and made peace. Wallenstein swept along the Baltic shore.

Ferdinand pushed for the forced conversion of all Protestants, while Wallenstein counseled moderation. "Give the peasantry plenty of time," he told the Emperor. "Do not press the lower orders too hard about religion."

Ferdinand, though, could not be moderate about religion. Neither could the princes of the Catholic League. Besides, both the Emperor and the princes thought the Czech general had too much power. Ferdinand made Wallenstein Duke of Mecklenburg. Then, encouraged by the princes, he relieved him of command. To everyone's relief, Wallenstein went back to Bohemia, but he took part of his army with him, and warned the Emperor of a new menace in the north.

The Snow King

Gustavus Adolphus did not resemble Wallenstein in anything but military genius. The King of Sweden, a fair-haired, burly man, was no nouveau riche adventurer, but genuine royalty. He had inherited one of the most powerful countries in Europe and made it more powerful by creating a new army.

Before Gustavus, the most up-to-date armies were modeled on the Spanish. They were built around massive blocks of pikemen, who provided shelter for musketeers. Artillery consisted of enormously heavy cannons that, once in place, usually stayed in place. Cavalry wore plate armor to their knees and relied more on pistols than on lances or swords.

The Swedish army still had pikemen and musketeers, but the pikes were shorter and the muskets lighter. More importantly, the formations were smaller. There were no huge, unwieldy squares of pikemen. Gustavus could maneuver his smaller units easily. Many of the musketeers carried the wheellock or the Baltic firelock, ancestor of the flintlock, instead of the cumbersome matchlock that was standard equipment in other armies. They used paper cartridges, which made loading faster.

His artillery was unlike anything seen before. The guns were light—some light enough to be manhandled into position. These were placed on line with the infantry, and the gunners could push them to keep up with the foot soldiers. They fired cartridges containing both shot and powder, and they could fire faster than the muskets.

The cavalry dispensed with most armor, a steel helmet and a heavy leather "buff coat" being all most wore. The horsemen carried only two pistols and a sword. Instead of cantering up to the pikemen and firing their pistols, the usual German method, the Swedes charged at a gallop, swords in hand. Gustavus usually led the cavalry himself. Like Alexander the Great, Gustavus liked to deliver the decisive stroke with cavalry. In brief, the Swedish army could move faster than any other army in Europe could, and it had vastly more firepower.

With Wallenstein, war was a means to an end: his own enrichment. With Gustavus, war was an end in itself. He was always fighting, with the Russians or with the Poles, wars that were interrupted by truces but which never ended. Wallenstein recognized the Swedish King's tactical genius, but the Empire's nobles scoffed. The "Snow King," they said, would melt as he approached the southern sun.

In its first test, the Swedish army crushed and scattered the Catholic League forces under Tilly at Breitenfeld. Old "Father Tilly," who had been fighting since he first enlisted as a teenage pikeman, received the last of his many wounds when a Swedish cannon ball took off his leg resulting in death. Reluctantly, Emperor Ferdinand turned to the only man who seemed likely to stop the doom from the north: Wallenstein.

Gustavus Adolphus: liberator or conqueror?

The Thirty Years War was a religious war. Most of the English-speaking sources on that war were Protestant. Consequently, modern American readers are likely to get the idea that Gustavus could be identified by his halo and Wallentein's floppy hat hid a pair of horns. Actually, both generals were princes of plunder. Discipline in both armies was strict. Neither Gustavus nor Wallenstein had any compunction about hanging soldiers who plundered without permission. But permission to plunder was by no means rare. Both generals made war pay for itself and both were besieged by would be recruits looking for a chance to rob and rape legally. Other generals were equally liberal about pillaging, but these two won battles.

"Now you have in front of you, for the first time," Gustavus told his troops before Breitenfeld, "a camp filled with precious booty, afterwards a road which passes the sumptuous villages and fertile fields of the Catholics. All that is the price of a single victory."

Pillage was a way of punishing enemies. After smashing Tilly's army, Gustavus's lieutenants urged him to march on Vienna. The King, however, chose to reward his troops by letting them rob, rape, and murder their way through Catholic Franconia. But pillage for neither army was restricted to enemy territory. Wallenstein's depredations in Catholic lands were powerful reasons for sacking him, and Gustavus himself, in a letter to his minister, Axel Oxenstierna, wrote, "we are obliged to carry on the war *ex rapto*, with great injury and damage to our neighbors." Rape and murder went

Gustavus Adolphus

along with this robbery. A peasant who tried to withhold property from these military brigands was lucky if his end was swift. Catholic armies routinely killed Protestant clergy, and Gustavus's troops tortured all the Catholic priests and nuns they found to death.

Gustavus's army was Swedish only in the sense that its leader was the King of Sweden. The soldiers, besides Swedes and Finns, included Scots, English, Danes, Slavs, and huge numbers of Germans. Wallenstein's army was equally heterogeneous. In each army, Catholics, Protestants, and atheists fought side-by-side. There may have been a few Muslims, too. Turkish mercenaries were not unknown. Wallenstein's second-in-command and best friend was Georg von Arnim, a Protestant, who, after Wallenstein retired, led the army of Johan Georg, the Protestant Duke of Saxony. Wallenstein and Arnim kept up correspondence after the Czech left the field. Both generals, the Catholic and the Protestant, now had the same aim: German unity and the absence of foreigners.

"Should the war last longer," Arnim wrote to Wallenstein, "the Empire will be utterly destroyed. He who has an upright, honest mind must be touched to the heart: when he sees the Empire so afflicted, he must yearn for peace. So it is with me. Therefore, I have let no opportunity escape...but have urged peace on friend and foe...our beloved Germany will fall a prey to foreign people and be a pitiable example to all the world."

Arnim, of course, was a friend of Wallenstein. Frederick, ex-King of Bohemia and former Elector of Palatinate, was not, but he refused Gustavus's offer to return him to the Palatinate as a Swedish vassal. "The King of Sweden is hard to content," Frederick remarked to another Protestant noble. Gustavus dropped a hint on what might make him content. "If I become Emperor..." he speculated in a conversation with the former Duke of Mecklenburg.

The clash of titans

Gustavus was laying waste to Bavaria, but Wallenstein was in no hurry to get back into the war—he let Ferdinand beg, and then he dictated terms. The terms were written down, but they have never been found—probably because the Emperor had them destroyed. From the evidence, it seems that Wallenstein got full control over the army, sole power to negotiate peace terms and conclude treaties, exclusion of the Emperor's son from any command, and exclusion of Spain from any influence on the conduct of the war. Some said Wallenstein was also promised the title of Elector. Gustavus, the king, and Wallenstein, the adventurer, each had full control of his part of the war.

Wallenstein's first operation was a curious campaign against his former comrade, von Arnim, and the Saxon army. Arnim had invaded Bohemia while Wallenstein was negotiating with the Emperor. When he had obtained his commission, Wallenstein pushed von Arnim out. Both the invasion and its repulse were strangely bloodless. All through the campaign, Wallenstein, through von Arnim, was begging Johan Georg, the Duke of Saxony, to support a new all-German league, pledged to religious toleration and home rule.

Johan Georg, however, was deathly afraid of the King of Sweden. Wallenstein tried to convince the Duke that Gustavus was not the only person to fear. He invaded Saxony and began treating it as Gustavus was treating Bavaria. Wallenstein was also giving the Swedish monarch a lesson in grand strategy. His base was Bohemia, the center of Central Europe. He needed neither Bavaria nor Austria. But if he controlled Saxony, he could threaten to again invade Denmark. The King of Denmark would no doubt make peace. Then Wallenstein could use the Danish navy to control the Baltic. Gustavus, cut off from Sweden, would be stranded at the foot of the Alps.

Gustavus turned north, but Wallenstein managed to join his army to what was left of the Bavarian army. Gustavus fell back and Wallenstein pursued. The Czech knew his army could not match the Swede's in mobility and firepower. He fortified a position near Nuremberg across Gustavus's line of communications. The Swedes had thoroughly ravaged the area; there was no food to be had. If the king stayed in place, his troops would starve. If he retreated, he'd lose prestige. If he fought, he'd be outnumbered and his army's mobility wouldn't count. He fought—and he lost. He resumed burning Bavaria to draw Wallenstein after him. Wallenstein resumed burning Saxony. He drew Gustavus after him.

The fast-marching Swedes caught up with Wallenstein near Lutzen, before Johan Georg could change his mind and join the new all-German league. Gustavus took a leaf from Wallenstein's book and entrenched his position outside Moritzburg. Wallenstein had no intention of attacking the entrenched and heavily armed Swedes.

For some reason, he let Gottfried Heinrich von Pappenheim take his private army, the Black Cuirassiers, and some infantry to attack Halle. Or Pappenheim, a flamboyant and notoriously insubordinate mercenary, didn't even ask permission. This left Wallenstein with only 8,000 infantry and 4,000 cavalry. Gustavus would not miss an opportunity like that. He led his 14,000 infantry and 5,000 cavalry out of camp. Wallenstein sent a courier galloping after Pappenheim and prepared to do battle.

Who won?

Wallenstein formed his infantry into five huge blocks, with pikemen 10 ranks deep supporting an equal number of musketeers. Four of these "battles" lined up behind a sunken road. Wallenstein put some musketeers in the road, hidden by its banks, while others were dug into trenches. The fifth battle, the right flank of his infantry, sheltered behind three windmills on a hill. Most of the cavalry, under Ottavio Piccolomini, covered his left flank. The rest of the horsemen connected the troops on Windmill Hill with those in the sunken road and with the village of Lutzen on the extreme right. In front of the troops, Wallenstein placed some 60 cannons. Suffering from gout, the general could not ride, and he had to inspect his troops from a litter.

With his march from Moritzburg slowed by Isolani's Croatian cavalry, Gustavus arrived at Wallenstein's position the night of November 15, 1632. He lined up his 26 heavy guns and his 40 quick-firing light guns in front of his infantry. His cavalry, spread wide on both the flanks, was backed up by musketeers who were ready to give attacking horsemen an unpleasant surprise.

Dawn did not exactly break the next day. The fog was so thick that the soldiers could hardly see each other, let alone the sun. It was noon when Gustavus gave the order to charge. Gustavus led the right wing cavalry. He crossed the sunken road and the trenches, collecting a musket ball in the leg as he did so. The Imperial musketeers, crouched in the sunken road, blasted the Swedish horsemen from below, then fell back to shelter behind the blocks of pikemen. Gustavus led his horsemen on and drove back Piccolomini's cavalry. In the center, his infantry captured some of Wallenstein's guns.

When he heard that, Wallenstein mounted his horse in spite of the gout and led a cavalry and infantry charge that drove back the Swedish center. A cannon ball clipped off one spur and several musket balls penetrated his coat, but he was unhurt.

Bernard of Saxe-Weimar, leading the Swedish left, ran into trouble, and Gustavus took some troops to that flank. He had just arrived when an Imperialist pistol ball hit him in the chest. Weak and in shock, he had ridden to the rear. For some time, he was not missed. When Saxe-Weimar realized what must have happened, he just told his men the king was in another sector. In a short time, events would prove that his idea was a good one.

Pappenheim and his Black Cuirassiers suddenly appeared. When he received Wallenstein's message, the dashing Pappenheim left his infantry behind and rushed to the battle. He hit the Swedish right wing, which Gustavus had originally led, with an old-fashioned hell-for-leather charge. The Swedish line buckled. Then, Gustavus's idea of reinforcing his cavalry with small groups of musketeers paid off. One of the musketeers mortally wounded Pappenheim. The Black Cuirassiers were a private army, so ultimately, they owed allegiance only to Pappenheim. With their leader gone, they hesitated, and the Swedes rallied.

The confusion of Pappenheim's army was what Saxe-Weimar tried to avoid by covering up the loss of Gustavus. But someone found the King's body anyway. The effect was not what Saxe-Weimar feared. The effect on the Swedes was like the effect of Theodoric's death on the Visigoths (**see Chalons, page 174**).

"They have killed the King!" a soldier screamed. Others took up the cry: "They have killed the King! Avenge our King!" Gustavus's army charged Wallenstein's all along the line. The Imperialists eventually fled. The Swedes, however, were too tired and cut up to pursue.

It was a Swedish victory, but the cost was great. The Swedes and the Imperialists both went into winter quarters. The spring would bring new surprises.

The second giant falls

Wallenstein's army had not been smashed. He not only kept it together, but he enlisted many eager recruits. He did not convince the Saxons to join his new all-German league, although he continued negotiating with them and other Protestant states through Armin. In the spring, the Saxon army joined the Swedish, now commanded by the Bohemian, Count Turn. In what B.H. Liddell Hart calls his "military masterpiece," Wallenstein separated the Saxons from the Swedes and surrounded the Swedes. This time Thurn was not leading a mob against two unarmed politicians. He surrendered his whole army to Wallenstein on condition that the officers go free and the men enlist in the Imperial army.

The victory brought no joy in Vienna. Ferdinand was outraged that Wallenstein had released the arch rebel, Thurn. That, and the fact that he had been negotiating with the Protestants and promising religious freedom led to a suicidal decision: Wallenstein must die. Ferdinand sent a secret commission to Piccolomini depriving Wallenstein of command and declaring him an outlaw to be taken "dead or alive."

At midnight on February 24, 1634, Colonel Walter Butler, an Irishman, Captain Walter Devereaux, an Englishman, and six other mercenaries in Imperial service, aided by two Scots named Gordon and Leslie, broke into Wallenstein's quarters and murdered the Czech-born German patriot. The Thirty Years War ground on and on until 1648.

Results: real and imagined

Lutzen is often hailed as the battle that preserved the Protestant cause. It was hardly that. When the Protestant Reformation began, there was little resistance from a lax laity and a self-serving clergy. But the fires of religious passion had been burning for more than a century, and by 1632, they were white hot. That passion made it impossible for a king or a duke to decide what religion his subjects would profess. The last king to do so was Henry VIII just about 100 years before. As Wallenstein and von Arnim saw, the day of forced conversions was over.

On the other hand, Lutzen did not determine that Germany would never become a Swedish province. It might have become one if Gustavus had lived and Wallenstein had died. That situation, though, would not have outlived Gustavus. The idea of Sweden absorbing Germany is something like a cat digesting an elephant.

The death of Gustavus, followed by the death of Wallenstein, insured that the war would go on until all parties were exhausted, which had serious consequences.

It was once estimated that the Thirty Years War wiped out three-quarters of the population of Germany. Modern research has scaled back the death count drastically. Nevertheless, the war was a social disaster. An entire generation grew up knowing nothing but war, slaughter, and anarchy. Hundreds of thousands of men knew no trade but soldiering. When peace broke out, some became mercenaries in the smaller wars on the continent. Others became the nearest civilian equivalent to soldiers (as soldiering was practiced in the Thirty Years War): they became bandits.

The war occurred in an era when kings in the western countries—Spain, France, and England—were consolidating their power and turning their nations into unified states. But in Germany, the war increased the disunity of the many statelets. Not for another two and a half centuries would Germany, the largest nation in Europe west of Russia, become a united state able to play a major part in international affairs.

Battle 46

Dewey's flagship, Olympia.

Manila Bay, 1898 AD
"...To see that you behave."

Who fought: Americans (George Dewey) vs. Spaniards (Patricio Montojo y Pasaron).

What was at stake: The aspirations of the United States to great power status.

"Well, Commodore, good luck," said Prince Henry of Prussia, the younger brother of Kaiser Wilhelm II. "I may send some ships to Manila—to see that you behave."

"I should be delighted to have you do so, Your Highness," Commodore George Dewey replied. "But permit me to caution you to keep your ships from between my guns and the enemy."

To Dewey, it seemed that Prince Henry, commanding the German Asiatic Squadron, had been going out of his way to be irritating. During the time both naval commanders were stationed at Hong Kong, Henry had remarked that he did not believe the European powers would allow the United States to annex Cuba. Dewey told him the United States did not intend to annex Cuba, but it could not allow the conditions there to continue.

Prince Henry's attitude was generally typical of Europeans. Only Britain seemed sympathetic to the United States. To the British, their "American cousins" were something of a joke, but cousins were, after all, cousins. The Spanish definitely were not cousins. There had been British sympathy for Spain when Spain was fighting the Cuban rebels. Winston Churchill, then a journalist in Cuba, wrote dispatches about the fighting that were consistently favorable to the Spanish military. But there was more than a little racism behind that sympathy.

The Continental Europeans saw the conflict as one between a large, uncouth, and not-quite-civilized country—the United States—and an ancient kingdom that was down on its luck. In the American Civil War, a generation earlier, the United States introduced the use of machine guns, armored warships, and railroads for mass troop movements. It fielded the most powerful army and navy in the world at that time. Still Helmuth von Moltke the elder, the Prussian field marshal, said there was nothing to be learned from "two armed mobs chasing each other around the country." In the eyes of Europeans, the Americans were bullies who wouldn't dare act toward other European states as they were acting toward Spain. Some Europeans even proposed testing that theory.

In a report to Berlin, Prince Henry said, "the [Filipino] natives would gladly place themselves under the protection of a European power, especially Germany."

If Henry thought he could intimidate Dewey, he could not have been more mistaken. Dewey was not a rash young man: he was a crazy old man, which is why he had command of the American China Squadron. He had been sent there to cope with a situation that began 10,000 miles away—on the island of Cuba.

Troubled waters

Of all Spain's possessions, Cuba and the Philippines were the most troublesome. There had been no problems in Puerto Rico, Guam, or the Marianas, but during the 19th century, the Caribbean island and the Asian archipelago had been in almost continual revolt.

Americans neither knew nor cared about the Philippines. All they knew was that the islands were in the "South Seas"—that semi-legendary domain of cannibals and hula dancers. Cuba was another story. American sympathy was entirely with the Cubans. The Cubans were a colonial people, as the Americans once were, resisting the harsh rule of a "mother country" thousands of miles away.

The Cuban revolt raging in the late 1890s was being waged with appalling brutality on both sides. The aim of the Cuban rebels was to make it unprofitable for Spain to keep the colony, which meant destroying the sugar crop, Cuba's main revenue producer. If that meant, as it did, thousands of people would be out of work and probably starve, then so be it—that was the price of liberty. To fight the rebels, the government developed even more repressive measures. The Spanish captain general (governor), Arsenio Martinez de Campos, who had put down the last revolt, decided he couldn't stomach the measures needed: "I do not think I have the qualities for such a policy. In Spain, only Weyler has them."

So the government appointed a new captain general, General Valeriano Weyler y Nicolau. Weyler invented a device that would plague the next century: in South Africa, in the Philippines, in Germany, and in German-occupied Europe the concentration camp. Hundred of thousands of people were herded into camps so they couldn't aid the rebel guerrillas. Tens of thousands died there from lack of food or medical care.

Weyler was one of the two people who made war between the United States and Spain inevitable. The other was President William McKinley.

An amiable man, McKinley had the knack of getting people to push him in the direction he wanted to go. Henry Adams called him the "first genius of manipulation." He needed that genius, because although Spain was universally disliked, American opinion was by no means unanimous on what the United States should do.

Some like Mark Hanna, the Republican boss who mistakenly thought McKinley was his tool, saw an opportunity to acquire colonies. Horace N. Fisher, a contemporary financial analyst, wrote, "Even now, our domestic consumption can not take more than 75 percent of our manufactured products…Hence the necessity for great foreign markets for such surplus, with the alternative of the curtailment of production or of wages." In that era of protective tariffs, "foreign markets" to most people meant colonies. Also, to most people, colonies were the mark of a great power. Why didn't the United States have colonies? Hanna and the wealthy businessmen he represented wanted colonies, but they didn't want war. War disrupted business and was an unproductive expense.

More Americans wanted war but didn't want colonies. They wanted to punish Spain and liberate Cuba, but the idea of owning colonies was repugnant to many people in this former colony.

Then there was the third group that wanted both war and colonies. Its most prominent spokesman was the assistant secretary of the navy, Theodore Roosevelt.

"All the great masterful races have been fighting races," he said in an address at the Naval War College. "No triumph of peace is quite as great as the supreme triumphs of war…the diplomat is the servant, not the master, of the soldier."

McKinley, like Roosevelt, wanted both war and colonies. Unlike Roosevelt, he preferred to let others do the campaigning. In his inaugural address, McKinley said, "We want no wars of conquest; we must avoid the temptation of territorial aggression." But in a memo to himself, McKinley had scribbled, "While we are conducting war and until its conclusion, we must keep all we get; when the war is over, we must keep what we want."

One of the members of Roosevelt's clique of war hawks was Commodore George Dewey. Dewey had attracted Roosevelt's attention by his eagerness for battle during a dispute with Chile. Roosevelt managed to have Dewey appointed to command of the China Squadron while his boss, Secreatry John D. Long, was absent. In the event of war, Dewey was to proceed to the Philippines, attack Spain's Pacific Fleet, and take the islands in the name of the United States. Roosevelt was a disciple of Captain Alfred Thayer Mahan, the American naval officer whose *The Influence of Seapower on History* is to sailors what Carl von Clausewitz's *On War* is to soldiers. Mahan stressed the need for naval bases at strategic spots in modern war. In the days of sailing ships, navies could operate worldwide for months at a time. In the late 19th century, they needed bases to refuel. The Philippines would give the United States a base from which it could exercise power in the Far East.

Remember the Maine!

McKinley continually pressed Spain to get rid of Weyler, to improve conditions in the concentration camps, to give the Cubans autonomy. Gradually, Spain complied. But with each concession, McKinley said it was too little and too late. There were anti-American riots in Havana. In spite of what the U.S. public believed, all Cubans were not prepared to greet Americans as liberators. McKinley decided to sent a U.S. warship to Havana on a "friendly visit." Even his rabidly anti-Spanish counsel-general in Havana, General Fitzhugh Lee, advised that sending a ship there would only aggravate relations with Spain. So McKinley sent the battleship *Maine* to Havana.

"After warning the Spanish ambassador that an anti-American outburst in Cuba would compel him to send troops," wrote historian Walter Karp, "the President ordered the warship to Havana to provoke an anti-American outburst."

There was an explosion, and *Maine* sank in Havana harbor with a heavy loss of American life. Modern researchers say the best explanation for the explosion was that spontaneous combustion in one of the ship's coal bunkers ignited a magazine. The American public suspected a mine planted by the Spanish government. Lieutenant Philip Alger, the navy's top ordnance expert, said no submerged mine could cause the damage done to *Maine*—a statement that made Roosevelt fly into a rage. McKinley appointed a commission to investigate. Of course, they found that the cause was a mine that must have been planted by the Spanish government.

McKinley sent an ultimatum. Spain must close the concentration camps, and it must lay down its arms and accept the "friendly offices" of the United States in reaching an agreement with the rebels.

Spain agreed to everything, but McKinley said it was too late. He asked Congress for a authorization to intervene in Cuba. In his message, significantly, he did not ask for recognition of the Republic of Cuba. That would preclude annexation.

But American support for the liberation of Cuba was too strong. Senator Henry M. Teller of Colorado slipped an amendment into the intervention bill: the United States might not exercise "sovereignty, jurisdiction or control" over Cuba. There was no mention of other Spanish colonies, such as Puerto Rico or the Philippines. Nobody was interested in them. Puerto Rico was apparently content with Spanish rule. The Philippines definitely were not. Filipino rebels were just about to push the Spanish into the sea, but to the American public, the Philippines were *terra incognita*.

Of course, to Roosevelt, McKinley, or Dewey, they were not. When he heard that the war had begun, Commodore Dewey set out for the Philippines. His British friends saw him leave with grave misgivings.

"The prevailing impression, even among the military class," Dewey recalled, "was that our squadron was going to certain destruction.

> "In the Hong Kong Club it was not possible to get bets, even at heavy odds, that our expedition would be a success, and this in spite of a friendly predilection among the British in our favor. I was told, after our officers had been entertained at dinner by a British regiment, that the universal remark among our hosts was to this effect: 'A fine set of fellows, but unhappily we shall never see them again.'"

Manila Bay

Dewey had nine ships, including three cruisers. One was merely a revenue cutter. They weren't the newest ships in the U.S. Navy. All were steel. The Spanish had 40 naval vessels in the Manila area. Manila harbor's entrance was narrow, with the fortress island Corregidor in the middle of it. On one side of Corregidor was Boca Chica ("Little Mouth"), a channel only two miles wide. On the other side of Corregidor was Boca Grande ("Big Mouth"), four miles wide. But in the middle of Boca Grande was another fortified island, El Fraile. The harbor entrance was reportedly mined. Merchant skippers entering the harbor had to take a zigzag course to avoid mines. Dewey, though, had served in the Civil War under Admiral David "Damn the Torpedoes" Farragut.

Dewey was confident. His opposite number, Admiral Patricio Montojo y Pasaron, was not. Most of his 40 ships were gunboats—old, small, and useless in a modern naval battle. His bigger ships were decrepit, and one was wooden. The cruiser *Castilla* had developed a leak in its propeller shaft housing on a short trip up the coast. The Spanish sailors plugged the leak with cement, which immobilized the propeller. Now *Castilla* could not move under its own power. Only five of the 14 mines available had been placed in the channels. Madrid had said 70 mines were on the way, but they wouldn't get to Manila before the Americans. Then Montojo learned that the four 150-mm guns he thought were guarding the bay entrance were still not in place.

Montojo would fight, but he knew he couldn't win. He moved his ships to shallow water, close to shore, to give his men the best chance of survival.

On the night of April 30, 1898, the American squadron, with Dewey's flagship, *Olympia*, leading the column, steamed through Boca Grande, past the guns of Corregidor. The column was almost through the channel when soot in the funnel of the revenue cutter, *McCulloch*, caught fire. The Spanish gunners on El Fraile noticed the flash. They fired a couple of rounds that missed. *McCulloch* and the cruiser *Boston* fired back, and the Spanish guns were silent. Dewey's ammunition was limited, and he didn't want to waste it firing on shore batteries, especially at night. No mines exploded.

When the sun came up, Dewey saw the Spanish warships anchored in line near the Cavite naval base. He brought his squadron in close. The Spanish began firing, but their shooting was wild. When his column was about 5,400 yards from the enemy, Dewey told Captain Charles V. Gridley of *Olympia*, "You may fire when ready, Gridley."

The Americans steamed past the Spanish ships on their port side, turned around and blasted them, now on the starboard side, again. A third time, they turned and unleashed another series of broadsides. The smoke was so heavy they couldn't see what damage they had done. Five times, they passed the Spanish line, firing as they went. Gridley told Dewey he had only 15 more rounds for his five-inch guns. Dewey moved the squadron back out of range to redistribute ammunition and assess damage to his own ships.

The pause was reported to be a break for breakfast, which made the Americans sound even more confident than they were. The Americans did eat breakfast while officers gathered data. Dewey learned that Gridley had miscounted: they had plenty of ammunition. Observing the Spanish fleet when a breeze had cleared away much of the smoke, Dewey later wrote, "It was clear that we did not need a large supply of ammunition to finish our morning's task." The Spanish fleet had been devastated. American casualties amounted to six wounded. One officer had died of heat prostration the night before the battle.

Dewey returned to the battle. Only one Spanish ship, *Don Antonio de Ulloa*, was left, and it was quickly sunk. The Spanish naval base hoisted the white flag.

The Battle of Manila Bay, a victory so lopsided it was almost a massacre, was over.

The garrison of Manila held out. Dewey established a blocade of Manila while the Filipino *Insurrectos* besieged the city. The Spanish commander refused to let Dewey use his cable to notify Washington of the victory, so Dewey dredged up the cable and cut it, cutting off himself and all the Philippines from communicating with the outside world. Dewey sent a ship to Hong Kong, the nearest cable terminus, to let the world know.

The United States went wild. Dewey was instantly promoted to admiral. The rest of the world was shocked. Nobody (except some Spaniards) seriously expected Spain to beat the United States in the long run, but nobody expected the news from Manila Bay.

"Mein Gott, mein Gott!"

Somehow, the implications of the battle didn't seem to sink into the consciousness of Prince Henry of Prussia. Henry seemed to have been a rather insensitive soul. Certainly, he didn't understand George Dewey. Still believing that the Filipinos might welcome a German protectorate, he sent some warships to Manila to observe the situation.

Dewey, suspicious and belligerent, thought the Germans were there to snatch the islands out from under his nose. His suspicions grew as more Germans arrived, until the naval detachment under Admiral Otto von Diedrichs had more tonnage and more guns than his own squadron. The situation wasn't helped by the fact that Dewey and von Diedrichs had different understandings of the role of neutrals in a blockaded port.

Dewey thought neutral warships should not only identify themselves but heave to so the blockading force could board them. The Germans didn't.

Finally, Dewey had had enough. The German cruiser *Cormoran* was sighted coming up the bay by *McCulloch. McCulloch's* skipper, Lieutenant T. F. Brumby, ordered his ship to approach *Cormoran* to board. *Cormoran* turned and steamed away. Brumby signaled "I want to communicate," but *Cormoran* ignored the signal. The little revenue cutter fired a shot across *Cormoran's* bow. The German cruiser stopped, and Brumby boarded her.

The next day, von Diedrichs sent an officer to Dewey to protest. An American officer who overheard the interview told a reporter:

"As soon as the German officer was shown into the presence of the Admiral, the latter began to discuss the situation. The Admiral has a way of working himself up to a state of great earnestness as he thinks out a question. Commencing in a subdued tone, he gradually became querulous and then emphatic as he spoke of the activity of the Germans. Growing more earnest, his voice took a higher pitch until he complained in vigorous terms of what had been done.

"If the German Government has decided to make war on the United States, or has any intention of making war, and has so informed your Admiral, it is his duty to let me know."

Hesitating for a moment, he added: "But whether he intends to fight or not, I am ready."

The German made hurried apologies and left murmuring, "Mein Gott, mein Gott!"

"There was no further interference with the blockade or breach of the etiquette which has been established by common consent of other foreign commanders," Dewey wrote.

Manila Bay established in the eyes of the world what should have been apparent after the Civil War: The United States was a Great Power.

Battle 47

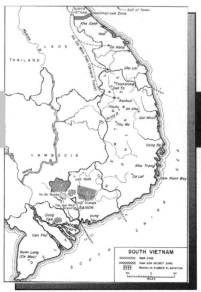

SOUTH VIETNAM
WAR ZONE
CAO SON SECRET ZONE
MICHELIN RUBBER PLANTATION

The Tet Offensive, 1968 AD
New Year's Fireworks

Who fought: Americans and South Vietnamese allies (William Westmoreland) vs. Viet Cong and North Vietnamese (Vo Nguyen Giap).

What was at stake: The survival of the anti-Communist South Vietnam government; also the domestic credibility of American officials.

Tet, the celebration of the New Year on the ancient Oriental Calendar of the Twelve Beasts, had begun. Many of the soldiers of the South Vietnam army were home to greet the Year of the Monkey. At 3 a.m. on January 31, 1968, a man named Nguyen Van Muoi slowly drove a black Citroen sedan through the quiet streets of Saigon. He headed for the United States embassy. After he'd traveled a few blocks, he glanced at his watch, leaned out of the car's window and yelled, "Tien! Tien!" ("Charge! Charge!").

Nineteen young men wearing red armbands suddenly appeared out of the shadows and ran toward the embassy as explosions rocked the city from one end to the other. Rockets and mortar shells were falling on Saigon from all directions.

Vo Nguyen Giap, North Vietnam's master strategist, was unleashing his biggest surprise, the attack that would be known as the Tet Offensive.

North Vietnam Army (NVA) troops and Viet Cong (VC) guerrillas simultaneously hit 100 strategic locations, including 38 cities and towns. Giap's forces made their greatest headway in Hue, the old imperial capital. Some 3,000 Communist troops took over the whole city. They killed 1,000 government employees, some by burying alive.

They didn't do so well in Saigon. The assault on the American embassy, a key target in Saigon, was a resounding flop. One of the attackers fired a Russian-made RPG 7, a combination recoilless gun and rocket launcher that projected a large, shaped-charge anti-tank shell. The shell hit the 10-foot wall around the embassy and blew a gaping hole through it. The Viet Cong attackers dived through. Two U.S. army MPs opened fire, killing the first man through the hole, but the second man killed both of them with a burst of automatic fire. The attackers ran to a gate in the wall, shot off the lock and let in more raiders.

Marine Sergeant Ronald Harper heard the firing and shut the door to the embassy building. The RPG man fired again. The RPG shell was designed for penetration: When it detonated, the shape of the explosive concentrated a jet of fire that could burn through the thickest known tank armor and fill the interior of the tank with flame and molten metal. It penetrated the door, blasting a two-inch hole through it. The thick cherry wood door, however, did not shatter like the masonry wall. The blast wounded one of the marine guards, but did no other damage.

The RPG man fired more rounds at the embassy building. They hit the terra cotta sunscreen around the building, breaking some tiles and expending their lethal jets of fire on the air. Marine guards and army MPs inside the building returned the attackers' fire, and "reaction forces"—more marines and MPs—began arriving. At 7 a.m. Private First Class Paul Healy led a counterattack by the reaction force troops, killing five Viet Cong personally and reaching the embassy building. An hour later, two platoons of paratroopers landed on the embassy roof by helicopter and moved out onto the grounds. One of the retreating Viet Cong raiders got into the home of retired army Colonel George Jacobsen. Jacobsen, a mission coordinator, had no weapon. He leaned out of a second story window and yelled to an MP. The soldier threw him a pistol, and Jacobsen used it to kill the machine gun-toting VC—the last of the embassy attackers.

The embassy was by no means the only target in Saigon. Major General Tran Do of the North Vietnam army, in charge of the Saigon operation, had smuggled some 4,000 troops, both North Vietnam regulars and Viet Cong guerrillas, into the city. Some wore civilian clothes, and some wore South Vietnam police uniforms. Weapons arrived in empty gasoline trucks, inside hollow logs, and under truckloads of watermelons. Some weapons had been brought in earlier, placed in empty coffins, and buried in cemeteries. Outside the city, Tran had thousands of more troops with heavy mortars and rockets. At precisely the same time, the Communist forces attacked the embassy, the prison, the radio station, and the South Vietnam Army armor school and tank park. After capturing the tanks, they were to attack Tan Son Nhut Airport and Westmoreland's headquarters. Surprise was complete, in Saigon and in the length and breadth of South Vietnam.

What made the surprise utterly complete was the gullibility and arrogance of the American high command—gullibility in falling for Giap's trickery and arrogance in refusing to change their minds in spite of the evidence.

The Year of the Monkey's monkey trap

Vo Nguyen Giap had taken an idea from his country's monkey hunters. Country people caught live monkeys for foreign zoos and pet stores by boring a hole in a coconut, placing a shiny bead inside it and leaving it where monkeys had been seen. A monkey would see the bead in the coconut and reach for it. The hole would be too small for the animal's clenched fist to pass through. But the monkey would not let go of the bead. Weighed down by the coconut, he would be easily caught by the hunter.

Giap's coconut was a place called Khe Sanh. The bead was the apparent massing of North Vietnam Army troops in the Khe Sanh area. U.S. aerial observers saw a network of NVA trenches surrounding the U.S. base near Khe Sanh. General William Westmoreland, the U.S. commander, was sure the North Vietnamese intended to take Khe Sanh and pour into South Vietnam. It was a situation he had dreamed of: getting the elusive NVA and VC forces in good old-fashioned knock-down-and-drag-out battle. He moved the bulk of his forces north to meet the North Vietnamese offensive head on.

On January 25, Westmoreland's briefing officers told the press that "the largest battle of the war" would soon take place near Khe Sanh. They said only the base at Khe Sanh was blocking the North Vietnam Army from flooding into the south. They also said the NVA had 20,000 troops surrounding the base. They did not explain: (1) how, if Khe Sanh was blocking the North Vietnamese, 10,000 of them (the southern part of the besieging forces) had gotten behind it; or (2) how one base could block an army that moved mainly by footpaths.

Such quibbles didn't bother Westmoreland. He was convinced Giap was attempting a replay of the destruction of the French base at Dien Bien Phu, and he knew he could wipe out the attackers.

Back home, the American public was growing more and more impatient with the war. Their leaders had told them that if South Vietnam became Communist, all the nations in Southeast Asia—Malaysia, Singapore, Indonesia, and the Philippines—would fall like a row of dominoes. Month after month, the public had been told how body counts showed the enemy was losing, how U.S. commanders had seen the "light at the end of the tunnel," how enemy activity was lessening. The war went on. People were beginning to doubt the "domino theory." Protesters, mostly draft-age youths, were marching and demonstrating. But now Westmoreland was promising the big battle that would end the war, and this time, he could present facts to back up his optimism.

When the Tet Offensive began, Westmoreland called it a feint to distract him from the offensive that would begin at Khe Sanh. He sent more troops north. The VC and North Vietnamese were able to overrun Hue because "Westy" refused to send his nearest troops, two brigades of the U.S. First Cavalry Division (Air Mobile), to aid the South Vietnam troops in Hue. The Air Cavalry troops were on standby to counterattack when Giap's Khe Sanh offensive began.

Bold plan, timid action

Giap's minions created havoc. They destroyed 100 airplanes and helicopters on the ground, practically wiped out the South Vietnam "revolutionary development" plan to pacify the countryside, opened dozens of jails, and killed hundreds of allied military and civil service personnel. Radio Hanoi urged the South Vietnamese civilians to revolt: "Everybody must stand up and attack the hideouts of the Thieu-Ky clique," it proclaimed, attacking the two most prominent South Vietnamese leaders.

But there was no uprising. After the first week, the Communist troops were on the defensive everywhere.

The plan could not have been bolder, but its execution was too cautious. The Communist generals were afraid to commit enough troops. They assigned platoons tasks that required battalions and battalions to jobs that called for brigades. Tran Do's underestimation was gross. About half of the Army of the Republic of Vietnam (ARVN) soldiers in Saigon were home with their families, but the Communist forces failed to take all their key objectives there. They captured a few points, such as Phu

Tho Racetrack, but nothing worthwhile. They captured the armor school, but as it turned out, that wasn't important. There had been a major intelligence failure. The tanks that were supposed to be there had been moved.

The Americans struck back with tanks, artillery, planes, and helicopters, causing even more devastation than the attackers. Westmoreland now said the Tet Offensive wasn't a surprise—he had been expecting it. He did not explain why half the ARVN troops were off duty when the attack was expected.

U.S. headquarters estimated that 30,975 VC and NVA troops had been killed. Like most "body count" data, this was probably a wild exaggeration. But there was no doubt that the Communists had suffered heavy losses and gained no new ground.

During the counterattack, Westmoreland continued to keep an eye on Khe Sanh, where he still expected the major Communist attack. When no attack came, Westmoreland stopped waiting. He moved to relieve the strongpoint. U.S. bombers dropped an enormous tonnage of bombs on the besieging trenches around Khe Sanh, including armor-piercing bombs to destroy the tunnels the North Vietnamese were supposed to be digging. On April 1, the Air Cavalry launched Operation Pegasus, history's first large-scale helicopter assault by ground troops. It was, correspondents said, a "textbook operation."

The air-mobile troopers got to Khe Sanh and found—nothing. Or almost nothing—some rockets, rifle cartridges, a few rifles, machine guns, and no troops. The trenches that looked so formidable from the air were much less imposing from close-up. "The trenches are only 14 to 20 inches deep and wide enough for just one man at a time to crawl toward the Marine positions," Douglas Robinson of the *New York Times* reported. They were nothing the NVA could use to launch a major assault, but they were enough to let it demonstrate hostile intent to the marines. There were no tunnels.

To the American public, it began to look as if Westmoreland had fallen for the biggest ruse since the Trojan Horse. He rejected that notion, claiming, "The enemy by my count has suffered at least 15,000 dead in this area." As few bodies were found in the area, Westmoreland's "count" had another basis. According to *Air Power and the Fight for Khe Sanh*, the official U.S. Air Force history of the battle:

> "General Westmoreland's Systems Analysis Office prepared four mathematical models from which its technicians concluded that the total enemy killed and wounded numbered between 49 and 65 percent of the force that began the siege—between 9,800 and 13,000 men. The generally cited estimate, 10,000, is half the number of North Vietnamese troops believed committed at the outset of the operation."

The American public began to doubt official reports on the progress of the war. Counting non-existent bodies by computer didn't improve the army's credibility. After Tet, public confidence in the Johnson Administration's handling of the war dropped from 58 to 35 percent. No politician was more astute at reading the political entrails than Lyndon Johnson. He said he would not seek another term. Hubert Humphrey, his vice president, tried to run as a peace candidate, but he was too closely associated with the war. Richard Nixon promised to end the war, and he was elected.

Nixon talked tough and continued bombing to appease the American "hawks," but he steadily pulled U.S. troops out of Vietnam. The last American soldier left August 11, 1972. On October 26, 1972, the government of North Vietnam said it had reached a tentative agreement with the United States in secret peace talks. Twelve days later, Nixon was reelected in a landslide.

A war of negative results

In 1975, North Vietnam took over all of South Vietnam. The United States had lost the first war in its history. Only that of Japan before World War II surpassed its winning streak of two centuries. The impact was not as strong as the loss of World War II had been on Japan, of course. But it was real.

First, there was the almost subconscious desire of Americans to expunge the shame of the loss. It was great enough for the public to hail the invasion of the flyspeck island of Grenada as a great victory. Victory in the Gulf War—the defeat of a fourth-rate military power following the orders of a tenth-rate strategist—made instant heroes of American generals.

Second, it led American military leaders to believe that the press had betrayed them. In the Gulf, the army arrested reporters who tried to get to the battle areas and spoon-fed correspondents self-serving communiqués at headquarters. Americans at home got the idea that their bombs never missed and that their anti-air-craft missiles were certain death to either enemy planes or rockets. These notions were untrue; in the case of the anti-aircraft missiles, spectacularly so. Allowing the military or any other group to so distort reality is extremely unhealthy.

Third, the official lying exposed by Tet led to a huge loss of faith in their leaders by the American people. The credibility gap by the end of the war was

An American soldier examines a Russian-made
Viet Cong submachine gun.

a psychological Grand Canyon. Take the "domino theory" for example: Somehow, all of those Southeast Asian dominos remained standing. The public began to examine the motives of leaders more closely, and it became less willing to forgive deception. The first fruit of this attitude was Watergate. Before the war was officially over, Nixon, who had been reelected by one of the most lopsided majorities in American history, had resigned the presidency in disgrace. Scandal followed scandal. The Iran-Contra shenanigans marred Ronald Reagan's last term, and there was the impeachment trial in Bill Clinton's last term. Each of these controversies revived the sort of bitter division that had appeared during the Vietnam War.

The United States was untouched physically by the Vietnam War. But the war left marks that will not disappear for a long time.

Battle 48

Romans fighting Gauls.

Rome, 390 BC
King Brennus's Laughter

Who fought: Romans (Marcus Furius Camillus) vs. Gauls (Brennus).

What was at stake: Classical civilization. Rome's defeat led to the invention of the Roman legion—a military instrument that established the Roman Empire and put an everlasting classical stamp on the West.

The envoys of Rome asked to speak to King Brennus, who was besieging the city of Clusium. Brennus's tribe, the Senones, were Gauls. The Gauls were bad news. From somewhere in Central Europe, north of the Alps, they had spread east and west. There were Gauls in Spain, in Britain, even in Ireland, at the very edge of the world. In the east, they had settled on the borders of Macedon and even penetrated Asia Minor. Everywhere they went, the Gauls brought their language and customs, forcing the conquered people to adopt them. To the Romans, it seemed that the Gauls were the most numerous people on earth. Fortunately, they were divided into many tribes, usually at war with each other. Now it looked as if the Gauls were trying to conquer the south. They had already destroyed the Etruscan city-states in the Po valley and were pressing into central Italy.

Clusium was an Etruscan city. The Etruscans and Romans had a long relationship, sometimes very bumpy. But Rome was now the greatest power in central Italy, and the people of Clusium asked them to warn off the Gauls. The Romans sent three ambassadors, members of the noble Fabius family.

As the ambassadors walked through the Gallic camp they saw not only warriors, but women and children. Brennus had brought his whole tribe. The warriors had metal helmets, and some of them, presumably the richer ones, wore mail shirts. All carried very long swords and spears.

When the ambassadors reached the King, they asked him why he was attacking Clusium—what injury had the Clusinians done to him. Brennus roared with laughter.

When he calmed down he said, "The Clusinians do us the same injury that the Albans, Fidenates, and Ardeates did to you. Being able to till only a small parcel of land, they possess a great territory and will not yield any part of it to us. You and we are being neither cruel nor unjust, but following the most ancient of all laws, which gives the possessions of the feeble to the strong.

"Cease, therefore, to pity the Clusinians whom we besiege lest you teach the Gauls to be kind and compassionate to those that are oppressed by you."

The Romans saw that they could not persuade the Gaul to leave. They went back to the city and encouraged the Clusinians to sally out against the besiegers. The Etruscans opened their gates and charged. At the height of the battle, one of the ambassadors, Quintus Ambustus Fabius could not bear to be a bystander. He put on his armor, got on his horse, and joined the fight.

Brennus saw him. He was outraged that an ambassador had broken the law of all nations by engaging in combat. He broke off the siege and prepared to march on Rome.

Back in Rome, the Senate charged Quintus Ambustus with violating his sacred duty as an envoy. But to the people of Rome, Quintus Ambustus was a hero. They refused to convict him and appointed the three Fabius brothers military tribunes to lead their army against the Gauls. When he heard who the Romans had elected to lead their armies, Brennus gave the campaign against Rome top priority.

The Roman army of those days copied the tactics of the Greeks. It fought as a phalanx, six or eight ranks deep. The front line was composed of the richest soldiers—the First property class—who wore Greek-type armor: metal helmet, corselet, and greaves, with a round wooden shield. Less affluent warriors, members of the Second and Third classes, wore native Italian armor. Second-class soldiers had to have a helmet, a pectoral (a bronze plate worn on the chest), greaves, and a shield; Third-class men did not need greaves. Fourth class soldiers had only a shield, and Fifth class didn't even have that. All carried spears, and the richer soldiers had swords, too. The best-armed men fought in the front of the phalanx, the Second and Third classes behind them. The Fourth and Fifth classes were light infantry skirmishers. They opened the battle, then sheltered behind the phalanx. The Roman army was almost entirely infantry. The richest men rode horses, but Roman cavalry were too few to be effective.

The Gallic cavalry, on the other hand, were numerous and effective. The Gauls invented horseshoes, which allowed their mounts to travel farther and over rougher terrain. The Gauls also invented, or copied from the Scythians, a four-pommel saddle. By pressing his thighs against the front pommels, the rider could maintain almost as secure a seat he would have with stirrups. The Romans had nothing like that saddle. The long Gallic sword was a good weapon for a horseman. The Gauls would throw their spears at an enemy then close to use their swords.

The Gallic footmen used the same tactics. Unlike the Romans, they did not move in an orderly phalanx. With the Gauls it was every man for himself. But the Gauls made up for their lack of discipline with their size and their utter ferocity. All of the Gauls were huge by Roman standards and all loved battle. There were even berserker Gauls who not only disdained armor but fought entirely naked.

"Woe to the vanquished"

On Midsummer Day, the Fabii led out 40,000 infantry to meet the Gauls, an army fully as large as any Brennus could command. The Gauls charged the Romans in a wild stampede, attacking from the front and both flanks. They threw their spears at the legionaries before they were within reach of the Roman pikes. They chopped off the ends of the pikes with their long swords and they chopped through the Romans' wooden shields. The Roman left wing broke and was driven into the Allia River and slaughtered. Then, the right wing fled into the hills, from which many made their way to the Etruscan city of Veii. The Romans not struck down were able to outrun the Gauls, who were, as Polybius says, "weary of the slaughter."

The defeated soldiers, the Roman aristocracy, and any other Romans who could, fled to the Capitol hill, the strongly fortified heart of the city. The Gauls sacked the rest of the city, burned it, and massacred many of the citizens. The Gauls tried to enter the Capitol by stealth, but though the guards were sleeping, the sacred geese at the temple of Juno began cackling and woke up the garrison, who repulsed the Gauls. The Romans then threw the captain of the guard headfirst off the cliff.

Unable to break into the Capitol, Brennus agreed to leave in return for a large quantity of gold. As payment was being made, some Romans noticed that the weights they must balance with gold were heavier than the weight agreed to. They complained to Brennus.

The Gallic king took off his sword belt, scabbard, and sword and tossed them onto the weights to be balanced.

"Woe to the vanquished," he said.

Marcus Furius Camillus

Marcus Furius Camillus was the most successful Roman general of his time, but he had been accused of keeping more than his share of the spoils from his latest conquest. Rather than pay a fine, he left the city and was living in exile. When he heard about Rome's defeat and disaster, he raised an army in the city where he was living. A messenger from Camillus sneaked into the Capitol, and the Senate agreed to commission Camillus dictator. Camillus set out to discomfit the Gauls.

Camillus improved both the equipment and organization of his army. He had smiths rim his men's shields with bronze or iron so the Gauls couldn't cut through them with their swords. Most importantly, he organized a new formation to replace the phalanx. Instead of a solid line, the men would be group in *manipuli* (handfuls) of 120 men. The manipuli would be in a checkerboard formation, with those in the second line covering the intervals in the first line. Instead of long pikes, the men in the manipuli would have a pair of heavy javelins so the spear-throwing Gauls could not outrange them. For close-in work, they had short swords. The manipuli formed the first two lines in the new organization. The third line was a phalanx armed with long pikes. There was far more open space and depth in the new formation than in the phalanx. A flanking attack on it would be much harder. And the manipuli gave the Romans much of the flexibility the Gauls had demonstrated while it retained the Roman discipline.

While Camillus was developing his organization, the Gauls were besieging the Capitol and foraging in the countryside. Camillus did not wait until he perfected his new army. He led his men out at night and attacked the camp of a Gallic foraging party. The Gauls had celebrated their successful pillaging by getting thoroughly drunk. Most of them had passed out when the Romans attacked. Almost all of them were dead when the Romans went home. After that, Camillus began attacking Gallic foragers wherever he found them, and the Gauls gave up foraging. While they were besieging the Capitol, their food started to run out. Camped as they were in the marshy ground around Rome, sickness broke out. Hunger and sickness were what induced Brennus to agree to leave upon payment of gold.

The Romans were still weighing out gold when Camillus and his new model army appeared. Camillus told Brennus to take his scales and weights and go, because Rome would be ransomed "with iron, not gold." Brennus snatched up his sword and fighting broke out, but neither side could do much in the streets and alleys of Rome. The Gallic and Roman armies both left the city and fought the next day. Camillus's new army lived up to his hopes, and the Gauls were scattered.

The grateful Romans dubbed Camillus a "second Romulus," the second founder of the city.

The title was deserved, because the military system Camillus devised was the basis of all other Roman armies for the next 500 years and the instrument that made possible the Roman Empire.

Battle 49

Russian cavalry charge French infantry.

Sedan, 1870 AD
The Heir

Who fought: Germans (Helmut von Moltke the elder) vs. French (Napoleon III)

What was at stake: The creation of a really unified German state for the first time in Germany's long history. Also, once again, whether Napoleonic "republicanism" or reactionary monarchy would triumph, part of Europe's bumpy road toward true democracy.

Charles Louis Napoleon Bonaparte found that being the nephew of a famous man—the most famous and most powerful man of his time, in fact—did not necessarily make life easier. Young Louis—the Charles was dropped soon after his birth—did not grow up in poverty, of course. His mother, Queen Hortense, was the wife of Emperor Napoleon's brother Louis, King of Holland, and the daughter, by a previous marriage, of Empress Josephine. Louis abdicated as King of Holland, and the couple was divorced. Napoleon, however, liked Hortense and her young son, so he gave her a healthy pension and let her keep the title of queen. When Napoleon was sent off to Elba, Hortense managed to ingratiate herself with the new Bourbon king, Louis XVIII. Louis rescinded her title of queen, but made her a duchess and continued her pension. When Napoleon returned, his second wife, Marie Louise, refused to leave Austria, so the Emperor made Hortense first lady of France.

279

After Waterloo (**see page 240**) everything changed. Hortense took Louis into exile in Switzerland, several times escaping arrest and execution during the "white terror" that followed the fall of Napoleon. When she was finally able to settle down, however, money was no problem. She had inherited a fortune from Josephine that produced an annual income of about $600,000 in today's money.

Louis Napoleon grew up in Switzerland, leading the life of a rich young playboy, until he met his older brother, Napoleon Louis, in Italy. Napoleon Louis had been in the custody of his father, ex-King Louis, and living in Italy. He had joined an Italian secret society dedicated to the unification of Italy. Louis joined him. Both brothers were unmasked as revolutionaries and driven out of all Papal and Austrian lands in Italy. While they were fleeing the Austrian authorities, Napoleon Louis died of measles. Hortense caught up with Louis Napoleon and helped him escape to England. Soon after, Emperor Napoleon's only legitimate son, called Napoleon II by French imperialists, died in exile in Austria.

Prince Clemens von Metternich, the Austrian chancellor and leader of the forces of reaction in Europe, was concerned. The fall of Napoleon had not brought stability to Europe. In 1830, there had been another revolution in France. A constitutional monarch, Louis Philippe, had replaced the king, Charles X. Metternich warned his ambassador to France about "the character of the man who will replace the Duke of Reichstadt [Emperor Napoleon's son]…The young Louis Bonaparte is a man tied up with the plots of the secret societies…The day of the Duke's death, he will look upon himself as called to rule France."

Chasing a throne

All Louis did was return to Switzerland. But he was soon intriguing with French army officers. In 1836, defying a law that forbade any Bonaparte from setting foot in France under penalty of death, Louis returned to France and attempted to lead a mutiny of French troops in Strasbourg. He was arrested within two hours, his co-conspirators were tried as traitors, but Louis was merely deported to the United States. King Louis Philippe did not want to create a martyr. The co-conspirators were acquitted. But to keep the young Bonaparte quiet as long as possible, the ship took him to the United States by way of Africa and South America. He was at sea for four months. His assessment of the United States—after 11 weeks in the country—was typically European, but had an interesting insight:

> "The country has immense material strength but it totally lacks any moral strength, The United States created itself a nation from the moment it had an administration elected by itself and two legislative chambers but it has only reached the stage of being an independent colony. Even so, each day you can see the transition: the caterpillar is shedding its cocoon and freeing its wings to fly ever higher as a magnificent butterfly; but I do not think this transition will take place without crises and upheavals."

The American Civil War was only 24 years away.

Louis returned to England. Then, with a bogus passport, he reached Switzerland, where his mother was dying. With her death, he inherited an immense fortune and went back to political intrigue. The French government demanded the Swiss expel Louis and even massed troops on the border. The Swiss said non, nein, and no to the French demand. Louis wrote to the Swiss authorities, admiring their independence, but saying he would leave anyway to prevent trouble. Actually, he had tried to provoke the French demands so he could appear to be a martyr to the French people.

Once again an exile in England, Louis again attempted a coup. On August 7, 1840, he landed weapons and armed men on the beach near Boulogne. This *putsch* was crushed even more easily than the last one. Louis was arrested, tried and sentenced to life imprisonment. In prison he wrote a treatise on artillery (his uncle's military specialty) and several on socialism. He advocated such radical ideas as universal suffrage (for men) instead of making the vote dependent on property ownership. In 1856, he escaped from the prison, walking out disguised as a workman.

In London, an English friend, Lord Malmesbury, chanced on the Compte Louis de Noailles, a French attaché.

"Did you see him?" Malmesbury asked the diplomat.

"Who?"

"Louis Napoleon. He is in London. He just escaped."

Malmesbury later wrote in his diary, "De Noailles dropped the lady who was on his arm and made but one jump out of the room. I never saw a man look more frightened."

Two years later, a riot in Paris turned into a revolution. The French revolution of 1848 touched off revolutions all through Europe: Austria, Hungary, Italy, and Germany all saw fighting in the streets and the sacking of palaces. Even in England there were the Chartist riots. In France, Louis Philippe lost his job. He, his wife, daughter, and grandson were forced to flee, and the Second Republic was proclaimed.

Louis Bonaparte went into politics. He was elected simultaneously from four departments even though, as a Bonaparte, he could not legally enter France. That didn't matter, because the Second Republic quickly turned into anarchy. The workers of Paris again took to the barricades. General Louis Cavaignac, the war minister, crushed the revolt in three days of bloody fighting and became a dictator. Louis, the self-proclaimed champion of the working man, was still in London. He joined the volunteers helping Wellington and the British Army crush the workers of London in the Chartist riots.

France held another election. This time Louis was elected from five departments with a huge lead in all. When the results were in, he left for Paris so quickly that a friend later found his bed unmade and the water still in his bath. Three months later, he ran for president of the Republic, beating Cavaignac, his nearest rival, five to one. He got 75 percent of all the votes cast, and 60 percent of the total electorate.

Three years later, claiming that reactionary forces in the Chamber were planning a coup d'etat, Louis executed a coup of his own. On December 2, 1851, his allies in the police arrested all hostile legislators, and Louis proclaimed a new constitution giving the president a 10-year term and dictatorial powers. He ordered a plebiscite to confirm it. Before voting could begin, his opponents took to the streets. Government forces quickly put down the revolt. Hundreds were killed, and tens of thousands were arrested and imprisoned. The plebiscite showed that the people overwhelmingly favored Louis's new constitution: 7,145,000 for it and 592,000 against it. The French population obviously thirsted for the imperial glory of Napoleon the Great, and Napoleon the Little was happy to provide it. A year later, the French Senate, all of whom had been appointed by Louis, proclaimed the president Emperor Napoleon III.

Napoleon III, an inveterate but inept intriguer, with none of his uncle's military genius, had been boosted to a throne by the French thirst for glory. But now he was about to collide with one of the century's great intriguers, who was also associated with a very peculiar sort of military genius.

The Iron Chancellor

German unity, the dream of Wallenstein and von Arnim **(see Lutzen, page 255)** had not died entirely. Napoleon had abolished the Holy Roman Empire, which traced its origins back to Augustus Caesar, with breaks repaired by Charlemagne (**see Tours, page 175**) and Otto the Great (**see Lechfeld, page 100**). Over the centuries, the Empire had changed from being Roman to almost entirely German. It had gone from being the tightly-controlled state of Augustus to a loose conglomeration of states large, small, and minute. And during the 16th century, that conglomeration was sharply divided between the Protestant (north and east) and the Catholic (south and west).

The Congress of Vienna, which attempted to remake Europe after Napoleon I, did not resurrect the Holy Roman Empire. It was, after all, as Voltaire said, neither holy, nor Roman, nor an empire. The Congress created the Germanic Confederation to promote peace among the 38 German monarchies, with a Diet at Frankfort-am-Main. More important was the *Zollverein*, or customs union, which in 1844 eliminated import duties between all German states but Austria. The Revolution of 1848 aimed at German unity, but Germany was still split along religious lines. Religion was a factor to reckon with, but by no means as powerful as it was 200 years before. More important now was nationalism and dynastic ambition. There were two large states in Germany—Austria and Prussia—and a swarm of lesser kingdoms. The question was whether Austria or Prussia would lead a unified Germany.

The question was decided by a tall, bull-necked Prussian Junker (landed nobleman), Prince Otto von Bismark. Bismark is remembered as the "Iron Chancellor," and he loved to wear a military uniform. Actually, his military experience was sketchier than Napoleon III's. His talent was for intrigue, but unlike Napoleon III, his schemes all aimed to benefit someone else: his king, Wilhelm I of Prussia.

His schemes frequently involved war, but Helmuth von Moltke, chief of the Prussian General Staff, handled the military side. Moltke was the first modern military bureaucrat, quite possibly the most able ever. Railroads had been used to move troops before—they provided some of the transportation in the Crimean War. In the American Civil War, they moved troops faster and for longer distances than Moltke's ever did, but neither Union nor Confederate armies were entirely dependent on railroads. In his most famous campaign, the "March to the Sea," William Tecumseh Sherman abandoned his own railroad communications and devoted himself to destroying Confederate rail transportation. For Moltke, in contrast, railroads were the backbone of strategy. He plotted timetables, capacities of trains, and depots, the location of marshalling yards, lines, spurs, and bridges with a precision unknown in any other military organization. He knew precisely how much ammunition was on hand and where, the availability of medical supplies, and even the condition of uniforms for the army. He believed that rapid mobilization and concentration were the essence of victory. He also made sure the Prussian army had good weapons, its artillery was excellent, and its infantry had a breech-loading rifle that did not require a soldier to stand up to load.

In 1848, Prussia had fought Denmark, which was trying to absorb the German-speaking duchies of Schleswig and Holstein. Prussia won the war but was forced by a coalition of nations led by Britain and Austria to give the duchies back to Denmark. In 1864, Bismark managed to play Britain, France, and Russia against each other so that no other nation opposed him when he invaded Denmark and took Schleswig and Holstein. Europe was still opposed to the annexation of the duchies by Prussia, but Bismark worked out a deal with Austria so that the duchies would be independent but jointly protected by Austria and Prussia.

Next, Bismark provoked a dispute with Austria over jurisdiction in Schleswig-Holstein. That led to war. Two Prussian armies fully prepared and equipped with the breech loading "needle gun," swept into Austrian Bohemia and hit the allied armies of Austria and Saxony from two sides. The "Seven Weeks War" removed Austria as a contender for the leadership of Germany.

But there was still a split between the Catholic south and the Protestant north, with states grouped into either the North German Confederation or the German Southern Union. To end that situation, Bismark counted on the inadvertent cooperation of Napoleon III.

Conning Napoleon

Napoleon III had been riding high after taking the throne. His new empress, Eugenie, who replaced (for a while) a legion of young mistresses, added a dash of glamour to his court. For military glory, he joined Britain in a complicated dispute that became the Crimean War. Having helped to humble Russia, he became a champion of Italian unification against Austria. Louis actually led the French Army into Italy and defeated the Austrians in two bloody battles, Magenta and Solferino. The sight of all those bodies was too much for the Emperor, and he made peace as quickly as possible. France gained Savoy and Nice; Austria kept Venetia. The Pope continued to reign in the Papal States, but his domains were occupied by French troops. All the rest of Italy was united under King Victor Emmanuel.

In 1862, things began to change for Napoleon III. He sent troops to Mexico to make an Austrian prince, Maximilian, Emperor of Mexico. Mexican guerrillas resisted strongly. When the American Civil War ended, weapons and volunteers began to flow across the border. The Americans sent a large army under the young, smart, and very aggressive Philip H. Sheridan to Texas. U.S. President Andrew Johnson sent a note: "The sympathies of the American people for the Mexican republicans are very pronounced and the continuation of French interference in Mexico is viewed with considerable impatience."

Napoleon ordered his troops to leave Mexico and urged Maximilian to accompany them. Maximilian, genuinely believing that he could help the Mexican people, refused. Maximilian's wife, Charlotte, came to Paris and begged Napoleon to keep the troops in Mexico. He said he could not, and Charlotte went insane.

As he had isolated Denmark before he invaded it, Bismark tried to isolate Austria. He especially wanted to keep France from aiding the southern empire. So he offered to give Napoleon a free hand in Belgium or the Rhineland if Napoleon would persuade Austria to sell Venetia to Italy. He knew Austria would not give up Venetia, and that her failure to do so would antagonize Napoleon III. He also kept all correspondence on the subject.

Napoleon III still hungered for the left bank of the Rhine to complete France's "natural frontier." Bismark had dangled the bait then snatched it away. After the Austrian War, Napoleon began claiming the left bank. Fear of France drove the German states into the arms of Bismark. They entered military alliance with Prussia, and two of the larger states, Saxony and Bavaria, agreed to send troops if France made war.

In 1868, there was a coup in Spain. Queen Isabella was ousted and Marshal Juan Prim became regent. Prim went looking for a monarch to lead the country. Bismark saw an opportunity. He began talking with Prim, and then, in 1870, the Spanish regent offered the throne to Prince Leopold of Hohenzollern-Sigmaringen, a distant relative of the king of Prussia. Leopold agreed, provided the king of Prussia and the emperor of France had no objections. Wilhelm of Prussia, who had no knowledge of the negotiations, did not approve. Bismark leaked the suggestion to the newspapers. Napoleon was not only surprised but profoundly shocked. He saw the ghost of the Hapsburg, Charles V, who as both Holy Roman Emperor and King of Spain had surrounded France on all sides. The French public became practically hysterical.

Napoleon asked his ambassador to Prussia, Count Benedetti, to request that the king persuade Leopold to turn down the offer. Wilhelm assured the ambassador he had no intention of encouraging Leopold to go to Spain. The French public was not satisfied. The French remembered the days of the first Napoleon, when no one dared to offend France, and before that, to the time of the 14th Louis, the Sun King, the monarch all Europe revolved around. Some of that seemed to have affected Napoleon III, whose only setback had been Mexico, thousands of miles away across a stormy ocean. He told Benedetti to demand that the king of Prussia forbid the Prince to become king of Spain. Wilhelm told the ambassador that his cousin was an honorable person. He had rejected the offer and would not change his mind. And that was that.

When Bismark heard of these personal approaches by the French ambassador, he begged the king to refuse any more direct interviews and go back to regular diplomacy through ambassadors. Wilhelm agreed and refused another personal audience with the French diplomat. He sent a memo to Bismark, telling him of the latest incident. Bismark asked for and got the king's permission to publish it.

Bismark said he edited the report to make it shorter and easier for newspapers to fit in. He added no words. But he edited it so artfully, that it looked insulting to France and the French Emperor. That went to French newspapers. To English newspapers, he sent his correspondence with Napoleon in which the French monarch expressed his desire to take over Belgium. The prospect of France controlling the Belgian channel ports would not induce Britain to help Napoleon.

As Bismark had expected, France declared war, and all the German states came to Prussia's aid.

Sedan

Moltke's mobilization machine, now including Prussia's German allies, roared into action. Regulars and reservists appeared on schedule. Trains took them to the French border from all over Germany. Every soldier had his equipment; supply trains deposited munitions, rations, and draft animals at prearranged depots; breech-loading, rifled cannons rode flat cars to the frontier.

Not all Prussian equipment was state of the art. The single-shot needle gun was obsolescent. It was greatly inferior to some of the rifles used in the American Civil War and was neither as powerful nor as accurate as the French Chassepot rifle, also a breech-loader. The French also had a secret weapon, the de Reffeye Mitrailleuse, which was one of the first machine guns. But the Prussian equipment, and the Prussian men, were all where they were supposed to be.

That was not true of the French. The French mobilization was slower than the Prussian, but the French generals decided to attack before all their troops were in place. The troops that were in place lacked guns, transportation, and ambulances. Magazines and fortresses that were supposed to supply troops as they neared the frontier were unstocked. A general at the front wrote to the minister of war:

> "In the supply depots, no camp kettles, dishes or stoves; no canteens for the ambulances and no pack saddles; in short no ambulances neither for division nor corps. Up to the 7th it was all but impossible to obtain a mule litter for the wounded. That day, thousands of wounded men were left in the hands of the enemy; no preparations were made to get them away....On the 6th an order was given to blow up a bridge, no powder could be found in the whole army corps, with the engineers, or with the gunners."

France's secret weapon, the mitrailleuse, had been kept so secret that none of the troops had a chance to train with it. It was a cluster of 25 rifle barrels, which were loaded by a clip at the breech. One man loaded and one turned the crank that fired it. It was capable of a cyclic rate of 250 rounds a minute. The trouble was that it looked like a cannon. The French used it as if it were a cannon. On a few occasions it fired on infantry at close range and did frightful execution. Mostly, though, the French gunners used it at long range, firing from well behind the front lines. As soon as they did, the German artillery knocked the guns out of action.

Napoleon had planned to invade southern Germany and to make an amphibious landing at the mouth of the Elbe River. But the confused French Army never got the invasion force to the southern German frontier, and the French invasion fleet sailed for the Elbe without any soldiers. Marshal Achille Bazaine, who led the Mexico invasion force, was in the Saar area, based in Metz. The Prussians were on top of him before he knew it, and then they swung around behind him, so that in the main battle he was facing Paris and the Prussians were facing the Rhine. Bazaine withdrew into the fortress of Metz, where there were not enough rations to last long.

Back at Chalons, Marshal Marie-Edme-Patrice de MacMahon desperately tried to organize an army of reservists, marines, national police, and refugees from other battles. Besieged by a welter of confusing orders, he set out to relieve Metz. He marched north, almost to the Belgian border, to flank the advancing Prussian armies. When he got the report, Moltke could not believe that any general could be so stupid as to march across the front of an advancing army. The Germans hit MacMahon in the front, then swung up from the south behind him. Some of his troops crossed the Belgian border, where they were interned. The rest crowded into Sedan. Among them was Napoleon III. The Emperor left the direction of the battle to his generals. He could not have done worse.

Sedan was even less well prepared for a siege than Metz. Bavarians, Prussians, and Saxons hemmed the French into tighter and tighter space. MacMahon was seriously wounded. He appointed General Auguste-Alexandre Ducrot to succeed him. But Ducrot knew nothing of MacMahon's plans or the French situation outside his own area. Unknown to either MacMahon or Ducrot, General Emmanuel-Felix de Wimpffen had been sent by the war minister to take over in case MacMahon were killed or incapacitated. Waving his commission, Wimpffen now took over. With the army disintegrating around him, Wimpffen ordered an attack and notified the Emperor. Napoleon was not the military genius his uncle was, but he had a modicum of common sense—which made him a rarity in the French high command. He ordered a white flag hoisted over the citadel of Metz. On September 1, 1870, he formally surrendered.

Napoleon III's reign was over. The Prussians and their allies surrounded Paris, which held out until January 18, 1871. The fall of Paris was followed by another revolt. The Paris Commune took power for a short time, but the revolt was put down by French troops under MacMahon.

Prussia annexed the French provinces of Alsace and Lorraine and received a large cash indemnity. But most important, all the German states except Austria proclaimed Wilhelm of Prussia to be Kaiser Wilhelm of Germany.

For centuries, France had been the greatest power on the continent of Europe. English-speaking readers, who remember the English victories at Crecy, Poitiers, and Agincourt, often forget that France won the Hundred Years War. But in 1870, France ceased to be the paramount European power, and many who are by no means French would agree that this was not necessarily a good thing.

Battle 50

Peter the Great.

Poltava, 1709 AD
A Boy on the Throne

Who fought: Russians (Peter the Great) vs. Swedes (Charles XII).

What was at stake: Russia's aspirations to be a great power in Europe.

It was payback time, Augustus believed. Gustavus Adolphus of Sweden had ravaged Poland. Gustavus's nephew, Charles X, had almost destroyed it. Charles's son, Charles XI, had increased the strength of his war-drained country and left his son, Charles XII, an empire that turned the Baltic Sea into a Swedish lake. But now Charles XI was dead, and Charles XII was barely 15.

Augustus, Elector of Saxony, had also been elected King of Poland. He is often called Augustus the Strong, a mistranslation of his German nickname, Augustus the Potent, which he had earned by fathering so many illegitimate children. Augustus knew he wasn't particularly strong. That's why he made a proposal to the ruler of Poland's ancient enemy, Russia. The Tsar of Russia, Peter, was strong. A tall, physically powerful man with the will power to match his body, he was the absolute monarch of a country with enormous undeveloped resources. He and the youthful Charles would soon demonstrate that they were among the most outstanding characters of the early 18th century.

Charles was young, but, like his father, his grandfather, and his great great-grand-uncle, he had been brought up to be a soldier. After Gustavus Adolphus had been

286

killed at Lutzen **(see page 255)**, his daughter, Christina succeeded the Swedish king, but Christina did the unthinkable: She became a Catholic. She was forced to abdicate, and Charles X took her place. Charles learned to master the intricate military machine Gustavus had created. He established a Swedish protectorate over Poland and West Prussia. A Polish revolt drove the Swedes out, then Russia, Denmark, and Austria joined the Poles against Sweden and Brandenburg in what became known as the First Great Northern War. The war ended with Sweden as the paramount power in northern Europe. Charles XI beat the Danes and Dutch at Lund and, although his fleet was defeated by the Danish navy, concluded the war on favorable terms. He ruthlessly reformed and updated the army, making it unequaled in Europe for its offensive spirit and reliance on cold steel. At the same time, he instituted civil reforms to make his state economically stronger.

Charles XII enlarged the army from 65,00 to 77,000—an enormous size for a small agricultural country such as Sweden. He was able to recognize talent and rapidly promoted officers who showed it. He also enlarged and improved his navy so it could match the powerful Danish fleet. Young Charles prepared for war, because he saw nothing but enemies around Sweden. The Danes and the Poles were the most obvious, but the scariest were the Russians, those mysterious people now being ferociously modernized by their tsar, Peter.

Peter the Great

Peter had been born only a little more than a century after Ivan the Terrible freed Russia completely from the Mongol yoke **(see Kazan, page 249)**. After English merchants had discovered the existence of Russia, Ivan tried to facilitate trade with the West by invading Livonia (parts of modern Latvia and Estonia) to get an outlet on the Baltic. Then Livonia became the prize in a long series of wars involving Russia, Poland, Denmark, and Sweden. When it ended, Sweden had closed that outlet. In 1682, when Peter became Tsar, life in Russia had not changed much since the time of Ivan the Terrible.

Peter knew that to catch up with his neighbors to the west, Russia must change its ways. But first he had to secure Russia's frontiers. He ended the long feud with Poland in 1686, and in 1696 he allied Russia and Poland. Then, he was able to turn east and take Azov from the Turks. After that, he launched the Grand Embassy to all the Western powers, asking their aid against the Turks.

Peter traveled with the Grand Embassy, but he went disguised as a sailor. The tsar knew Russia must have a merchant marine to trade with the West advantageously, and to protect those ships, it must have a navy. As Peter Mikhailov, seaman, he got a hands-on course in navigation. He took a job in an English shipyard, again incognito, and learned shipbuilding from the ground up. He later built a frigate with his own hands.

While abroad, he learned that the Strelsy, the musketeer corps, had revolted. Their victories over the Mongols and Turks had filled the Russian musketeers with a sense of their own importance. Peter returned, put down the revolt, and executed the ringleaders. In some cases, he was the headsman. Then he began to reform the army.

In the time of Ivan the Terrible, the Russian clergy was scandalized when they heard that some soldiers had shaved their beards. Shaving, they declared, was against the will of God, and it made their soldiers look like the impious "Latins." Peter ordered all Russian men to shave and he saw to it that all the soldiers did. He personally sheared off the beards and mustaches of the Russian nobles. Peter forbade the wearing of traditional Russian clothes. He introduced conscription and brought Russian commoners into the army for the first time. By the end of his reign, the Russian army was 210,000 strong, not counting another 100,000 irregulars and reserves. Peter often drilled the soldiers personally.

The Second Great Northern War

Peter knew the war was coming because he had helped plan it when he visited Augustus the Potent on his way back from western Europe. The plan also involved Denmark, still smarting from defeat at Swedish hands. The Danes were to draw Swedish forces to the west, while Saxons, Poles, and Russians would gobble up Swedish-controlled areas on the Baltic shore.

In 1700, Tsar Peter, after concluding a treaty with Turkey, led 40,000 men into Livonia and laid siege to Narva, on the Gulf of Finland. Then he heard that the teenaged Charles, leading "an innumerable army," was approaching. What happened was that King Frederick of Denmark, trusting his navy to keep the Swedes in Sweden, had invaded the Duchy of Holstein, a Swedish protectorate. But Charles had arranged for an Anglo-Dutch naval demonstration to distract the Danes and crossed the channel into Denmark while Frederick's navy was watching the English and Dutch. With Copenhagen threatened, Frederick made peace. Charles took part of his army up the Baltic. He intended to relieve Riga, under siege by the Saxons, but he heard the Russians were at Narva. He decided to deal with the most dangerous enemy first.

Charles had only 8,000 men, but Peter didn't know that, and panicked. He appointed Prince de Croy commander of the army and returned to Moscow. Charles attacked in a snowstorm. "Now is the time, with the storm at our backs," he told his troops. "They will never see how few we are." The Russians fled.

The next spring, Charles left 15,000 men to defend the Baltic provinces and invaded Poland. He routed the Poles and Saxons, although always outnumbered, and declared Augustus dethroned. He appointed a Polish nobleman named Stanislaus the new king of Poland and pursued Augustus into Saxony. A Swedish army in the Holy Roman Empire worried the Austrians and British who were fighting a major war against Louis XIV. Under Austrian pressure, Augustus renounced his claim to the Polish throne and his alliance with Russia. That left Charles free to invade Russia. He refused to discuss peace with Peter and took his army from Poland into Russian territory.

Charles gathered 44,000 men, an army that appeared well adapted to campaigning on the Russian steppes—24,000 of them were cavalry. He left 8,000 behind to keep Poland in line, but he still outnumbered the 35,000 Peter was able to concentrate. Peter avoided a pitched battle. He responded to the invasion with what would become a classic Russian strategy. He sent nomad horsemen into Poland and Silesia to attack Charles's rear areas. As Charles advanced, Peter retreated, leaving, as the Russians said in World War II, only "scorched earth" for the enemy. Charles did catch up with a Russian force near Holowczyn. He defeated them, but these Russians, fighting in their own country, did not flee in panic. It was a portent.

While Charles was campaigning, he got a message from Ivan Stefanovich Mazeppa, leader of the Ukrainian Cossacks. Both Russia and Poland claimed Ukraine, but it was really controlled by Cossacks, Russian runaway serfs and rebels who had established their own republics in several locations on the steppes. If Charles would put Ukraine under his protection, Mazeppa said, he would support him with 30,000 Cossacks. Tsar Peter's scorched earth strategy was giving the Swedes serious supply problems. To Charles, the food and grass in a friendly Ukraine looked even better than 30,000 horsemen, so he turned south.

Meanwhile Swedish General Adam Lewenhaupt had already set out from Riga to reinforce Charles with 11,000 men, cannons, and supplies. His officers counseled Charles to wait for Lewenhaupt, but he got another message from Mazeppa urging him to hurry so the Cossacks wouldn't change their minds before he arrived. Charles continued his march.

Lewenhaupt, trying to catch up with his impulsive king, ran into a huge Russian force. He was defeated. He hurriedly buried his artillery and burned his supply wagons so they wouldn't fall into the hands of the enemy, then took the 6,000 men he had left to join Charles. Another Swedish general, Lybecker, also had trouble. Marching out of Finland, he intended to burn St. Petersburg, founded by Tsar Peter only a few years before. The Russians fell on his 12,000 men before they reached the new city and drove him back to Finland with a loss of 3,000 men and 6,000 horses.

Charles finally met Mazeppa, but the Cossack leader had only 1,500 men with him. The Cossack rebel was trying to cope with a rebellion among his fellow rebels, who were being helped by the Russians. Five days after the meeting, the Cossacks deposed Mazeppa entirely, Charles found himself in a hostile country with no native support, and winter had come to the steppes.

In February, when the spring thaws began, Charles had only 20,000 men and 2,000 of them were wounded. He had only 34 cannons, and most of his gunpowder was wet. Charles sent orders for King Stanislaus, his puppet king of Poland, to join him. On May 2, he laid siege to Poltava, a fortified town on the Vorskla River. Peter, after putting down another Cossack rebellion, took an army to the Poltava area and built a fortified camp.

Poltava

The siege went on and on. Charles was wounded in the foot. In bed, trying to recover, he received a message from King Stanislaus stating that conditions in Poland prevented him from going to Ukraine. When Peter, in his fortified camp, heard that Charles was prostrate, he led his troops out of camp to induce the Swedes to give battle. Under cover of night, he led his troops to within two miles of Poltava and built another camp.

Charles took up the challenge. He detached 2,000 men to maintain the siege lines, 2,400 to guard his baggage, and 1,200 to stay on the western bank of the Vorskla to guard his rear. Most of the artillery stayed in the siege lines.

With 12,500 men, half infantry and half cavalry, and only four cannons, the Swedes would attack some 50,000 Russians in a fortified camp. The south and east sides of Peter's camp were protected by woods and a river. To reach the north and west sides of the camp, the Swedes would have to pass through a gap between the river and more woods. Peter had built six redoubts to cover the gap. Behind the redoubts, the tsar had stationed a strong force of infantry and cavalry.

The Swedish infantry attacked in four columns, followed by the cavalry in six columns. Charles went with them, carried in a horse litter. The Swedish left wing passed through the gaps between the redoubts and pushed back the Russian troops behind them. The general commanding the right wing, however, tried to capture the redoubts one by one and got bogged down. Charles halted his left wing's advance so the right wing wouldn't be cut off. But Peter had launched a counterattack.

Both monarchs led their troops with conspicuous bravery. Charles's litter was smashed by a cannon ball, and 21 of his 24 bodyguards were killed. Peter had a musket ball go through his hat. Another hit his saddle, and a third glanced off a metal cross he wore around his neck. Of the Swedish army, 3,000 were killed or wounded and another 2,800 made prisoners. Russian casualties came to 1,300. Charles tried to reorganize the remnants of his army and retreat to the Turkish border. Only he and 1,500 troops made it.

The war went on, with Charles receiving help from Turkey. Finally, the Turks expelled Charles. He rode across Europe, back to Sweden, and was killed on December 12, 1718, while besieging a Norwegian fortress.

The Second Great Northern War ended with the Stockholm treaties of 1719 (between Sweden and Russia's allies) and 1721 (between Sweden and Russia). But the course of the war had been decided at Poltava, a decade before. Sweden was finished as a Great Power, its control of the Baltic broken forever. Russia gained Livonia, Estonia, Ingria, and part of Finland. Peter got his outlet on the Baltic, and he forced his huge hermit kingdom to become part of Europe.

Honorable Mentions
Other Battles, Other Lists

Back in 1851, a British lawyer and history professor named Edward Shepherd Creasy published *Fifteen Decisive Battles of the World*. Creasy must have been a pretty good lawyer, because in 1860 he was appointed Chief Justice of Ceylon and became Sir Edward. That he was more than a pretty good historian is obvious. *Fifteen Decisive Battles* has been in print for a century-and-a-half, and it has inspired a number of other decisive battle lists.

That other lists do not all agree with Creasy's does not detract from the old lawyer's achievement. A lot of things have changed since 1851. None of Creasy's contemporaries could have envisioned a world that was not economically and largely politically dominated by white Europeans. History to Creasy's readers was conceived as a stream that began with a spring in Greece, flowed through Rome into northern Europe, across the English Channel, and culminated in the British Empire.

There have also been a lot of battles since 1851. Even adopting Creasy's Eurocentric world view it would be necessary to at least look at the American Civil War, the Franco Prussian War, World War I, and World War II. Joseph Mitchell expanded Creasy's list to 20, but why only 20? J.F.C. Fuller in his *A Military History of the Western World* covers more than 100 major battles. And he misses a lot. The Battle of Britain gets less than a page and a half in Fuller's opus, compared to the 24 pages on the Battle of Warsaw in the Polish-Russian War of 1920. And Fuller was a retired British general. As a matter of fact, he was a distinguished general. With his colleague, B. H. Liddell Hart, (a military critic and journalist, not a general, who also made battle lists), he was one of the world's pioneers in armored warfare. But neither he nor Liddell Hart had much interest in protracted affairs such as the Battle of Britain or the Battle of the Atlantic.

Most battle lists overlook the psychological aspects of victory or defeat. Several years ago, the present author published a book called *Fatal Victories*—battles in which the winner was undone by his victory. The reason for this unexpected result was usually the battle's effect on the minds or morale of either the winners or the losers. Some of them were decisive enough to make this book. Some were not.

Here are some of the battles that had to be considered but did not make the top 50:

The Battle of the Metaurus

This was a battle in which Claudius Nero defeated the army of Hannibal's brother, Hasdrubal. This prevented badly needed reinforcements from reaching Hannibal, who had been devastating Italy for a decade. But even with the reinforcements, Hannibal would not have been strong enough to besiege Rome or any other major city in populous, intensely hostile Latinium. Hannibal had already lost the war with his overwhelming victory at Cannae, nine years earlier. He had gambled that a great victory over the Romans would induce Rome's subject nations to revolt. No victory could have been greater than Cannae, but almost no Roman vassals joined him.

The Battle of Blenheim

This battle is a popular choice. The victory enabled Jack Churchill to build the enormous palace of the same name, but it didn't end the war. Churchill, the Duke of Marlborough, actually lost the war five years later with his Pyrrhic victory at Malplaquet. Malplaquet did more than end the War of the Spanish Succession, it paved the way for the American and French Revolutions.

Wolfe's victory on the Plains of Abraham

This battle, which resulted in the British capture of Quebec, makes many lists. Quebec was the key to the St. Lawrence River, which leads to the Great Lakes and the river-and-lake communications of much of North America. But the French had already been pushed out of most of North America, and with British control of the sea, they had no hope of rebuilding their strength. The deaths of both Wolfe and Montcalm make the battle a dramatic story, but it wasn't that decisive.

The raising of the siege of Orleans by Joan of Arc

Another English-French conflict that's frequently chosen. St. Joan's career is certainly a dramatic story, and the French did, in fact, win the war. But Joan was betrayed and martyred, and the war went on for another two decades. And given the disparity of the populations of France and England at the time, a permanent English victory in the Hundred Years War was most unlikely.

The Battle of Salamis

The battle in which the Greek fleet, under the Athenian Themistocles, wiped out the Persian fleet, serving Xerxes. The Greek victory destroyed Xerxes's plan for the conquest of Greece. But that was a plan Xerxes's predecessor, Darius, had already rejected as almost impossible. Darius knew that the conquest of Greece would require subtlety and subversion. His general, Datis, ruined the Great King's plan by his sacking of Eretria, which discouraged the Athenian fifth column. Darius planned on that fifth column opening the gates of Athens after Datis had lured the Athenian army to Marathon.

The Roman defeat in the Teutoburger Wald

Creasy and many others have listed this battle in their writings. It supposedly meant that the German tribes would not be incorporated into the Roman Empire. The result was that, many centuries later, the German tribes destroyed the Roman Empire of the West. Actually, some of the western and southern Germans were incorporated into the Empire. In 1985, the German city of Augsburg celebrated the bimillennial anniversary of its founding by the Romans. Those Germans on the fringe of the Empire were comparatively civilized. The bulk of the Germans, in the north and east, were not. Roman culture was based on cities. The Celts of Gaul and Britain were already somewhat urbanized. The restless German tribes were not. No matter what happened in the Teutoburger Wald, the Roman Empire would not have been able to absorb the Germans in that stage of development. Teutoburger Wald may give German and English historians a warm, fuzzy feeling about their ancestors, but it wasn't decisive.

The siege of Constantinople

The siege of Constantinople (717–18), has a better claim to being considered decisive. The East Romans, under Leo the Isaurian, beat back the Arab army and navy under the Caliphs Suleiman and Omar, introducing Greek fire in the process. The Roman victory stopped almost unbroken string of Arab victories. But Constantinople was an extremely tough nut to crack, as waves of Goths, Huns, Avars, and Slavs could testify, and it was not likely that the Arabs, basically desert fighters with a leavening of Levantine seamen, would succeed where the others had failed. A few years later, the Muslims had a better chance of success at the other end of Europe, in Gaul. But they were defeated in a toe-to-toe slugging match near Tours that did make this list of battles.

Manzikert

At Manzikert, new recruits to Islam, the Turks of Alp Arslan, defeated and captured the East Roman emperor, Romanus Diogenes, in 1071. That was a serious setback for Christendom. It was, however, one of the factors that caused Christendom to launch the Crusades, which for a century were a serious problem for Islam. During the Crusades and for a long time afterwards, the Eastern Roman Empire remained a power to be reckoned with.

The Turkish failure to take Vienna

This battle was in 1529 and often makes lists of decisive battles. But the Turkish army that circled the crumbling walls of Vienna was one that had lost its taste for sieges at the gory and nominally successful siege of Rhodes (which is included here).

Plassey

At both Rhodes and Vienna, the West was on the defensive against an assault from the East. (We're talking culture here, of course, not geography.) A clash in which the West was on the offensive also makes our "honorable mention" list of battles. Robert Clive, leading a British and native army, defeated the army of the Nawab Siraj-ud-daulah at Plassey, making possible the British conquest of India. That was pretty decisive for both Britons and Indians, but the British Raj is long gone now. At Tenochtitlan, Hernan Cortes pioneered the conquest of a non-European empire by European troops who were allied with native troops. The pattern recurred many times before Plassey. Tenochtitlan also had the effect of opening the Pacific link between the East and the West.

The Battle of the Chesapeake

A couple of decades after Plassey and on the other end of the world, is another also-ran. There an inferior British fleet failed to stop de Grasse from cutting off Yorktown. That is sometimes called the battle that won the American Revolution. It did ensure Cornwallis's surrender. But that surrender was simply the straw that broke the British camel's back. Two other battles were more decisive: Bunker Hill showed that the colonists would not be deterred by the regular army and navy deployed in superior strength and used in pitched battle, and Burgoyne's surrender at Saratoga resulted in France, Spain, and the Netherlands joining the American colonists, a combination too great for even the mighty British Empire.

Biographical Glossary

Following are thumbnail sketches of military leaders who are featured in at least one chapter and are mentioned in others. The list does not include purely political leaders or political leaders who participated in military campaigns other than those described in this book.

Gustavus Adolphus

Born in 1594, the son of the King of Sweden, Gustavus became king in his own right at the age of 16. By that time, he was already an experienced soldier. Gustavus inherited what was probably the best army in Europe, and he made it better. He instituted a fair system of conscription and radically reorganized the army to increase its mobility and firepower. He created an extremely sophisticated instrument, which needed an extremely sophisticated general to lead it: his ability to use the tactical potential of his army, not his strategy, led to his many victories. At Lutzen, in 1632, he confronted Wallenstein, a greater strategist leading an army with an outdated organization. Wallenstein lost the battle but retained control of his army. Gustavus was killed, and his army, lacking its genius-general, lost its efficiency.

Alexander the Great

Son of Philip II of Macedon, Alexander, born in 356 BC, was a cavalry commander when he was 18, became king at 20, conquered the Persian Empire when he was 26, and died in 323 BC, before he was 33. He wanted to conquer the world, or at least the civilized world, but in India, his troops refused to march any farther. Cruel and ruthless to those who opposed him, he nevertheless proclaimed the brotherhood of man and tried to break down barriers of prejudice between his Greek and Asian subjects. He died of a fever in Susa, the old Persian capital, after returning from India.

Attila

Attila is believed to have been born in 406. He became joint king of the Huns with his brother, Bleda, after the death of his uncle, Rugila in 435. Attila killed Bleda in 444 or 445 and became sole ruler. He warred periodically with the Romans and continually with the nomad tribes of Europe until he had incorporated them all into his empire. It was his desire to conquer those who sought refuge in the Roman Empire that led him into Gaul in 451. He invaded Italy in 452, but turned back after meeting Pope Leo I. Attila died the next year. He is said to have had a nosebleed and drowned in his own blood while in a drunken stupor. Although the story sounds made up, evidence indicates that that's what really happened.

Belisarius

Born in the Balkans in 500, Belisarius became a bodyguard for the Roman Emperor, Justinian. Justinian demonstrated his uncanny ability to spot talent when he made the young soldier governor of Mesopotamia in 527. He was appointed master of soldiers in the east in 529, and the next year he wiped out a greatly superior Persian army at Daras. He played a key role in crushing the Nika Rebellion in 532. He conquered the Vandal kingdom in Africa in 534 and Sicily in 535. Invading Italy, he drove the Goths into Revenna and captured their king in 540. He returned to Constantinople and defended it against a Hunnish invasion, but the war in Italy flared up again and was finally ended by Narses.

"Gentleman Johnny" Burgoyne

Born in 1722, reputedly the bastard son of a lord, Burgoyne joined the British Army in 1740. During the Seven Years War, he took part in commando-style raids on the French coast. He raised a light horse regiment and took it to Portugal, a British ally, which was being invaded by Spain. He routed the Spanish at the Battle of Villa Vilha, where he showed extraordinary enterprise and daring. Lionized in London, he became a playwright and member of parliament. He used his political clout to get approval for a plan to end the revolt in America. His campaign ended in disaster, partly because of the incompetence of officials in London but mostly because he didn't understand the situation. His surrender of his army at Saratoga was the turning point in the American Revolution.

Davy Crockett

Born in 1786, David Crockett was a son of the frontier. He became a member of Congress from Tennessee. Crockett was famous as a humorist and for his marksmanship, but he was never famed for his modesty. He wrote an autobiography in 1834, which established his reputation as "king of the wild frontier." As a soldier, he served under Jackson in the Indian campaigns and in the War of 1812. He moved to Texas, leading a small group of Tennessee riflemen, to fight at the Alamo in 1836. He survived that fight long enough to be brought before Santa Anna, who had him executed.

Enrico Dandolo

Born in 1122 to one of the leading families in Venice, Dandolo served his city-state all his life as a military leader and as a politician. As a military man (soldiers and sailors were interchangeable in Venice) he had fought the Pisans, the Genoese, and the Byzantine Greeks. He suffered a wound fighting the Greeks that killed his sight, but that didn't end his activity. He was Doge in 1203 when crusaders approached him to get transportation to Egypt. Dandolo skillfully turned the crusade into an expedition against Constantinople, which he captured for the first time in its history.

Hannibal

Hannibal was the son of Hamilcar Barca, Carthage's most successful general. He was born in 247 BC, during the First Punic War. After the war, Hamilcar went to Spain to conquer a new empire for Carthage and took Hannibal with him. After the death of Hamilcar and his brother-in-law, Hasdrubal, Hannibal inherited the Carthaginian army in Spain. When war broke out, he marched over land to Italy, defeated the Romans overwhelmingly in a string of battles and tried to induce a revolt of Rome's subject peoples. There was no revolt, and Hannibal was called back to Africa. There, leading an inexperienced army, he lost to Scipio, a talented Roman with an experienced army and horde of Libyan cavalry. Hannibal continued to fight the Romans as an advisor to Antiochus of Syria. Defeated again, Hannibal moved to the Black Sea coast where, pursued by the Romans, he committed suicide in 182 BC.

Sam Houston

Sam Houston, like Davy Crockett, was a son of Tennessee. But as a boy, Houston had run away from home and joined the Cherokees. Later, like Crockett, he had campaigned under

Andrew Jackson. Houston, though, was a lieutenant in the regular army. At that time, the army was in charge of Indian affairs, and because Houston spoke fluent Cherokee, he became the government's representative to the tribe. He felt the tribe was not being treated fairly, so he accompanied several Cherokee chiefs on a visit to Secretary of War John C. Calhoun. Houston went not as an army officer but as a Cherokee. He appeared before the starchy Calhoun in a loin cloth and a blanket. Soon after that, he left the army. He went into politics and became governor of Tennessee at the age of 30. Following the breakdown of his marriage and a period of depression, he went to Texas. He became commander in chief of the Texas Army and wiped out Santa Anna's Mexican forces at San Jacinto. He opposed the secession of Texas when the Civil War broke out but died before the end of the war.

Ivan the Terrible

The son of the Prince of Moscow, born in 1530, Ivan had himself proclaimed Tsar of all the Russians. A mediocre general but a skilled diplomat, Ivan warred against the weakening Mongol Khanate of Kazan and in 1552 broke the Mongol yoke that had been fastened on the Russians by the heirs of Genghis Khan. Two years later, he conquered the Khanate of Astrakhan. The Khanate of the Crimea, the last descendant of the Mongol Golden Horde, became part of the Ottoman Empire. Ivan initiated Russia's march to the East and at the same time started its return to the European mainstream. In the later years of his life, Ivan began to grow insane and lived up to his nickname. He died in 1584.

Genghis Khan

In 1162, Yesukai the Valiant, chief of the Yakka Mongols had his first son and named the boy Temujin. Nine years later, Yesukai was murdered. Clan enemies tried to wipe out Yesukai's family, but his wife, Houlun, led her family from refuge to refuge. Temujin grew up as a fugitive, but that sharpened his ability to plan and to think fast. That ability, plus his bravery, earned him a group of dedicated followers such as Subotai Bahadur and Chepe Noyon. By 1206, he had conquered most of the nomads of the Gobi who, in a great council, proclaimed him Genghis Khan, emperor of all men. He conquered the Chin of North China and took their capital, Yen King (modern-day Beijing). He moved into Central Asia and destroyed the Kingdom of Hia and the Empire of Black Cathay (Kara Kitai). His campaign against the vast Karesmian Empire led his generals, Subotai and Chepe Noyon to invade Europe. By the time he died, on his way to punish rebels, the khan had conquered the greatest empire ever seen. His heirs expanded it further, which caused immense changes in world trade and the diffusion of ideas.

Erich Ludendorff

Although he looked like a typical Junker, Ludendorff was born, in 1865, into modest circumstances. Because of his lack of social status, he was commissioned into one of Germany's dowdier regiments. However, his energy, intelligence, and devotion to work attracted the attention of the Great General Staff. At the beginning of World War I, he took advantage of an opportunity and led troops into the Belgian city of Liege, through the ring of forts defending it. He became a hero and was sent to the Eastern Front to help von Hindenburg against the Russians. With the help of the brilliant, gluttonous Max von Hoffmann, he showed Hindenburg the way to victory in the Masurian Lakes. The firm of Hindenburg-Ludendorff-Hoffmann went on to more victories in the East. Then the two senior members were transferred to the west. The pushy Ludendorff soon made himself, in effect, German commander in chief. When the Western Front collapsed, Ludendorff resigned. He came back again as an aide to Adolf Hitler, but Hitler soon found the old general's political ideas too wacky even for him. He died in 1937.

Called the "world's first great artilleryman," Mohammed II was born in 1430 to Sultan Murad II of the Ottoman Empire and an Albanian slave. He became sultan himself at the age of 21 and resolved to take Constantinople. The Christian stronghold levied a toll on all movements of Turks between their lands in Anatonia and in the Balkans. For the siege, Mohammed collected the world's largest guns and the most cannon any country ever fielded. His artillery, however, did not conquer the city. Some Turkish troops found an unused postern gate and sneaked in. They were able to hit the defenders from behind during a Turkish assault on the walls. The victory earned Mohammed the nickname "the Conqueror." He failed, however, to conquer Rhodes and died the next year.

Helmut von Moltke the Elder

Although he was born in Germany in 1800, Helmut von Moltke first served in the army of Denmark. He left that force and joined the Prussian Army, but while in Prussian service he traveled to Turkey. While there, he served in the Turkish Army during its war against Mehmet Ali, the sultan's supposed vassal in Egypt. Back in Prussia, he headed the general staff in the Prussian-Danish war. Before Moltke, the general staff was not highly regarded. Moltke's study of railroad systems and how they could affect war changed all that. Victories over Denmark, Austria, and France proved the value of railroads and staff work as well as Moltke's peculiar genius. He stayed in the service until 1888 and died in 1891.

Helmut von Moltke the Younger

Von Moltke the elder was such a success that Kaiser Wilhelm appointed his nephew, also Helmut von Moltke, chief of the Great General Staff. The nephew, who was born in 1848, always referred to himself as "the lesser thinker." Unfortunately for Germany, he was quite right. He had inherited the Schlieffen Plan for the conquest of France, which some authorities say was unworkable. The younger Moltke ensured it would not work by bowing to pressure from German royalty, especially the Crown Prince of Bavaria. After the repulse at the Marne, Erich von Falkenhayn replaced him. He died in 1916.

Napoleon I

Although he was born in 1769 into the minor nobility of Corsica, Napoleon's family embraced the French revolution. He first attracted attention by fighting counterrevolutionists in Toulon and later by putting down a royalist rising in Paris. In 1796, he was given command of the revolutionary army in Italy, a ragged, hungry, and dispirited force. He restored morale, resupplied the troops, and led them to victory. He invaded Austria, and when he was 25 miles from Vienna, the Austrians surrendered. He invaded Egypt and fought in Syria, but when the British defeated his fleet at the Battle of the Nile, he returned to France. In 1799, he was made first consul of the government, which gave him total control of France. In 1804, he made himself emperor. He ran into trouble simultaneously at both ends of Europe: Russia and Spain. To a large extent it was caused by his inability to deal with guerrillas. His enemies took advantage of French weakness and defeated him at Leipzig in 1814. He was forced to abdicate, but he returned to France in 1815. His defeat at Waterloo ended his career. He died in 1821.

Napoleon III

Louis Napoleon Bonaparte proved that being the heir of a famous and powerful man is not always a ticket to the good life. He was an inveterate plotter and a wily enough politician to make himself emperor, like his uncle. He lacked his uncle's military talent, although he had good ideas on the design and use of artillery. His main weakness as a general was that he hated to see people killed. And as emperor, he neglected the army's preparedness and allowed incompetents to staff its higher offices. When war broke out with Prussia, he joined the army at Sedan in 1870 but he allowed his generals to make the decisions. That was a mistake.

Narses

Narses, one of history's most underrated generals, was born in Persarmenia, the part of Armenia occupied by Persia, in 473. He was a slave and had been castrated so he could guard Persian harems. The fact that he was a eunuch may account for his obscurity. It seems most historians like their military heroes to be macho. Somehow, Narses ended up in the slave market at Constantinople. Justinian, that genius at finding genius, bought him and set him free. The ex-slave became the highest civilian official in Justinian's palace. He was not only brilliant, honest, and utterly loyal, he was totally fearless. He proved that by walking alone into a bloodthirsty mob during the Nika Rebellion. He was a keen theoretical student of war. Justinian, having despaired of any of his generals winning the war in Italy, gave the command to Narses. Narses trounced the Goths and drove them out of Italy. Then he beat the Franks and escorted the Lombards back across the Alps. Italy remained at peace until the new emperor, Justin II, retired the old eunuch and brought him back to Constantinople. As soon as he was gone, the Lombards flooded into the Po Valley. Narses lived on in Constantinople for ten more years, dying at the age of 97.

Suleiman the Magnificent

Born in 1495, Suleiman the Magnificent, son of Selim the Grim, was a child of the Renaissance. When he became sultan his main aim was increase relations, particularly trade relations, with Christian Europe. In his first campaign, against Hungary, he exhibited none of the supposed Turkish ferocity. But that was an easy war. The siege of the "stronghold of the Hellhounds," the Knights of Rhodes, was not easy. Suleiman and his army never quite recovered from that. The army lost its capacity to press a siege, and at Vienna actually refused to fight. Suleiman lost his love of humanity and became a hard, bitter old man. He died in 1566 during the siege of the obscure fortress of Szigetvar. His ministers secretly embalmed his body and kept it on a throne so his men wouldn't know the sultan was dead and run away.

Arthur Wellesley, Duke of Wellington

The fourth son of a man who was described as "an impoverished Irish peer," Wellesley was born in Ireland in 1769 and educated at Eton and at a French military academy. His father was not so impoverished he could not buy young Arthur a commission in the British army at the age of 16 in 1785. Lord Mornington continued to purchase commissions for his son so that by 1793, Wellesley was a lieutenant colonel. In the meantime, when he was a mere lieutenant, Arthur Wellesley managed to be elected to parliament. He served in India against French allies and the formidable Tippu Sultan. He campaigned against Napoleon's troops on the Iberian Peninsula from 1808 to 1813, aiding Spanish guerrillas. In 1814, he was fighting on French soil when Napoleon abdicated. When Napoleon returned from Elba, Wellington commanded the allied forces that finally defeated the French emperor. In politics, he is remembered as a towering reactionary, but he introduced the Catholic Emancipation Bill and a bill for Parliamentary reform. He died in 1852.

Glossary of Military Terms

Words in italics refer to other entries in this glossary.

Abatis: Trees felled in front of a defensive line, with the tree tops pointing toward the enemy. If time permits, the ends of the branches are sharpened. It served the same purpose as barbed wire.

Aircraft carrier: A large ship from which warplanes can take off and land.

Army: In general, all the soldiers of a particular country. In the United States and most other armies, an organization composed of several *corps*.

Arquebus: An early firearm with a stock and a *matchlock*.

Artillery: Usually *cannons*, but also such mechanical projectors as *catapults*, *ballistas*, and *trebuchets*. In the Middle Ages it was also applied to archers.

Assault rifle: A rifle capable of both *automatic* and *semiautomatic* fire. It fires a cartridge less powerful than the previously issued hand-operated and semiautomatic rifles. The lower power facilitates handling when the weapon is fired automatically. All modern armies use assault rifles.

Automatic: Any weapon that will keep firing as long as the trigger is held down.

Ballista: An ancient weapon with two arms set like a giant *crossbow* but with each powered by the elasticity of twisted rope. With this, as with the *catapult*, hair—human or animal—made the most elastic rope.

Baltic lock: A very primitive form of *flintlock* used primarily in Sweden during the 17th century.

Battalion: A military unit consisting of several *companies* and smaller than a *regiment*.

Battleship: A large armored ship with the heaviest guns in a navy.

Bayonet: A bladed weapon attached to the front of a rifle or musket.

Bomb: An explosive device. In British usage, a *hand grenade* or *mortar* shell. In the United States, usually an aerial bomb.

Bomber: Usually a plane that drops *bombs*.

Breech-loader: Any firearm, from *cannon* to *pistol*, that is loaded behind the barrel. Breech-loaders were not very successful until the invention of the metallic *cartridge*.

Brigade: A military unit smaller than a *division* and composed of more than one *regiment* or of several *battalions*.

Bullet: A projectile fired from small arms. It may be loaded separately, as in *muzzle-loaders*, or as part of a *cartridge*.

Cannister shot: Small shot, smaller than *grape shot*, packed in a metal cannister and fired from a *cannon*. It has the effect of a huge shotgun.

Cannon: Any firearm larger than a .50-caliber *machine gun*.

Cannon ball: A round projectile approximately the diameter of the cannon that fires it. Cannon balls were used with smoothbore cannons to get the greatest range when used against troops and the greatest hitting power when used against walls.

Caracole: In military usage, a column of cavalrymen who would ride up to the enemy and, just outside of pike range, fire their *pistols*, turn, and ride back to the end of the column where they would reload.

Cartridge: A package containing a projectile and propelling powder. Sometimes it also contained the *primer*. *Flintlock* and some *percussion lock* cartridges were usually paper. The soldier would bite the end of the cartridge and, if he had a *flintlock*, spill a little powder into the prim-

299

ing pan. Then he would ram the whole thing, paper, powder, and *bullet*, down the barrel of his weapon. The paper cartridge for the Prussian needle gun contained a primer, and there was no biting. Generally, though, there was no primer in the cartridge until the invention of metallic cartridges. Metallic cartridges made efficient breech-loaders possible, including repeaters, semiautomatics, and automatics.

Catapult: An ancient engine with a single upright arm used for throwing boulders at an enemy. A skein of twisted rope powered the arm. In modern times, a device for launching an airplane from the deck of a ship.

Chain shot: *Cannon balls* or half-cannon balls linked by a short length of chain. It was used to demast sailing ships.

Cohort: A Roman formation of approximately 600 men. In the Roman Army as reorganized by Marius, six cohorts made a legion.

Company: An army formation consisting of several *platoons* and smaller than a *battalion*.

Composite bow: A bow made of different materials. The most common are composed of strips of horn, wood, and sinew. Composite bows are more flexible than bows composed of one material. Therefore, they can be made shorter. Short composite bows are easy to manage on horseback and became the basic weapon of Asian horsemen for centuries.

Corps: An army unit larger than a *division* and smaller than an *army*. It consists of more than one division.

Crossbow: A bow set at right angles to a stock. Because it can be drawn with both hands, or with a mechanical device, it is usually far stronger than a hand bow.

Cruiser: A naval ship smaller than a *battleship* and larger than a *destroyer*. Originally intended for commerce raiding, cruisers became naval workhorses, handling a large number of missions.

Destrier: The huge horse used by an armored knight in battle.

Destroyer: A fast ship smaller than a *cruiser* and often armed with torpedoes as well as guns. Destroyers, like modern cruisers, are now armed with a variety of missiles. They were originally called "torpedo boat destroyers" and were designed to fight off torpedo boats—small craft that at the turn of the 19th and 20th centuries posed a major threat to *battleships*.

Dive-bomber: A bombing plane that releases its bombs while diving directly at its target. The concept was invented by the U.S. Navy and used most successfully by it and by the Japanese Navy, although the German Stukas got the most publicity. Because they present an almost stationary target while diving, dive-bombers are extremely vulnerable to ground fire and are seldom used now.

Division: An army unit larger than a regiment and smaller than a corps. In some military groups that have abandoned *regiments*, a division consists of many *battalions* or a few *brigades*.

Fascine: A bundle of sticks used to fill in a ditch or dry *moat*.

Fighter plane: Small, fast, and heavily armed airplane used primarily to shoot down enemy planes.

Flintlock: A firearm designed to ignite its propelling charge with sparks caused by a piece of flint striking steel. Strictly speaking, the flintlock was the most refined version of this system. Older systems include the *Baltic lock*, the snaphaunce, the miguelet, and the dog lock.

Frigate: In the age of sail, a naval ship equivalent to a modern cruiser—smaller than a *line of battle ship* but a formidable fighting vessel. Later, a light escort naval vessel.

Front: Russian term for a combination of armies.

Gabion: A wickerwork tube filled with earth to provide shelter for *cannons* or musketeers.

Grapeshot: Small balls packed in a bag on a wooden base. It was fired from muzzle-loading cannons as an anti-personnel weapon. Grapeshot had larger and fewer balls than *cannister shot* and longer range.

Grenade: Generally a small explosive charge that may be thrown by hand or fired from a *rifle* or a *grenade thrower*. Some grenades may contain gas, smoke, or incendiary material instead of explosives. Ancient European manuscripts sometimes refer to artillery shells as grenades.

Grenade thrower: Usually a single shot gun that may be used alone or attached to a rifle. There are also automatic grenade throwers that look like a *machine gun* on steroids.

Gun: Any firearm. In artillery, a long-barrel cannon designed to have a higher velocity and flatter trajectory than a *howitzer* or a *mortar*.

Hand grenade: A *grenade* thrown by a soldier.

Hoplite: A heavily armed Greek infantryman who fought in a *phalanx*.

Horse archer: A cavalryman, usually a light cavalryman (lightly armored or unarmored), who uses a bow and arrows as his main weapon. Horse archers dominated the Eurasian steppes for a millennium.

Howitzer: An artillery piece lighter and with lower velocity and higher trajectory than a *gun*, but heavier and with more velocity and a lower trajectory than a *mortar*.

Javelin: A spear, usually a small one, that is thrown.

Lamellar armor: Armor consisting of small plates laced or riveted together. It was extensively used in Asia.

Land mine: An explosive charge detonated by a person (anti-personnel) or vehicle (anti-tank) passing over it or by remote control.

Legion: Roman military unit. Originally the Roman Army, later, six cohorts. In the late 18th century, especially in the American Revolution, it was a force of infantry and cavalry operating independent of the main army—for instance, Tarleton's Legion.

Line of battle ship: Ancestor of the modern *battleship*; a sailing vessel mounting a large number of guns.

Long bow: An all-wooden bow approximately as long as a man. The length was to give it enough flexibility to shoot an arrow about 30 inches long. The length itself did not give it power, but the longer the bowstring can push against the arrow, the faster the arrow flies. Long bows had been used in Europe since the Stone Age, but the English tactic of massed shooting made it a formidable military weapon.

Machine gun: Strictly speaking, an *automatic* weapon using rifle cartridges or cartridges just a bit larger (for example, Browning .50 caliber) and firing from a mount. Light machine guns may sometimes be fired without a mount. In common usage, *submachine guns* and automatic rifles, including *assault rifles*, are machine guns.

Mail: Armor made of interlocked rings. It was apparently invented by the Celts.

Maniple: Smallest unit of the old Roman legionary army.

Matchlock: A firearm fired by bringing a smoldering piece of cord (a "slow match") in contact with gunpowder.

Mine: Originally a tunnel under a fortification. After the invention of gunpowder, charges were placed in the tunnel to blow up the fortification. By extension, an explosive charge floating in the sea was called a mine. Marine mines were originally called torpedoes, but then torpedo was applied exclusively to what its inventor called the "automobile torpedo." There is no tunneling involved in placing a marine mine, of course. Nor is there any in the latest extension of the term, the *land mine*.

Moat: A ditch around a fort. It may be either water-filled or dry.

Mortar: A short barrel cannon with low velocity and high trajectory. Mortars were originally used to shoot over the walls of forts. Because they are extremely light for the power of their shells, mortars are widely used by infantry. Most modern mortars are muzzle-loaders, the only modern artillery that is.

Musket: Originally, a *matchlock* that was heavier than an *arquebus*. It was so heavy that it had to be fired from a rest, but it penetrated armor so well that soldiers generally gave up wearing steel suits. Later, lighter, and with a flintlock, it was the prime weapon of the infantryman. When rifles were adopted for all infantrymen, the common weapon was called a "rifled musket."

Muzzle-loader: Any firearm loaded from the muzzle, or in the case of percussion *revolvers*, from the front of the cylinder.

Percussion lock: Instead of a powder-filled priming pan, the percussion lock used a *primer*, usually a small cap filled with fulminate of mercury, which would explode when struck by the gun's hammer.

Phalangite: A soldier who fought in a *phalanx*.

Phalanx: Formation of massed infantry armed with spears and protected by shields. It apparently was invented by the Sumerians. It was perfected by the Greek city-states. The Macedonians under Philip, Alexander, and their successors used a slightly different form with lighter armor and longer spears.

Pilum: The Roman spear, a javelin with its point on a long iron rod that was mounted on a heavy wooden haft. There were two weights of pila. The lighter one was thrown first, then the heavier one. They were designed to stick in an enemy's shield and could not be cut off. The legionary aimed to step on the dragging pilum haft and pull down the enemy shield so he could finish him off with his sword.

Pistol: A small firearm designed for one-hand use by cavalrymen. Later, it became a last-ditch weapon for soldiers manning crew-served weapons and for staff officers.

Plate armor: Armor made of large plates that reached perfection in 15th-century Europe.

Platoon: A military unit smaller than a *company* and composed of several *squads*.

Primer: Early firearms, flintlocks, wheellocks, matchlock, and so forth fired their charges by bringing fire or sparks in contact with powder. Later guns ignited the powder with a small explosion created by striking a shock-sensitive explosive in a small container called a primer.

Recoil-less gun: Isaac Newton said every action has an equal reaction. He also knew that momentum (the action and reaction) equals mass times velocity. The recoil-less gun eliminates recoil by creating equal action at both ends of the barrel. Gas at an extremely high velocity—thanks to a carefully designed venturi—blasts out of the breech at the same time the shell leaves the muzzle. Because of the back-blast, standing behind the gun could be fatal. So could firing it with a wall close behind you.

Regiment: A military unit larger than a *battalion* and smaller than a *brigade*.

Repeating rifle: A rifle with a magazine that can be loaded with a number of *cartridges*. The cartridges are then loaded into the firing chamber by a quick hand movement.

Revolver: A firearm with charges held in a cylinder, which revolves to bring each load into firing position. All modern revolvers are pistols, but there were revolving rifles in the 19th century.

Rifle: A long arm with a rifled barrel—that is, grooves have been cut inside the barrel to rotate the bullet. The gyroscopic effect of the rotation keeps the bullet traveling point-first. Because of that, a rifle can fire a heavier projectile than a smoothbore musket. Pistols are rifled—so are machine guns and artillery pieces—but only hand-held long arms with rifled barrels are called rifles.

RPG-7: A Russian anti-tank weapon that appears in every brush-fire war in the world. In spite of U.S. Army public information officers in the Vietnam War, RPG does not stand for "rocket propelled grenade." It's the initials of three Russian words meaning "hand-held anti-tank weapon." The Russians had a gadget called an RPG-43, which was a hand grenade propelled by the user's arm. The RPG-7 is a combination *recoil-less gun* (copied from the German Panzerfaust) and a rocket.

Sap: A trench dug from your main line toward a besieged fortress. Engineers—"*sappers*" the British called them—would stop digging forward at intervals and dig other trenches parallel to the fortress walls. When close enough, they would site artillery and start digging *mines*.

Sapper: Not shock troops, as some Vietnam War sources call them, but engineers who spent more time digging than shocking.

Semiautomatic: A weapon that fires one shot for each pull of the trigger and does not require any additional movement for reloading the chamber. Semiautomatic rifles are obsolete in all armies.

Shell: A hollow artillery projectile filled with explosives, gas, or incendiary material. A shell is also part of a small arms cartridge, the part also called the case. The term "shell casing" is redundant, illiterate, and widely used.

Small arms: Formerly, weapons that could be held and fired by one man. Now it includes *machine guns*, rifle caliber, or .50 caliber ("heavy," in British terminology).

Spanish square: A mass of pikemen formed in a square, supporting, in most cases, an equal number of musketeers. It was the most popular formation in the early modern period when artillery was rather immobile. It was invulnerable to cavalry and to any other infantry formation. Artillery directed at the square, however, could cause horrible slaughter. The Swiss, leading exponents of the square with the Spanish, eventually refused to face artillery.

Squad: The smallest infantry formation. In British terminology a "section," in German, a "gruppe."

Submachine gun: An *automatic* weapon firing pistol cartridges. It is generally used with two hands. Gen. John T. Thompson, who developed the Thompson submachine gun, coined the name. Submachine guns are generally obsolete in modern armies, having been replaced by *assault rifles*.

Submarine: A ship that travels underwater. Originally small, fragile craft that could stay below the surface for only limited periods, subs are now enormous, whale-shaped crafts that can stay under almost indefinitely and make great speed submerged. They have always been armed with *torpedoes*. Now they also have rockets.

Torpedo: Originally a marine mine, now it is a miniature, unmanned submarine tipped with an explosive warhead. Some are guided to their targets by wire. Some others are guided by the sound of the target's engine and propellers.

Torpedo plane: An airplane that launches *torpedoes*. The torpedo plane came into its own in World War II, but like those other great WWII weapons, the *dive bomber* and the *submachine gun*, it may never be used that way again. Because it must fly low and straight approaching the target, it's even more vulnerable than the dive-bomber.

Trebuchet: A medieval weapon consisting of a long pivoted beam, heavily weighted on the short end and with a sling on the long end. When the long end was released, the short end fell rapidly. The long arm swung up and launched a missile at the enemy. Trebuchets were necessarily large, but far more durable and efficient than torsion-powered missile throwers. They were invented in China and got to Europe as a result of the Mongol conquest of most of Eurasia.

Wheellock: A firearm that produces sparks by spinning a steel wheel against a piece of iron pyrites. The mechanism was complicated, easy to break, and hard to repair. There was much less delay between pulling the trigger and discharging the shot than with the *flintlock*, but the cheaper, more rugged *flintlock* replaced it entirely.

Timelines

The chapters as presented here jump all over the historical record. To help the reader see how things developed, we have some additional timelines. The first is a straight chronology, from the earliest battles to the latest. The second relates to the development and spread of democratic government. The third traces the ancient clash between Western and Eastern cultures, including the long confict between Christianity and Islam. The fourth traces the development of European nations and the spread of Western hegemony over the world. Finally, the fifth traces the reaction against European hegemony.

An attempt like this, to chart the currents of history, necessarily means that there will be some overlap. Bunker Hill, for example, was a milestone in the spread of democracy, and it was also the first reaction against European colonialism.

Timeline 1: chronology of the 50 battles

Marathon, 490 BC

Rome, 390 BC

Arbela, 331 BC

Cannae, 216 BC

Emmaus, 166 BC

Carrhae, 53 BC

Adrianople, 378 AD

Chalons, 451 AD

The Nika Rebellion, 532 AD

Busta Gallorum, 552 AD

The Yarmuk Valley, 636 AD

Kadisiyah, 637 AD

Tours, 732 AD

Lechfeld, 955 AD

Hastings, 1066 AD

Gupta, 1180 AD

Hattin, 1187 AD

Constantinople I, 1203 AD

Las Navas de Teloso, 1212 AD

Constantinople II, 1453 AD

Diu, 1509 AD

Tenochtitlan, 1520–21 AD

Rhodes and Malta, 1522 and 1565 AD

Kazan, 1552 AD

Lepanto, 1571 AD

The Armada, 1588 AD

Lutzen, 1632 AD

Poltava, 1709 AD

Malplaquet, 1709 AD

Bunker Hill, 1775 AD

Saratoga, 1777 AD

Valmy, 1782 AD

New Orleans, 1814 AD

Waterloo, 1815 AD

The Alamo and San Jacinto, 1836 AD

Wu-sung, 1862 AD

Chickamauga, 1863 AD

Sedan, 1870 AD

Manila Bay, 1898 AD

Tsushima, 1905 AD

Marne, 1914 AD

Tanga, 1914 AD

Dublin, 1916 AD

Petrograd, 1917 AD

France, 1918 AD

Battle of the Atlantic, 1939–45 AD

The Battle of Britain, 1940 AD

Midway, 1942 AD

Stalingrad, 1942–43 AD

The Tet Offensive, 1968 AD

Marathon, 490 BC
The Nika Rebellion, 532 AD
Busta Gallorum, 552 AD
Malplaquet, 1709 AD
Bunker Hill, 1775 AD
Saratoga, 1777 AD
Valmy, 1782 AD
New Orleans, 1814 AD
The Alamo and San Jacinto, 1836 AD

Chickamauga, 1863 AD
Sedan, 1870 AD
The Marne, 1914 AD
Dublin, 1916 AD
France, 1918 AD
Battle of the Atlantic, 1939-45
The Battle of Britain, 1940
Midway, 1942
Stalingrad, 1942–43

Timeline 3: East vs. West

Marathon, 490 BC
Arbela, 331 BC
Emmaus, 166 BC
Carrhae, 53 BC
Chalons, 451 AD
The Yarmuk Valley, 636 AD
Kadisiyah, 637 AD
Tours, 732 AD
Lechfeld, 955 AD
Gupta, 1180 AD
Hattin, 1187 AD

Constantinople I, 1205 AD
Las Navas de Teloso, 1212 AD
Constantinople, 1453 AD
Diu, 1509 AD
Rhodes and Malta, 1522 and 1565 AD
Kazan, 1552 AD
Lepanto, 1571 AD
Wu-sung, 1862 AD
Tsushima, 1905 AD
Midway, 1942 AD
The Tet Offensive, 1968 AD

Timeline 4: European nationhood and hegemony

Rome, 390 BC
Cannae, 216 BC
Adrianople, 378 AD
Chalons, 451 AD
Busta Gallorum, 552 AD
Tours, 732 AD
Lechfeld, 955 AD
Hastings, 1066 AD

Las Navas de Teloso, 1212 AD
Constantinople II, 1453 AD
Tenochtitlan, 1520–21 AD
Kazan, 1552 AD
The Armada, 1588 AD
Lutzen, 1632 AD
Poltava, 1709 AD
Sedan, 1870 AD
Manila Bay, 1898

Timeline 5: the reaction against European hegemony

Bunker Hill, 1775 AD
Saratoga, 1777 AD
New Orleans, 1814 AD
Tsushima, 1905

Tanga, 1914
Dublin, 1916
Midway, 1942
The Tet Offensive, 1968

Bibliography

Adcock, F.E. *The Greek and Macedonian Art of War*. Berkeley, CA: University of California Press, 1962.

Adler, Mortimer J., ed. *The Revolutionary Years*. Chicago: Encyclopedia Britannica, 1976.

Alexander, Bevin. *How Great Generals Win*. New York: Norton, 1993.

Aspery, Robert B. *War in the Shadows*. Garden City, NY: Doubleday, 1975.

Ayton, Andrew, and J.L. Price. *The Medieval Military Revolution*. New York: Barnes & Noble, 1995.

Bain, David Haward. *Sitting in Darkness*. Boston: Houghton Mifflin, 1984.

Bakeless, John. *Turncoats, Traitors and Heroes*. Philadelphia: Lippincott, 1959.

Barr, Stringfellow. *The Mask of Jove*. Philadelphia: Lippincott, 1966.

Bartlett, Thomas, and Keith Jeffrey, eds. *A Military History of Ireland*. New York: Cambridge University Press, 1997.

Beeler, John. *Warfare in England, 1066-1189*. Ithaca, NY: Cornell University Press, 1995.

— *Warfare in Feudal Europe, 730-1200*. Ithaca, NY: Cornell University Press, 1971.

Bell, J. Bowyer. *The Secret Army*. New York: John Day, 1970.

Bellesiles, Michael A. *Arming America*. New York: Knopf, 2000.

Berton, Pierre. *Flames Across the Border*. Boston: Little, Brown, 1981.

Billias, George Athan, ed. *George Washington's Opponents*. New York: Morrow, 1969.

Billings, Malcolm. *The Cross and the Crescent*. New York: Sterling, 1988.

Birnbaum, Louis. *Red Dawn at Lexington*. Boston: Houghton Mifflin, 1986.

Black, Jeremy. *War and the World*. New Haven, CT: Yale University Press, 1998.

Bobrick, Benson. *Angel in the Whirlwind*. New York: Simon & Schuster, 1997.

Bowers, John. *Chickamauga and Chattanooga*. New York: Avon, 1994.

Boxer, C.R. *Four Centuries of Portuguese Expansion*. Johannesburg: Witwatersrand University Press, 1961.

Boyle, Andrew. *The Riddle of Erskine Childers*. London: Hutchinson, 1977.

Bradford, Ernle. *The Sword and the Scimitar*. New York: Putnam, 1974.

Bresler, Fenton. *Napoleon III*. New York: Carroll & Graf, 1999.

Brice, Martin. *Forts and Fortresses*. New York: Facts on File, 1990.

Brockelmann, Carl. *History of the Islamic People*. New York: Capricorn, 1960.

Brownstone, David, and Irene Franck. *Timelines of War*. New York: Little, Brown, 1994.

Burn, A.R. *Persia and the Greeks*. New York: Minerva Press, 1962.

Bury, J.B. *The History of the Later Roman Empire*. New York: Dover, 1958.

— *The Invasion of Europe by the Barbarians*. New York: Norton, 1967.

Cannon, John, and Ralph Griffiths. *The Oxford Illustrated History of the British Monarchy*. New York: Oxford University Press, 1988.

Carr, Caleb. *The Devil Soldier*. New York: Random House, 1992.

Carrington, Henry B. *Battles of the American Revolution*. New York: Promontory Press

Carver, Michael, ed. *The War Lords*. Boston: Little, Brown, 1976.

Casson, Lionel. *The Ancient Mariners*. New York: Minerva Press, 1959.

Caulfield, Max. *The Easter Rebellion*. Boulder, CO: Roberts Rinehart, 1995.

Chambers, Anne. *Granuaile*. Dublin: Wolfhound Press, 1986.

Chandler, David. *The Art of Warfare on Land*. London: Hamlyn, 1974.

Chandler, David, ed. *The Dictionary of Battles*. New York: Henry Holt, 1988.

Chandler, David G., ed. *Great Battles of the British Army*. Chapel Hill, NC: University of North Carolina Press, 1991.

Chidsey, Donald Barr. *The Siege of Boston*. New York: Crown, 1966.

Childers, Erskine. *The Riddle of the Sands*. New York: Dover, 1976.

Churchill, Winston S. *My Early Life*. New York: Scribner's, 1958.

Cipolla, Carlo M. *Guns, Sails and Empire*. New York: Minerva Press, 1965.

Clari, Robert de. Edgar Holmes McNeal, trans. *The Conquest of Constantinople*. New York: Norton, 1964.

Clauswitz, Carl von. *On War*. Princeton, NJ: Princeton University Press, 1984.

Coe, Michael D., Peter Connolly, Anthony Harding, Victor Harris, Donald J. Larocca, Thom Richardson, Anthony North, Christopher Spring, and Frederick Wilkinson. *Swords and Hilt Weapons*. New York: Barnes & Noble, 1994.

Coogan, Tim Pat. *Eamon de Valera, The Man Who Was Ireland*. New York: Barnes & Noble, 1993.

— *Michael Collins, The Man Who Made Ireland*. Boulder, CO: Roberts Rinehart, 1996.

— *The IRA*. Boulder, CO: Roberts Rhinehart, 1994.

Coogan, Tim Pat, and George Morrison. *The Irish Civil War*. London: Weidenfeld & Nicolson.

Cooper, Matthew. *The German Army, 1933-1945*. Lanham, MD: Scarborough House, 1978.

Cox, Tom. *Damned Englishman: A Study of Erskine Childers (1870-1922)*. Hicksville, NY: Exposition Press, 1975.

Cumming, William P., and Hugh Rankin. *The Fate of a Nation*. London: Phaidon Press, 1975.

Danvers, F.C. *The Portuguese in India*. London: W.H. Allen, 1894.

Davidson, Basil. *The Lost Cities of Africa*. Boston: Little, Brown, 1959.

Dawson, Christopher. *The Making of Europe*. New York: Meridian, 1959.

De Camp, L. Sprague. *The Ancient Engineers*. Garden City, NY: Doubleday, 1963.

Delbruck, Hans. *History of the Art of War*. Lincoln, NE: University of Nebraska Press, 1990.

Descola, Jean. *The Conquistadors*. New York: Viking, 1957.

de Rosa, Peter. *Rebels: The Irish Rising of 1916*. London: Corgi Books, 1991.

Derry, T.K., and Trevor Williams. *A Short History of Technology*. New York: Oxford University Press, 1960.

Diagram Group, The. *Weapons: An International Encyclopedia from 5000 BC to 2000 AD*. New York: St. Martins, 1990.

Diaz del Castillo, Bernal. *The Bernal Diaz Chronicles*. Garden City, NY: Doubleday, 1956.

Doblhofoer, Ernst. *Voices in Stone*. New York: Viking, 1961.

Dos Passos, John. *The Portugal Story*. Garden City, NY: Doubleday, 1969.

Duffy, Christopher. *Siege Warfare*. New York: Barnes & Noble, 1996.

Duggan, Alfred. *The Story of the Crusades*. Garden City, NY: Doubleday, 1966.

— *The Cunning of the Dove*. Garden City, NY: Doubleday, 1966.

Dunan, Marcel, ed. *Larousse Encyclopedia of Ancient and Medieval History*. New York: Harper & Row, 1963.

Dupuy, R. Ernest, and Trevor N. *Compact History of the Revolutionary War*. New York: Hawthorn Books, 1963.

Dunnigan, James F., and Albert A Nofi. *Dirty Little Secrets*. New York: Morrow, 1990.

— *Dirty Little Secrets of World War II*. New York: Morrow, 1994.

Eden, Stephen. *Military Blunders*. New York: Metro, 1995.

Eggenberger, David. *An Encyclopedia of Battles*. New York: Dover, 1985.

Einhard and Notker the Stammerer. *Two Lives of Charlemagne*. Baltimore: Penguin, 1969.

Ellis, John. *The Social History of the Machine Gun*. New York: Pantheon, 1975.

Esposito, Vincent J. *The West Point Atlas of American Wars*. New York: Praeger, 1960.

Falls, Cyril. *A Hundred Years of War, 1850-1950*. New York: Collier, 1953.

Faragher, John Mack., ed. *The American Heritage Encyclopedia of American History*. New York: Holt, 1998.

Fichtenau, Heinrich. *The Carolingian Empire*. New York: Harper, 1964.

Fischer, David Hackett. *Paul Revere's Ride*. New York: Oxford University Press, 1994.

Fletcher, Richard. *The Quest for El Cid*. New York: Knopf, 1990.

Fleming, Thomas J. *Now We Are Enemies*. New York: St. Martin's, 1960.

Franklin, Benjamin. *Writings*. New York: Library of America, 1987.

Frantz, Joe B. *Texas: A Bicentennial History*. New York: Norton, 1976.

Fuller, J.F.C. *A Military History of the Western World*. New York: Da Capo, 1987

Ghirshman, R. *Iran*. Baltimore: Penguin, 1964.

Gordon, C.D. *The Age of Attila*. Ann Arbor, MI: University of Michigan Press, 1966.

Grant, Michael. *Dawn of the Middle Ages*. New York: Bonanza, 1986.

Greaves, C. Desmond. *1916 as History*. Dublin: Fulcrum Press, 1991.

Grousset, Rene. *The Empire of the Steppes: A History of Central Asia*. New Brunswick, NJ: Rutgers University Press, 1970.

— *The Rise and Splendour of the Chinese Empire*. Berkeley, CA: University of California Press, 1959.

Gudmundsson, Bruce I. *Stormtroop Tactics*. Westport, CT: Praeger, 1989.

Herodotus. *The Histories*. Baltimore: Penguin, 1960.

Hogg, Ian V. *The Complete Machine-Gun*. New York: Exeter, 1979.

Holy Bible. New York; Catholic Book Publishing Co., 1949.

Horsman, Reginald. *The War of 1812*. New York: Knopf, 1969.

Jackson, Robert. *Fighter*. New York: St. Martin's, 1979.

James, Marquis. *The Life of Andrew Jackson*. Indianapolis : Bobbs-Merrill, 1938.

James, Simon. *The World of the Celts*. London: Thames & Hudson, 1993.

Jennings, Patrick. *Pictorial History of World War II*. Norwalk, CT: Longmeadow, 1975.

Jobe, Joseph. *Guns*. Greenwich, CT: New York Graphic Society, 1971.

Johnson, Curt. *Battles of the American Revolution*. New York: Rand McNally, 1975.

Johnson, J.H, *1918: the Unexpected Victory*. London: Arms and Armour Press, 1997.

Joinville, Jean, Sieur de, and Geoffroi de Villehardoin. M.R.B. Shaw, trans. *Chronicles of the Crusades*. Baltimore: Penguin, 1970.

Josephus. *The Jewish War*. Baltimore: Penguin, 1959.

Karsten, Peter, ed. *The Military in America*. New York: Free Press, 1980.

Keegan, John. *A History of Warfare*. New York: Vintage, 1994.

— *The First World War*. New York: Knopf, 1999

— *The Mask of Command*. New York: Viking, 1987.

— *The Second World War*. New York: Peguin, 1990.

— *Six Armies in Normandy*. New York: Viking, 1982.

Keegan, John, and Andrew Wheatcroft. *Who's Who in Military History*. New York: Morrow, 1976.

Kemp, Peter. *The History of Ships*. London: Orbis, 1978.

Kennedy, Paul. *The Rise and Fall of the Great Powers*. New York: Random House, 1987.

Ketchum, Richard M., ed. *The American Heritage Book of the Revolution*. New York: American Heritage, 1958.

— *The Battle for Bunker Hill*. Garden City, NY: Doubleday, 1962

Kippenhahn, Rudolf. *Code Breaking*. Woodstock, NY: The Overlook Press, 1999.

Krauze, Enrique. *Mexico*. New York: Harper Collins, 1997.

Lamb, Harold. *Charlemagne*. New York: Bantam, 1958.

— *Genghis Khan*. New York: Bantam, 1953.

— *Theodora and the Emperor*. New York: Bantam, 1963.

— *The Crusades*. New York: Bantam, 1960.

Leckie, Robert. *The Wars of America*. New York: Harper & Row, 1968.

Levathes, Louise. *When China Ruled the Seas*. New York: Simon & Schuster, 1994.

Liddell Hart, and Basil H. *Great Captains Unveiled*. Novato, CA: Presidio Press, 1990.

— *Strategy*, New York: Praeger, 1960.

— *The Real War: 1914 to 1918*. Boston: Little, Brown and Co., 1930.

Lincoln, W. Bruce. *Red Victory*. New York: Simon & Schuster, 1989.

Lind, Michael. *The Alamo*. Boston: Houghton Mifflin, 1997.

Linn, Brian McAllister. *The U.S. Army and Counterinsurgency in the Philippine War, 1899-1902*. Chapel Hill, NC: University of North Carolina Press, 1989.

Livy. *The War With Hannibal*. Baltimore: Penguin, 1965.

Lord, Walter. *A Time to Stand*. New York: Bonanza, 1987.

Lucas, James. *War on the Eastern Front 1941-1945*. New York: Bonanza, 1979.

Luttwak, Edward N. *The Pentagon and the Art of War*. New York: Simon & Schuster, 1985.

Macardle, Dorothy. *The Irish Republic*. New York: Farrar, Straus and Giroux, 1965.

McEvedy, Colin. *The Penguin Atlas of Ancient History*. New York: Viking Penguin, 1988.

Machiavelli, Niccolo. *The Art of War*. New York: Da Capo, 1965.

McKissack, Patricia and Frederick. *The Royal Kingdoms of Ghana, Mali and Songhay*. New York: Henry Holt, 1994.

McNeill, William H. *The Pursuit of Power*. Chicago: University of Chicago Press, 1982.

McPherson, James M. *Battle Cry of Freedom*. New York: Ballentine, 1989.

Manchester, William. *The Arms of Krupp*. Boston: Little, Brown, 1968.

Marrin, Albert. *1812: The War Nobody Won*. New York: Athenem, 1985.

Marsden, E.W. *Greek and Roman Artillery: Historical Development*. Oxford: Clarendon Press, 1999.

Marshall, S.L.A. *The American Heritage History of World War I*. New York: American Heritage, 1964.

Massie, Robert K. *Dreadnought*. New York: Ballentine, 1991.

Mathew, K.M. *History of the Portuguese Navigation in India (1497-1600)*. Delhi: Mittal Publications, 1988.

Melegari, Vezio. *Great Military Sieges*. New York: Exeter Books, 1981

Messenger, Charles. *The Blitzkrieg Story*. New York: Scribner's, 1976.

Middlekauff, Robert. *The Glorious Cause*. New York: Oxford University Press, 1982.

Miller, John C. *Alexander Hamilton and the Growth of the New Nation*. New York: Harper & Row, 1964.

Millis, Walter. *Arms and Men*. New York: Mentor, 1958.

Mitchell, Joseph B. and Edward Creasy. *Twenty Decisive Battles of the World*. New York: Macmillan, 1964.

Morison, Samuel Eliot. *The Oxford HIstory of the American People*. New York: Oxford University Press, 1965.

— *The Two Ocean War*. Boston: Atlantic Monthly Press, 1963.

Morris, Eric, Curt Johnson, Christopher Chant, and H.P. Wilmott. *Weapons and Warfare of the Twentieth Century*. Secaucus, NJ: Derbibooks, 1976.

Morrison, Sean. *Armor*. New York, Crowell, 1963.

Montross, Lynn. *War Through the Ages*. New York: Harper & Row, 1960.

Moody, T.W., and Martin, F.X., eds. *The Course of Irish History*. Cork: Mercier Press, 1978.

Murray, Williamson, and Millett, Allan R. *A War to be Won*. Cambridge, MA: Belknap, 2000.

Nalty, Bernard C. *Air Power and the fight for Khe Sanh*. Washington: Office of Air Force History, 1973.

Nevin, David. *The Texans*. New York: Time-Life Books, 1975.

Nickel, Helmut. *Warriors and Worthies*. New York: Atheneum, 1971.

Ni Dhonnchadla, Mairin, and Theo Dorgan, eds. *Revising the Rising*. Derry, No. Ireland: Field Day, 1991.

Norman, A.V.B., and Don Pottinger. *English Weapons and Warfare. 449-1660*, New York: Dorsct, 1985.

Nowlan, Kevin B., ed. *The Making of 1916*. Dublin: the Stationery Office, 1969.

Oakeshott, R. Ewart. *The Archaeology of Weapons*. New York: Praeger, 1960.

O'Brien, Conor Cruise. *States of Ireland*. New York: Vintage Books, 1972.

O Broin, Leon. *Dublin Castle and the 1916 Rising*. New York: New York University Press, 1971.

O'Connor, Frank. *An Only Child*. Boston: G.K. Hall, 1985.

— *The Big Fellow*. Dublin: Clonmore & Reynolds, 1965.

Oliveira Marques, A.H. de. *History of Portugal*. New York: Columbia University Press, 1972.

Olmstead, A.T. *History of the Persian Empire*. Chicago: University of Chicago Press, 1960.

Oman, Charles. *The Art of War in the Middle Ages*. Ithaca, NY: Cornell University Press, 1960.

O'Malley, Ernie. *On Another Man's Wound*. Dublin: Anvil Books, 1997.

— *The Singing Flame*. Dublin: Anvil Books, 1997.

O'Rahilly, Aodogan. *Winding the Clock: O'Rahilly and the 1916 Rising*. Dublin: The Lilliput Press, 1991.

O'Toole, G.J.A. *The Spanish War*. New York: Norton, 1984.

Parker, Geoffrey. ed. *The Times Illustrated History of the World*. London: Times Books, 1995.

Payne, Robert, and Nikita Romanoff. *Ivan the Terrible*. New York: Crowell, 1975.

Payne-Gallwey. *The Crossbow*. London: Holland Press, 1986.

Pearson, Michael. *Those Damned Rebels*. New York: Putnam, 1972.

Pernoud, Regine, ed. *The Crusades*. New York: Putnam, 1962.

Peterson, Harold L. *Arms and Armor in Colonial America*. New York: Bramhall House, 1956.

— *Book of the Continental Soldier*. Harrisburg, PA: Promontory, 1968.

— *Round Shot and Rammers*. New York: Bonanza, 1969.

Pflanze, Otto. *Bismark and the Development of Germany*. Princeton, NJ: Princeton University Press, 1963.

Piggott, Stuart, ed. *The Dawn of Civilization*. New York: McGraw-Hill, 1961.

Pitt, Barrie and Frances *The Month by-Month Atlas of World War II*. New York: Summit, 1989.

Platt, Colin. *The Atlas of Medieval Man*. New York: St. Martin's, 1980.

Plutarch, *Plutarch's Lives*. New York: Modern Library.

Polybius. *The Histories of Polybius*. Bloomington, IN: University of Indiana Press, 1962.

Pope, Dudley. *Guns*. London: Hamlyn, 1969.

Pope, Saxton. *Bows and Arrows*. Berkeley: University of California Press, 1962.

Powell, T.G.E. *The Celts*. New York: Praeger, 1958.

Powell, E. Alexander. *Gentlemen Rovers*. New York: Scribner's, 1913.

Pratt, Fletcher. *The Battles that Changed History*. Garden City, NY: Doubleday, 1956.

Prawdin, Michael. *The Mongol Empire*. New York: Free Press, 1961.

Prescott, William H. *Conquest of Mexico*. Garden City, NY: Blue Ribbon Books, 1943.

Preston, Richard A., Sydney F. Wise, and Herman O. Werner. *Men in Arms*. New York: Praeger, 1962.

Procopius. *History of the Wars, Secret History* and *Buildings*. New York: Washington Square Press, 1962.

Regan, Geoffrey. *SNAFU*. New York: Avon, 1993.

— *The Guinness Book of More Military Blunders*. London: Guinness, 1993.

— *The Guinness Book of Naval Blunders*. London: Guinness, 1993.

Reid, William. *Weapons Through the Ages*. New York: Crescent, 1976.

Ring, Jim. *Erskine Childers*. London: John Murray, 1996.

Robinson, H. Russell. *Oriental Armour*. New York: Walker, 1987.

Rodgers, William Ledyard. *Greek and Roman Naval Warfare*. Annapolis, MD: U.S. Naval Institute, 1964.

— *Naval Warfare Under Oars*. Annapolis, MD: U.S. Naval Institute, 1967.

Ropp, Theodore. *War in the Modern World*. New York: Collier, 1962.

Runciman, Stephen. *Byzantine Civilization*. Cleveland: World Publishing, 1961.

Russell-Wood, A.J.R. *The Portuguese Empire, 1415-1808*. Baltimore: The Johns Hopkins University Press, 1998

Schele, Linda, and David Freidel. *The Untold Story of the Ancient Maya*. New York: Morrow, 1990.

Serjeant, R.B. *The Portuguese Off the South Arabian Coast*. Oxford: Clarenden Press, 1963.

Severin, Timothy. *The Oriental Adventure*. Boston: Little, Brown, 1976.

Showalter, Dennis E. *Tannenberg*. Hamden, CT: Archon, 1991.

Simkins, Michael. *Warriors of Rome*. London: Blandford, 1988.

Smith, W.H.B. *Small Arms of the World*. Harrisburg, PA: Stackpole, 1960.

Snodgrass, A.M. *Arms and Armour of the Greeks*. Ithaca, NY: Cornell University Press, 1967.

Southern, R.W. *The Making of the Middle Ages*. New Haven, CT: Yale University Press, 1962.

Spence, Jonathan D. *God's Chinese Son*. New York: Norton, 1996.

Stone, George Cameron. *Glossary of the Construction, Decoration and Use of Arms and Armor*. New York: Jack Brussel, 1961.

Sturluson, Snorri, Magnus Magnusson, and Hermann Palsson, trans. *King Harald's Saga*. Baltimore: Peguin, 1966.

Sulzberger, C.L. *The American Heritage Picture Book of World War II*. New York: American Heritage, 1966.

Tarassuk, Leonid, and Claude Blair. *The Complete Encyclopedia of Arms and Weapons*. New York: Bonanza, 1979.

Taylor, A.J.P. *English History, 1914-1945*, New York: Oxford University Press, 1965.

— *The Second World War*. New York: Perigee, 1983.

Taylor, Telford. *Sword and Swastika*. New York: Barnes & Noble, 1980.

Tebbel, John. *Turning the World Upside Down*. New York: Orion, 1993.

Terraine, John. *To Win a War*. Garden City, NY: Doubleday, 1981.

Thompson, William Irwin. *The Imagination of an Insurrection*. New York: Harper & Row, 1972.

Toynbee, Arnold, ed. *Cities of Destiny*. New York: Oxford University Press, 1950.

Trask, David F. *The War With Spain in 1898*. New York: Macmillan, 1981.

Treece, Henry. *The Crusades*. New York: Random House, 1962.

Tuchman, Barbara. *The Guns of August*. New York: Dell, 1963.

Tucker, Glenn. *Chickamauga: Bloody Battle in the West*. Indianapolis: Bobbs Merrill, 1956.

van Creveld, Martin. *Technology and War*. New York: Free Press, 1989.

van der Vat, Dan. *The Pacific Campaign*. New York: Simon & Schuster, 1991.

Vasiliev, A.A. *History of the Byzantine Empire*. Madison, WI: University of Wisconsin Press, 1964.

Vernadsky, George. *Ancient Russia*. New Haven, CT: Yale University Press, 1969.

von Hagen, Victor W. *The Aztec: Man and Tribe*. New York: Mentor Books, 1960.

— *World of the Maya*. New York: Mentor Books, 1960.

Wallace-Hadrill, J.M. *The Barbarian West*. New York: Harper & Row, 1962.

Wedgwood, C.V. *The Thiry Years War*. Garden City, NY: Doublday, 1961.

Weir, William. *A Well Regulated Militia*. North Haven, CT: Archon, 1997.

— *Fatal Victories*. New York: Avon, 1995.

— *Written With Lead*. Hamden, CT: Archon, 1992.

Wilkinson, Burke. *The Zeal of the Convert*. Sag Harbor, NY: Second Chance Press, 1985.

Wikinson, Frederick. *Edged Weapons*. Garden City, NY: Doubleday, 1970.

Wrixon, Fred B. *Codes and Ciphers*. New York: Prentice Hall, 1992.

Young, Peter. *The Machinery of War*. New York: Crescent, 1973.

Young, Peter, ed. *Great Battles of the World*. New York: Bison Books, 1978.

Young, Peter and J.P. Lawford, eds. *History of the British Army*. New York: Putnam, 1970.

Younger, Calton. *Ireland's Civil War*. London: Fontana Press, 1979.

Index

About the Author

William Weir was an army MP, and later served as an army combat correspondent in the 25th Infantry Division during the Korean War. He was a newspaper reporter in Missouri and Kansas, which included being military editor at the *Topeka State Journal*. While a public relations specialist for a large telephone company, he wrote some 50 magazine articles, many of them on military history and weaponry. Since retiring from his public relations job, he has written four books, *Written With Lead: Legendary American Gunfights and Gunfighters, Fatal Victories, In the Shadow of the Dope Fiend* and *A Well Regulated Militia: The Battle Over Gun Control*. He now lives in Connecticut where he and his wife, Anne, watch with pride the activities of their three children, Alison, an Air Force officer, Joan, a special education teacher, and Bill, a newspaper reporter.